797,885 Books

are available to read at

www.ForgottenBooks.com

Forgotten Books' App
Available for mobile, tablet & eReader

ISBN 978-1-331-90581-3
PIBN 10252287

This book is a reproduction of an important historical work. Forgotten Books uses
state-of-the-art technology to digitally reconstruct the work, preserving the original format
whilst repairing imperfections present in the aged copy. In rare cases, an imperfection in
the original, such as a blemish or missing page, may be replicated in our edition. We do,
however, repair the vast majority of imperfections successfully; any imperfections that
remain are intentionally left to preserve the state of such historical works.

Forgotten Books is a registered trademark of FB &c Ltd.
Copyright © 2017 FB &c Ltd.
FB &c Ltd, Dalton House, 60 Windsor Avenue, London, SW19 2RR.
Company number 08720141. Registered in England and Wales.

For support please visit www.forgottenbooks.com

1 MONTH OF
FREE
READING

at

www.ForgottenBooks.com

By purchasing this book you are eligible for one month membership to ForgottenBooks.com, giving you unlimited access to our entire collection of over 700,000 titles via our web site and mobile apps.

To claim your free month visit:
www.forgottenbooks.com/free252287

* Offer is valid for 45 days from date of purchase. Terms and conditions apply.

English
Français
Deutsche
Italiano
Español
Português

www.forgottenbooks.com

Mythology Photography **Fiction**
Fishing Christianity **Art** Cooking
Essays Buddhism Freemasonry
Medicine **Biology** Music **Ancient**
Egypt Evolution Carpentry Physics
Dance Geology **Mathematics** Fitness
Shakespeare **Folklore** Yoga Marketing
Confidence Immortality Biographies
Poetry **Psychology** Witchcraft
Electronics Chemistry History **Law**
Accounting **Philosophy** Anthropology
Alchemy Drama Quantum Mechanics
Atheism Sexual Health **Ancient History**
Entrepreneurship Languages Sport
Paleontology Needlework Islam
Metaphysics Investment Archaeology
Parenting Statistics Criminology
Motivational

English Dialect Society.

Vol. XXXI.

LOSSARIES OF WORDS

USED IN

HETTON-LE-HOLE, DURHAM,
IN LAKELAND, AND IN
EAST ANGLIA ;

BY

THE REV. F. M. T. PALGRAVE,

THE REV. T. ELLWOOD,

AND

WALTER RYE.

(Numbers 74, 77, 75.)

London:

PUBLISHED FOR THE ENGLISH DIALECT SOCIETY
BY HENRY FROWDE, OXFORD UNIVERSITY PRESS WAREHOUSE,
AMEN CORNER, E.C.

CONTENTS.

—◆—

𝔄 𝔏𝔦𝔰𝔱

OF

WORDS AND PHRASES

IN EVERY-DAY USE

BY THE

NATIVES OF HETTON-LE-HOLE

IN THE COUNTY OF DURHAM

BEING

WORDS NOT ORDINARILY ACCEPTED, OR BUT SELDOM FOUND

IN THE

STANDARD ENGLISH OF THE DAY

EDITED BY THE

REV. F. M. T. PALGRAVE

SOMETIME CURATE OF HETTON

London

PUBLISHED FOR THE ENGLISH DIALECT SOCIETY

BY HENRY FROWDE, OXFORD UNIVERSITY PRESS WAREHOUSE
AMEN CORNER, LONDON, E.C.

PE
1884
H4P35

Oxford
HORACE HART, PRINTER TO THE UNIVERSITY

PREFACE

ONLY two forms of speech are here described : (1) literary, conventional, or Queen's English ; and (2) dialectal English, as spoken in the county of Durham. Let no reader, then, complain that I have inserted words not peculiar to Durham county, or even to the North of England, for South-country words may be found in this glossary.

What I mean is that such words are used in Durham county, and are yet, so far as I know, not accepted in polite English. I have not gone into the intricate question of derivations, except in a few obvious cases, knowing how easy it is for a dabbler in etymology to lay himself open to the well-deserved ridicule of competent critics.

The dialect differing little in vowel-pronunciation from the accepted speech, it has been thought unnecessary to overburden these pages with a phonetic rendering of each word. Where the glossic, however, is used, it is either to mark an unusual word where the pronunciation might be ambiguous, or as a typical example of other words of a like character. Where the word 'fine' occurs in the text, it means something more refined than the dialect pure and simple, introduced in the presence of one more highly educated than the speaker.

I began by affixing 'J. G.' to several words, but as
time went on and I received more and more help from
Mr. Gleghorn, I have discarded this, and beg to acknowledge here my deep obligations to him for his many
contributions to this glossary, which have swellèd it to
quite twice its original size.   To him and to Mr. R. Welsh,
both of Hetton, I am most grateful for kindness received
in compiling this word-list.   Imperfect I know it to be,
yet the responsibility rests entirely upon me : a great deal
of interesting matter must necessarily have escaped one
who was only three years resident in the district.

Perhaps I may add here a few items of interest, which
could not well have found a place elsewhere in this book.

With regard to proper names, double Christian names
are often employed in addressing one another, as, 'John
Henry,' 'Mary [maa·i] Lizzie,' 'Mary Ellen,' in the same
way that Marianne is often used elsewhere.   Names ending
in ' -son ' are probably our commonest surnames, as Robin-
son, Robson, and others.   Heslop, Teesdale, Young, Hopper,
are all common local names.   The following is a small
list, showing peculiarities of pronunciation :—

Atkinson,	pronounced	Atchison
Dobson	„	Dŏbison
Gleghorn	„	Glegram
Hodgson	„	Hodgin
Matthew	„	Martha [maath·u]
Smithson	„	Smitson
Stevenson	„	{ Stĕvison { Stĭvison
Tonks		Trunks
Turnbull	„	Trummel

Red is the Tory colour, and blue the Liberal, in this
county.

It is by many miners considered unlucky to sleep above the ground-floor, or to meet a woman during the early hours of the morning, while going to their work down the mine. Some men will turn back for no other reason.

Cup and saucer are set on the left side of the plate, and this has often been done to me in my lodgings. The most noticeable furniture in a miner's cottage consists of a handsome brass bedstead, tall chest of drawers, knife-box (and spoon-case combined) hung against the wall, 'longsettle,' weight-clock in case, sewing machine, 'poss-tub' and 'wringer' (upright clothes-wringing machine). Fires are raked in at night, and thus kept burning day and night, so that in some cases it is true that a fire has not been lighted afresh for ten or twelve years.

Bakers', poulterers', and fishmongers' shops are not usually seen in colliery villages. A 'village,' moreover, may contain as many as 5,000 people, or even more, while 'town' stands for such places as Sunderland or Shields. Bread is always baked at home, even in such places as Bishop Auckland. Fish is hawked about.

It is my opinion that, in spite of a rather congested population, the standard of morality is higher than in the South, while there is more kindness shown towards animals, though this does not apply, unfortunately, to pit-ponies, whose lot is too often a miserable one. Rabbit-coursing is also a flagrant exception. There is a good deal of brag and loud talk, exclusiveness and Pharisaism, amongst the miners as a class, but they cannot be called a degraded class by any means, nor more addicted to their peculiar temptations than any other class. Soaking in public-houses on pay-Saturday is very general, and great extravagance in living. But their home life compares well with that of men in any rank, and the miner, as he returns black from his work, may often be seen surrounded by his 'bairns,' perhaps with one on his shoulder. The genuine 'pittie' (coal-hewer) is very rarely a church or chapel-goer; neither is his wife, for the matter of that. Indeed, throughout this district, there is not the same disproportion between male and female worshippers observable in the South, the male element not uncommonly preponderating with us.

F. M. T. P.

26, VICTORIA PLACE, DEVONPORT,
    May 23, 1895.

TABLE OF SOUNDS

—•◆•—

[*The letters in square brackets represent Mr. A. J. Ellis's Glossic System.*]

ă as in 'man,' and

à as in 'master,' are pronounced [aa], the same *a* as in Fr. 'avez-vous,' except where otherwise noted. As a matter of fact, these two examples are exceptions in the dialect, becoming [maa·n] and [maa·stu]. 'Cat' varies between [kaat] and [kaa·t].

ar will be found written throughout [ăā]—the symbol adopted by Mr. G. P. R. Pulman in his *Rustic Sketches* (South-western dialect), this being the nearest sound that I know, although Pulman's vowel is slightly more nasalized.

ĕ in many words is pronounced very distinctly, a purer sound than that generally heard in lit. Eng. For instance, -*es* (pl. noun) -*ed* (past part.) are pronounced with a distinct *ĕ*, which is neither [i] nor [ú], as generally spoken not only in Southern dialects, but even in lit. Eng.

ee (as sounded in lit. Eng., whether spelt so or not) becomes [ae, ae·] in the dialect. This is the vowel in 'see,' 'sea,' and 'so;' 'he,' 'she,' 'me,' &c.

f is pronounced pure in 'of,' not as in lit. Eng. 'ov.' [ovf], not [ofv].

g, ending the pres. part., is not sounded.

h sounded as in lit. Eng.

ī, as in 'my,' 'mind,' is something between the literary sound [uy] and the Devonian [aa·y], and is therefore marked [aay]. 'Sight,' 'night,' 'right,' &c., however, become [saet], [naet], [raet]. 'Find' is always short = finnd, cp. German *finden*. So also, 'blĭnd,' 'hĭnd legs,' 'ahĭnt' (behind). Contrast 'wĭnd' (our 'wĭnd,' except in poetry), while to wind a watch is to 'wĭnd't.'

ĭ in many words is pronounced very distinctly, a purer sound than that generally heard in lit. Eng.

ng pronounced pure, not as ngg; e. g. 'fing-er,' 'long-er,' 'young-est.'

ŏ, as in 'not,' &c., is pronounced in continental fashion, and should be correctly written [ao]. [Au] (not [au·]), however, has for convenience been adopted in the text—a slightly coarser sound than the true one.

ŏ in a few cases remains as in lit. Eng., e. g. 'off' = [of] in the dialect, not [au·f]; 'soft' = 'sofft;' 'cross' = [kros], not (kraus] nor [krau·s]; 'brokken' (broken).

ough pronounced ow, as sowt, thowt, nowt. Cp. 'Howton' (Houghton-le-Spring—always so called).

ow. This is not the pure oo heard in Tyneside, although, for want of a better sign, [oo·] has often been adopted in these pages. It is rather a mixture of [oo·], [oa·], and [uuw·], and, like the last, [uuw·], is decidedly guttural.

My plan, therefore, has been to write down in the text whichever of these three vowels seemed to me to predominate over the other two. Occasionally the ow was so open that I have written [aaw·].

Vowel-sounds are apparently far more varied in a dialect than in received English, the vowel often changing its quantity, or becoming modified, according to the nature of the consonant by which it is followed.

r, except where initial, is a mere vowel, as in lit. Eng. It is never rolled as in Scotland, nor reversed as in South-western English.

s is pronounced pure, in 'is,' 'was,' and not as if iz, waz. Not [sz], but [zs]. So written at beginning of word-list, although later on the simple s has been adopted for convenience' sake.

t is pronounced in 'hasten,' 'fasten,' &c.

th hard in 'although' (as in lit. Eng. 'thin '). Var. dial.

ŭ, as in 'shut,' 'come,' is always pronounced ŏŏ [uo]. This is a test-vowel of Northern or Midland speech.

VOWEL-TRANSPOSITIONS AND OTHER CHANGES

—+—

ā becomes ă, as, mak (make), tak (take), stapple (staple).

ā becomes ī [aay], as, nīber (neighbour), wite ('weight, blame), wy (weigh), strite (straight). Contrast the pron. of eight [ee·út], though I have heard 'ight.'

ā becomes yă, as, Jyan, syam, tyabble, kyak, nyam (Jane, same, table, cake, name).

ā becomes yĕ, as, [fyes], [plyes], (face, place).

ai becomes ĕ, as, acquent, Renton (Rainton, near Hetton).

ai or ay becomes ëa, as, plee-a (play), wee-a (way), ree-un (rain), ee-ut (eight). This last is common, though not so pure, I imagine, as 'ight.' Contrast the pron. of 'idea' [aa·y·-dae], almost [aa·y·dai·], (accent on first syllable). This pron. is not confined to speakers of the dialect. "Thoo hesn't getten won i-day i' thy heed."

air becomes ăr, as, thar (there), war (where), har (hare). 'Here' is [hae·n] or [hai·u].

au becomes â, as, [aa·l], [haa·l], (all, hall). Call is [kaa·l].

d becomes th in lether (step-ladder), sowther (solder), showther (shoulder), thereckly (directly).

ĕ becomes ă, in sattle (to settle), tallifo (telephone), parish-ment ('perishment'). So, vice versâ, wesh, hesp (wash, hasp).

ĕ becomes ee, in weel (well), heed (head), &c.

er becomes re, as, [paat·rún], pattern. Cp. brunt (burnt). So also Soothren, Southern(er). Cistern is always 'cistren';

thirteen is 'thriteen,' A.-S. *threotyne*.   On the other hand, 'grinning' often becomes *girnin'*.

f is dropped in 'self,' as in other dialects.   Mysel', &c.   "It will ... smooth *it sell* against you."—Boy's essay.

g becomes **k** in 'stacker' (stagger).

ī becomes ē [ae·] in 'thee' (*th* hard; = thigh), reet (right), seet (sight). Short-sighted is always 'near-seeted.'   Boys selling matches cry, "box o' leets."   "Good neet."   "A'll mak the blōōd *flee* fra thy heed (head)!"   In [ae] (short) the [ai·] sound seems to predominate, in [ae·] (long) the [ee·] sound.

ĭ becomes ĕ in 'steng' (sting).   And conversely, ĕ becomes ĭ in 'stritch' (phrase—"at a stritch"), yis, yit (yes, yet).   A finer pron. is 'yass,' but *yes* is 'fine' in all its forms; the only genuine word in the dialect is 'ay.'

ir or **ur** becomes **or** [au·], as, dorty (dirty), forst (first), chorch (church), Morton (Murton—a common name), hort (hurt).   And so with 'word' (pronounced as spelt), 'work,' 'world' [wau·d, wau·k, wau·ld].

Contrariwise, **or** becomes **ur**, as in 'hurse' (horse).   "Try to make things for the people for the *informary*" (infirmary, —never 'hospital').—Extract from a boy's essay.

l is dropped, while ō becomes **â**, in [kaa·d, aa·d, haa·d], cold, old, hold.   Cp. [aa·n], own (adj.).

n is dropped in 'in,' which becomes *i'* before a consonant.

n.   A favourite letter in the dialect, e. g. win (with), bin (by), fon (for), sin (since), tin (to).

ō becomes **â** (see under 1)—snaa (snow), raa (row = terrace), knaa, thraa, craa (noun).   Joe is invariably 'Jo-a,' echo [ek·oa·u], and *no* ('fine' talk for 'nay') is always 'no-a.'

ŏ becomes ă in lang, haliday (A.-S. *haligdæg*), slaps (slops), lap-sided.   Contrast ŏny, mŏny, Jock (any, many, Jack).

ō becomes ŏ in brŏken, brok (broken, broke).   So, *sloth* is 'slŏth,' and *soda* is 'sodda.'   'Sloth,' however, is not true dialect, 'slot' being always used (meaning a sluggard).

ō becomes yă, as, styan, alyan, nyan, yam (stone, alone, none, home).
Cp. Yorks. 'beean,' bone. So, we say 'byath' or 'beeath' (both).
The A.-S. for *none* is nán = ne-án, so that Durham preserves
the most primitive form of all.

ō or ōō becomes ā or ē, as, [wae·] (= who. N.B. 'who' in the
dial., as pronounced in lit. Eng., could only mean 'how' [hoo·]),
[wae·z] (whose), [nae·baud·i] (nobody), [tae] (too, to; *two* is
pronounced [tuw]), dae (do), sae (so). Thus have is [hae·];
clothes are always [klae·z]; more, sore, are mair, sair; both
is baith (oftener byath); and most is maist [mee·úst]; while
no is nay. So [sae], sew [syoo·], sow [soa·u] or [saa·]
are all distinct in the dialect, but [saa·] also stands for 'saw'
(noun); [nae, sae, dae], however, are by no means so clear,
as may be seen from the following :—

> "Nae (nay, no); it's nae (no) good."
> "A's gannin doon to the sae" (sea).
> "A tell'd 'm sae" (so).
> "A's gan to sae" (see).
> "What's thoo gan to dae?" (do).
> "He's gan to dae" (die).

These sounds are almost identical, although 'no' (adv.) seems to
have more of the ā sound about it, 'no' (adj.) more of the
ē sound ; whilst *die* is pronounced, I should say, with a distinctly
longer vowel than *do*, and with rather more of the ē sound.

oo becomes ow, as, shower (sure); [aa·z shuw·u] "I'm sure"
(very common). [Aa·z shaaw·u aa· kaan·u see·n], "I'm suie
I can't say," is the usual assertion of ignorance. 'Byowtiful,'
tow [tuw·] (two). Cp. 'fower,' as in other dials.; A.-S. *feówer*.
So, *vice versâ*, ow becomes oo, as in thoo, hoose, noo, hoo, &c.

s or c becomes z in looze (loose, vb.), prozession (procession),
converzation, dezolate, abzorb, dezease (decease). So, contrariwise, Wesleyan is 'Wessleyan,' collision is 'collisshion' ([sh],
not [zh]).

t in 'it' is often dropped, e. g. 'in't' (in it), 'keep't,' &c.
"A dinna think't," the regular phrase for "I don't think so."
"He gave me't," never "he gàve it me," *it* always coming last
in such sentences.

u becomes **i** in 'honey' [hin·i] (term of endearment), [dis·únt] (doesn't), while **i** becomes **u** in duzzy [duoz·i] = dizzy.

u becomes **o** in one—'wonn' (always). 'Yan' is only heard from old people. So tong (tongue). See also under **ir.**

u [u] becomes **ŏŏ** [uo], as in the convent. Eng. pron. of bush, butcher, put, &c. N. country shibboleth. [knom hae·u] (come here) is perhaps a little 'fine' for 'har away.' [u] sometimes, instead of becoming [uo], becomes [oo] (not [oo·]), as, [kloob, roon, joog, moog, hooz], club, run, jug, mug, us (occasionally). Cup, muck, 'bus, however, would be short, [uo]. "And ever give *ous* cause."—From the National Anthem, as copied down by a boy. So, *vice versâ*, 'bush,' 'cushion' are often pronounced with the lit. *u*, and 'sugar' is always 'shugger' [shug·u].

ur becomes **ar** in warse (worse), warship (worship).

v dropped, as in ha'e (have), owre (over, too-). Becomes **f** in 'of' (not *ov*), naff (nave of wheel).

y inserted before **ōō**, e. g. skyool, school (always). So, fyool, byook, abyoon (above), gyoose, nyoon, syoon (soon). Cp. syoo (sew). Often spelt elsewhere 'beuk' or 'buke,' &c.

y becomes **ă**, e. g. varra [va·ru] very, Soonda [Suon·du] Sunday, &c.

NOTES ON GRAMMAR AND SYNTAX

a, an, both used, as in lit. Eng.

-ie. Common diminutive, e. g. laddie, lassie, Jimsie, Robertie, bairnie, doggie, 'wee bittie cattie,' 'brownie.'

Some words are only used in the plural; see under **Canes.**

by often becomes 'bin,' but not before a true consonant. "Bin hersell," "A's bi misell," "Bin itsell."

on. *n* dropped : "To lie o' the grass." (='on' or 'of'?) Used instead of *for* in the following :—"Gan on ! she's waitin' o' tha."

thy and **thine** are both used, e. g. "This boot is thine," "This is thy boot."

to becomes 'tae' before a consonant; 'tin' before a short vowel— "tin us," "A went tin'm" (to him, or to them); 'tiv' before a long vowel—"He went tiv oor hoose."

with becomes 'wi' before a consonant, 'win' before a short vowel, and 'wiv' before a long one (?); wimma (with me; emphat. wi' *me*), wi' tha, win 'm (him or them), win us, wi' ya (emphat. wi' *ye*). We always say, to travel 'with the train' for 'by train.' This is not confined to dialect speakers. 'With' is always [with], never [widh]. 'With' often stands for 'to,' e. g. 'used with,' 'well taken with,' 'kind with' (see under **Clap**).

it is becomes 'it's,' as in lit. Eng. "It's a grand day." "Ay, is't, a's shower" (or, "ay, a's shower is't"). Also used in cases where 'it is' would be found in ordinary English, e. g. "Where is't?" "There it's."

is it becomes 'is't' (Shakes.) [ist] (always). Not only in interroga-
tions, as, [wae· ist, wāā ist] (who is it? where is it?), but also in
asseverations, as, "A din-ah we ist" (I don't know who it is).
Notice the absence of any trace of *z* in *is*; or of *r* in *where*, even
before a vowel.

-en, past part. act., e. g. getten, hadden, letten, putten, litten.
So in SW. dial. 'boughten bread' is shop-bread, where -en
marks the p. p. *pass.*

I is [aa·z], 'thou is' [dhoo·z], invariably for 'I am,' 'thou art.'
When *thou* is not the first word, and is not emphatic, *tha*
[dhu] is the form, which stands also for 'thee' (unemph.).
'Thou' in such cases is emphat.—"A winna be bet (beaten)
bi [dhoo·]" (I'll not be beaten by *thee*). "Isn't tha" (aren't
you)? For the subjective and objective cases of pronouns
reversed for emphasis (so common in SW. dial.), cp. 'us is'
[hooz is] for 'we are,' heard occasionally from Board School
children—a species of 'fine' talk (!).

tell'd or **tell't**. Told (invariable). Cp. sell'd (sold).

seed, saw.

was and **were** are never transposed, but always used correctly as
in lit. Eng. Neither do we say 'I loves' or 'they loves.'

can't, won't, don't, unknown. We say 'cannot' or 'canna'
(= canno'), 'winnot,' 'winna,' 'dinnot,' 'dinna,' the form
in -t when used absolutely, or when followed by a word
beginning with a vowel. The following are idiomatic: "Can
you not?" (= can't you?), "think you?" (do you think?) e. g.
"Can you not do it, think you?" Cp. the frequent question
put to newcomers, "What think you of Hetton?" or more
familiarly, "What's tha think of Hetton?" P.—"What!
Is that water there?" Dungeon Ghyll guide—"It's not water,
isn't that."—Heard in Cumberland, but equally common at
Hetton.

ACCENT AND PRONUNCIATION

It is impossible for me to indicate the intonation of the Hetton dialect in ordinary conversation, still less those nicer refinements in which dialects are so immeasurably richer than the standard English; but, roughly speaking, the accent is evenly distributed on each syllable, without any being slurred over. This fact was very clearly brought home to me by the cry "Vote for [fau·] Fenwick!" the 'for' not being contracted into *f'r* or *f'*, even in the repeated cry of a tipsy man (July 12, 1892).

In 'accent (vb. and n.), accept, advent, expense,' both syllables are equally accented, not as in lit. Eng. accépt, 'xpénse, &c., and the e's are correctly pronounced, [aad·vent] not [ad·vúnt]. So also, 'object' (vb.) is sounded exactly the same as 'object' (subst.). 'House,' however, in compounds becomes *'us*, as in *workus*, *bake'us*. A few words are added, showing the prominent syllable in North-country pronunciation : secretáry, apóstolic, melanchóly (short o), circumstánces, arrangemént, steadfást, testimóny, trespáss, Whitechápel, párishioner.

We always say prōgress, trēfoil, &c.

WORDS AND PHRASES

Abbut [aab·út]. An introductory word. 'Ay, but,' or 'ah ! but.' E. g. "abbut a will."

Abed. In bed. Var. dial.

About [u·boot]. Around. "A'll twist yer neck about."—May 27, 1892.

Abune [u·byoon]. Above.

Ahĭnt. Behind.

Aliblaster. A large marble made of alabaster.

All [aa·l]. Quite. Var. dial. Used of time or distance. "How far is't? One mile?" "Ay, it'll be âll that." Note the future tense, where in the south the present would rather be used.

Alley. A glass marble used by boys in playing marbles. Probably from *alabaster*. The game of German Tactics, played with these, always goes by the name of 'Glass alleys.'

And all. A common pleonasm, often signifying nothing, though it may stand for 'also.' "He was there and all."

Any [on·i] (always). At all. "Can ye sing ony?" I have also heard the double form 'any at all' from one speaking 'fine.'

Arnicks. The bulbs of the buttercup-tribe.

B

Ask. A small lizard, or newt.

Ass. Ashes.

Aud-farand. Cunning; sagacious beyond one's years. (Spelling copied from Halliwell.)

Ay [aaˑy]. Yes (always). 'Yis' is fine, for gentlefolks' ears. Children are often corrected for answering 'ay' instead of 'yes' to their betters. Yet the native word sounds far more expressive. It is also very common as a mark of approval or attention, in listening to a narration.

Backcast. "We canno' backcast it," said by a widow of her son's illness, meaning, 'We cannot now order it differently.'— Feb. 25, 1892. This is not the general meaning. The word usually means a relapse. · "Thoo's getten a backcast" (i. e. you've got a relapse).

Bad [baaˑd]. Poorly. Var. dial.

Badly liked (of persons). Disliked (always). So, to be 'badly taken with' (unpopular), to be 'badly used' (ill-used).

Baff [baaf]. Techn. The alternate, or 'off' day or week ('Baff Saturday,' 'Baff week') when the fortnightly wages are not paid to the miners. Opposed to 'Pay Saturday.'

Bag. To give a rabbit the 'bag' is to overfeed it and thus cause its death.

Bairn or **Barn**, a sound between [baan] and [bāān]. Child (always). So 'grand-bairns.' This latter probably imported from Northumberland.

Bait-poke. Linen bag in which workmen carry their food.

Bally [baaˑli]. A lever for turning points on a railway; so called from a big iron ball on the stem.

Bank [baangk]. Hill. The word 'hill' is practically unknown in the dialect. Also techn. for the 'pit'- surface, top of 'shaft.' To 'work at bank' is to do the colliery work above ground.

Barley [bāā·li]. To claim, to speak for first ; as, "Barley me the big 'un."

Bat. Stroke, blow (always).

Bath [baath]. vb. trans. To wash any one in a bath. Children are always 'bath'd.' For *bathe*, lads often say 'bāve,' and 'bāvin' hole' (piece of water dammed up).

Beck. Used indifferently with 'burn.' A stream.

Bedfast. Bed-ridden (always).

Bedstraw. Heard once in Hetton from a South Shields person :—"He was a thin man,—looked as if he lived on his own bedstraw."

Belong [bu·lang]. Belong to, hail from. A man, on being asked where he 'belongs,' says, "I belong Hetton," meaning his home, or place of birth, according to circumstances. "War dis thoo belang ? " "Aa belang canny Shields."

Berries. Generic name for all fruit of the berry kind.

Betimes. Sometimes ; at times.

Bid. Invite to a funeral. "Was thou bid ? " When a miner dies, a 'bidder' goes round to all his fellow-workmen to bid them attend his funeral.

Bide. Stop, remain. Var. dial. 'Stop' is more generally used, but is finer. "Mind thou bides away." "Don't let them *bide* out night."—Extract from boy's essay.

Bill-knife. A knife used by butchers for cracking bones.

Bird's-eye. Germander Speedwell. "*Bird's-eyes* in summer."—Boy's essay.

Bit. Used adjectivally, as, 'a bit garden' (a little garden), 'a bit lad,' or 'a bit laddie,' 'a bit lass' or 'lassie' (a little boy or girl), &c. (always). We never say 'a bit of a—.' "Have a *bit* sport such as football," &c.—Boy's essay.

Bitch. A female. "Gan on, you bitch"(said in my hearing by a tiny child). Common term of abuse. A saying sometimes heard is, "Every dog has its day, and a bitch two afternoons."

Bite. A bit, morsel. " Not hadden a bite the day " (=to-day, [dhu dee·u]), is a beggar's usual plea. Two common sayings are : " Bite the bridle and bear it," of ' lumping ' anything disagreeable ; and, " I could bite a double tack nail in two " (a sign of hearty hunger).

Blackclock. Cockroach (always).

Blare. To cry. " A'll gi' th' something to blare for, if aa start wi' th'." " Thoo's always blarin'." So, ' blary,' noisy, of an infant.

Blather [blaadh·u]. Gabble. " She blathers away when there's no one here," said of a baby's attempts to talk.— May 7, 1891. " Hard (hold) thy blatherin' tongue."

Blazer. A piece of sheet iron, put between the grate and the mouth of the chimney, in order to make the fire draw.

Bleck. Dirty grease, found on coal waggon-ways where rollers are used.

Bleeberry [blae·beri]. Bilberry. The ĕ in 'berry' is quite distinct in compounds in the dialect, never as in lit. English (' blea-berry,' not ' bleab'ry ').

Blindy [blin·di]. Blindman's Buff. The usual form is ' Billyblindy.' See **Willy blindy**, p. 51.

Blob. To bubble. " It blobs up."

Blood-alley. A bone-marble with red streaks in it.

Bloody [bluod·i]. A favourite epithet amongst many pitmen, to be heard several times in every sentence from certain individuals.

Blush. Blister (subst. and vb.). " His hand's all blushed " [hizs haandzs aa·l bluosht].

Bogey (_g_ hard). Agric. A low, two-wheeled sleigh-cart for carrying hay to the stack without the trouble of pitching. The 'pikes' are drawn on to this cart by a rope, the ends of which are wound round a windlass-roller at the front end of the cart. Also, a square wooden truck on four wheels, for the purpose of removing heavy goods a short distance, called also a 'tram.' Down the pit, a bogey with an iron pin about two feet long, at each of the four corners, to prevent the timber and rails from falling off, would be called a 'horney tram.'

Bonny. Fine, pretty, handsome. "Thou's a bonny bairn." 'The Bonny Pit Lad' is an inn so-called in Easington Lane, near Hetton. "That's a bonny loss when ye're nae scholar"—May 8, 1891.

> "Lee laa, let,
> Ma bonny pet."

("Lie low, 'light," &c.,— said to a butterfly, in chasing it. [Lae·t]=alight, settle.) 'Bonny bord' (bird), [baun·i bau·d].

Bottles. Medicine (always).

Bottom. "We must all stand on our own bottoms," a common saying, equivalent to Gal. vi. 5. [Wae muos aa·l staan iv oo·r aa·n baut·mz.] Sometimes varied as follows:—"Every tub must stand on its own bottom."

Bowdie [boo·di]. A sherd, or piece of broken earthenware.

Bowl [boo·l]. Stone ball. The game is common in the North among pitmen. The one who throws the longest distance in three throws is declared the winner. Weight of 'bool' 5 oz., 15 oz., 20 oz., and upwards. For the pronunciation of this somewhat difficult vowel, found also in bowl (cricket), see under **Ow**, p. viii.

Bowrie [boo·ri]. The ring in which boys place their marbles, whilst playing.

Bracken. Brake-fern.

Braffen [braaf·n]. Horse-collar.

Brambles [braam·búlz] (always). Blackberry bushes and their fruit. 'Blackberry,' if used, would be 'black-berry' (the two words distinct,— see under **Bleeberry**). Blackberry jam is always 'bramble jam.' "Apple and bramble tart," "Bramble pudding" (from a *menu* at the North of England Café, Durham).

Bran-spanking-new. Quite new.

Brattice. In the house, a wooden boarding fastened at right angles to the door-frame, on the side where the door opens, so as to screen the room from draughts. Also, wood or canvas used in mines to help the air to travel.

Bray. Beat, thrash. " A'll bray tha weel."

Breed [braeˑd]. Bread. Compounds of bread are transposed : e. g. 'cheese and bread,' 'butter and bread,' 'jam and bread.'

Breed. To spread (of manure). Not heard about Hetton, but used in the county.

Brent. Steep (of stairs, ladders, and such-like erections).

Brimming. Boarward (of a sow), *maris appetens.*

Brinkside. River bank. "It's i' the brinkside" (said of a bird's nest).

Brock. Badger. "Aa's sweatin' like a brock." (A.-S.)

Broth. A pl. word, as in other dialects. 'A little broth' is always 'a few broth.'

Brownie [brooˑni] (always). Brown linnet. Singing competitions of these' birds for a wager are held in public-houses, where they are always advertised as Brownie Matches.

Brung. past part. of 'bring.' 'Browt' and 'brung' are both used, the former being the commoner form. The word generally used in the dialect, however, is 'fetch.'

Buck-stick. The game of 'Trap, Bat, and Ball.' Called 'Spell and Nurr' by old men. The game is now obsolete, but the implements were as follows. (Bat or Mallet), the 'buck-head' was about the size and shape of a small Yorkshire Relish bottle, with one side flat, though some players preferred to have it round. The stick inserted in the 'buck,' and fastened to it with cobbler's wax-ends, was generally a cane about a yard long. (Trap), the 'trippets' were of two kinds. The *wooden trippet,*—a strip of wood with hollowed cup at the heavier end, and a heel underneath towards the other end to obtain leverage, like the trapstick in Trap, Bat, and Ball. The *spring trippet,*—a rod of steel, was fixed at one end in a frame, and the other end was then bent down and inserted between the teeth of an upright notched stick fixed in the other end of the frame. This saw, or toothed 'catch,' being struck outwards, released the steel rod or trippet, and this threw into the air a ball, called a 'pot quoit,' which had been placed in a cup soldered on to the trippet. The scores were counted by the number of 'rigs' over which the quoit was hit. The little lads who collected the 'chucks' or quoits were called 'chuckiers,' and their reward was a certain number of shots.

Buffet [buof·et] (emphasis on the final syllable). Corner cupboard, the top half of glass, like a bookcase.

Bullet. A sweet(meat). The usual term. A large sweetshop in a certain North-country town is inscribed in large capitals —The Bullet King.

Bummeler. Bumble-bee.

Burn [bau·n]. A stream.

Butcher. The stickleback, without a red belly. See **Doctor.**

Butcher's Plums. Meat (?). On saying to some one I was visiting, "Who lives next door?" I was answered, "The butcher. That's where we get our butcher's plums." Only heard once.

Buzzer. Techn. The steam whistle or 'fog-horn' that warns miners of the times for returning to and from work.

Buzzum [buoz·um]=besom, a kind of broom made of heather or ling. *Bosom* is always pronounced [boo·zúm].

Byreman. A man who works among cows. Fr. 'byre,' a cowhouse. "Keep the cows *bier* clean."—Extract from boy's essay.

Caff. Chaff.

Cage. Techn. The lift which goes up and down in the shaft of a mine.

Call [kaa·l]. E. g. 'What do they call you?' The invariable equivalent to 'What's your name?' this latter form of inquiry being generally unintelligible to children, as I have found by experience. Also, to abuse. "Please, sir, he called me," a schoolboy's common complaint of another boy to his master.

Callant. Boy, or girl. Imported from Northumberland.

Caller [kaal·u]. Fresh. The cry of fishwives is still, 'Caller hair'n (herring)! Fresh, caller hair'n.' Also, [kaa·lu], a man paid to go round at various hours of the night and early morning, 'calling' miners to get up to go to work, by rapping on their doors. Hence, 'Calling Course,' the time a caller goes his rounds.

Calven [kaa·ven]. Of cows, that have lately calved.

Cam [kaa·m]. Rising-ground. " Tak' some o' that cam off."

Camp-bed. Four-poster, with a curved top on, formed of wooden laths with cross-bars let into them. The framework opens in the middle, for taking down.

Can and **Could**, besides their literary use, are also used in a peculiar sense for the vb. to be able. "They'll not can get any food"=not be able to. "I haven't could get across the doors," i.e. I've not been able to get out (v. common).— April 7, 1891. "I doubt I'll not can get" (I expect I shan't be able to come). This last is one of the commonest phrases, to be heard every day.

Canes. The schoolmaster's cane. Always in plural thus, "She's getten her canes" [kae·unz]. Cp. 'teas' (pl. noun) [tae·z], though used somewhat differently, e. g. 'We'll have our teas,' 'I'll have my tea.' Cp. also **Crickets**, **Taws**, **Gases**. This last means gas-jets, as in a gaselier. "Having the *gases* lit."—Boy's essay.

Canny. A North-country catchword. 'A canny few'=a fair number, a 'canny man' is one with some sense in his head, a 'canny little body' would be a dapper little person, with some notion of briskness and neatness. "It'll tak' a canny bit," i. e. take some time. Also, careful, gentle. A child is told to be 'canny' with a jug, a baby, or other perishable article entrusted to him. A juvenile letter to some one at Shields was inscribed on the envelope, "Please, Mr. Postman, be canny with this letter." 'Ma canny hinny,' a term of endearment.

Cant. To set on edge, and so turn over. "It canted owre."

Cap. A piece of leather put on a shoe.

Carling Sunday. Fifth Sunday in Lent, on which day the traditional dish is one of 'carlin's' cooked in melted butter A carling [kaa·lin] is a kind of pea, of a dark grey or brown colour. They are used by lads on 'Carlin' Sunday' for throwing at one another, and are boiled by publicans for their customers on that night.

Casket. Cabbage-stalk.

Cat [kaat, kaa·t]. "Let the cât dee" (die), i. e. let the swing (see **Shuggy**) run down of itself (constantly).—School treat, July 27, 1892. Also, the game of Tipcat, often called 'kit cat.'

Cat-haws. Hawthorn-berries, often shot by boys through a hollow hemlock-stalk.

Cat-knockles. The peculiar way some boys hold their marbles when shooting.

Cavil [kyav·l]. The station of each miner engaged in hewing coals is called his 'cavil.' These are changed every quarter by the drawing of lots.

Chaffs. Jawbones (plural only).

Chancetimes. Occasionally (very common).

Checkers. The game of Draughts (only word in use).

Checkweighman (miners' techn. term). Name for both the owner's and the people's representative, each appointed to check the other's dishonesty, in weighing coal-laden tubs, as they come from the pit.

Cheese and Bread. The young leaves of the hawthorn are pulled and eaten by children under this name. (See under Breed, p. 6.)

Chemmerly. Urine kept in a large stone bottle and used for washing clothes. This must undoubtedly be what Halliwell mentions as "Chamber-lie. Urine.—*Shak.*"

Chimla. Chimney. Hence 'chimla-piece.'

Chinnerly. To separate the larger pieces of coal from the dust.

Chisel. A kind of bran with which boys feed rabbits.

Chuck. Food, provisions.

Chucky. A young fowl.

Clag. To clog, stick ; so 'clagged'=stuck.

Claggum. Toffee.

Clap. To stroke, pat. "If you *clapped* them, they will be kind with you."—Boy's essay on Kindness to Animals. Observe the 'with,' which is very idiomatic.

Clarts [Clääts]. Mud. 'Clarty,' dirty. For the vowel-pronunciation, see under **Ar,** p. vii. It may be very adequately represented by 'air,' so 'clairts.' As villages are often denoted by some epithet, so we have on Tyneside 'Canny Shields,' 'Bonny Newcastle,' 'Clarty Walker.'

Clash. Disturb. 'Clash'd and slap'd,' of milk which has been agitated by hasty carriage. "He's been clash'd about, poor fellow" (i. e. often shifted). Met. "I'll clash thy brains out." Also, to 'clash' the door, is to bang it. "Dinno' clash the door so [dur sae·]."

Claze or **Cleze** [klae·z] (= clō's). Clothes. Hence the compounds, *Claze-prop,* a long pole to prop up the *Claze-line ;* *Claze-stick,* a short stick to thrust clothes down when boiling in the pan ; *Claze-swill,* a basket made of peeled willows, used for holding clothes on washing-days.

Cletching. Brood of chickens. (Final *g* inferred.)

Clever [kliv·au]. In good health ; well, properly. "If the window had been open, we could have seen clever." "He's not over-clever to-day," i. e. not very well. (Very common phrase), [naut uw·u kliv·au dhu dee·u].

Click. To catch one in the side, of a sudden twinge of pain, &c. "She was click'd away very sharp," was said to me of a woman dying suddenly. 'Click up,' catch up. To 'click' hold of any one (clutch).

Clip. To shear. "*Clip* the sheep in the summer."—Boy's essay.

Clish-clash. Idle talk. "There's been a lot o' clish-clash about it."

Clock. To sit, of hens. "She's not gan to clock yet." "Yon hen's clockin'." A 'clocker' is a sitting or broody hen.

Clog. A log. 'Yule-clog.'

Close. vb. [-z] and adj. [-s]. Shut. *Shut* is considered vulgar, *close* somewhat fine ; but both are heard.

Clout [kloo·t]. A cloth, or old rag (always).

> "Never cast a clout
> Till May is out,"

a local proverb, illustrating the inclemency of a North-country Spring. The vowel is not pure. Also, a blow on the head. [oo·] ; see under **Ow**, p. viii.

Coggly. Crooked, from side to side, as of an uneven swing's motion. Walking on high heels, or sitting in a hay-cart, would be so described.

Cotterill. A split pin for fastening handles on to cranks.

Coup Cart [koop]. The common dung- or coal-cart.

Cow [koo·]. A long iron rod fastened to the last 'tub' of a 'set,' so that in case the rope breaks, the rod sticks in the ground and holds the tub fast. Dray-carts and others have such rods dangling at the axle-tree, to take the strain off horses on a 'bank.'

Cowp [kuwp]. To exchange ; also, to overturn.

Crack. Talk. "Sit doon an' let's heh (hear) tha crack a bit." To have a 'bit crack' is the invariable way of expressing a bit of a gossip. 'Not much to crack on' is the usual expression for indifferent health. Cp. the lit. 'crack jokes.' Also a talker (for this, cp. double use of the word 'gossip'). "Thou's a good crack."

Cracket. A low stool, found in most cottages. When coal is low, miners sit on a cracket to their work, one end of which is higher than the other. A cracket stands on legs which in shape are not unlike a pair of bootjacks. A 'steul' [styool] has three separate legs, and a 'cobbler's stool' has four.

Cradle [kred·l]. A pig's ladder. Also, scaffolding in a 'shaft.' Also, a baby's wooden bed, on rockers, to be seen in use in every cottage. It is stiff and Noah's-ark-like in appearance.

Crake [krae·uk]. The crier's rattle, used when a meeting of miners is cried through the street, is called his 'crake.' The likeness· between this sound and the cry of the corn-*crake* is obvious.

Cray [krae·]. A hutch, as 'pig's cray,' 'pigeon-cray,' &c. The only word in use.

Crible. To curry favour.

Crickets. The game of cricket is always spoken of in this plural form. See under **Canes**, p. 8.

Crowdy [kraaw·di]. A kind of porridge. (Teaspoonful of oatmeal, in plate of hot water, and half a glassful of milk added, when cold.)

Cuddy. Donkey (always,—'donkey' unknown). 'Cuddy-handed' is left-handed.

Cush [kuosh hau·, kuosh haa·, kuosh huop] and other variations. A call to cows at milking-time.

Da and **Ma.** Papa and Mamma. " Where's tha (thy) ma? " " Tha da's coming ! " [kuom·ún].

Daft. Foolish, of persons. Of things : " They're the daftest things a child can have, to play with " (Mrs. R—, of some keys, Oct. 30, 1891). Var. dial.

Dawd. Slice. "Cut him a dawd o' breed."

Deadborn. Stillborn.

Dear knows [dae·u naa·z]. The superlative of ignorance, corresponding to 'goodness only knows.' On asking a woman when her husband will be in, she frequently gives this answer.

Deave [dae·v]. To trouble, bother (=deafen ?). " Next to George's integrity and generosity of character, was his love of country and patriotism. He was always ' deaving' us about his native Cumberland."—George Moore's Life, by Smiles, p. 29. " It's eneugh to deave one " (the noise children make).

Debiliated. Mispron. of ' debilitated.'

Delve. To dig.

Dene [dae·n]. The picturesque wooded hollows, each traversed by a stream, which line the sea-coast of Durham, are called ' denes.' " Cowslips in spring in the *deen*."—Boy's essay.

Dickises. " A'll dee (do) the dickises," i. e. something that another cannot do, e. g. walk on a wall, jump a stream, &c.

Dickyhedgie. The ' hedge-sparrow' (*accentor modularis*).

Doctor. The stickleback, with a black head and reddish belly.

Doors. "I haven't been across the doors," i. e. across the threshold, out of ' doors.' Notice the pl. in both cases.

Doorstaingels (*g* soft, as in ' angel '). Door-frames.

Doorstead [dur-stae·d]. Threshold.

Dothering. Same as 'dothery.' ' Dotherin' ducks,' the *quaking grass*.

Dothery [daudh·uri]. Shaky, failing ; of old age.

Doubt [aa· doo·t] (I doubt). The equivalent to 'I think.'

Dough [doo·]. Cake. 'Yule-doo' is a kind of currant cake made in shape of a baby and given to children at Christmas. Not so many years ago the 'putter lad' expected his 'hewer' to bring him the 'yule-doo.' If the hewer failed to bring one, the putter would take the hewer's clothes, put them into a 'tub,' fill it up with rubbish, and send it 'to bank ' ; or if the 'doo' was not well made, the putter nailed it to a tub and wrote the hewer's name underneath.

Doving [doa·vún]. Dozing.

Dowly [daaw·li], which seems to point to 'Doly '=doleful, as the true spelling. Dull (of persons or things). "Chorch is se dowly."—June 16, 1891.

Drawk. Soak. "A've gotten drawked throu' " (wet).

Duckstone. A boys' game, played by any number of boys. Each player chooses a nice round stone about the size of a cricket-ball, and calls it his 'duck.' A mark is made on the ground, and at a distance of about six feet from the line or 'bye' a large stone is placed, on which one of the players sets his duck. The game begins by choosing who has to set his duck on the stone. This is done by all the players pitching or rolling their ducks as near the stone as possible ; the one farthest off 'lies on.' Then the rest of the players 'toe the bye,' and try to knock his duck off. If the 'man ' can touch a player carrying his duck back, before he reaches the bye, this player then becomes the 'man.' The duck must always be on the stone when a player is touched,— else it is no go.

Duds. Clothes. Var. dial.

Duff [doof]. Fine coal, or coal dust (the only name in use). Hence, duffy, trashy, cheap and nasty (of sugar) ; small, like flour (of coal) ; ticklish, hard, awkward. The vowel in 'duff,' 'stuff,' &c., is longer than the ordinary vowel, being [oo], a sound halfway between [uo] and [oo·].

Dunch. To nudge or jog any one.

Dwarmy [dwaa·mi]. Faint, languid.

Dyke. A hedge. This word is never used to mean a ditch. The word hedge is only used in fine talk. " Toss't owre the dyke."

Een [ae·n]. Eyes. " Aa'll put thee een oot ! " Only used in this single expression, and that by old people. This is the sole relic of the old Saxon plural that I know of in the dialect.

Eh! aa din-aa ("dinna ken"—Bp. Auckland). "Indeed, I don't know." The commonest of expressions. ' Eh ! ' [ae] is a true North-country exclamation, capable of various meanings, according to intonation and context.

Eneugh [u·nyoo·f]. Enough.

Enjoy. Bad health is ' enjoyed,' equally with good health. This is a common use of the word in Eng. dial.

Enter-common. A place open to everybody. For instance, Hetton Hall grounds, being presumably private, during the strike were ' enter-common,' roamed over at will, used by anybody.

Ettle. To intend, try. " A ettled to gan to Hetton."

Evenly or **even-y.** adv Even ; probably, likely. (Probably a Tyneside word, as it is apparently unknown in or about Hetton. Frequently heard from a Tynesider.)

Eyesight. Never abbreviated into ' sight.' We always ken folk by ' eyesight.'

Face. The innermost part of the pit, where the hewers or stonemen are engaged at working into the solid coal or stone.

Fad [faad, faa·d]. Farmyard, littered with straw, for keeping stock in.

Fair. vb. intr. To improve, become fair (of weather).

Farntickled. Freckled.

Fash [faash]. To bother (vb. trans.). To be 'fashed' with anything, is to be troubled by it. " Lad, dinna fash yersel." "He disn't fash the hoose mŏŏch" (said of one seldom in); or, as we should say, 'trouble the house.'

Fat. This word is used by boys playing marbles. If a player shoots his marble into the ring, he is said to have 'spun fat,' and ceases playing.

Feck. Portion. "He did the main feck of the work."

Feckless. Helpless and feeble. The regular epithet of contempt for any one unable to shift for himself.

Femmer. Frail ; of persons and things. (Always.)

Fend. To shift for oneself, to do well. (Hardly dialect.)

> "A man may spend :
> He'll always *fend*,—
> That is, if the wife be owt (anything);
> But a man may care :
> He'll always be bare,—
> That is, if the wife be nowt."

Fetch up. Bring up, rear (always). To 'bring' is generally to 'fetch.' So, my mother (Yorks.).

Fettle. vb. and noun. North-country catchword. To 'fettle' or 'fettle up' [fetl uop], the regular expression for to 'right up,' 'get in order,' 'repair.' 'In good fettle'(good condition). "When mountain sheep sniff the breeze, as you come upon them, it is a sign of their being in good fettlin'."—Sep. 11, 1890. A woman has enough work to do with her children, "măkin', mendin', and fettlin' for their bellies." Also as a salutation : "Well, —, what fettle?" "Oh, canny." "I'll fettle ye up" (=punish).

Fiddy faddy. Trivial, elaborate, e. g. of fancy work. Not common.

Fine tasted. Fine flavoured. Dialect ?

Finger calves [fing'u kaafs]. More commonly called 'sucking calves ' [suok'n kaafs].

First [fau·st]. Instead of 'next —day' we always say '—day first.' This phrase is always used in local advertisements of entertainments, sales, &c. "— will be glad to see him to tea Monday *first* at 5 p. m."—From letter, Aug. 27, 1892.

Fladges. Snowflakes. Often called 'flatches.'

Flat. Min. tech. The station to which the 'putter' pushes the full 'tubs.' Here they are hitched together, and taken by the driver,—ten or twelve tubs at a time—to the 'landing,' which is a larger flat. From this flat they are drawn by the engine to the 'shaft.'

Fley. To scare. "Lad, dinna fley the galloway."

Flinches. A boys' game. This is played by a number of boys placing their caps in a row against the wall. Then the players in turn take a ball, and standing at a distance try to roll the ball into a cap. The owner of the cap which contains the ball picks it out and throws it at one of the players. If he fails to hit a boy, a small stone is put into his cap, and he is said to be 'one egg.' As soon as he is 'three eggs,' he takes up his cap, and this goes on until there is just one player left. The rest of the players must now place their hands against the wall in turn, and the winner is rewarded by having three shots with the ball at each player's hand. If a boy flinches or takes his hand away, he suffers three shots more for each flinch. I ought to have said that when a player takes the ball out of his cap, to throw at a boy, he may call on him not to 'stir flesh;' but if the other boy is quicker, and calls out 'flinches,' he is allowed to dodge.

The game is sometimes played in another way, as follows : —The players take the names of the days of the week. 'Sunday' will then throw the ball against the wall, and call out another name, e. g. 'Friday.' If 'Friday' succeeds in catching the ball or 'keeping' it before it touches the ground, he throws it against the wall and calls out (say) 'Wednesday!' If 'Wednesday' fails to 'kep' it, he picks up the ball and throws it at a player, shouting out 'nee (no) flinches,' whereupon the player stands fast. If

' Wednesday ' hits the player, the player tries to hit some one else, and so on until there is a miss. The one who misses throws the ball out and ceases playing, and thus the game goes on till only one player remains : then follow the rewards and punishments.

Flipe.   Hat-brim.

Flit.   To ' shift' or remove from a house by night, unknown to anybody.   " A Friday's flit
                                   Will never sit."

Foalfoot.   Coltsfoot, *tussilago* (always).

Folk.   People, e. g. ' menfolk,' ' womenfolk.'

Folly tar.   A game played with marbles, while walking along. One boy shoots his marble, and the other tries to hit it.   If it comes within the span (hand's-breadth), it is called 'Spangy Oneses' (' wonnzes ') ; but if it hits, it is called ' Knocky Twoses ' (' towsers '). Formerly so, but now played differently.   They just hit, and count that *one*, and so follow on.

Fon.   prep.   For.   In certain cases and by certain people.   We should always say, " I'll work for thee " [aa·l wau·k fur dhu], and ',fur me,' ʻ fur ye ; ' but some would say, ' fon it,' ' fon us,' ' fon 'im,' ' fon 'er,' ' fon 'em,' whereas most people would probably say ' fo' them ' [faudh·m].

Fond.   Foolish ; hence ' fondie.'   " Thou's a fondie."

Footing, first.   Properly, the first person who enters one's doors on New Year's Day.   This refers to the custom of going round to various houses on the morning of the New Year, soon after the old year has passed, and being regaled by those who humour the custom by keeping open house (bread and cheese, meat and drink, especially the latter) for the first callers.   Men go around in bands, it being held unlucky for a female to usher in the new year.   The cat is generally locked up beforehand, as it is also considered unlucky for animals to appear on these occasions.

Forbý.   Besides (accent as in ' besides ').   Prep. and adv. " There was other six forbý me."

Forebears [fau·bae·uz]. Ancestors. Sometimes called 'fore-elders.' "Our fore-elders have all lived here."

Fore-head. Always pronounced as two distinct words. This pronunciation is by no means confined to dialect speakers.

Forenénst [fu·nenst] (accent on last syllable). Facing opposite (always). Of houses in a street: "He lives right f'nenst us." Also metaph. "They're not doing right forenenst me," "He gov us sixpence forenenst it" (i. e. towards it).

Forthless. Worthless, useless.

Fortnighth [fau·t-núth]. Fortnight (always).

Fozy. Unsound, of vegetables. A 'fozy' turnip is a woolly one.

Fratchy. Cross-tempered. I have also heard 'fratch,' but these words are imported from Tyneside.

Fray [frae]. From. So, 'tee' [tae·] = to, too (*two* = [tuw]) ; cp. hae (have), hennot (háve not). A 'finer' pronunciation from pitmen for 'hennot' is 'hev'n't.'

Fremd. Strange. "He was mair like a frem'd body na a friend." "A fremd body wad dae that" (reproof given to a churlish man who refused to confer a benefit even on a relation in distress).

Fresh. A thaw. "There's a heavy (or, thick) fresh on." Common word among countrymen.

Fret. A mist, or sea-fog. To [frae·t] is also, to fret, whence adj. *freetin'* (fretful).

Gaffer. A 'masterman' or foreman. Var. dial.

Gait [gyet] (=way, road). A mining term signifying a short journey, e. g. from flat to shaft and back again ; hence, last journey. A workman, removing a heap of soil or stones, if asked how much still remains, will sometimes answer, "Another gyet 'll takd up," meaning one more journey. "Aa just hev another gyet to gan." "He niver knew what gyet it went" (what became of it).

Galloway [gaal·u·wu]. Pony. The only term in use. Pit-ponies are always spoken of as 'galloways.'

Gan. Go. A.-S. *gan.* "Gan on!" = 'now then!' 'start!' to be heard from children in the street all day long. The vowel in this word is very short, and nearly approaches the lit. short ă: the same sound is heard in 'yam' (home). 'Going' (pres. part.) is 'gannin,' when used absolutely; but when used as an auxiliary verb, it becomes 'gan;' e. g. "Is thoo gannin'?" (Are you going?), "A's gannin' doon to the [sae·]" (sea); but "A's gan to' [sae·]" (see), "A's gan to dae't" (I'm going to do it). This is sometimes heard :— " Ye're like the weel-off that hevn't a hoose to gan te" (You are like the well-off that haven't a house to go to), of those who have no need to trouble about finding a lodging for themselves, because they have a residence of their own.

Garth [gāāth]. A potato-ground, also called 'Taty-garth.' More generally, a small grass-field, enclosed, near a dwelling. A common element in place-names, as Hallgarth (Pittington), Briggarth in Easington Lane, &c.

Gather. v. i. Make a collection ('gathering') in money.

Gee. Pronounced Jee. A call to horses to go to the right, or off-side. Sometimes 'Gee-ba!' [jae·baa·] is heard. So Gee-back! Gee-up! (Forward).

Gee-y. Crooked, twisted. "It's all a-gee-y" [u·jae·waay].

Geordie [jau·di]. A miner; cp. Jack Tar, Tommy Atkins, or 'Johnny,' 'Tommy,' as generic names.

Get. One of the commonest uses in the dialect is that in which 'get' is used absolutely, for 'manage,' 'reach' (a place); hence, 'be present.' "I couldn't get" = I could not (manage to) get (there).

Get away. To die. Past part. getten, e. g. [get·n u·wee·u] i. e. dead. Also imperat., meaning, 'You don't say so!' Exclamation of surprise, doubt, or disbelief. An equally common expression is 'Gart' (slang rather than dialect).

Get off. 'Get up,' learn by heart (always). "*Get* some songs *off.*"—Several boys' essays.

Ghyll [gil]. A bit of wild ground hollowed out by nature ; a ravine. A common place-name in the Lake country.

Gill [jil]. A halfpint. Used of liquids.

Gimmers [jim·úz]. Rascal. "Ye gimmers, a'll smash tha l"

Gis gis [gis·gis]. Call to a pig.

Give over [giv uw·u] = 'Don't !' 'Stop that !' (very common). Imperat. of vb. meaning 'to cease.'

Gliff. Startle. "She gliffed me there."

Glower [gluw·u]. To stare with anger or amazement.

Gook, by [baa·y gauk]. An everyday expression of surprise, &c. Quasi-oath. "By gock, thoo's a quare 'un."

Gome. To heed. "He niver gomed me there."

Gorecap [gau·n kaa·p]. A quasi-oath. (Should be written *Go-cap ?*)

Gowk [guuwk] or 'gowkie.' A soft person. An April fool is often called 'April gowk.' 'Gowk' is also the core of an apple.

Grand. Common epithet of weather. [Graan dee·u] is the usual salutation on a bright, sunny day.

Grape. To grope, search. Also, a kind of shovel (sometimes called 'gripe '), or huge fork-like implement used in filling coke, and by farmers for removing manure.

Greybird [gree·u bau·d]. Commonest name for the song-thrush.

Greyhen [haen]. A jar in basket-covering, containing spirit.

Ground. "He hadn't been to ground for— days."—Mar. 2, 1892. To 'gan to groond,' a common expression for going to the closet.

Grozer [grau·zu]. Gooseberry.

Grunge. To grunt. 'Grunt' unknown. "They will shew their teeth at you and *grunge* at you."—Boy's essay.

Guisen [gaa·yzn]. To become dried and contracted, of rain-tubs or wooden cisterns, so that the water 'sipes' out. "Yon tub 'll guisen."

Guising [gaa·yzn]. Play-acting by ' guisers,'—men and boys in disguise (with blackened faces and paper caps), who go about performing a rough Christmas play. "Have *guisers*," "most of the boys *guise* near Christmas."—Boys' essays. The play is much as follows :—

CHARACTERS :—*The Leader, King George, Doctor Brown, Johnny Funny.*

Leader. The moon's gone down, and I've lost my way,
And in this house I mean to stay.
If you don't believe the word I say,
Step in, King George, and clear the way.

(Here comes in King George.)

King George. King George is my name,
A sword and pistol by my side ;
I hope I win the game,
The game of the sword,
The game of the sword.
Let's know your power,
I'll slash you into mincemeat
In less than half-an-hour.

Leader. You, sir ?

K. G. Yes, me, sir !

Leader. Take the sword, and try, sir !

(They fight and Leader falls.)

K. G. Ho, ho ! What have I done ?
I've killed his father's only son.
Send for the ten-pound doctor.

J. F. There's no ten-pound doctor.

K. G. Send for the twenty-pound doctor.

Dr. Brown. Here comes in old Doctor Brown,
The best old doctor in the town.

K. G. Who made you the best doctor ?

Dr. B. By my travels.

K. G. Where did you travel ?

Dr. B. Italy, France, and Spain ;
Three times there, and back again.

K. G. What can you cure ?

Dr. B. A dead man.

K G. Cure him.

Dr B. I've got a little bottle in my pocket, goes tick-tack. Rise up, Jack !

(Leader rises.)

*All sing :—*My brother's come alive again,
We'll never fight no more,
We'll be as kind as ever,
As ever we were before,
A pocket full of money,
A cellar full of beer,
I wish you a merry Christmas
And a happy New Year !
The weather's very clarty,
My boots is very thin,
I've got a little money-box,
To put my money in.

(Each then sings a solo.)

Gulley. Carving-knife, bread-knife. . Also, a crevice (gully).

Gusset. A tongue of stuff inserted as a patch ; a gore.

Gyoose. Goose. "Like a gyoose cut i' the head," i. e. bewildered, 'all abroad' as we say.

Ha woy. A call to horses to come to the left or 'near' side.

Hack. Min. tech. A heavy pick, weighing about 7 lbs., with head about 18 in. in length. There are various kinds, e. g. Tommy hack (round head and chisel point), Jack hack (round head and sharp point), Pick hack (sharp head and chisel point). Also, filth, dirt. "Aa canna get the hack off tha."

Hain. To shield, exculpate.

Halleluias. Salvation Army folk. The usual term.

Ham [haam]. Repeat. "He ham'd it o'er and o'er."

Handball [haand-baa·l]. The game of Rounders. More commonly called 'roondies.' Played by girls with shells ('williks') and a ball, whilst these words are recited :—

"Set a cup upon a rock,
Chalk me one a pot.
One, two, three, four,
One at a time," &c.
"One up," &c.

Handhollow [haan·daul·u]. Used by girls when playing the game of 'hitchy-dabber' (hopscotch). Often the 'dabber' gets so near the line that a girl cannot insert the breadth of her hand between, in which case she must give up the 'dabber' to her opponent to play.

Hand's-turn. A stroke of work (common) ; often, of a 'good turn.'

Hant. Habit. "He has a nasty hant of doing that."

Happen. This verb is used transitively, e. g. "he happened it" (i. e. it happened to him), "she happened a bad accident."

Har away [haa·wee·u, haa·ru·wee·u, haru (' harra ') wee·u]. The shibboleth of this county, heard every day and almost every five minutes. Be off! Come along! Here !

Heck. Call to a horse to come to the left or 'near' side.

Hemmels. Originally, a thatched shed, stable, or byre ; now the same, though seldom thatched. The word, although still understood, is going out of use. A field opposite Hetton Rectory, which once contained stables, is always called 'the hemmels field.'

Hempy. Up to tricks and pranks, mischievous. Very common. Also, 'hemp,' a scamp. (The word has nothing to do with *impudent.*)

Hench or 'hinch.' Haunch.

Hew [hyóo·, hyóa·] (vowel strongly emphasized). vb. t. & i. To hack away at the coal down a mine. Hence, 'hewer,' one who hews coal, a miner. (The vowel is peculiar, and should be heard to be appreciated.)

Hey [hae]. A common exclamation of surprise or indifference ; "hey! aa din-aa " (really, I don't know).

Hilly howley [hil·u huwl·(u)]. Hill and hole. In tossing the bat for innings, 'hill' is the oval side uppermost, 'howl' the flat side. "Hill or howl for innings, lad." Also used in Quoits.

Him. "Him wi' the " 'hat !' 'cap !' 'stick !' as the case may be. Children's salutation of chaff to a stranger in any way attired out of the common.

Hind (the 'i' long). A farm-labourer. (The only term in use.)

Hing. Hang.

Hipsy dixy (of evidence). Trumped up. (Is this *ipse dixit?*) A rare word about Hetton, heard from a Tynesider.— Oct. 31, 1891.

Hitchy-bay. The game of Hopscotch. Properly speaking, 'hitchy-bays' are the courts marked out. The square bit of wood is called 'hitchy-dabber.'

Hogger. Hose-pipe. Also, the following stocking-arrangement. The coal-hewer formerly wore his stockings with the 'feet' cut off, so that when small coals got into the stocking-foot, he had only to pull off this, and not the whole stocking; consequently his ankles were bare, while the stocking-leg covered his calf. He still swears by his 'hoggers,' as, "Dash mi hoggers !"

Hoit. Slut. "Ye mucky hoit !"

Hold. "Hold thy hand" [haa·d dhi haand, emphat. haa·nd] means 'Hold hard!' 'Stop!' 'Don't!' An expression to be heard every day in playing games.

Honey [hin·i], or [huon·i] (fine talk). The standing epithet of endearment to children, and used in the N. in much the same unrestrained way that 'my dear' is used in the S. W. 'Hooney hinney' is sometimes heard. "Behave, hinny," the stock admonition to a child at table.

Horney tram. See under **Bogey.**

Horntop. Only heard in the simile, "as slaa (slow) as a horntop."

Hotes. "Hoats, lad !" 'Hush!' or, as a North-countryman would say, 'Whisht !'

Howdie [haaw·di]. Midwife. "Thoo's niver been weshed since the howdie weshed th',"—sometimes said to a very dirty person.

Howk. To dig or hew out, as, for instance, with a 'hack.' "He's howked all the flowers up."

Hoy. To throw. "Let's see wee'll (who will) hoy the far-est."

Hunkers. Haunches. 'Sitting on the hunkers' means squatting, as miners do in the streets (sitting on the toes, with the thighs resting on the calves).

Hup [huop]. Whip (always).

Hupstitch=Every now and again, only in the phrase 'every hupstitch,' e. g. "she bakes every hupstitch." "He does it every hupstitch," or, "he does it *with the good constant*," i. e. constantly, or oftener than seems to be required.

Insense. Make to understand, 'render sensible,' inform. "You didn't insense me what your name is, did you?" "We insensed him intid" (into it).

Italian iron. A 'tallion iron' is an iron tube about 6 in. long and pointed at one end. Into the tube is inserted a heater. It is used to make the waves in the frills of old women's caps. The word is not dialectal, but probably few ordinary readers would be able to name the article, which is still to be seen in many cottages.

Jackjaw. The common mispron. of jackdaw.

Jolly Miller. A round game.

"There was a jolly miller, and he lived by himself,
  As the mill went round he made his wealth ;
One hand in the hopper (also, 'copper'), and the other in the bag,
  As the mill went round he made his grab (or, 'brag')."

These are the words they sing when playing. They go, two and two together, round and round, and there is always an odd one in the middle. When they come to the last word 'grab,' he makes a grab, forces another to come out, and takes his place ; they then start again, singing as before.

Jowl [juuwl]. The flesh on a pig's jaws. Also (vb.), to knock on the coal, while working down the mine, so that workmen on the other side may know by the sound how near they are to one another.

Jumly. Muddy. 'Jumly water.'

Kail-pot. A crock to boil cabbage (kail), &c., in. "The kail-pot's callin' the yetlin' smutty" (common proverb).

Keeker. The overlooker on a pit-heap.

Keep. "How are you keeping?" i. e. How are you (in health)? Very common, and—I fancy—more or less characteristic of Northern speech.

Kellick. Unfledged bird.

Ken. 'Kend,' 'kent'=know, knew, known. Of recognizing, or being acquainted with, people : "aa kenned 'im"(universal). [Aa· din·u ken], common about Auckland, is not so common around Hetton as [aa·din·aa] or more strictly [aad·i·naa] ('I don't know'). Yet I have heard the former pretty frequently from children and pure speakers. The form 'kenna' is also found, e. g. 'Diz thoo kenna?' (dost thou know?).

Kenner. Time to cease work. The common expression is 'lowse' (vb.).

Kenspreckled. Well known, marked.

Ket. Not good for food. (Often applied to sweatmeats.)

Kibble. Min. tech. A big iron tub, for filling with rubbish, in sinking a shaft.

King's evil. Erysipelas, a gathering in the face.

Kist. Chest. A chest of drawers is a 'kist.'

Kit. A small tub for washing in, used by pitmen.

Kite. Belly. "Deil be the kite!" (often said of a greedy child).

Kitling. Kitten.

Kittle. Ticklish, awkward to manage. A 'kittle' cough is one that tickles. Boys try to set a trap 'kittly.'

Kitty. Policeman's lock-up. (General.) Also, a short straw, about 6 in. long, filled with powder, and used by miners in firing.

Kitty cat. Game of Tipcat.

Knees, 'sitting on the,' the regular expression for kneeling. "He canna sit on's knees noo" (of an invalid). "He tell'd her to sit upon her knees, so down they sat."   .

Lad [laad]. Boy, youth. 'Boy' is never used. Also, a common way of addressing horses.

Laggans. The pieces of wood which go to form a 'tub.'

Laid off. Discontinued. The invariable description of a pit which is not working is 'laid off' or 'laid in.'

Lang. Long. 'Lang-settle,' 'Lang-legs' (nickname). "Short reckonings make lang friends." 'Nice and lang' (sarcastic expression of length).

Lap. To wrap. "Has thou lapped it up?"

Lass [laas]. 'Girl,' in the most comprehensive meaning of the word. (Universal.) "Mr. Shaw is keeping well, and me and my little *lass* are both well."—From letter, Oct. 28, 1890.

Lat. A lath.

Lay in. To 'lay in' a pit, or lay it idle; to leave off working it, as when it becomes exhausted of coals. See **Laid off.**

Lead [lae·d]. To lead a horse and cart; practically 'leading' is equivalent to 'hauling.'

Learn. Teach (as in other dialects).

Liberty. Leave, permission. Var. dial.

Library [laay·bu·ri]. A book got from a library (always). "Hes thoo getten a lib'ry?" The word is also used as in polite English.

Lignies. Quoits made of *lignum vitae* wood, used in the game 'Spell and Nur.' Also, a word used by boys when playing out their last marbles. "Them's mi ligganies" means his last, all he has.

Like. Likely. 'Like to fall'—nearly falling.

Limbers [lim·uz]. Shafts of a carriage. The only name for shafts of a 'tub' down the mine, which are made in one piece and detachable.

Linings. Pitmen's drawers, fastened at the knee by strings.

Lippen. To depend on, or trust to a person to perform a certain work. "I lippen on him doing it."

Lisk. Thigh.

List. Desire, energy. "I haven't list to gan across." "He hesn't list to did" (do it). Preserved in the lit. *listless*.

Loggerhead. A coloured butterfly. Large moths are also sometimes called 'loggerheads.'

Longcart [lang·kāat]. A two-wheeled hay-cart, somewhat between an ordinary cart and a rolley.

Longsettle [lang·set·l]. A long seat like a form, with back and arms.

Lonning. 'Laning,' i. e. lane. The only form known. [lon·ún.] "Gan ōōp the bâck-lon'." "We find swiney up Mousely (Moorsley) *lonen*."—Extract from boy's essay on Wild Flowers.

Looks-tha=look'st thou? [looks dhu]. An expression to gain attention, or mere pleonasm, used by boys to one another, the familiar form of 'Look you!' which latter is addressed to strangers or superiors.

Loop [luwp]. To leap, jump. "See we can lowp the far'est." "When I was young and lusty, I could lowp a dyke."

Loose [laawz]. To finish work. "What time diz thoo louz?" or, to a stranger, "What time do ye (yae) louz?" (When do you leave off working?)

Loppit. Sour milk, curd milk.

Lops and lice. Hips and haws. So called by children.

Love-begot. Born out of wedlock. (An unjustifiable eu-phemism.)

Low [luw]. A flame. Hence '*low-rope*,' hempen rope steeped in tar, to burn as a torch.

Lowpy-lang-lonnen (=leapy long lane?). Leap-frog.

Lug. Ear (always). "I'll skelp thy lug." The 'u' is generally long, [loog] rather than [luog].

Lum. Chimney. "Thou's as black as the lum."

Ma. See under **Da.**

Make. To 'mak' gam'' (make game) of anybody, to make fun of, ridicule. Generally, in the form *makkin' gam'*. To 'mak' sha'p,' or 'be sharp;' equivalent to the commoner 'look sharp.' I have heard 'sharp' used adverbially, meaning quickly. [Aa·l shääp dae·d] (I'll do it quickly).

Man. As throughout North, used in exclamations. 'Noo, mon!'=Now, sir. "Eh, mon, aa din-aa"=Indeed, sir (or, mate), I don't know. Also used irrespective of sex, e. g. I overheard a big girl say to a little one, "Look oop that râ, mon" (look up that row, child). In other uses man is always long [maa·n].

Manishment. Mispron. of 'management.'

Mark. 'Dressed up to the mark,' i. e. in the extreme fashion. So, 'up to the nines,' 'up to the knocker,' 'up to Dick and down to Richard.' All more properly slang than dialect.

Marra (marrow). Mate. So, of things, the 'fellow.'

Matterless [maat·u·lús]. "It's matterless," our everyday ex-pression for 'No matter,' 'It's immaterial.'

Maybe [meb·i]. Perhaps.

May-cat. The superstition is, that a cat littered in May will suck infants' breaths, if allowed to climb up into the 'creddle.' Nobody will keep a May-cat.

Meat. Food. Var. dial. Bib. Only used in this wide sense, when speaking of animals' food, e. g. "Give the hens their meat."

"Give them good *meat.*"—(From a boy's essay on Kindness to Animals.)

Mense. Politeness, kindness. When you invite your friends to dinner as a duty, and they cannot come, you are said to 'save your meat and your mense.' "It'll be more menseful" (courteous, hospitable-looking)—said of serving up a joint entire, to some guests, rather than the same joint cut up into chops. "Mense is a great thing in this country" (*re* funeral extravagance as a token of respect).—A. R., July 4, 1892. Decency. "I did it for mense's sake." Vb., to decorate, e. g. 'mense the window.'

Mettle. "He's ower sharp mettle" (too hasty tempered).— Mr. B., of his brother, July 21, 1892.

Mickle. 'Little or mickle' (much). Not common. "I'd rather have the scrapin's o' the muckle (or 'mickle') pot than the wee pot full."

Middenstead. Ash-heap.

Midgy. Also called a 'Mistress.' These names were given to a kind of lamp used by putter lads. The height of the lamp was about 8 in., width 3 in., with open front. When first invented, they were simply little wooden boxes, with a hole at the bottom, through which the candle was thrust, and another hole at the top to let out the heat. Afterwards tin took the place of wood. The flame was sheltered by a piece of wood or tin about 2 in. high from the bottom of the lamp, and a similar piece from the top. The 'midgy' has now gone out of use.

Mind. Remember. Var. dial.

Mistress. Used interchangeably with 'Missus,' the former being used rather of strangers.

Moley rat. The only name known for the common mole.

Muffler [muof·lu]. A neckerchief or 'comforter' (always).

Must. Often used where we should say 'shall' in lit. Eng. "Would you like your milk to drink, Mr. P.?"   "Yes, please."   "*Must* I bring you 't, then?"

My word [maa·wau·d]. Our commonest exclamation of surprise. Answers to 'indeed,' 'well, I'm sure,' of other parts. "My ward, thoo'll get wrang."

Native. Native place (always so).

Nay [nae·]. No. The adjective is pronounced with more leaning towards [ee·] sound, else the two are identical in the following: [nae·, aa·zh shuw·u dhaz nae· paath hae·u] (*no*, I'm sure there's *no* path here).

Neif [nae·f]. Hand. "Dŏŏble yer naif (or, '*naiv*') lad." "A'll gi' tha my neif directly!"   'Double-neif,' the clenched fist.

Nevvy. Nephew (always). Var. dial.

Nicely. "How are you?"   "Nicely," a 'polite' expression for 'varry canny,' or, 'aa canna com-plee-an' (complain).

Niffnaffs. Nick-nacks.

Night. Used, as in country parts in S., of any time after noon. Heard a woman parting from another at 3.30 p.m., say, "Good night."—July 7, 1890.

Nimmy.
> "Nimmy, nimmy, nak,
> Which hand will tha tak'?
> The reet or the left,
> Or the bonny bord's (bird's) heft?"

Counting-in rhymes recited in starting a round game.

Nine. "He's like a 9 with the tail cut off" (of a man good for nothing).—April 27, 1892. Favourite simile.

Noll. To strike [naul].

Nor. Than (always). Cp. the Welsh *na*; or is it only a transposition of *than*; or can it be really *nor* (=and not, instead of than (=*then*, next in merit)? For transposition, cp. 'int I' for 'nit I,' in S.-W. Eng.

Noration. A confused crowd. A noise.

North-countryman. One from Northumberland or over the Border. "He cooms fro' the West," would mean Weardale, Teesdale, or Cumberland. 'Sooth' (south) means anywhere south of the speaker; 'West-countryman' would be unintelligible, of a Cornishman,—he would be a Southern [sooth rún]. 'Countryman' means an agricultural labourer.

Nought [nuwt]. Nothing. So, 'thowt'=thought. "What's thoo daein'?" "Nowt." "Aa thowt sae" (always).

Now [noo·]. Often used for emphasis, a mere pleonasm. "He's a nice mân, he is, noo." "He came here, he did, now," &c. Used for 'well' in other parts; e. g. 'noo then' (emphasis on word 'noo') [noo·dhn]='well, then' (in narrative).

Nows and thens. Common for 'now and then.'

Null [nuol]. Annul. Mr. R., an invalid, rubs his legs to 'null the pain' [nuol dhu pee·un].

Of. (1) [u]='Like,' in the phrase, "or onything o' that."
    (2) [iv]='in,' in the phrase, "He's getten such a pain iv his legs." "He canna lie iv it" (i. e. in the bed). This may not be a form of 'of,' but a transposition of 'in.'
    (3) [of]='for.' To 'wait of' any one is to wait *for* him. (Invariable.) So, "he's shootin' of us" (he's shouting for us).

Oftens [of·ns]. Often.

On. Of. E. g. "a bit on't," "tak' hard (hold) on't." But we say 'a cup o' tea.' When 'of' is used, it is never pronounced *ov*, any more than 'is' becomes *iz*.

One [won]. Used with indef. art. "I saw a one yesterday" (cp. the phrase, 'a dozen,' &c.). This would only be used, but always, where 'one' was not used numerically, as opposed to any other number, but merely as a unit.

Open out. To open, the 'out' being superfluous. Of parcels, new buildings, &c. Not by any means confined to dialect speakers.

Other. Used as in St. Matt. xxv. 16, 17, 20. "We had a sale of work and made £20, also a social and dance, and made *other* twenty."—From a letter, Feb. 13, 1894. (In lit. Eng. we prefix *an* before *other*, whereas in the dialect *a* is prefixed to *one*.)

Our. Used in calling members of a family. Mothers may be heard shouting at the top of their voice, "Har away, oor Jeäne Marry Lizzie" (all Christian names are generally given, as here, referring to one child). "Coom hayer, oor Jumzie!" (Come here, our James). Used indiscriminately by boys to one another; "dinna do that, our Fred."

Out of the way [oot dhu wee·u]. Of people, ungodly, attending no place of worship, disrespectable, or vicious (varied according to context). "He's been an out of the way man iv his time."

Outbye. Out of the way, remote. Also, techn., of a miner coming towards the 'shaft' in order to get 'to bank.' The corresponding term is 'inbye,' i. e. further along underground, towards one's 'cavil.'

Over [uw·u]. Too; 'owre big,' 'owre smarl' (small). (Always.)

Oxter. Armpit. 'Oxter-bound,' stiff in arm and shoulder.

Panker-bowdie [paeng·ku buw·di]. A game played with marbles. The 'panker' or 'penker' is a large marble, made of stone or iron. Each boy puts four marbles in a ring, and proceeds to knock them out of the ring with a panker. What he knocks out he gets; but if he fails to knock one out, the next boy aims at his panker, and so puts him out. The line from which they start, five yards from the ring, is called the 'bye.'

Past. "He's gone past hissel," i. e. lunatic. "A's sixteen past," i. e. sixteen, past my sixteenth birthday. Contrast S.-W. equivalent, "I be into my seventeen."

Paste-eggs (i. e. Pasch-eggs). Eggs, dyed in a decoction of logwood chips and onion peel, and sold in shops or prepared at home during Easter, are so called (always).

Pawky [paa·ki]. Dainty.

Pay [pee·u]. "I'll pay your bottom," a common threat to children.

Peedee. Something small, as a tiny marble.

Peesweep [paez·waep]. Lapwing, or peewit.

Peggin'-top. A peg-top.

Pen-point. Nib of a pen.

Pen-shank. Pen-holder.

Perishment. A violent chill is always described as a 'perishment of cold' [pa·rish·múnt u kaa·d].

Pick at. Find fault with, abuse (very common).

Piffolo. Piccolo (always).

Pike. A large haycock, often six feet high. The small haycocks only are called 'cocks.'

Pipe-stopple. Stem of tobacco-pipe. Sometimes called 'pipe-shank.'

Pit. The only word in common talk for a *mine*. So, a miner is always 'pitman' or 'pittie,' and pit dress is 'pit-claes.'

Pittering [pit·rún]. Low-spirited, complaining. "Ay, he's pitterin' on" (said of one who was continually fancying he was just about to die).

Planting. Plantation. "Gan up past yon plantin" [plaan·tn].

Playlaking. A simpleton. To 'mak' a playlakin' of' any one, to make a fool of him.

Please. 'Please yes,' 'please no,' a schoolchild's answer to his teacher. "Tommy, do you know your lesson?" "Please yes."

Plodge. To wade through any liquid substance. What is called 'paddling' in polite English, we always call 'plodging.'

Pluff. Plough (very seldom). 'Plough Inn' is called 'Pluff Inn.'

Poke. A sack, or bag (common). 'Flour-poke.'

Poked. Offended. "He's getten hissel' poked."

Pollis. Police. 'The pollis'=the policeman. "I'll fetch the pollis,"—frequent threat to a naughty child.

Pompey. A small boy ; a dwarf.

Poss. To wash clothes by putting them in a 'poss-tub' of soap and water, and thumping them with a 'poss-stick,' or short-legged staff,– in some places called 'dolly.'

Pot-pie. A boys' game. All caps being placed on a lad's back, the rest vault over him, 'leap-frog' fashion, and the one who displaces a cap becomes *vaulting-horse* in his turn.

Potted head. Stewed meat, as sold in butchers' shops.

Priest [praest]. A clergyman is always so called. "I have being to church and heard the *priest.*"—Boy's essay.

Proggle. A thorn.

Puddings. Intestines. "A'll pull thy puddin's oot !" (Hence, Pigs'-puddings, Black-pudding.)

Put. Min. techn. term. The 'putter' is a lad who 'puts,' or shoves the full tubs from the hewer's 'cavil' to the 'flat' (q. v.), and takes the empty ones in to him. The empty or 'tume' tub is often called the 'led 'un ' (=led one, i. e. the tub led in).

Putting through. A scolding.

Quey stirk [waay stau·k]. Two-year-old heifer.

Quoit. Besides the usual meaning (a common game amongst miners), this word also means a large white marble made of earthenware, and called a 'pot quoit.'

Rageous. Outrageous (violent and delirious).

Raise. To 'raise the place' [ree·úz dhu plyes], to make an uproar. "He's raised the place to gan there" (of a boy who had pestered his parents to send him to school, and gone wild over it with excitement).

Rame. To ply one with questions, as children love to do. Mrs. R.—April 1, 1892. "What's tha ramin' o' me for?" "He just ramed my life out for sixpence." Here it means to 'bother.'

Range [rae·unj]. To rinse. "Range the pot out."

Rank. The distance a 'putter' puts the coal from face to flat. The first 'renk' might be 80 yards from the hewer, and as the distance increased, the putter received an additional penny for every 20 yards. This was the case formerly, but putters are paid differently now.

Ranters. Primitive Methodists.

Rasp. Raspberry. Strawberry is pronounced straa-bérry (not 'straubry'). See **Bleeberry.**

Rattle-scawp. A frolicsome, mischievous fellow.

Rax. Stretch. Dry flesh, stretched tight, would be 'rax'd.' Hence 'raxy,' stiff. "He raxed his-sel' oot" (stretched his arms).

Readimadeasy. Reading made easy [raed·úmúd·ae·zi]. The term is only used by old people, and refers, I imagine, to a once popular spelling-book of that name. "How far did ye get through the readimadeasy?" "Oh, I got as far as the 'Crâ and the Jug,' and the 'Man with the Scythe in his Hand.'"

Rear. Underdone (of meat).

Recking-crook [krook] not [kruok]. A crook hanging over the fire for pans to hang from.

Reckling. The weak pig in a litter.

Reek [rae·k]. Smoke. 'Baccy-reek,' 'Powder-reek.'

Reest. To be lazy. When a horse refuses to draw a load, we say it has 'tune (taken) the reest.'

Reesty. Rusty (of bacon).

Rend. Tear. "I rended the lard out of a pig," i. e. took the fat to boil down.

Ribbing-plough. A plough without wheels.

Ricket. A badly-castrated animal.

Riddle. A sieve. Var. dial.

Ride. To 'ride the water with' anybody is, to trust him. "He's not safe to ride the water with."

Riggy. Ridgy, as of a grass-field in furrows. Furrows are called 'rigs.'

Rīnd. Rime, boar-frost. "There's a heavy (or, thick) rind on."

Rip. Rascal. Often said of children.

Rive. To tear. "Rive that handkerchief in two." "Please sir, he's ruvven a leaf out." "He's ruvven his breeches." [raayv, ruov, ruovn.]

Road. Way (metaph.); as, 'out of the road' ('out of the way' means something quite different), 'in the road,' 'no road' (by no means), 'any road' (anyhow). This use of *road* is found in the Midlands, and extends a considerable way South.

Rolley. What is called a 'trolly' in some parts, i. e. an open waggon for carrying heavy goods, such as beer-barrels or packing-cases.

Rolypoly [raaw·li paaw·li]. Rolling over and over, as children do on a slope.

Rook [roo·k]. Thick fog, damp. "It's a thick rook the neet (to-night)." Adj. 'rooky.' Cp. 'reek.'

Roopy. Husky (of the voice). (Always.)

Rown [ruuwn]. Roe of a fish. The milt is called 'melt.'

Rozzle. Resin. Also, to warm oneself. "He rozzled his hide."

Rummle cundy. A ditch filled up with loose stones, for water to drain through.

Sackless. Foolish, senseless.

Safety. Pronounced as a trisyllable, 'safe-ity.'

Sag. To bend down in the middle, yield (as a plank does by its superabundant weight). *Shakes.*

Salamander. A poker with a flat, thickened end, heated red-hot in the fire, for thrusting into an unlighted fire. (Mentioned in *David Elginbrod.*)

Sally Walker. A round game. The players form a ring, joining hands, and go round a girl in the middle of the ring, singing—

"Rise, Sally Walker, rise if you can,
Rise, Sally Walker, to follow your good man.
Choose to the east, choose to the west,
Choose to the bonny lad that you like best."

The girl in the middle then takes the young man of her choice, and the rest sing—

"Now ye're married I wish you joy,
First a girl and then a boy.
Seven years over, seven years to come,
Now is your time to kiss and be done."

They then kiss and go out, to give place to another couple, the game going on as before.

Sandlark. Meadow-pipit.

Sark [saaˑk]. Shirt.

Satisfised. The invariable mispronunciation of 'satisfied.' [saatˑisˑfaaˑyzd.]

Scallion. A young onion, before the bulb has formed. A favourite dish is scallion and lettuce.

Scobbie. Chaffinch. Not so common as 'sheelie.'

Score. Line. 'On the scores, out!' This word is used by boys in their game of marbles, when the marble is not knocked clean out of the ring, but lies just on the line : then the cry is raised, 'It's on the score.'

Scoreprice. Pitmen's wages, the price current for filling a 'score,' i. e. 21 (or, in some places, 25) 'tubs.'

Screed. A man, speaking of various-sized scraps of glass, cut into squares and long strips, called it "only screed-glass." (Only heard once.) Same as *shred?*

Scribe. A scribble or scratch, in the phrase, "He hadn't the scribe of a pen for it," meaning he had not even a receipt or written guarantee.

Scrike. vb. and subst. Shriek.

Scringe. When a boy sharpens his slate-pencil with a knife, he says it makes his teeth 'scringe.'

Scrubter [skruob·u]. A wooden harrow, made of boards fixed on a frame Venetian blindwise, for breaking 'clots' (clods).

Scuffler [skuof·lu]. The same as a 'scrubber.' Also, a turnip-plough.

Scumfish. Suffocate.

Scunner. To flinch, or give signs of pain. "He never scunnered that blow on the heed (head)."

Second-handed (always thus). (At) second-hand.

Seek. Look for. (Invariably.) [saek.]

Seggar [seg·u]. Soft stone lying on coal-seams, used for making into bricks and coping-stones.

Set. subst. Work, to-do. "A've had-en a bonny set win 'm." Also, a train of coal-waggons or tubs. To 'set' means, to escort, convoy.

Set on. Sew on, of buttons, &c. Also, to put 'tubs' into the 'cage' down a coal-mine, the man, whose business this is, being called 'set-on,' or 'on-setter.' 'Set' is the ordinary expression for 'put;' e. g. "set on the dishes," "set out the fowls" (drive them out of doors), &c.—see **Put.**

Settlings. Sediment.

Shades [shae·udz]. Window-curtains (always). "Shades cleaned at 1s. 9d. the pair," painted on a laundry-cart in Sunderland. 'Window-curtain,' when used, only refers to that kind which is strung across the lower half of a window.

Shaft. Min. The perpendicular entrance to a mine, in which the 'cage' works. There is a double shaft to every mine. [shaaft.]

Share. Cow-dung.

Sheelie [shae·li]. Chaffinch.

Shift. To remove, change one's residence. To move, e. g. "Shift them gates" (of opening or shutting railway-crossing gates). A 'shift,' tech., is a turn at work, mining work being divided into 'day-shifts' and 'night-shifts,' each of eight hours' duration.

Shinny. The game of hockey. 'Hockey' is unknown.

Shire. To pour off water or any liquid in such a way as to leave the sediment.

Shithering bout [shith·rún boot]. Shivering fit, feeling of cold all over the body.

Shive. Slice. "It is easy from a cut loaf to steal a shive." See *West Somerset Wordbook.* This proverb may be found in Shakespeare (Tit. Andron. Act ii. Scene 1). ·

Short-tongued. A person who cuts his words short, slurring them over, is sometimes said to be 'short-tongued.'

Shot. Rid, as to be 'shot' of any person or thing (always so). "A's well shot on't" (I'm well rid of it).

Shotstick. A round stick on which a paper cartridge is rolled (mining term).

Shuggy. subst. and vb. int. Swing. "Give me a shuggy; he's shuggied all the afternoon [aaf·tu·nyoon]." (S. Sch. Treat, Aug. 13, 1891.) The word 'swing' seems to be quite unknown in this connexion. 'Swings' are swing-boats, to be seen at every fair. A 'shuggy' is also a see-saw.

Siddle. To pick out or choose the best of anything.

Sin. Since, ago. 'Zyne' is sometimes heard among the old, and 'langzýne' (accent on the penult.).

Singing hinny. A kind of girdle-cake, common among old folk. (Name imported from the North.) Now generally called Spice Cake. (Not to be confused with **Spice**, q. v.)

Sipe. Leak. "The watter's sipin' oot."

Skeel. A peculiarly-shaped bucket (broader at bottom than top, with upright stave projecting from rim, to serve as a handle), formerly used in colliery villages to carry water for household use. They were carried on women's heads on a 'wase' (q. v.), and a piece of wood was made to float on the top, to prevent the water from splashing over.

Skelp. Smacking blow. "A got a good skelp at him." Infants are threatened with having their 'botts (or 'bottomies') skelped.'

Skelper. Anything very large,—a 'whacker.' Cp. 'banging,' 'slapping,' as epithets of size.

Skemmy. The common blue or farmer's pigeon, often kept by boys as a pet.

Skimmering. 'Skimmerin' clean,' the acme of cleanness. Of a doorstep, linen, &c. (Communicated by A. T. D.)

Skinch. "Let be! I'm not playing." When a boy wishes to stop playing at any running game, he shouts "Skinch!" meaning he is not liable to be caught and made prisoner.

Skitling. Same as 'hempy.' "The skitlin' rascal!"

Slack. A hollow or dip in the land.

Slip. Child's pinafore.

Slippy. Slippery (always).

Slogger. To walk with the stockings hanging loosely.

Sloken [slauk·n]. Slake, quench.

Slowed [sluwd]. Drùnk.

Slum. Slumber. "He's slumming" [sluom·ún].

Small, in the phrase, 'Small family,' means a family of small children.

Smally [smaa·li]. Small. "That's a smally bit bairn."

Smit (='smite'?). An infectious disease is said to 'smit,' or to 'be smittle' (always). "He'll get the smit" (i. e. catch the disease). "Is't smittle?" (Is it 'catching'?)

Smout [smoot]. A hare's 'run' through a hedge.

Smush. To smoulder away, as touch-paper used by miners. The 'touch' is made by soaking in saltpetre.

Snap-apple. The game of Bob-apple.

Sneakly. Quietly (generally with a notion of slyness).

Sneck. A door-latch (always). Also, vb., to latch.

Snot. Candle-snuff.

Soft. Wet (of the weather). The common salutation on a rainy day is, "Soft!"

Sonsy. Nice, jolly-looking, stout (of persons). Imported from the North, and not commonly heard.

Soss. A heavy fall. "He went down with such a soss."

Sour docken. A small plant children pull and chew,—the Common Sorrel.

Spang. Span, i. e. the distance stretched between thumb and little finger.

Spanish. Licorice, or Spanish juice. (Pron. 'Spennish.')

Speer. Inquire. This word is rare, being an importation from the North.

Spelk. A thorn or splinter in the flesh. The usual term. Also of anything insignificant. "A spelk of a thing." "He's just a spelk of a lad."

Spell and Nurr. See **Buck-stick.**

Spew. To vomit.

Spice. The only name known for currant-cake. 'Cake' always means tea-cake.

Sprag. Min. A bar of wood inserted between the spokes of a coal-waggon, to act as a drag.

Spuggy. Sparrow. Boys' nickname for the house-sparrow. "Looks tha, thar's a spuggy, man!"

Squander [skwaa·ndu]. Scatter (always).

Staithes [stae·uths]. Tech. The shipping stage belonging to a colliery.

Standard. A stager, well-known inhabitant of any place. "Another old standard . . . passed to his rest the week before."—From a letter, Aug. 29, 1895. (Very common.)

Steer. Strong (of the voice).

Stent. One's fill. "He's had his stent" (i. e. satisfied).

Stick and Clout. Cant name for an umbrella.

Stime. "A canno' see a stime," often said by one whose eyesight is bad.

Stirk [stau·k]. Yearling calf.

Stirken. To cool and stiffen, as gravy does. [stau·kn.]

Stite. Equally, as soon. "Stite him as me" (the sense is often 'much rather').

Stithe. pron. 'Steith' [staayth], not [-dh], cp. **Staithes.** Stench, or a very close atmosphere.

Stobbie. Unfledged bird.

Stonie. Stallion. [styan·i.] A stone is always a 'styan.'

Stook [stoo·k]. Bundle of sheaves set up in the corn-field.

Stour [stuuw·u]. Dust in motion.

Strait. Narrow. (Common.) "Yon's a strait place." Cp. St. Matt. vii. 13, 14.

Stramp. Trample.

Striddly-pigeon. A boys' game. A boy is blindfolded, generally by pulling his cap over his eyes, and stands with his legs stretched out. The other boys shy their caps between his legs. When all the caps have been thrown, the boys shout, "Strite (straight) on, striddly-pigeon!" The boy then walks straight on, until he touches a cap with his foot. The owner of the cap snatches it up and runs to a certain place and back again, the rest of the boys 'bleaching' him, that is, thrashing him about the head with their caps. As soon as the boy returns to the starting-place, he becomes 'pigeon.'

Stubbie. Same as 'stobbie.'

Sump. 'Sump wet,' wet to the skin.

Sup [snop]. Drop. 'A sup rain' (a drop of rain); "he likes a sup" (fond of a drop too much); "ha'e a sup milk, will tha?" vb., to sip or drink. "Give them (cats) clean milk to *sup*."—Boy's essay.

Swalley [swaul·i]. A hollow place. "The village lies right in a swalley." Said also of the throat, e. g. "My throat is sore just in the swalley."

Sweel. To gutter, flare, of a candle.

Swiney. Common Sow-thistle or Milk-thistle. See under **Lonning.**

Taistrel. An ill-mannered boy; one given to playing pranks.

Take with. Take to, appreciate. "——'s well tune with," i. e. is very popular. [tyoon] is p. p. of [tak].

Tanner. Root of a boil, corn, or tooth.

Tappy-lappy. Pell-mell, helter-skelter. Halliwell has, "In haste with the coat-laps flying behind through speed," with the following example :—"Nanny Bell's crying out : I just gat a gliff o' Gweorge runnin', *tappy-lappy*, for the howdey."

Tarry towt. A single strand of rope steeped in tar.

Tarsy [taaˑzi]. A round game. The players form a double ring by standing in a circle with a space between each, while each player has another standing immediately behind him. There is one odd player who stands, as third, behind any of the other two. A player standing in the centre then tries to 'tig' or touch the inside player who has *two* behind him, while the latter, to avoid being caught, must either run behind the two standing behind him, or behind any other two in the ring. Thus another is brought to the front rank, and if caught before he can place himself behind another couple, becomes in his turn the pursuer, while the late pursuer takes his place in the ring.

Taw [taaˑ]. A boy in playing marbles always has his fancy marble to shoot with : this he calls his 'taw.' Var. dial.

Taws [taaˑz, taaz]. A leathern strap for punishing naughty children, to be seen hanging up in many cottages. It is like a carriage-window strap, cut into a fringe at one end.

Teas. Used in the plural thus :—"She haves her teas (=frequent teas) sometimes at the Sewing Meeting" (A. R.). "No, thank you, we've hadden our teas" (but, 'my *tea*'). See under **Canes.**

Teejy. Tedious, peevish.

Teem. vb. i. and tr. Pour. The only word known. Rain 'teems in' through a leaking roof. To 'teem out' is to pour out liquids. A teapot with a well-turned spout is called a 'good teemer.' Shakes. has 'beteem.'

Teethache. Toothache. "He's getten the teethache."—Oct. 19, 1892. Also called 'tyoothwark.' "My tooth's working, I've get-en the toothwork."

Tew [tyoa·]. To tire, pull about, tease. "She fairly tewed his life out." So 'tewing,' of work, means tedious, and 'tew,' generally, means, to toil, labour. For pronun., see under **Hew.**

The night [dhu nae·t]. To-night; so, 'the day.' (The usual expression.)

Throng. Busy; inconveniently crowded (always).

Thropple. Throat, windpipe.

Throstle. The song-thrush is sometimes called 'thros'le,' but more often 'greybird.'

Tice. Entice, encourage.

Tidy betty. A short fender across the grate, without a bottom.

Tied. Used metaph., like the lit. Eng. 'bound.' So found in Jeremy Taylor. "A's tied te gan" (forced to go).

Tig. To touch. (Used by children at play.)

Tiggy. The child's game of 'Touch.'

To. By. 'What are you to trade?' "She's getten a son tin 'im" (lit. 'got a son *to* him,' i. e. by him). Also, = For. "What'll ye take to your breakfast?"

Token. Min. techn. A ticket, of tin or leather, affixed to each tub of coals, stating details.

Toom [tyoo·m]. The day or time for the dismissal of hinds, when they are hired afresh. Met., "A've had-en a sair tume (spell) abune six moonths." "He canna bide a tume now" (a change, of raiment or position,—of an invalid). This word does not seem to be generally known. Also, empty (only used of coal-waggons).

Toothwork [tyuoth·waa·k]. Toothache.

Toughcake [tyoof kyak]. A water-cake, or white-cake, baked on the girdle. No currants used.

Tram. Min. techn. term. Very much the same as **Bogey**, q. v. Strictly speaking, a bogey has the flange on the wheel, while in the case of the tram, the flange is on the rail. Also, the tram had fast and loose wheels, having more play on the axle, to allow them the better to take a curve.

Trippet and quoit. The game of Trap, Bat, and Ball, more commonly called 'Buck-stick.'

Troon [truuwn]. A mason's trowel.

Trow [truw]. Trough.

Truth. "The truth goes farthest," the common overture to a confession, to be heard any day.

Tub [too·b, toob, tuob]. Min. A coal-waggon used down the pit, holding from 6 to 8 cwt.

Tug. To rob (a nest).

Tune or **Teun.** Taken (always).

Tup [tyoop]. A 'tupe' or 'teup' is a ram. Var. dial.

Twist. Quarrel, disagreement. "They're all atwist." "Hes thoo hadden a twist?" So, 'twisting,' discontented.

Twitch-bell. Ear-wig (=twitch-belly? Cp. S. W. 'angle-twitch'=a worm. Ear-wig=arse-wriggle).

Unpatient. Impatient.

Upcast. Throw in one's teeth, taunt with.

Upgrown. Grown up, adult (always).

Uproar. No idea of noise implied, but only of confusion, as of a house 'upside down.' To 'be in an uproar,' is to have an untidy room, as on washing-day, &c.

Upstanding. Regular, fixed, constant (of wages).

Used with [yoaˑzd with] or [yuwˑzd with]. Used to, accustomed to. Cp. 'taken with.'

Vast. 'A vast [vaast] of'=number of; a 'vast o' years,' the only expression for a long time. "There has a *vast of* People died here lately."—From a letter, March 27, 1895.

Viewer. The manager of a coal-mine. So, 'under-viewer' (under-manager).

Vine. A lead-pencil (always). 'Pencil' always means slate-pencil. "A piece of *vine*."—Boy's essay.

Wad [waad]. Would.

Wag. 'Play the wag,' to play truant.

Waggon-way [waagˑn weeˑu]. Tech. A colliery line of rails.

Warden [wāādn]. Church warden. This abbreviation is universal, and used by all classes.

Warsh [waaˑsh]. Faint, from loss of food. (adj.)

Wase [waeˑz]. A folded cloth, or bundle of straw, placed upon the head, on which to rest the 'skeel,' q. v. I have altered the spelling of this word from 'weeze' to 'wase,' in accordance with Halliwell.

Waysgoose. Day trip of the workpeople belonging to a firm or company, especially a newspaper staff. Same as 'bean-feast.' Var. dial.

Week-end. In the North always signifies Saturday till Monday, when working-folk sometimes go away for a visit. The common expression of educated and uneducated alike, and by no means confined to the North. 'Week-end trips' are now advertised on most of the lines.

Weeny. Tiny. Only heard once, from a native of S. Shields.

Wey ay [waiˑaaˑy] (why, ay!). Interj. To be sure! (v. common.)

Whaing [hwaeng]. Boot-lace.

What cheer [chai·u, chae·u]. Commonest greeting of man to man, answered back in the same words. A nautical phrase imported into the dialect (?), equivalent to 'hoo is tha?' For the pron. of *cheer*, cp. 'here,' 'hear,' which are both pronounced [hai·u] or [hae·u]. [Kaan dhoo· hae·u mu] (Can you hear me?).

What for. For the commoner 'what . . . . for?' Standing at the beginning of a sentence, like the literary 'why' [waut fur hez dhoo baen u·wee·u sae lang] 'What for,' i. e. 'why,' 'hast thou been away so long?' N. B. The glossic [fur] exactly represents its equivalent in lit. Eng., in speaking of the 'fur' of any animal (= Fr. feu). 'What' is used for 'that' or 'which,' as in the following :—"Give them your things *what* you cant eat."—Boy's essay.

Whaten. 'What'n' or 'what'na'= what kind of? (always). Cp. 'whichen a one' (which), 'suchen a' (such a).

Whiles. Once (*olim*); sometimes.

Whin. Gorse.

Whirligig [hau·li·g̈ig]. A boy's iron hoop. The wooden hoop only is called a 'hoop.'

Whisht [hwisht]. Hush! 'Hush' is quite unknown.

Wick. Quick. (subst.) "He's cut his finger into the wick."

Wife. Woman. "An aad wife." So, 'fish-wife,' 'hen-wife.' Cp. 1 Tim. iv. 7.

Wig. A tea-cake. Same as 'Doo.'

Wiggery waggery. Loose motion in walking.

Will. Used for 'shall,' e. g. "Will I like it, think you?" So, 'would' for 'should.' "Aa wad like 't, aa wad noo" (I should like it, I should indeed). This is not confined to dialect speakers, as the following extracts from letters will testify :—"I will be glad to hear from you soon;" "I will be pleased to do my best to meet your wishes;" "We will be very glad if you will give us the pleasure of your company," &c. ; "We will be very glad to see you." For this use, cp. the following from two boys' essays :—"You might run to the man and say, take some bricks off (an overloaded cart), or else the horse *shall* fall down ;" "letting us see the Magic Lantern, and telling us where we *will* see the place."

Willy blindy [blin·di]. A game played by boys. One boy is blindfolded, and the rest tie knots in their handkerchiefs, and strike him on the head or shoulders, until he catches hold of one of them. This one then becomes the 'willy.'

Wingeing. Whining. "He's winjin' on now," "She's so winjy."

Winter. The bracket hooked on to the bars of a grate, upon which anything may be heated in front of the fire.

Wishful. Desirous.

Wite. Weight; blame. "He got the wyte on't." Cp. 'neighbour,' pronounced 'nighbour.'

Wobbit. An introductory word. "Wobbit thou'll not."

Wor [wau]. Our. 'Oo-ur,' spoken fast, produces 'wor' or 'wur.' Cp. probable origin of the lit. pronunc. of *One*.

Work [waa·k]. To ache. "Mi airm warks." This is a common Wykehamist 'notion,' except that it is pronounced 'wurk.'

Wowl [wuwl]. To howl, cry.

Yam. The invariable pronunciation of 'home.' An example of purely short *a*; cp. 'gan.' "Aa's gannin yam, aa is."

Yard [yãad]. Common abbreviation for 'churchyard.' Cp. **Warden.**

Yetling. A small crock. See under **Kail-pot.**

Yewfir [yuof·u]. A young fir-tree about the girth of a man's arm.

Yoke. To 'put in' a horse (to a vehicle). This is distinct from 'harnessing,' or putting the harness on his back, &c.

Yon (adj.), **Yonder** (adv.). That, there; generally, of objects pointed out. Sometimes, of distant things. I was much amused once, when going over the castle at Durham, to hear a man who had lately seen the sights of London, comparing the antiquities of the castle with what he had seen 'yonder,' or 'in yon place,'—all his remarks began, 'When I was *yonder*,' &c.

Yowley or 'yellow yowley' [yuw·li]. The yellow-hammer.

Yule. Christmas. Hence 'Yule-dough' (see **Dough**), 'Yule-clog' (see **Clog**). 'Yuletide' is becoming commoner than it was a short time ago, but most people say 'Christmas.'

OXFORD: HORACE HART, PRINTER TO THE UNIVERSITY

LAKELAND AND ICELAN

BEING

A Glossary of Words

in the

Dialect of Cumberland, Westmorland and North Lancashire

WHICH SEEM ALLIED TO OR IDENTICAL WITH THE
ICELANDIC OR NORSE

TOGETHER WITH

*COGNATE PLACE-NAMES AND SURNAMES, AND A SUPPLEMEN
OF WORDS USED IN SHEPHERDING, FOLK-LORE
AND ANTIQUITIES*

BY THE

REV. T. ELLWOOD, M.A.

RECTOR OF TORVER

AUTHOR OF 'LEAVES FROM THE ANNALS OF A MOUNTAIN PARISH
IN LAKELAND'

𝕷onbon

PUBLISHED FOR THE ENGLISH DIALECT SOCIETY

BY HENRY FROWDE, OXFORD UNIVERSITY PRESS WAREHOUSE
AMEN CORNER, E.C.

Oxford
HORACE HART, PRINTER TO THE UNIVERSITY

INTRODUCTION

———◆◆———

In the year 1869, and for one or two years following,
Dr. Kitchin, now Dean of Durham, took up his abode at
Brantwood, near to this parish and on the opposite margin
of Coniston Lake, and while there he had in hand, as a
Delegate of the Clarendon Press, Oxford, the proofs of
Cleasby and Vigfusson's *Icelandic Dictionary*, which was
then passing through the press. As a native of Cumberland, I had long before this been in the habit of collecting
characteristic old words of the Cumberland and Furness
dialect, and Dr. Kitchin kindly asked me to look over
those proofs to see whether I could suggest any affinities
between the Icelandic and our Northern forms. A careful
comparison convinced me that there was a remarkable
resemblance in some words, and an identity in others,
both in form and meaning ; that this resemblance was so
general that it could not be owing to any mere accidental
circumstance ; and that the older the words found in our
dialect, the more closely did they and the Icelandic seem
to be allied. It occurred to me then that the task of
collecting such words of the dialect of Cumberland, Westmorland, and Lancashire North of the Sands, as seemed to
have identity or close affinity in form and usage with the
Icelandic, would be one means of tracing out the origin
of this dialect, and hence in some measure the origin of

those by whom this dialect was spoken; and as we have in Lakeland words and usages almost as primitive as they have in Iceland, we could, I thought, trace some portion at any rate of our native language a great way towards its primitive or parent stock.

I thought also that, as many of the old customs and superstitions in Lakeland are fast dying out, just as the old Norse words that represent them have become or are rapidly becoming obsolete, it must be now or never with me in commencing the undertaking, if I wished permanently to note down the customs and vocables of the people amongst whom the whole of my life has been spent.

I have worked at intervals at the task of collecting these words for a period of now upwards of twenty-seven years; and though I have doubtless in some instances done over again what others have done much better before me, yet in other instances I imagine I have unearthed and identified words·and customs of the Northmen yet to be found amongst our Dalesmen, of which not any notice had been taken before.

Dr. A. J. Ellis, in his fifth volume of *Existing Dialects as compared with Early English Pronunciation*, gives fifteen varieties of the Cumberland dialect, ten of the Westmorland dialect, and seven of the dialect of Lancashire North of the Sands, that is, of Furness and Cartmel. These differences are, I think, only phonetic, and do not include any radical or derivative differences; and if you find any undoubted Norse word in the dialect of any portion of that area of which I have spoken, the chances are that it has survived in every other rural portion of that district, provided that that portion has 'an oldest inhabitant' with years long enough and memory keen enough to retain the customs and vocables of sixty or seventy years ago. I refer to Dr. Ellis in this connexion with great pleasure. I corresponded with him on the subject of the Cumberland and Furness dialect from 1872 close up to the time of his death. At times for weeks a voluminous correspondence kept passing between us; he took the dialect in its phonetic, while I tried so far as I could to examine it in its derivative aspect; but throughout this correspondence Dr. Ellis was always most willing to communicate anything I required from his unrivalled word lists and researches. The last communication I received from him was with the present of the concluding volume of his great work[1] upon the subject; and shortly afterwards, having completed in these volumes what may, I think, be regarded as his life-work, when his task was over he fell asleep.

It seems in many instances to be the opinion of philologists who have treated upon our dialect as derived from the Norsemen that, as they were plunderers, so all names and habits of plundering must be referred to them. A careful study, however, of the words of the following Glossary seems to point to a very different conclusion. The remarkable thing about them is that they evince the peaceful disposition of those who first settled here and left their language. The great bulk of the words are field names and farm names—the terms applied to husbandry operations, and names for the keeping and rearing of sheep and cattle or used in their care or management; words applied to butter-making, cheese-making and dairy

---

[1] The general title of this work is 'On Early English Pronunciation with Especial Reference to Shakespeare and Chaucer.' Published for the Early English Text Society and the Philological Society, London.—Part I in 1869—Part V in 1889. Part V deals more especially with existing dialects as compared with Early English Pronunciation

operations generally, and the domestic duties and concerns of everyday life. In pursuing this study it has been of great service to me that I have never lived outside the district in which the words peculiar to this dialect are still retained; and that I have lived generally in the most rural, the most isolated, and consequently the most unchanged portions of it, that my word lists were obtained where my life was spent—amongst a people where the earliest words and customs are retained if they are retained anywhere; and from living amongst them I have always had opportunities of getting these words from those who speak them in their earliest and, therefore, their purest forms.

The country bordering upon the Solway is often pointed out as being the most rich in Cumberland in unchanged dialect forms. It was in this country I was born and lived, being conversant with almost every part of it until I was between seventeen and eighteen years of age. For three years I lived near the Cumbrian Border to the East of Carlisle, where phonetically a very different dialect is spoken, approximating very much to the Lowland Scotch of Annandale, still however retaining the characteristic Norse forms.

After this, for two or three years, as a master in the St. Bees' Grammar School, a foundation then *free* for every boy native of Cumberland or Westmorland, I had an opportunity in this, a central Parish on the West Cumberland sea-board, of hearing the dialect of boys who had been born in well-nigh every large and important parish of Cumberland, and also to some extent of Westmorland; while for the last thirty-five years of my life, in a remote mountain parish of the Lancashire Lakeland, I have certainly, in my searchings and wanderings, had the most ample opportunities of studying the dialect and folk-speech of every nook and corner of the lake country, and of every parish and valley in Lancashire North of the Sands.

I have said that many of the old words of Lakeland (by which term I mean what may be called larger Lakeland, i. e. Lakeland as it includes the whole of Cumberland, Westmorland, and Lancashire North of the Sands) are, like many of the objects and customs which they represent, rapidly becoming obsolete, that the dialect, as represented ˙by its most characteristic words and phrases, is fast disappearing; yet in Cumberland at any rate we have a series of dialect poets, extending over great part of 200 years, who have embalmed in their songs and poetic sketches the words and phrases of our Cumbrian everyday life. They have been poets of the people, and their words and measures still live in the converse of Cumbrians: with those words and measures I have been familiar from childhood, and I seem to have retained them viva voce [1] from my earliest recollections. In illustration of the meaning of the words in the Glossary I have quoted copiously from those local dialect poets. Briefly, therefore, I will sketch the position and writings of the chief of them, extending from the early part of last century to the present time.

The first Cumberland dialect poet was the Rev. Josiah Relph. He was born shortly after 1700, and died of consumption in 1743. He became perpetual curate of his native village, Seberingham, and also, as the custom then was, he taught the parish school. Many of Relph's pieces are pastorals and translations into the dialect from Horace,

---

[1] Most of the editions of the Dialect Poets are so incomplete, omitting even the best pieces, that they have to be retained viva voce if retained at all.

Virgil, and Theocritus; and in some of his poems he has very faithfully pourtrayed the chief characters of the village in which he lived.

Stagg, the next dialect poet, was born about the year 1770 at Burgh-upon-Sands, near Carlisle, and died at Workington in 1823. He was deprived of his sight very early in life. He kept a circulating library at Wigton, and eked out his living partly by acting as a fiddler at dances, fairs, hakes, and merry nights. His pieces, published first by Robertson of Wigton, exhibit truthful pictures of Cumberland scenes, manners and customs, as they existed one hundred years ago. His poem, *The Bridewain, or Bringing Home the Bride*, is the most truthful picture of the keen neck-or-nothing galloping and other amusements which took place at a Cumberland wedding of the olden time. It is a literal description of a marriage which took place in the Abbey Holme, where it is still spoken of as 'The Cote Wedding.'

Sanderson is the next Cumberland poet. Born in 1759, he seems to have lived most of his early life at Seberingham. He spent the closing years of his life at Shield Green, Kirklinton, where he lived the life of a recluse. He was a great collector of old Cumberland dialect words; and in some of the oldest forms in the following word-lists I have had hints from his sketches. He was the compiler of the first, or at any rate one of the very first, of our Cumberland Glossaries. I have a copy of it which I suppose to be of the earliest, probably of the only edition; it bears the imprimatur 'Jollie, Carlisle, date 1818.' He died in 1829. His end was a melancholy one. The cottage in which he lived by himself, from want of care on his part, took fire in the night; the neighbours were alarmed, and ran to the rescue; he escaped, dreadfully burned, from the flames, and lay down (he was in his seventieth year) under a tree, much exhausted, a few yards from his own door. His friends meanwhile tried to save what they could of his property. He inquired most anxiously after a box in which his MSS. had been deposited, with the view of the publication of a laboriously corrected edition; being told that the box was consumed, he expired a few minutes after, saying, or rather sighing out, 'Then I do not wish to live.'

Mark Lonsdale was born in 1759 in Caldewgate, Carlisle, and passed through life partly as a teacher and partly as an actor in London and the provinces. He died in 1815 in London, and was interred at St. Clement Danes. He wrote much for the stage. Of his writings in the dialect, *The Upshot* is the ablest and most original dialect poem that has appeared. It is the free sketch of such a Cumberland gathering (see Glossary, under 'Upshot') which really took place about 1780. It consists of about 300 lines, and I know of no piece that approaches it in the correct use and application of old Cumberland words. After continuing for many years in MS. it was published in 1811 in Jollie's *Sketch of Cumberland Manners and Customs.*

Robert Anderson is the Cumberland poet whose works[1] are most widely and most generally known. He was born shortly after 1770, in Carlisle, and died in 1833, at the same place: he was a pattern-drawer by trade. His life was like more lives, a hard struggle for existence, and he fell in his later years into habits of intemperance, which may possibly have had something to do with those feelings of bitterness and misanthropy which he exhibited in the decline of his life. He is matchless as a truthful exponent of the dialect, manners, and customs of Cumbrians. He

---

[1] Most of the editions of Anderson are very imperfect and incomplete. The most complete I know was published by Robertson, Wigton.

carries us into their homes and their domestic scenes, and lets us hear their quiet fireside chat. He brings us to their fairs and merry-makings, their weddings, their hakes and dances. He depicts their wrestlers and other athletes as the greatest heroes, and lets us know in almost every portion of his writings that, in comparison with other counties,

'Canny ole Cummerlan caps them o' still.'

In the Glossary I have quoted so copiously from his writings that a good idea of his style and language may be gathered therefrom.

Rayson was born in 1803 at Aglionby, near Carlisle, and died in 1857. Great part of his life was spent as a country schoolmaster. He was a great favourite with the farmers, writing their letters and making their wills, and received as the principal part of his fee for teaching their children free whittlegate with them, as was customary at that time. His best piece is *Charlie McGlen*.

Dr. Gibson, M.R.C.S. and F.S.A., is, in point of time, the next writer in the Cumberland dialect. Next to Anderson I consider him to be its most successful exponent. For seven years he lived about two miles from here, and had a medical practice which took in Coniston, Torver, Seathwaite, and the Langdales, and this I believe was the time of his greatest literary activity, in which he composed most of his dialect works They all appeared in a volume entitled, *Folk-speech, Tales, and Rhymes of Cumberland and some districts adjacent*, published by Coward, Carlisle, in 1868.

Of the pieces it includes, I consider *Bobby Banks Bodderment* the best. To this last piece, which I consider the masterpiece of prose in the Cumberland dialect, I have frequently alluded in the Glossary, under the initials B.B.B.

Dr. Gibson was born at Harrington in 1813, and died at Bebington, Cheshire, in 1874.

John Richardson, who spent a long and useful life as parish schoolmaster in the lovely and sequestered Vale of St. John's, near Keswick, has published two volumes of *Cumberland Talk* (Coward, Carlisle, 1871 and 1876). They consist of sketches of Cumberland home life in poetry and prose: they are, especially the first volume, a faithful reflex of the Cumberland dialect and Cumberland habits at present, more especially as they exist in the neighbourhood of Keswick, Threlkeld, and the Vale of St. John. I have quoted from them frequently [1].

In addition to these, I have referred to and quoted from some local poets and anonymous dialect verses which I had either remembered or written down in a list of my own. To these I have referred as *Local Songs*, &c.

For many years I have been a careful reader of, and at times a contributor to, *Notes by the Way*, and other discussions on Westmorland dialect [2] and place-names in the pages of the *Westmorland Gazette*. This has confirmed my opinion upon the very close connexion and identity that exists between the dialect of Cumberland, Westmorland, and Furness in their place-names and dialect words. Some words I have obtained colloquially, without being able to say exactly when or where ; but I can, I think, safely affirm that there is no single word in the Glossary which cannot be evidenced either to· exist or to have existed in

---

[1] Miss Powley, who died at Langwathby in 1883, has written some excellent pieces (prose and poetry) in the Cumberland Dialect, under the title of *Echoes of Old Cumberland*, published by Coward, Carlisle.

[2] Authors chiefly referred to for Westmorland Dialect are :— *Ann Wheeler's Dialogues*. Rev. T. Clarke's *Specimens of Westmorland Dialect*. Kendal, Atkinson & Pollitt, 1872 ; and *A Bran New Wark*, by Rev. W. Hutton, 1785 (re-edited for English Dialect Society by Professor W. W. Skeat in 1879).

the meaning assigned to it in the dialect of one or more of the three counties I have named.

Recurring to the Norse element, Mr. Magnússon[1] has most carefully vised and revised, and corrected when required, every word and every phrase of the Norse or Icelandic portion of this work. I am not likely to meet with contradiction when I say that I could not have a greater authority upon that subject.

The fact that this work professes to be a Glossary of the dialect, and not a treatise upon Comparative Philology, precludes me from bringing forward the close connexion between it and the Icelandic so prominently as has been done elsewhere; but I think any one who reads over carefully the words of the one and the other will be convinced that there is a most striking and radical affinity between our Northern English dialects and the words that in language, place-name, and folk-lore are found in the Icelandic or Norse.

---

[1] Editor of the revised edition of the Icelandic Version of the Bible for the British and Foreign Bible Society, 1866, Joint Translator of the Saga Library, and Author of *Legends of Iceland*.

GLOSSARY

Á. A river, Icelandic. Used very largely as suffix for river-name, as Hvítá, white river, formed from a glacial moraine. Hitá is hot river, as formed from a hot spring. At page 76 of *Landnáma* it is said of a settler, 'he took land between the hot river and cold river, Hitá ok Kaldá.' In *Edda* over one hundred North-English and Scottish rivers or *a*'s are mentioned. In Lakeland this *á* is frequently found suffixed as a river-name, e. g. Rotha, Bratha, Greta, Wisa. Torver is in old documents called Torfa, the name of the river upon which it stands, whose waters (being discoloured by the mossy uplands through which it flows) are therefore called Torfa, that is The turf *river*.

Addle or **Ettle**. In Cumberland, to earn.
'*Addlin* brass,' earning money.

Agate. On gate. See *gate*, discussed in **Whittle Gate.**
We're gitten *agate* = We are making progress.

Akin. Related, of the same race. Icel. *kyn*, race or generation. 'Frá kyni til kyns,' from generation to generation.

Alegar. Vinegar. In West dialect spelled Allegar = Ale eager or Ale fermented.

> 'Ya drop o' *allegar*.'—*Bran New Wark.*

*B

Ang-nail. (A.-S. *ang-naegl*, a whitlow.) A piece of nail upon the finger growing out from the other nail, and at times occasioning great pain.

Angry. Painful or inflamed. Icel. *angr*, pain.

Ark. A chest. Meal *ark*, the meal-chest. *Arklid*, a place-name near foot of Coniston Lake. Icel. *örk*, A.-S. *arc*, Lat. *arca*.

Arr. A scar. Icel. *arr*, a scar ; Cleasby.

Arval, *adj.* Anything connected with heirship or inherit-ance, from Icel. *arfr*, inheritance ; used chiefly in refer-ence to funerals. The friends and neighbours of the family of deceased were invited to dinner on the day of the interment, and this was called the Arval dinner, a solemn festival to exculpate the heir and those entitled to the possessions of deceased from the mulcts or fines to the lord of the manor, and from all accusation of having used violence. In later times the word acquired a wider application, and was used to designate the meals provided at funerals generally. Icel. *arfi*, inheritor ; Ulph. *arbi*, A.-S. *yrfe*, Dan. *arv*. From *arfr* comes Icel. *erfða-öldr*, Dan. *arveöl*, a funeral feast in Iceland and Denmark corresponding apparently, in solemnity and the general nature of the invitation, with the Arval feast of the North of England. *Arveol = arv + öl*, Danish, inheritors' ale, is the nearest etymological equivalent of dialect *arval*. Compare **Bridal.**

Arval Bread. Cakes which each guest received at a funeral.

Arvals. Used of meat and drink supplied at funerals. To drink off the *arvals =* To consume what has been left at a funeral.

Ask, a lizard. Gael. snake or adder.

Assal tooth. A grinder, from Icel. *juxl*, which Cleasby defines as a jaw tooth or grinder.

At. That, an indeclinable relative pronoun. Corresponds with the Icelandic indeclinable pronoun *at*.

At. Is in Furness used in the sense of 'to' before the infinitive, e.g. 'He telt me *at* gang,' He told me to go. Icel. *at* or *að*, the mark of the infinitive, as '*at* ganga, *at* hlaupa, *at* vita,' to go, to run, to know. Icel. 'Hann bauð theim *at* ganga' = Furness, 'He bad them *at* gang.'

Atter. A spider, from *atter*, poison. Icel. *eitr*, poison.

Attercob. A spider's web (cobweb), from *atter*, poison, and *coppa*, a cap or head.

Awns. In Furness, and West and South Cumberland, called *angs*, the beards of barley. Process of separating described under **Fotr**. Icel. *angi*.

Aye. Always or ever. Icel. *æ* = ever or always, *æ grœnn*, ever green. In the *Landnáma* it is said of the How or burial-mound of Torf-Einarr that in winter and summer it was 'æ grœnn' = ever green.

Bain. Near. Icel. *beinn*, straight or short. *Bainest* way, in Cum. and Fur. = *beinstr vegr* in Icel. In the dialect all the degrees of comparison are found—*bain, bainer, bainest.*

Bairn. A child; lit. anything born. Icel. *barn*, A.-S. *bearn*.

Bakston. An iron plate upon which oat-bread was baked. The name and process seem to correspond with name and use of Icelandic *bakstr-járn*, an iron plate for baking sacramental wafers. But *bakstr-ofn*, baking oven, comes nearer.

Bale-fire. Icel. *bál*, a flame. A series of signal-fires lighted upon the Scottish and Cumbrian borders to denote the outbreak of war. Chancellor Ferguson gives a list of stations for bale-fires extending along the border from the Solway to the Tyne. Such stations are found commonly in Lakeland, e. g. the Beacon Mountain in High Furness, the Brandrith Mountain at the head of Ennerdale. *Lay of Last Minstrel*, canto iii. 25:

> 'Is yon the star o'er Penchryst Pen,
> That rises slowly to her ken,
> And, spreading broad its wavering light,
> Shakes its loose tresses on the night:
> Is yon red glare the western star?
> O, 'tis the beacon-blaze of war.'

Bang. A blow. Icel. *bang*, hammering, an onomatopoeic word.

Bank. Wards, as denoting direction: as up-*bank*, upwards; down-*bank*, downwards. Icel. *bakki*.

> 'While trees they grow up-*bank*,
> While rivers run down-*bank*,
> We nivver maun leuk on his marrow agean.'-ℭANDERSON.

Barrin-oot. The locking-out of the schoolmaster by the scholars at Christmas, who exacted as the conditions of his admittance a certain period of holiday. This is well illustrated by Richardson's humorous sketch in the dialect entitled *T' Barrin-oot*.

Barrow, Barf, or **Berg.** (Icel. *berg*, a mound.) A mound; then a hill. Frequent as place-name and surname in Lake district.

Bauk. Beam to support the roof of a house. Icel. *balkr*, a beam; naval bulk-heads.

Bauks. The crossbeams of a loft upon which the hay was laid.

Bēēs or **Beece.** Used of cows or cattle generally. Evidently a contraction of beasts; or cp. Icel. *báss*.

Beck. (Icel. *bekkr*, Dan. *bæk*.) A small stream or rivulet, found very generally as common noun and compound of place-name in North of England. *Beckermet*, a village in Cumberland; literally, 'the meeting of the waters.' *Beckermote Scar* is a steep cliff in limestone at the angle of the Nidd (Yorkshire), where it sinks into the ground. *Beckermonds* is the name of a tongue of land in Yorkshire between two streams at their confluence. So the river Eamont was formerly called Amot, from *a*, a stream, and *mot*, meeting. Amot is also the name of a river in Norway, and of several places there situated at the confluence of two streams. In speaking of the vale of Avoca, amongst the Wicklow mountains, Moore has beautifully recorded the strong impression made on the mind by the meeting of waters :

'Oh! there's not in the whole world a valley so sweet
As that vale in whose bosom the wild waters meet—
Oh! the last rays of feeling and life shall depart
Ere the bloom of that valley shall fade from my heart.'

Beel or **Beller**. To bellow. Icel. *baula*. Used of the bellowing of cows or bulls. See under the word **Dow.**

Beild. A shelter. (Properly, anything bylled or built, from O. E. *bylle*, to build.) On high and exposed fells, a shelter of loose stones to protect the sheep from storms. The lair of a fox is also called its *beild*, and seems to correspond with Icel. *bæli*, a den. In the *Creed of Piers Plowman* we have :

'Swich a *bild* bold
Y build upon erth heighte.'

The wild and lonely pass of Nan Beild, at the head of Kentmere, doubtless took its name from such a beild. Near to it is still pointed out the place where a father and his three sons, who had been shepherding, were found dead, locked in each other's arms, under the shelter of a stone wall, where they had been starved to death. Burns uses the word *bield* in the sense of a shelter in his *Address to a Mountain Daisy*:

> 'The flaunting flowers our gardens yield
> High shelt'ring woods, and wa's maun shield;
> But thou beneath the random *bield*
>   O' clod or stane,
> Adorns the histie stibble field,
>   Unseen, alane.

Berrier. A Thresher. 'Bed-time for *berriers* and supper time for carriers.' Old Cumberland Proverb.

Berry. To thresh with a flail. Icel. *berja*, to strike or thresh.

Bete. To mend or improve the fire. (Icel. *bœta*, A.-S. *betan*, to mend or improve. Fires bete.—Chaucer.) To mend, applied to the fire. Hence, rectangular pieces of turf cut from the moss and used for burning, were called *betes* or *peats*, from being used to repair or mend the fire. One of Anderson's songs, dated 1808, is entitled *Peat Leader's Complaint*. In many parts of Cumberland and Lakeland, the peat stack entirely supplied the place of coals. Many houses had only hearth-fires, i. e. fires without grates, consequently nothing but chats and peats could be used for fire-elding. On baking days, when the brandrith was in use or otherwise, a large fire was required; the office of beting the fire was sufficient to employ one person. At night such fires were not altogether extinguished, but the peat embers were 'raked,' as it was called, i. e. the embers were so raked over that they would smoulder until morning. Consequently many fires in the Lake district had never been altogether extinguished for years; and I know the case of a man who possessed his grandfather's fire—the fire never having been altogether extinguished for three generations.

Bewce. A stall for oxen. Icel. *báss*, a boose or stall in a cow-house, as 'binda kú a bás.' Cow and bás go together as in an Icelandic nursery rhyme—'sofa, sofa, selr i eyju, kýr á bási, köttr i búri.'

Bicker. A wooden dish or drinking vessel. Icel. *bikarr*, a large drinking vessel.

Bid. To bespeak attendance. (Icel. *bjóða*.) Applied chiefly to marriages and funerals. The district within which all were invited to funerals was called 'a bidding.' 'As many as ye shall find, *bid* to the marriage.' In the *Landnáma*, the harvest feast is called the 'haust boð' or harvest bidding.

Bigg. Barley. (Icel. *bygg*, Dan. *byg*.)

> 'Ya Thursday he went wi' some *bigg* to the market
> An drank wi some neebers he little kent how.'—ANDERSON.

Biggin. A building. Cf. A.-S. *Byggan*, Icel. *Bygging*. Used also in proper names, as Newbiggin, Sunbiggin.

Birk. (O. N. *björk* [collect. *birki*], Dan. *birk*.) The Birch. Names of farms are derived from this word, as The Birks in Seathwaite; so used elsewhere. The surname *Birkett* seems formed of this word with the Norse article suffixed.

Birler. The person who handed round the ale at a Cumberland feast, and whose duty it was to see that the guests generally were provided with drink. Icel. *byrla*, which Vigfusson defines as signifying, to wait upon or hand round the ale at banquets. Magnússon says, 'the word in Icelandic corresponding to *birler* is *byrlari*; and in Iceland the men who assist in carrying drink about to guests at weddings and other feasts are even now so called.'

Bizen. (Icel. *býsn*, a wonder; A.-S. *bisen*, an example.) This word, which in the dialect means a warning or example, generally goes with 'shem.' 'She's a shem and a *bizen* to aw the hail toun.'—Anderson.

Blained. Half-dry. Generally applied to linen hung out to dry. Dan. *blayne*, to whiten. *Blain* is found in Craven in the sense of whiten; also, to dry, as above.

Blea. Lead-coloured; also blue. Icel. *blá-*, in *blár*, blue. Blea Tarn, between Great and Little Langdale.

Blea-berries. Whortle-berries. Icel. *blá-ber*, Dan. *blaaber*, blue berries, from their blue or livid appearance.

Bleate. Bashful. Icel. *blautr*, timid, effeminate.

> 'Great is thy power, and great thy fame
> Far kenn'd and noted is thy name
> And though yon lowin' heugh's thy hame
>   Thou travels far
> And, faith! thou's neither lag nor lame
>   Nor *bleate* nor scaur.—Burns.

Blin Bile. Blind boil, a boil that does not come to a head, or run.

Blin Tarn. A tarn without visible outlet; Icel. *blindr*, blind. So we have 'a *blind* alley,' without exit.

Bloomery. Ancient smelting furnaces in Cumberland and High Furness, the remains of which are still to be found. The word may be connected with Norse verb *blása*, used for to smelt in *Landnáma Bók*.

Board. Anciently meant table. Still so retained in the phrase 'bed and board,' board and lodgings; 'Board of Trade.' In the Icelandic it still retains the double meaning of board and table. John xii. 2, 'Og Marta gekk fyrir borðum,' Martha served at table.

Bole. Trunk of a tree. Icel. *bolr*.

Bower. The inner room in a cottage. Icel. *búr*. **Byre.** A cow stall. Both words seem to have come originally from Icel. *búr.* Common to all Teutonic languages, and in most meaning ' a chamber.'

Brandrith. (Icel. *brandreið,* a grate.) The brandrith in Lakeland was originally an iron tripod, held together by rims of iron, and employed in supporting the girdle-plate which was used above the hearth-fire for baking oat-bread. The name and thing named are gradually passing away, as hearth-fires are being supplanted by modern grates, and oat-cake by wheat-bread; yet there is hardly a valley in Lakeland in which a *brandrith* may not be found and is not yet occasionally used. The Three Shire Stones where the three fair counties meet together upon the top of Wrynose, near the source of the river Duddon, were called 'The Three-Legged Brandrith,' as being the place where the grate for the beacon-fires or bale-fires was placed. It is in a prominent position, and could be seen from each of the three counties— Cumberland, Westmorland, and Lancashire; in fact, the original grate or *brandrith* may have at this point stood partly in each one of them. This word has a still more local significance, for the usual term for the point, generally marked by a large boulder stone where the boundaries of three parishes met was called Brandrith. A mountain near the Great Gable bears the name of ' The Brandrith '; and the place where the rivers Brathay and Rothay meet at their confluence with Windermere is called ' The Brandrith,' because in old times an iron grate was placed there as a beacon which could be seen down the Lake of Windermere. So upon the river Reuss where it flows from Lake Lucerne is an old lighthouse or light-tower which is said to have given its name ' *Lucerna* ' to the Lake.

Brandrith Stean. A boundary stone at the meeting of

three parishes. There is a huge boulder-stone so called at the western extremity of this parish, which marks the point at which the three parishes of Torver, Blawith and Woodland meet.

Brant. Steep. (Icel. *brattr*, A.-S. *brant*, steep.) Proverb, ' as *brant* as a besom.' Brantwood, on the eastern margin of Coniston Lake, which has been successively the residence of distinguished *literati*, at present the residence of Professor Ruskin, is so called from the *brant* or steep wood which rises behind it.

Bridewain. Bidden wedding or Infaire. A marriage.

Brissett. A wooden frame.

Bruff or **Bur.** A faint luminous disk round the moon, called technically ' a corona.'

Bummel Bee. (Icel. *buml*, resounding.) The humble bee.

Burn. A stream, equivalent to Beck. (A.-S. *burn*, Gothic *brunna*, a spring; Icel. *brunnr*.)

Busk. A bush. ·(Icel. *búskr*.)

By. A very common termination of the names of villages. Anderson says :

> 'There's Harraby and Tarraby,
> An Wigganby beseyde,
> There's Oughterby and Souterby
> An *Bys* baith far an weyde.'—*Thuirsby Witch.*

In Iceland this is *bær*, *bær*, or *býr* ; in Norway, *bö* ; in Sweden and Denmark, *by*. This word is very frequent throughout the whole of Scandinavia ; and wherever the Scandinavian tribes went and settled the name *by* or *bö* went with them. In the map of Northern England the use of this word marks out the limit and extent of the Norse immigration ; e. g. the name Kirkby or Kirby. About twenty or thirty such names are found in maps of the Northern and Eastern counties, denoting churches built by the Norse or Danish settlers; e. g. Kirkby-in-Furness, Kirkby-in-Kendal, now usually Kendal. Compare *Kirkjubœr* in Iceland. In Denmark and Sweden names ending in *by* are almost numberless. (This note I have had in a great measure from Dr. Kitchin, Dean of Durham.)

Bye. Lonely, as a bye place = a lonely place, is connected with this word.

Caimt. Ill-natured or peevish.

Cald. Cold. Icel. *kaldr*, cold. Caldbeck = Icel. *kaldbekkr*.

Cam. The upper portion of a stone fence often formed of sharp serrated stones so as effectually to turn the Herdwick sheep. Icel. *kambr*. Such a cam is called a Yorkshire cam, a ridge or fence on the moors formed by digging two ditches and throwing up a ridge between them. Catcam on Helvellyn seems to be from this word, ' a *cam* fit to turn a cat.'

Cap. To top or surpass.

> 'Yer buik larn'd wise gentry, that's seen monie a country
> May preach and palaver and brag as they will,
> O' mountains, lakes, valleys, woods, watters and meadows
> Bit canny auld Cummerlan *caps* them aw still.'—ANDERSON.

Carl. A countryman or one of the commoner or meaner order. Norse *karl*, used in *Landnáma* in sense of 'libertus' or freedman. 'Nor the *churl* said to be bountiful.' Isa. xxxii. 5.

Carlings. Grey pease steeped in water and fried next day in oil or butter, eaten on mid-Lent Sunday or the second Sunday before Easter, called on this account *Carling* Sunday. We have this expressed in the old rhyme naming the Sundays before Easter:—

> 'Tid, Mid, Misserai
> Carling, Palm and Pace Egg-Day.'

It was a very common custom for boys and others to carry their *carlings* in their pockets and salute each other in the house or upon the roads with a handful of them. This Sunday was in earlier times called ' Carè Sunday,' and is said to be from *kœra*, given in Cleasby and Vigfusson as meaning, to make a *charge against* or *accuse*, and so called in reference to the charges or accusations made against our Lord at this time. The name and the custom have doubtless originated in a religious observance.

Carr. (Icel. *kjarr.*) Applied to fields or woods. In Norse *kjerr* is also applied to a small wood. In Cumberland small, hollow, cup-shaped fields, surrounded by alders or ellers, were called eller cars. Dillicars is a very usual appellation of fields so shaped, from *kar*, a cup, and *deila*, to divide.

Chaft. The jaw. Icel. *kjaptr*, N. *kjafter.*

Chats. Fuel formed of underwood and brushwood, very commonly used in Lakeland for keeping up hearth fires and other household fires.

Cheese-rims or -rums. Cf. Icel. *rim*, a rim. Circular wooden frames in which the curds were pressed in making cheese. They were usually composed of staves held together by wooden hoops. They were circular vessels of coopered staves without top or bottom in which the curds were confined and pressed from above by a beam from which a stone was suspended as a lever.

Choop. Pronounced shoop. Red seeds of the wild rose. ' Rotten as a *choop*.' Proverb.

Clagg. To stick. Dan. *klœg*, loamy.

Clam or **Clem**. To starve. Icel. *klemma*, to pinch.

Clap. A pat. Icel. *klapp*, a pat.

Clap. To pat. Icel. *klappa*, to pat.

Clap-bread. (Dan. *klappe bröd.*) Thin cakes beaten or clapped out with the hand.

Claver. To climb. Dan. *klavre.*

Clegg. (Icel. *kleggi*, a cleg or horsefly.) The horsefly or gadfly.

Cletch. A brood, as of chickens. Cf. Icel. *klekja*; Ulph. *klahs*; Dan. *klœkke.*

Clock lound. The downy seeds of the Dandelion are collectively called a clock from the idea that the number of times one must blow to bring them all off will indicate what hour of the day it is. They are blown off with the slightest puff, and when the wind is so still as not to disturb those seeds it is said to be *clock lound.* Cf. *lound.*

Cluif. A hoof. Icel. *klauf.* Connected with *cleave*, the cleft hoof.

Cote. (Icel. *kot*, a cottage or small farm; A.-S. *cote.*) The word is very frequently found as the name of places bordering on the Solway. In the Abbey Holme, for example, it is applied as the name of several farms; e. g. Raby Cote, Seaville Cote, East Cote, Skinburness Cote, Sea Cote.

Cow-ban or **Cow-bo**, pronounced kū. A large horseshoe-shaped wooden collar, generally of ash, to fasten cows to the *bewce.* It was fastened to a stake called a rid-stake. The two ends hung downwards and were joined by a crosspiece called the catch, and remained fastened by the elasticity of the bow. See *Jobby Cow-ban's Lawsuit*, a tale in the dialect, by Richardson. The name as well as the article are Scandinavian, Icel. *kýr, kú,* a cow, and *bogi,* a bow.

Cowp. To exchange or barter. Horse-dealers are called by Anderson 'horse-cowpers.' 'What aw trades 's bad as horse cowpers?' Anderson's *Carel Fair.* Icel. *kaupa,* to barter, *kaup,* a bargain. The root-word, as used by Ulphilas, means to strike. We have the idea in the phrase 'to strike a bargain,' the equivalent of *cowp* or *kaupa.* Hence also the Cumberland phrase of 'chopping off' cattle to any one, i. e. striking the bargain; and hence also the custom which cattle-dealers had of striking hands to show the bargain was concluded. The surname Cooper or Cowper seems to be derived from it.

Cratch. A curved frame to lay sheep on. N. *kraki,* a looped and trunked stem used as a staircase; still so used in Norway.

Creel. A hazel or willow basket used for holding peats; the peat creel. Icel. *kríli,* a basket.

Crewel. To work embroidery in mixed colours. 'To *crewel* a ball' is to cover it with variegated worsted work.

Creyke. A nook or opening formed in the sand of marshes by the tide. 'He stuck in a *creyke,'* Anderson's *Burgh Races.* From Icel. *kriki,* a nook or recess.

Cringle. Curved, from Icel. *kringla* a circle, in Cringle Craggs in Langdale; Cringle Gill.

Cronies. Boon companions. Dan. *kro,* a beerhouse.

> 'Cum sit down ma *cronies*
> A lal bit an lissen.'—ANDERSON.

Cross. See page xv of '*Landnáma as it illustrates the Dialect of Cumberland*' by T. E.

Cur. A Shepherd's or Farmer's dog. Magnússon says the Icelanders call any unknown dog a *korri.*

Cush. Addressed to cows, as *Gis* or *Griss* is addressed to pigs. From Icel. *kussa* or *kusa.* 'Kus! kus!' is the milkmaid's call to cows in Iceland, just as 'Cush! cush!' is in the North of England.

Cush man. A very common ejaculation expressive of wonder.

Daft. Simple or silly. Icel. *daufr.* Gaen *daft* = gone mad.

Daytal. Daily, as '*daytal* labourer,' a man who works by the day. *Tal* corresponds with Icel. *tal*, a count. Tell, to count, 'He telleth the stars.'

Deave. To deafen. Icel. *deyfa.*

> 'Fad sez when Dick streykes up "Jim Crow"
> Or Joe tries "Uncle Ned"
> Whisht! lads; yūr gaun ta *deave* us aw
> Its teyme ta gang to bed.'—*Local Song.*

Dee. To die. Icel. *deyja,* to die.

> 'What complaint had he, Betty,
> Says hoo aw' caunt tell,
> We neer had no doctor,
> He *deet* of hissel.'—EDWIN WAUGH.

Deeal. A division or share, as of a town or common field which, though unenclosed, has its produce divided or parcelled out into separate portions, the ownership of which changes annually in succession. Icel. *deila,* to divide; A.-S. *dœlan*; Goth. *deiljan*; Engl. To deal or divide, as of cards.

Deeal. A dale or valley. The Norse word *dalr,* plu. *dalar,* a valley, seems to correspond exactly in meaning and application with this word *deeal,* as found in Lakeland. As place-names they have a similar application, and in Iceland Þver-dalr, Djúpi-dalr, Breið-dalr, Langi-dalr, Fagri-dalr, correspond with Crossdales or Thwart-dales, Deep-dale, Broad-dale, Lang-dale, Fair-dale, in Lakeland.

Icel. *Vatzdalr* = Lakeland Wasdale. *Vatzdalr* is literally waterdale. See *Landnáma*, p. 71. In Iceland, as in Lakeland, they speak of *dala-menn*, i. e. dalesmen.

Deet or **dight**. To prepare or to cleanse, as corn from chaff.

> 'The cleanest corn that e'er was *dight*,
> May hae some pyles o' caff in ;
> So ne'er a fellow-creature slight
> For random fits o' daffin.'
>
> Burns' Version of Eccl. vii. 16.

Deetin-cleaith. A cloth used to dress corn upon.

Deetin-Hill. A hill near the homestead was used by Cumberland farmers to dress corn upon by throwing it up against the wind. 'The *deetin hill.*' In almost all old Cumberland barns : doors opposite to each other were provided, so as to secure a draught of air to cleanse or deet the corn.

Deetin Machines were a later invention which, by turning a handle connected with fanners, secured an artificial blast. The blast for bloomeries in High Furness was secured by having them placed in a narrow gorge or ravine through which the wind rushed furiously.

Deft. Skilful, neat.

> 'Aw heard a jeyke at window pane,
> An *deftly* went to see.'—RICHARDSON.

Degg. To moisten. Icel. *döggva*, to bedew, to moisten.

Des. To heap up or pile. Icel. *des*, a heap of hay ; *desja*, to heap up hay.

Dill. To lull to sleep. Icel. *dilla*, to lull.

Dillicar. (Icel. *deila*, to divide, and *ker*, Dan. *kar*, a cup.) A name generally applied to small, cup-shaped fields in Lakeland. A number of them laying together are called

Dillicars. There is an instance in this parish, where six such fields together, forming something like a circle, are called dillicars.

Dog-whipper. In old parish account books there is frequently an annual payment entered to the dog-whipper or for dog-whipping. Whipping dogs out of church was very essential where every shepherd was usually accompanied by two or three dogs, and a quarrel amongst the dogs that would thus assemble might have been a very serious matter. Latest entry for dog-whipping at Torver is May 21, 1748, in which occurs the item for 'Ringing Bell and Dog-whipping, 5s. 2d.'

Donk. To moisten or wet, as rain does. Dan. *dönke*, to make damp.

Donky. Wet or moistened. 'A *donky* day,' a wet day.

Donn and Doff. Dress and undress, do on and do off. Edwin Waugh, in *Lancashire Songs*, says :

> ' When th' order comes to us
> To doff these owd clooas,
> There 'll surely be new uns to don.'

Donnot. A worthless person. 'There's many a good looking donnet.'—*Local Proverb*. According to Fergusson, from *dow not*; Brockett, *do naught*.

Dordum. 'I take this word,' says Ferguson, 'to be from *dyra dómr*, thus explained by Malet : ' In the early part of the Icelandic commonwealth, when a man was suspected of theft, a kind of tribunal, composed of twelve persons named by him and twelve by the person whose goods had been stolen, was instituted before the door of his dwelling, and hence was called a *door doom*, or Icel. *dyra dómr*, i. e. door judgement ; but as this manner of proceeding generally ended in bloodshed, it was

* C

abolished. Hence in Iceland the word was generally synonymous with the tumult and uproar which generally characterized the proceedings.' Such a *dyra dómr* and its consequent disorder and bloodshed is described in *Landnáma.*

Dow. Good or help. When a person is not likely to recover from an illness it is said of him, ' He'll du nea *dow.*' Icel. *duga,* to help. Proverb :

> 'A whussling lass an a bellerin cow
> An a crowing hen ell du nea *dow.*'

Ann Wheeler, in *Westmorland Dialogues,* says of a scape-grace, ' Hes nwote at *dow.*'

Dowly. Lonesome or dull, as applied to a road or place. Icel. *daufligr,* deaflike, i.e. lonesome or lonely. This word is used in the same sense in Yorkshire. Blackah, in *Poems in the Nidderdale Dialect,* says : ' Bud t' hoose leaks *dowly* all t' week lang.'

Drape. To speak slowly.

Dree, *adj.* Icel. *drjúgr.* Slow but sure ; lasting. Besides Cumberland, Westmorland, and Furness, this word is well known in the dialects of Yorkshire and South Lancashire. In Waugh's ' *Cum whoam to the childer an me,*' we have :

> 'Av brong thi top cwoat dusta know,
> For t' rains cummin down varra *dree,*
> The hearthstones as wheyte as new snow,
> Cum whoam to the childer an me.'

Dree. To endure. (Icel.. *drýgja,* to lengthen.) On the Cumbrian and Scotch border, to ' *dree* his wreid,' is equivalent to endure his fate. In the *Guy Mannering* of Sir W. Scott, Meg Merrilies, whose dialect is of this district, says of Bertram, ' He had *dreed* his wreid in a foreign land till his twenty-first year.'

Dub. A pool or piece of deep water, the depth being the thing chiefly considered in the name. (Icel. *djúpr*, deep, also *dýpi*, depth; Dan. *dyb*.) This word is very commonly used in Cumberland as the name of watering-places near farmhouses. The deep pool bounding the Abbey Holme and finding its way into the Solway at Dubmill, is called from its depth, 'the Holme Dub'; we have also Dub Wath. The Great Doup, near the Pillar Rock, is a precipice of several hundred feet deep, by falling down which one of the most adventurous climbers in Lakeland, the Rev. James Jackson, lost his life. Icel. *djúp* means the *deep*, as applied to water. The word is also applied to deeps on the lakes and fiords of Norway, and there is a river in Normandy called Dieppe, or 'the deep,' which gives its name to the town which stands upon it.

Eaa. Channel of a stream. 'Hows t' *eaa*?' i.e. How is the water running? (Icel. *á*, a stream; A.-S. *ea*.) The Leven and Crake are thus at times called *ea* or stream. The Norse form *á* enters into the form of a great many river-names in this district, e.g. Brath*a*, Bel*a*, Cald*a*, Gret*a*, Liz*a*, and Wis*a*. In Iceland rivers from glaciers are called *Hvítá*, or white rivers; from hot springs they are called *Hitá*, or hot rivers, as opposed to Kald*á*, or cold river, which is another Icelandic river name = Calda in Cumberland.

Easings. Eaves. A.-S. *efesan*, eaves.

Efter. After. Icel., Dan., Swed., and A.-S. *efter*.

Elding. Fuel. (Icel. *eldr*, Dan. *ild*, fire; Icel. *elding*, fuel.) In Exod. iii. the flame of fire appearing to Moses is in the Danish Bible *eldslowe*. Fire *elding*, as applied to chats and peats, is the most general name for fuel in Lakeland.

Elf. Cognate with Dan. *alf*, Icel. *alfr*.

Eller. The alder tree. Icel. *elrir* (Dan. *œl.*) Elterwater, in Langdale, is a Tarn taking its name from the alder trees which grow near it. We have the name ellercar, applied in Denmark and the North of England to small, cup-shaped meadows surrounded by elder trees; from Norse *eller* and *kjarr*, copsewood or brushwood. Also in the proper names Ellerbeck and Ellwood. ' Birk an eller ' are often named together.

Fain. Pleased. Icel. *feginn*, fain.

> 'Wey Geordie aws *fain*
> To see thee again.'—*Local Song.*

Fairy. See **Elf.**

Fär. Norse for sheep, as in Fāroe Islands = Sheep Islands. Sheep pastures upon the Yorkshire moors are called *fār* pastures. This word *fār*, a sheep, seems to be found in the name Fairfield, which is in Lakeland applied to the flat, level sheep-pastures upon the tops of mountains. Fairfield, near Ambleside, is a notable example. Magnússon says ' in Iceland we have in old records *fár* and *fær*, for sheep. I take *fær* to be the direct source of Fair in Fairfield.'

Feal. To hide or cover. Icel. *fela*.

Feeal. To give way or decline, as in old age. It is said of an old man, ' He's feealin fast.' Icel. *feila*, to falter; adj. *feilinn*, faltering, connected with Lat. *fallere*, to shake.

Fell-fo. Fieldfare or Landrail. *Fare*, to go, as in fare, farewell, &c.

Fend to. To make a shift to gain a living. Icel. *féna* ?, to

gain or profit. Anderson says : ' How *fens ta* ? ' How
are you ?

> 'A man may spend, an still can *fend*,
> If his weyfe be owt, if his weyfe be owt,
> A man may spare, an still be bare
> If his weyfe be nowt, if his weyfe be nowt.'
>
> *Local Proverb.*

Fendy. Economical, thrifty.

Fess or **Fest.** To send out cattle to other farms to be
grazed (Dickinson). This word I take to be from
Icel. *festa,* which Vigfusson gives ' to settle,' ' make a
bargain, or stipulate.'

Fest. To bind an apprentice.

Festing Penny. Money paid to a servant upon hiring to
bind the agreement. Both these words are from *festa,* as
above. *Festar penningar* is given in Icelandic as meaning
pledge or bail. *Handfested* is applied to irregular
marriages or betrothals in the North of England, though
I am not sure that it is so used in Cumberland. It
evidently has its counter - part in Icelandic *festar,*
betrothals.

Fettle. Order, condition. Connected with Icel. *fella* (pron.
feddla) to join together, or to put into order, as þat er
vel felt=that suits well.

Fit. Foot in dialect, and in Icelandic web-foot. The
mouth of a stream is called beckfit, and a village on
the Solway, Beckfit, so derives its name.

Flack. A thin sod. Icel. *flag,* the spot where turf has
been cut.

Flacker. A person who cuts and spreads ' flacks.'

Fleet. See **Flet.**

Flet. To skim milk. A.-S. *flet,* Dan. *flöde,* cream. Magnússon says, 'The corresponding verb in Icelandic is *fleyta*, to skim anything that floats on the surface, especially cream.'

Flick. Flitch. (Icel. *flikki*, a flitch of bacon.)

> 'Blin Stagg the fiddler gat a whack,
> The bacon *flick* fell on his back
> An than his fiddle stick they brack.
>> Bit whist a'll sa nea mair.'
>>> ANDERSON'S *Worton Wedding.*

Flit. To remove, as of household goods and chattels. Such a removal, when made in secret and to avoid paying creditors, is called a 'moonlight flitting.' · Dan. *flytte dag*, moving day; Icel. *flytja, flyt flutti*, to remove. Gen. xii. 8, 'Og fluttist til fjallanna fyrir austan Betel,'=and removed to a mountain on the east of Bethel.

> 'When the hūse is whirlin roun about
> Its teyme enough *to flit*,
> For we've always been provided for,
> An sea wull we yit.'—*Local Song.*

Flowe. An expanse of mossy waste, as Wedholme Flowe in the Abbey Holme, Solway Flowe, Bowness Flowe. Icel. *flói*, a marshy moor.

Force. (Icel. *fors*, mod. *foss*, a waterfall.) Used of a waterfall in the Lake country, as Airey Force, Colwith Force, Stockgill Force, Force Forge.

Forelders. Ancestors. Icel. *foreldri*, parents, ancestors.

Forwarning or **Foreboding.** Cf. Icel. *forboð, fyrirboði*. The prophetic anticipation of some serious misfortune, as death. In illustration of the corresponding Icelandic idea, a remarkable instance is given in the *Erybyggia Saga.* See chapter xi of that Saga.

Fotr, Fotring Iron. (Icel. *fótr*, the foot.) A fotring iron was an instrument in the form of a square made of plates of sheet iron, and used by the Cumberland farmers for separating the awns from the barley. It was used between the feet, hence its name. The process was called *fotring*.

Fotr. A verb formed from the foregoing word.

Fots. Woollen substitutes for children's shoes, from *Fotr* a foot.

Fra. (Dan. *fra*; Icel. *frá*.) From.

> 'There were lasses *fra* Wigton, *fra* Worton, *fra* Banton,
> Some o' them gat sweethearts, while others gat neane,
> An bairns yet unworn 'll oft hear o' Burgh Races,
> For ne'er mun we see sec a meetin agean.'—Anderson.

Fremmed. Strange. Dan. *fremmed.* Mostly in phrase '*fremmed folk*,' as distinguished from those well known or 'natives.' In Bible of Ulphilas, 'Framatheis,' foreign or strange, ex. *fra*, from.

Fridge. To rub, as a stocking against a badly-fitting shoe.

Frith or Firth (is the Icel. *fjörðr*, dat. sing. *firði*,) a frith or bay, as Solway Frith, a Scandinavian word; but a small crescent-formed creek or inlet is called a *vik* or *wyke* in Windermere, and is less than *fjörðr*. In Iceland and Old Scandinavian countries the shore districts are frequently divided into counties bearing the name of *frith*, just as the inland part is divided into dales. The western and eastern part of Iceland are called West Firths and East Firths, and in Norway a county is called Firðir; over one hundred *firðir* are mentioned in Iceland. In *Landnáma Bók*, a frequent phrase for describing the homes of the early settlers is 'Milli fjalls ok fjöru,' between fell and foreshore.

Gain. Near = Bain. Gainer way = Icel. *gagn* in *gagn-vegr*, a short cut.

Galt. A male pig. Icel. *galti,* and *göltr.* This word is found in *Landnáma* in a remarkable passage describing the settlement of Ingimund, where a boar (*galti*) is said to have swum about till it died.

Gang, Gan, Gow, Gowa. Go. One of the oldest and most general words in the northern family of languages. Ulph. *gaggan;* A.-S. *gangan;* Icel. *gunga* or *gá;* Dan. *gange* or *gaa.* *Gowa* seems equivalent to 'Go away,' and is now *howay.* A thrifty and industrious housewife upon the Border, once describing her life to me, said : ' It 's gang, gang, aye gang, gang, an when aw canna gang nea langer awn dūne.'

Gangrel. (Used with 'body.') The old Border appellation for tramp.

Gap. Icel. *gap,* gap, an opening in a fence.

Gap. Used of the openings or passes amongst the mountains of Lakeland, e. g. Whinlatter Gap, Scarf Gap, Raise Gap.

Gap rails. Round poles let into stone, or wooden.posts, instead of gates.

Gapsted. (Icel. *staðr,* a place.) Entrance to a field is so called.

Gar. To compel. (Icel. *gjöra,* to make.) 'It garred me greet.' 'I'll *gar* thee,' I'll compel you.

Gards. Another form of the word **Garth,** applied to fields or enclosures. The word corresponds in a remarkable manner in its application in Iceland, Norway, Sweden, and Denmark, to the use in which we find it in Cumberland, Westmorland, and Furness. The oldest form is the Gothic *gards,* as found in the Bible of Ulphilas.

Garn. Yarn. (Icel. *garn.*) 'Spin *garn*' in Cumberland corresponds with Icel. *spinna garn* as given in Vigfusson.

Garn-winnels. A wooden cross from which the *garn* is wound. Cognate through the Icel. *vindil-áss,* windlass, as used in ships. Of this word Magnússon says, ' *Garn-winnels* corresponds, as to the *thing,* exactly to the Mod. Icel. *garn-vinda.* As to the *form,* winnels evidently descends from *vindill,* a winding instrument, which we have also in windlass = *vindil-áss,* a winding-beam.'

Garth. A garden ; also a small enclosed field close to the farmhouse. Sheep, calves, and pigs were put into it. Garth, surname. Icel. *garðr.*

Gate. Thoroughfare, a way, a road. ' Gaen his own *gate,*' gone his own road. From Icel. *gata,* a way or road, a thoroughfare. Ulph. *gatva* = πλᾰτεῖα. Dan. *gade,* street. Gate in Carlisle is also used of streets, as Botchergate, Rickergate, Caldewgate, &c. Similarly, Clappersgate, Mealsgate.

Gate. Used of rights of pasturing upon marshes or fells, as cattle gates, sheep gates.

Gaum. Sense or forethought. Icel. *gaumr,* heed or attention.

Gaumless. Evidently the accidentally unrecorded Icel. *gaumlauss,* a perfectly classical compound, heedless or senseless. Icel. *gaumr,* heed or attention, found in the phrase ' Gefa gaum at e-u,' to give attention to. ' Thou greet *gaumless* fuil.'—Richardson.

Gay or **Gey.** Very or thoroughly, as ' a *gey* feyne day.' Carlyle's mother speaks of him as being ' *gey ill ta leeve wi.*' See Froude's *Life of Carlyle.* Icel. *gagn,* through or thoroughly, as *gagn-hræddr,* thoroughly frightened.

Gesling. Young of geese. Icel. *gœslingr.* From this root we have the surnames Gasgarth, Gaskell.

Gildert. A number of snares attached to a hoop for catching small birds in the snow. (Icel. *gildra*, a trap.)

Gill or Ghyll. A deep, narrow glen, with a stream running at the bottom. The Icelandic word *gil* (Norwegian *giel*) has exactly the same meaning. If there be no stream another word is used. *Gill* is also found in Cumberland as surname.

Gimmer. Ewe lamb. Icel. *gymbr*, a gimmer or ewe that has not lambed; Dan. *gimmer-lamb*.

Gird. A wooden hoop used for enclosing or keeping together the rims of firkins. Icel. *gjörð*, *girið*, collect. Cognate with **Garth or Gards**, an enclosure.

Girdle or Gurdle. Sometimes also called the girdle-plate. An iron plate used for baking oat-cakes and bread over the fire.

Girdle or Gurdle. A flat pan or circular iron plate fitted with bule like a pan, and used for baking cakes generally

> ' Our weyfes for *gurdle* ceake an tea ;
> Bit aw's the chap for gud strang yell.'—Anderson.

Giss or Griss. A pig or swine. Icel. *gríss*, a young pig, Dan. *gris*, Sc. *grice*. In calling a pig the term used is ' giss ! giss ! ' or ' griss ! griss ! ' The proverb, ' He nowder said giss (or griss) nor sty ' (*stía*=sty), is equivalent to, ' He neither said pig nor sty.' *Griss* is found also in Grasmere or Gricemere, Grisedale Pass, Grisedale Farm, Grisedale Glen ; also Grizedale, a valley near Hawksland, and Grizebeck. Grice is a surname in Cumberland.

Gloppened. Astonished. Icel. *glúpnaðr*. ' Aw was fairly *gloppened*.'—*Ann Wheeler's Dialogues.*

Gloppers. Blinders for the eyes of horses. Cf. Icel. *gloppa*, opening, a hole.

Glour. To look earnestly. Cf. Icel. *glóra*.

Glumpen. To look surly. Icel. *glúpna*.

Gouk. The cuckoo. Icel. *gaukr*.

Goving. Adjective from **Guff**, with the same meaning. ' Greet *goving* fuil,' a great vapouring fool.

Gowl. To cry with a whine, as a dog does. To cry. Icel. *góla*, to howl or whine. Ps. lix. 14, ' A kveldin og góla sem hunda, og hlaupa um kring staðinn.' In the evening they will whine like a dog and run about the city. In *Landnáma*, p. 161, ' svá gól ' is used of a raven's croaking as foreboding a terrible conflict, from which it anticipates a feast. Magnússon says, ' The Icel. *gaula* has at the present day exactly the same sense that you give to *gowl*.'

Gowpen. (Icel. *gaupn*; Sc. *goupen*.) This word seems to be exactly the same in sound and significance in Cumberland and Iceland. It means (1) *the two hands held together in the form of a bowl;* (2) as a measure, *as much as can be taken in the hands held together.* Scotch, ' goud in *goupens*.' Within my own remembrance the beggars were furnished with a bag, and the charitable housewives put into it a *goupen* of meal or flour. The ballad of *Robin Hood* alludes to such a practice; when Little John is sent a begging, he says he must have

> ' A bag for my meal,
> A bag for my malt,
> A bag for my flour and my corn ;
> A bag for a penny
> If I get any—
> And a bag for my own bugle-horn.'

The Hebrew word *caph* represented such a measure, and

the Hebrew letter, of which *caph* is also the name, is represented by the bent hand.

Gradeley. Promptly or well. (From Icel. *greiðliga,* readily.) Also as an adjective, lasting or enduring.

> 'Ahve nea *gradely* comfort mè lass
> Except wi yon childer an thee.'—EDWIN WAUGH.

Grave. To dig. Icel. *grafa.*

Greeap. (A.-S. *grēp,* a furrow.) The space or furrow behind cows in stalls.

Greenhew. A word found in old manorial writings, used for the payment for cutting trees upon an estate by the tenant.

Greymin. A thin covering or spotting of snow.

Grip. To seize. Icel. *grípa.*

Grund. Farm, used as place-name. Sand grund or ground, &c. Icel. *grund,* a green field or plain. *Grund,* as farm name, occurs very frequently in High Furness, e. g. Sawrey Grund, Holm Grund, Park Grund. The same is the case in Iceland. H. Swainson-Cowper, F.S.A., kindly collected for me the names of this class. In Furness alone he enumerates forty-seven Grunds as portion of place-names generally joined with personal names.

Guff. A vapouring fellow. Icel. *gufa,* vapour, steam. In local names in Iceland, as Gufunes, Gufudalr, Gufuskalar, so called from the steam of the hot wells.

> 'When seck leyke *guffs* leame decent fowk
> Its teyme sum laws sud alter.'—See ANDERSON's *Village Gang.*

Haaf, *vb.* To fish with the large *haaf* or sea nets. Icel. *háfr* and *háf-net,* a· net with a poke-formed centre to collect the fish in. This word is so used by fishermen of the Solway, both on Scottish and Cumbrian side.

I have seen it in an old charter of the Burgh of Annan, describing the rights of fishing.

Haaf Net. Poke net.

Hack. A pickaxe. Dan. *hakke.*

Hag Worm. Viper. Magnússon gives me the following interesting note on this word. ' *Hagworm* is Icel. *högg-ormr* (=*hew*-worm, from the action of the reptile, when it bites, resembling the movement of the adze in the joiner's hand), a snake, a serpent. In Icelandic Bible " serpent " is always *höggormr.*'

Hald. Hold. Icel. *hald.*

Hancloot, Hanclaith. Towel. Icel. *hanklæði.* Magnússon says the mod. Icelandic is also *hand-klútr.*

Handsel. A bargain, generally applied to the money that crosses the hand for the first bargain. Corresponds with the Icelandic word *handsal,* which Vigfusson explains thus : ' A law term, usually in the plural, *handsöl,* handselling or hanselling, i. e. the transference of a right, bargain, or duty to another by joining hands : hand-shaking was with the men of old the sign of a transaction, and is still so used among farmers and others ; so that to shake hands is the same as to conclude a bargain. Lat. *mandare,* manu dare.'

Hank. To fasten. Icel. *hanka.*

Harbour. A place of reception, a room. Icel. *herbergi,* F-m. 1-104 alliteration ' hús ok herbergi,' house and hold, corresponding Cumberland phrase, turned out of ' huse and harbour,' harbour here being identical with Icel. *herbergi.*

Hause. Used of the passes over the lower fells which separate the valleys of Lakeland, as Scatoller Hause,

Gaits Hause, Esk Hause, Tarn Hause, Haws or Hause Water. Icel. *háls*, the neck, then a hill, a ridge, especially in Iceland, of the low fells which divide two parallel dales. Cf. Swiss *col* in the same use.

Haver. (Icel. *hafrar*.) Oats.

Heck. A swinging gate, used where a fence or wall crosses a beck. Also of the hurdles into which hay is put for cattle. Dan. *hekke*, Icel. *heggr*, a hedge.

Heckberry. The bird-cherry. Dan. *hœgebœr*, prunus padus.

Hell. This word is used as the name of several streams in Lakeland, called from it Hell Beck. Such streams generally proceed from recesses resembling caves, e. g. Hell Gill in Langdale, hence the name from Icel. *hellir*, a cave. Gen. xix. 30, 'Og hann var þar i helli,' and he dwelt in a cave.

Helm Wind. From Icel. *hjalmr*, Goth. *hilms*, A.-S., Eng., and Ger. *helm*, a Teutonic word derived from *hilma*, to hide. In this acceptation it is given by Vigfusson, as applied in popular tales, to a cap of darkness which makes the wearer invisible, and so also it is applied in Old Norse to the clouds as rendering the mountains invisible. There are several mountains in Iceland called Helm or Hjalmr, and in Norway called Hjalm; and we have Helm Crag near Grasmere, and the Helm near Kendal. *Helm* is also found as a surname. It is from the idea of covering or hiding, the original sense, that we get the name helm in helm wind, for the helm is the cap or covering of clouds which descends upon the summit of Cross Fell at the time when the helm wind blows. The places most subject to this helm wind are Milburn, Ouseby, Melmerly, and Gamblesby. Sometimes, when the atmosphere is quite settled, with hardly a cloud to be seen and not a breath of air stirring, a small cloud appears on the summit of the mountain, and extends itself to the north and south. The helm is then said to be on, and in a few minutes the wind is blowing so violently as to break down trees, overthrow stacks, and occasionally throw a person from his horse, or overturn a horse and cart. When the wind blows the helm seems violently agitated, though on ascending the Fell and entering it there is not much wind. Sometimes a helm forms and goes off without a wind; and there are essentially easterly winds without a helm.

Hem. To draw in. Icel. *hemja.*

Herdwicks. The black-faced breed of sheep found in Lakeland, noted for their climbing powers and ability to live on bare pasture.

Herry. To rob, as birds' nests. Icel. *herja,* to ravage or plunder. O. E. *harry,* ' Who harried hell.'—Milton.

Hesp. A fastening or catch for a door. S. Eng. *hasp,* Icel. *hespa.* A greedy and overreaching man is called ' an ole hespin.'

Hest. A horse. Icel. *hestr.* In proper names, as *Hestam*= hest and ham or heim, a dwelling. Hest Bank.

Het. Hot. Icel. *heitr.*

Hind or **Hine.** A man put in to occupy a farmhouse where the farmer has more than one. A.-S. *hina-hine,* a servant, Icel. *hjón,* an upper servant. *Hind* is also found in Cumberland as surname.

Hinder, Hind. Back or behind. Icel. *hindri.*

Hisk. To open, as of children gasping for breath, or sobbing. Cf. Icel. *hixta,* to hiccough, to sob.

Hocker. To bend. Icel. *hokra,* to crouch.

Hollin. The holly. This word apparently takes the Norse suffixed article *inn* or *in.*

Holm. An island, especially in a lake or creek ; also of low land near a lake or river, e. g. Silver Holme, Ling Holme, Rough Holme, and the many Holmes in Windermere and other lakes. Holme Island, near Grange, in Morecambe Bay; the Abbey Holme. Compare Icel. *holmr,* which exactly corresponds with it in those meanings. *Holme* is found in Westmorland as surname.

How. Originally a grave-mound, then a gentle eminence or mound, frequently in proper names in this sense. Silver How, Fox How, Torpen How, Brown How, The Hill of Howth in Dublin Bay. Miss Powley, in a *Plea for Old Names,* says that *how* is still in use in Cumberland and Westmorland for grave-mound; and Edmondson says *howie* still means a mound, tumulus, or knoll in the Shetland and Orkney Islands. Icel. *haugr* is a tumulus or burial-mound ; an Icelandic verb *heygja,* formed from this noun, signifies to *bury or inter with a mound over the grave,* signifying an honourable burial and a distinction conferred only upon chieftains. See *Landnáma Bók. How* is found as surname in Lakeland.

How. Bleak or exposed. *How* and *lænd* express the two opposite ideas. *How,* exposed ; *lænd,* sheltered.

Howk. To excavate. Swe., Goth. *holka.*

Hummer. A grassy slope by the side of a river. ' *Hummers* dark,' Gibson's *Folk Speech.* Icel. *hvammr,* a grassy slope or vale ; ' Very frequent as an appellation in every Icelandic Farm,' Vigfusson. It also means a swamp, and is in this sense applied in Lakeland to wet land. The word illustrates in a remarkable manner the varied history of the same word in different countries.

While in Lakeland it has become an obscure and almost obsolete word in the dialect: in Iceland as *Hvammr*, the name of the home of the noble and talented family of the Sturlungs, it becomes one of the most memorable and renowned place-names in the history of the Icelandic commonwealth.

Hurd. A herd of cattle. Icel. hjörð. Cf. Goth. *hairdeis*, a herd or shepherd, Icel. *hirdir*, a shepherd. John x. 'Eg em góðr hiriðr,' I am the Good Shepherd.

Ill, *adj.* Bad or evil. Icel. *illr*, bad or evil. ' It's an *ill* win that blows neabody good.' Proverb.

Illify. To defame.

Ings. Meadows. N. and A.-S. *ing* or *eng*, a field or meadow. As place-name, *The Ings*, near Windermere.

Intak. A piece of land enclosed near a farmhouse, an *intake*, evidently so called as having been originally *taken in* from the common or fell. ' As they wor o' trailin varra slā down Willy Garnett's girt *intak*.'—Gibson's *Folk-speech*. Of this word Magnússon says, 'This is a purely Scandinavian term, but unknown in the Cumberland sense except in Sweden, where a piece of a common enclosed for cultivation is called *intaka*.'

Intil. Into. Dan. *ind til*, Swe. *in till*.

Keld. A well or spring. (Icel. *kelda*, Dan. *kilde*, a well or spring), found in place-names, as Threlkeld, Iron Keld, Butterilket, Butterild Keld and Keldra, a well with an *á*, or spring flowing from it; also a hamlet called Keld in Westmorland.

Kemp. To strive, to contend. Icel. *keppa* (pp = mp), Dan. *kœmpe*, Swed. *kämpa*. Cf. also Icel. *kempa*, which Vigfusson defines as a champion. We have two instances

of the use of this word in Stagg, the blind Cumberland
poet:

'See how the *kemping* shearers run,
An rive an bind an stook their corn.'

And again :

'Auld Nick and Scott yence *kempt* they say,
Whan best a reeafe fra san cud twayne.'

The Scott here spoken of is Michael Scott, the wizard
mentioned in *The Lay of the Last Minstrel*. In more
contests than one Old Cumbrian traditions speak of him
as being able to hold his own against the devil.

Ken. To know. Icel. *kenna*, to know. 'D' ye ken John
Peel?'

Kenning. Recognition, 'oot ov aw kenning,' out of all
recognition. Icel. *kenning*, a mark of recognition.

Ket. Carrion. Icel. *kvett, ket, kjöt,* flesh; a Scandinavian
word found in neither Anglo-Saxon nor German.

Kep. To catch. Icel. *kippa*, to pull, to wrench, to pick.

Keslop. Rennet from a calf. (Icel. *kœsir,* explained
below, and *hlaup,* coagulated milk.) Used very commonly
by the housewives of Cumberland and other portions of
Lakeland for making cheese. Cheese-making is not near
so common now as it was formerly, when every farmhouse used to manufacture its own cheese. The Icelandic
gives us a striking parallel to this word and its meaning,
for in Cleasby *kœsir* is translated as rennet from a calf's
maw, *used to curdle milk, hleypa mjólk,* for making cheese
and *skyr*; and is frequent in modern Icelandic usage.
Hlaup is the curdled milk in its first unacidulated state,
while *skyr* is the sour curds stored up for food, and at
present a national dish with the Northmen.

Kink. To cough in convulsions. The hooping-cough is
called the *kink*-cough. Icel. *kinka,* to nod the head.

Kirk. Church. *Kirkja* in Iceland, *kirk* in Scotland, and *kirke* in Denmark. Also in derived proper names: Kirkfell in Wasdale Head, Kirkju Fell in Iceland.

Kirn or **Kurn.** A churn. Icel. *kirna*, a churn. This word gives its name to the harvest festival or feast of the ingathering in Cumberland, called *kurn* supper, from the fact that half-churned cream was one of the good things served up upon the occasion. Butter sops were also a very essential part of the feast formerly, and consisted of very thin wheaten cakes broken small and sopped in butter melted with sugar. I do not know what Ambrosia was like, but Butter sops used to seem to me to be a feast fitted for the gods. I believe that they are now almost, if not altogether, unknown. ' Up-and-down kurn,' a churn which was much in use in Cumberland and Westmorland formerly, although now obsolete. It was worked by an up and down process.

Kist. A chest. Icel. *kista*, a chest. Old oak *kists* and cupboards are to be found very generally in old farmhouses in Cumberland and the Lake district; they are very curiously and laboriously carved with the initials of the family to which they have originally belonged, with various flourishes and devices, and dates ranging from 1600 or thereabouts, to 1800 are carved upon them. A gentleman, Mr. Collingwood, who is well versed in wood carving, has assured me that some of the curious letters carved upon them are unmistakably Norse. *Eel kist* was the term applied by the monks of the Abbey in Holm Cultram to the pond near the river Waver in which they kept their eels alive. The road to it is still called *Eel Kist* lane; also the coffin was called *kista* in which Kveldulf drifted aland, see *Landnáma.*

Kitling. A kitten. Icel. *kettlingr.*

Kittle. To tickle. Icel. *kitla.*

Knab. A rocky projection, e.g. The *Knab* on Windermere. Icel. *knappr.*

Knep. To browse or nip grass, as a horse. Dan. *nappe,* to pick up rapidly small objects, to snatch.

Knot. A rocky excrescence, generally proceeding from the top of a mountain. (Icel. *knúta,* which Vigfusson explains as a knuckle-bone or the head of a bone.) The word is of frequent occurrence both in Norway and Lakeland. The Knott, Benson Knott, Knott End, Hard Knott, Harte Knot (= the hard knot) in Norway; and the idea seems to be taken from the close resemblance which some mountains bear to the round of the knuckles. '*Hnúta* is frequently applied to the tops of mountains in Eastern Iceland, which resemble the knob of the " femur " which moves in the socket of the hip-bone.'—Magnússon.

Kurn-supper. The Cumberland Feast of Ingathering.

Kyle. A boil or sore. 'As sair as a *kyle,*' Proverb. From Icel. *kýli,* a boil or abscess. 'Gripa á kýlinu,' to touch a sore place. 'Ódaun leggur af kýlum minum,' 'There is anguish from my wounds.'—Ps. xxxviii. 5.

Kysty. Fastidious. Applied generally to those who are difficult to please with the quality of their food, e.g. 'Thū lyle kysty fairy'='You little unthankful imp.' Often heard on the Border. Icel. *kveistinn,* fastidious, peevish.

Lad. (Icel. *hlaði*), a pile or stack. *Lad* stones, upon the top of Wetherlamb Mountain, are stones *piled up.* There is the same idea in the place-name Lad Cragg and Latrigg.

Læn'd or **Leen'd**, as above, used in High Furness for sheltered, as a *leen'd* place for sheep on the fell.

Laif or **Hlaif**. A loaf. Ulph. *hlaifs*, a loaf. Icel. *hleifr*. The word as used in the dialect seems to have the **H**.

Lair. Mire or dirt. Icel. *leirr*, clay, earth, loam ; Dan. *leer*. This *leir* or *lair* very frequently goes in this sense to form place-names in *Landnáma*, as *Leirhöfn*, the miry landing-place; *Leiruvágr*, the miry bight.

Lairy. Miry.

Lait or **Late**. To seek. (Icel. *leita*, to seek; Ulph. *wlaiton* ; Greek, περιβλέπεσθαι, to look around.) In the modern Icelandic Bible, John viii. 50, ' En eg *leita* ekki mins heiðurs; sá er, sem hans *leitar* og dæmir,' I seek not mine own glory; there is one that seeketh and judgeth.

> ' Lads i't dark, meeade rampin wark
> As cloaks and clogs were *laitit.*'
> MARK LONSDALE, The Upshot.

Lake or **Laik**. To play as children do. Icel. *leika*, to play ; Ulph. *laikan*, to skip or leap for joy. In the Maeso-Gothic Bible of Ulphilas, Luke xv. 25, ' Saggvins jah laikans,' is ' Songs and Plays.' According to De Quincey (*Lake Poets*), Wordsworth used to pun on the double meaning of this word as implying playing and visiting the Lakes (' Laking ').

Laikins. Playthings, toys. Cf. Icel. *leikinn*, playful.

> ' Here baby *laikins*, routh o' spice on sto's an' stands extended.'
> STAGG, Rosley Fair.

Lane. Alone. Icel. *leyna*, to conceal.

Lang. Long. Icel. *langr*.

Lang streekt. At full length. Dan. *langstrakt,* at full length.

Lapstone. A cobbler's stone upon which he beats his leather. Icel. *lappa,* to patch or cobble.

Lathe. A barn. Icel. *hlaða,* Dan. *lade,* a barn. Leathes, a village in Cumberland ; Watenlath, barn at the end of the wath ; and Silloth, may all come from this root.

Lee, Lea, or **Ley.** A scythe. Icel. *lé* with art. *léinn,* mod. *ljár* ; Dan. *le,* a scythe. The same word in the same meaning is found in Yorkshire, and Lucas thus describes it as found in Nidderdale :. ' It is a large heavy scythe with a straight handle, and blade flat with the handle, unlike those in the South, which are smaller, and have the blade turned at an angle.'

Leeze. To cleanse wool, *les* being applied to anything made of wool. Icel. *les,* knit woollens.

> '*Leeze* me on thee John Barleycorn,
> Thou King o' grain.'--BURNS.

Leister. A salmon spear, from Icel. *ljóstr,* a club, then a salmon spear. There is a graphic description of how the *leister* was used for spearing salmon on the Solway in the *Redgauntlet* of Sir W. Scott. A *leister* with three prongs of a somewhat different construction is used in Cumberland for leistering eels, the eels being brought up between the prongs.

Lig. To lay. Icel. *leggja.*

Lin. Flax or linen. Icel. *lín.* '*Lin* sarks.'—*Ann Wheeler's Dialogue.*

Lite. To depend upon or rely upon. Icel. *hlíta,* to depend or rely on.

Loave ! An interjection denoting wonder.

Loavins. Used in the same sense. '*Loavins*, what el Betty think, Betty think, Betty think.'—*B. B. B.*

Lofin Days! or **Lovin Days!** *Lofi deus*, or 'Praise God'; an interjection of wonder.

Look. To pluck out weeds from among the corn, generally performed by an instrument called looking tongs. The derivation of this word of very common use in Cumberland puzzled me for a long time. Vigfusson, however, seems to clear up the matter when he gives *lok* as meaning a fern or weed, and quotes in illustration the phrase, 'Ganga sem *lok* yfir akra,' to spread like weeds over a field. Dan. *luge*, to weed an orchard.

Looking-tongs. Looking-tongs, used as above.

Loppered. Coagulated, as milk.

Lound. Calm or still. *Lound* places, sheltered places. Icel. *leyndr*, hidden, covered; 'laun vogr,' a sheltered creek. Magnússon says, anent this word: 'It has clearly the same sense as Icel. *lygn*, Swe. *lugn*, Dan. *lun*, calm, sheltered against wind: the corresponding nouns being Icel. *logn*, Swe. *lugn*, Dan. *lun*. Perhaps in the Lakeland word we have at last a clue to the origin of Icel. *lundr*, Swe. *lund*, Dan. *lund*, a grove.

Lova me. In Cumberland=*lof-mér* in Iceland, both derived as above.

Lowe. A flame. Icel. *logi*; Dan. *lue*. The flame of fire spoken of as appearing to Moses, Exod. iii. 2, is in the Icelandic Bible, 'Eldsloga,' and in the Danish Bible, 'Ildslue.' Eldin being also applied to fire in Lakeland.

Lowe. To flame. Swedish, 'Elden begynner loga upp'= Cumbrian and Furness phrase, 'T' Eldin begins at low up.'

Lowse. To release, as children from school or horses from work. Icel. *leysa*, to release.

Lowse. Loose. Icel. *lauss*, loose.

Lug. Ears of a dog, horse, or sheep. Cf. Swed. *lugg*, forelock.

Lug-mark. The ear-mark of mountain sheep is so-called.

Mair. More. Icel. *meiri.*

> 'The last new shūn our Betty gat,
> They pinched her feet, the deil may care,
> What she mud hev them lady leyke
> Though she hed corns for ivver *mair.*'—ANDERSON.

Mak, *sb.* Make, shape, or kind.

Mak, *vb.* To meddle. 'Aw nowder *mak* nor mell.'
Proverb meaning, 'I do not interfere.'

Maks. Sorts. 'It tuks o' *maks* ta mak ivvery mak.'—Rev.
T. Clark, *Johnney Shepherd.*

Man. A conical pillar of stones erected on the top of
a mountain. Cf. Icel. *mön*, mane, ridge, top.

Mappen or **M'appen.** It may happen.

> 'Lal Dinah Grayson's fresh fewsome an free
> Wid a lilt iv her step an a glent iv her e'e
> She glowers ebben at me whativer I say
> An meastly maks answer. wid—*M'appen* I may
> M'appen I may she sez, mappen I may,
> Thou think's I believe the, an mappen I may.'
> GIBSON, *Folk-speech.*

Mazlin. A stupefied person. 'Whats ta meead o't meer
an car thou ole *mazlin*?'—B. B. B.

Mear-field. A field in which the several shares or owner-
ships are known by meer-stones or other boundary
marks. A field was so divided in this (Torver) parish
into three shares until last year, then the three shares
came into one ownership and the division ceased. Cf.
Icel. *mæri*, boundary, in *landa-mæri.*

Meean. A moan in Westmorland dialect.

Meean. Mane of a horse. Icel. *mön.*

Meer Maid or **Meer Man.** The Norse ideal of the Meer Man or Marmennill, is well illustrated on pages 76 and 77 of the *Landnáma*, where he is said to have been brought up by an intending settler while fishing, and is compelled to indicate to the settler a future landtake. The same foreboding or prophetic character is given to him in the North of England.

Meer Stones. Stones placed at the boundaries of undivided allotments to mark the limits of the owners. Many of the old allotments were thus divided, and there are still stones so standing and so named: seems to correspond exactly with the *Lýritr* of Norway (from *lýðr*, people, and *réttr*, right), which is explained in this way : ' When the boundary of a field or estate was to be drawn, the law prescribed that a mark-stone (*merkis-steinn*) should be raised upon the spot, and three other stones laid beside it, called landmark-stones (*lyrittar-steinar*), and by their number and position they were distinguished from all other stones in the field.' To meer corresponds Icel. *mœri*, boundary in *landa-mœri*.

Melder. A grinding of meal. Icel. *meldr*, meal.

> 'That ilka *melder* wi' the miller,
> Thou sat as lang as thou hed siller.'—BURNS.

Mell. To interfere. Cf. Icel. *miðla* (*m. málum*, to bring terms about in disputes). In *Ann Wheeler's Dialogues* Gossips are described as those who employ their time in ' Gangin frae house to house heerin news an *mellin* e ther nebbors.'

Mell Doors. The space between the outer door of a house and the inner = middle doors. Of this word, Magnússon says, ' In Icelandic farmhouses the term *milli-dyr* = middle door, is still heard ; it means a door which is somewhere between the front door and the door of the household sitting-room = *baðstofu-dyr.*'

Mense. Decency. Icel. *mennska*, manliness or propriety of conduct; what becomes a man, from Icelandic *menn-skr*, what belongs to a man.

Mensfu. (Icel. *mennskufullr*?) Hospitable or becoming. Derived as above.

Meol or **Meals.** Sandhills. (In Iceland sandhills are called *melr*, pl. *melar* from the meal-like appearance of the sand.) Found frequently in proper names, e. g. Millom = meol holm, Esk Meals, Mealsgate, Cartmel, Mealo. See a very interesting illustration in the *Landnáma.* See pages 77 and 78.

Mi. Mine. Icel. *minn, mín, mitt*, my.

Mickle. Large. Icel. *mikill*, large. Mickle dore, lit. Great Door, the deep chasm or opening between Scawfell and Scawfell Pikes.

Mind, *vb.* To ·give. one's mind or attention to. Icel. *minna*, to remind.

Mire. A moor or bog. Found in place names, as The Mire, Pelutho Mire, Mire Side. Icel. *mýrr*, a moor, bog, or swamp. Hence also in Icelandic place-names, Mýri, Mýrar.

Moud. Mold. Icel. *mold.*

Moudywarp. The mole. Icel. *moldvarpa.*

Muck. Dirt or mud. Icel. *myki.*

Muit or **Moot Ho.** Literally the *Meeting* Hall or Town Hall.

Mun. Must. Icel. *mun.*

Munnet. Must not.

Murry Neet, Merry Neet or **Old Wife Hake.** This, as its name imports, was a night dedicated to mirth and festivity. It took place at some village or country inn during the Christmas holidays, and was most characteristic of Cumberland and Lakeland. In the following verse from Anderson's *Bleckell Murry neet*, the scenes at such an entertainment are described :—

> 'Ay, lad sec a *murry neet*, we've hed at Bleckell,
> The sound o' the fiddle yet rings in my ear,
> Aw reet clipt an heelt war the lads and the lasses
> And monie a cleverlish hizzy was theer;
>
> The bettermer swort sat snug i' the parlour,
> I' the pantry the Sweethearters cutter'd sea soft,
> The dancers they kick'd up a stour i' the kitchin,
> At lanter the caird-lakers sat i' the loft.'

Naggin. Tormenting. Icel. *naga*, to gnaw ; colloquial : *nagga* and *naggra*, nag.

Narhand. Near to. Icel. *nœrhendis*.

Natterin. Peevish, cross. Icel. *gnadd*, grumbling ; *gnadda*, to grumble. Dan. *gnaddre*, to grumble.

Neaf. Fist. Icel. *hnefi*, the fist.

Neakt. Icel. *nekt*, nakedness.

Near. Stingy. Dan. *nœr*, close, sharp.

Neb. Beak. Dan. *nœb*, Icel. *nef*.

Neea. No. Icel. *neinn*.

Nuik or **Neuk.** Nook.

> 'They say a heedless woman woaks at sartin neets o' t' year
> An greeans an yewls at sec a rate as freetins fowk to heer
> I wadn't mind sec teals, bit yence I gat afreet mesel;
> I' Branthet *Neuk*, an hoo it was, just lissen an I'll tell.'
>
> GIBSON, *Branthet Neuk Boggle.*

Numerals. The following are the Icelandic numerals up to five :—*Einn*, one; *tveir*, two; *þrír*, three; *fjórir*, four; *fimm*, five. The numeral system of the dialect does not, so far as I have been able to compare them, bear any especial affinity to them. A very curious numeral system, however, has been found to prevail, with some phonetic variations, over the whole of the North-English district of which I am treating, having come down apparently *viva voce* from very early times. They have been generally spoken of as sheep-scoring numerals, though by no means confined to this. I subjoin three specimens :—

No. 1. BORROWDALE, KESWICK, CUMBERLAND.	No. 2. KIRKBY STEPHEN, WESTMORLAND.	No. 3. CONISTON, HIGH FURNESS, NORTH LANCASHIRE.
Yan	Yan·	Yan
Tyan	Tyaan·	Taen
Tethera	Taed·'ere	Tedderte
Methera	Maed·'dere	Medderte
Pimp	Mimp	Pimp
Sethera	Hai·tes	Sethera
Lethera	Sai tes	Lethera
HoVera	Hao·ves	HoVera
Dovera	Dao·ves	DoVera
Dick	Dik	Dik
Yan-a-dick	Yaan·edik	Yan-a-dik
Tyan-a-dick	Tyaan·edik	Taen-a-dik
Tether-a-dick	Taed·eredik	Tedder-a-dik
Mether-a-dick	Maed·eredik	Medder-a-dik
Bumfit	Buun	Mimph
Yan-a-bumfit	Yaan·eboon	Yan-a-Mimph
Tyan-a-bumfit	Tyaan·eboon	Taen-a-Mimph
Tether-a-bumfit	Taed·ereboon	Tedder-a-Mimph
Mether-a-bumfit	Maed·ereboon	Medder-a-Mimph
Giggot	Buomfit	Gigget

No. 1 was obtained from the shepherds of Borrowdale.
No. 2 Dr. A. J. Ellis obtained through Dr. Murray from Mr. W. H. Thompson, of Kirkby Stephen.
No. 3 my wife remembered from childhood as used by Coniston shepherds.

Offcum. Stranger, seems to correspond as to form with Icel. *af-kvæmi.* In the Fell dales, those who are not natives of a dale or district, or who have lately come into it, are called *offcums*, and it is sometimes very long ere they are looked upon as possessing the full freedom and social privileges of the dale or district.

Oft. Icel. *opt* or *oft*.

Oot. Icel. *út*, out.

> 'Thou's here ivery day just to put yan aboot—
> An thou moiders yan terrably—Jwohnny, git *oot.*'
>
> GIBSON, *Folk-speech.*

Peat. An oblong piece of moss or turf used for beating or mending the fire ; hence called *beats* or *peats*.

Peat Mull. The waste or débris of the above used for banking up fires, so that they may smoulder and continue alighted. Mull = Swed. *mull*, Dan. *muld*, Icel. *mold*. Icel. *mó-mold* answers exactly to peat mull ; *mó* from *mór*, peat.

Pell. A rattling shower of hail or rain. A Cumbrian, being questioned as to whether it rained much in his neighbourhood, replied, ' It douks and drizzles, bit nivver cums doon in nea greet *pell.*'

Pentas. Penthouse. A roof fixed to the side of a house. Common in the last century in farmhouses in Cumberland and Lakeland generally. With the modern improvements in farmhouses they have now generally passed away. There is still one at Low Torver Park in this parish, one I know in Langdale, and one till lately at Hause Bank, Coniston. Magnússon, who visited some of them when residing here with us, says he believes them identical with the outside galleries which formed of old a marked feature in Scandinavian houses.

Pot. Icel. *pottr*. The deep circular holes generally filled with water, from which peats have been dug upon the mosses, are called peat pots. The word is also applied to the deep circular holes which the action of a river forms amongst the rocks in the Duddon. The circular glacier mills in the rocks of Switzerland have been formed by a somewhat similar process. The word is applied to any basin-shaped hole. From this root are *kail pot*, the large circular pan used for boiling broth; *set pot*, the large circular pan built into a furnace.

Pun. Pound.

Punston. Poundstone; a pebble or cobble stone, as nearly as possible of the weight of twenty-two ounces. In old days butter was sold by the long pound, which weighed twenty-two ounces. Great care was exercised in selecting a round stone of the precise weight. I remember a round cobble stone so used by an ancestor of my own, which had been chipped a little to reduce it to the 'standard.' One of the oldest and heaviest penny pieces was selected in order to give the cast or overweight.

Quit. Free. N. *kvittr*, free. When a person loses at a game of chance, he sometimes says he will play again, 'double or quits,' i. e. quit or free from the obligation. It is found in the same sense in the Bible: 'The owner of the ox shall be *quit*.'—Exod. xxi. 28.

Raise. Applied originally to mounds or cairns raised over the dead, as Dunmail Raise, between Grasmere and Wyburn, said to be the grave of Dunmail, the last king of rocky Cumberland. Stone Raise is the name of a Cumbrian village thus derived. Of this word Magnússon says, 'Raise = Icel. *hreysi*; Dan. *rös* and *röse*; Swe. *röse*; Norw. *rös*, also Dan. and Swe. *sten-röse*, all = heap of stones thrown together anyhow by hands or nature; a cairn.'

Rake. Commonly used as name of a sheepdog, from Icel. *reka*, to drive, or *reki*, driver. Possibly, however = Icel. *rakki*, a cur.

Rake. In the Lake country, applied generally to the narrow paths along which sheep *are driven* to the fell. It is used in the same acceptation in Yorkshire. From Icel. *reka*, part. *rak*, originally *vreka*, to drive; *Outrake*, corresponding in sound and meaning with Icel. *út reka* (Joshua iii. 10, ' út reka kananita,' drive out the Canaanites), was a path by which sheep were driven out to the fell. There is one so named on Black Combe, one at Torver, one at Coniston. There seems to be one or more in most of the larger valleys in Lakeland, which are spoken of as ' the rake,' just as we speak of ' the fell.' There are also several farms in the district called 'The Outrake,' and I have observed that such farms generally stand at the entrance to a rake or fell drive. The Norse verb *reka*, also means to drive or drift, as the tide does; and we have this verb in the place-name of Wreaks End, near Broughton in Furness, derived from a point in the stream close by which makes the end of the tide flow or drift in that direction. On the Yorkshire moors sheep are said to 'rake out' when they go single file. Ulleraker = wool rakes, was formerly a realm of Sweden in the present province of Westmanland.

Ram. Strong, as of a pungent, offensive smell. Icel. *ramr*, *rammr*, strong, rank.

Rang. Wrong. Icel. *rangr*.

Rannel Boak. The house beam ; the large beam running across the chimney in old farmhouses. Icel. *rann*, a house (?) and *balkr*, a beam.

Rannel Tree. Another form of the above.

Rash. Active. 'As *rash* an' as young eighty-five.'— Anderson. Icel. *röskr*, Dan. *rask*, Swed. *rask*.

Ratch. To sneak about, to lay hold of meat, as dogs do. Cf. Icel. *rakki*, a hound or dog.

Ratch. A thievish, greedy animal, generally applied to an old sow which is spoken of as ' the ole *ratch.*' Sometimes applied to a thievish person, as in the following lines :

> 'An than t' ole body cums oot ta fratch
> She's a gudden ta fratch is yon un my songs.
> She co's me "a durty ole theeven *ratch*"
> An than we ga at it leyke hammer an tongs.'—*Local Song.*

Raup. An auction, from Icel. *hrópa,* to cry, *hróp,* a cry.

Reckling. The weakest member of a litter of pigs or of a brood of chickens, from O. N. *reklingr,* an outcast ; or it may be from *reck,* care, as describing that which requires most care.

Red. Iron-ore, so called in Furness, from Icel. *rauði,* the red iron ore, from which the Norse settlers wrought iron. *Landnáma* : ' Hann blés fyrstr manna rauða á Islandi, ok var hann af því kallaðr Rauða-Björn,' he was the first man who smelted (red) iron in Iceland, and from this he was called Red-Bjorn.

Redstake. The stake by which cattle are bound to the ' bewce.' A.-S. *wræd,* a band or tie, and *staca,* a stake.

Reean (in Furness), **Rein** and **Rane** (in Cumberland and Westmorland). The *reeans,* in Furness, were unploughed portions which were left round the cultivated fields, known in other portions of the country as ' head riggs.' The origin of the name seems, however, to have been from the uncultivated strips which, before town fields and commons were divided by fences, were left untilled in order to mark the boundaries. A neighbouring land-owner, aged somewhere near eighty, tells me that he remembers perfectly well when the town fields of Coniston and Torver were divided by such *reeans,* and every man's

division was called his *reean.* The same system was
known also in Westmorland, for J. B. Davies, Esq., of
Kirkby Stephen, says:—'The name *reeans* is used here
for narrow strips of grass land, a little higher than the
ground on either side, left in closes called field lands or
dale lands to mark the division of such land or dale.
We have fields called *raynes*, sloping land with riggs or
terraces, on the lower side of which there is usually a
reean or slightly elevated strip. These slightly elevated
strips have often been levelled down, but the name is
still retained.' The same system prevailed in Cumberland, and Dickinson, in his *Glossary of the Cum. Dialect*
(English Dialect Society) defines 'Rig and Rane,' a phrase
very common in Cumberland formerly, as 'an arable field
held in shares, which are divided by narrow green lanes
(*ranes*) and the intervals usually cultivated.' The system
is found still, or at any rate was found very recently, at
Tebay near Penrith in Westmorland. The system formerly prevailed in Yorkshire. O. N., Icel. *rein*, Swed.
ren, a grassy strip round a cornfield, which must not be
broken up by plough or spade; a field-boundary.

Reeap. Rope. Ulph. *raips*, Icel. *reip*, rope.

Reek. Smoke. Icel. *reykr*, smoke. Reykjavik, the capital
of Iceland, is literally 'smoke wick,' so called from the
steaming hot springs near it. Cf. 'the Auld Reekie,' or
Edinburgh, in Burns.

Reek. To smoke. Icel. *rjúka.*

Reet. Neat, properly equipped or fitted out.

> 'She's smart oot o' dooars, she's tidy i't 'hoose,
> Snod as a mowdy warp—sleek as a moose;
> I black goon, i blue goon, i green goon or grey,
> I tell her she's *reet*, an git m'appen I may.'
> GIBSON, *Folk-Speech.*

*E

Rice or Ris or Rise. Brushwood, thorns on hedges, &c.
Copsewood and brushwood generally. A person doing
anything with energy is said to be 'gaun at it leyke
a man haggen (i. e. cutting down), *rīse*,' implying that
rīse, from its thick, prickly and impenetrable nature,
requires energy in him who cuts it down. Icel. *hrís*,
a collective noun for shrubs or brushwood. (O. E. *rīs* or
rys.—Chaucer.)

Riddins or Ruddins. Clearings. See *Landnáma*, 126.

Rig. A ridge. Icel. *hryggr*, given in Cleasby as the
back or spine in men or beasts, then a ridge or mountain
ridge. It is very generally applied in this country to
a ridge, then an oblong hill, as Lantriggs, Latrigg; also
in Cumberland as surname.

Rig Reeap. The straw rope going over the ridge of a
stack.

Rim. An edge; from Icel. *rim*, a rim or outer edge, as of
a sword.

Rive. To tear. A 'slate *river*' is a splitter or divider of
slates. A boy who tears his clothes is called 'a *rive* rags.'
Icel. *rífa*; Dan. *rive*; Eng. *rive*.

Ross. From Icel. *hross*, a horse. Rosthwaite, Rossgid,
Rosley, noted for its horse fair; and Ross, a common
surname.

Roven. Riven. Icel. *rofinn*, part. of *rjúfa*.

Rowan Tree. The mountain ash. O. N. *reynir*; Dan.
rönnetræ. This word marks, perhaps more clearly than
any other, the intimate connexion between the words and
superstitions of Scandinavia and the North of England.
Reynir is found in a few Icelandic place-names, as
Reynir, Reynivellir; Reynis-Stadr, applied to mark
places at the time of the settlement, the only sort

of tree, except the dwarf birch, that was found in
Iceland. There is a place called Raynors, in Cumberland, which seems to mean 'The Mountain Ashes.'
Rowantree is also found as surname. The rowan tree
was a holy tree consecrated to Thor, and, according to
legends quoted in Vigfusson, very intimately connected
with the mysteries and superstitions of the Icelanders.
Reynir had its fame in Iceland from the supposed
magical influence of the tree against witches. In some
places in the North of England a piece of the rowan
tree was placed above the door to scare away evil
influences. Atkinson, in his *Forty Years in a Moorland
Parish*, says that in Yorkshire women often carried
with them a piece of the rowan tree to drive off evil
spirits, hence it was called *witch wood*; and in Lakeland the stick for stirring the cream was frequently of
the rowan tree wood, to counteract the malign spiritual
influence which at times bewitched the cream so that no
butter was forthcoming. Burns says :

'Thence countra wives, wi' toil and pain
May plunge and plunge the kirn in vain :
For, oh ! the yellow treasures taen
              By witching skill
And dawtit twal-pint hawkie's gaen
              As yell 's the bill.'

Rowt. To bellow (of cattle). Icel. *rauta*, to roar ; Swe.
ryta.

Ruddle. Red paint used for marking sheep, and made
from the red hematite found up the Wasdale Screes and
elsewhere among the Cumbrian Mountains. See the
mode of procuring it described in *The Old Church Clock*,
by Canon Parkinson. Icel. *ryd*, rust. Magnússon says,
'The corresponding Icelandic word is *rjóðla*, an iterative
of *rjóða*, to redden by besmearing, used in the common

language of Iceland for the act of lightly besmearing. The word is not recorded in the dictionaries, but it may be heard in all parts of the country.'

Rung. Round of a ladder.

Runnel. An open drain or runlet. Dan. dialect, *rönnd.*

Sackless. Simple or without energy. Icel. *saklauss,* innocent, free from blame. From *sök,* blame, and *lauss,* without. A 'neer-do-well' is sometimes called a *sackless.*

Saeng. A heap or bed of hay. Icel. *sæing, sæng,* bed.

Saim. Lard.

Sair or Sarr. Sore. Icel. *sárr.*

Sammel. Gravel.

Sand. Often used to form place-names. Icel. *sandr.*

Sark. Shirt. Icel. *serkr,* shirt.

> 'An cried out, "Weel dūne cutty *sark* !"
> When in a moment a' was dark.'—BURNS.

Scale. A wooden hut or shelter. Used of wooden huts put up as a temporary protection for turf, which are called 'peat *scales.*' It is also frequently found in place-names, as The Scales, Scale Hill, Bowscale, Seascale, Nether Scales, Scaleby, literally 'the booth dwelling.' Icel. *skáli,* a shed or hut put up for temporary use. It is said in the *Landnáma Bok* of the earliest settlers in Iceland, 'þar sér enn skála-topt þeirra ok svá hrófit.'

Scale, *vb.* To disperse or separate. Icel. *skilja,* to separate. This word is very generally used in the dialect of Lakeland. *Scaling hay,* spreading it out in the sun ; *scaling,* i. e. spreading, peats. The clouds are said to *scale* when they disperse.

Scar. The face of a rock, a cliff cut off or escarped; the rock itself. Cf. Icel. *sker*, an isolated rock, from *skera*, to cut; Swe. *skär*.

Sconce. A stone seat fixed in the wall in old farmhouses. Cf. Icel. *skonsa*, a nook in a house.

Scree. The débris or shale on the steep, almost perpendicular, side of a mountain, as the Screes of Wastwater; from Icel. *skriða*, or from the sound *scree*, which the shale makes in rushing down.

Scroggs. Stumps. Dan. *srog*, a stump.

Sebben. Seven. Ulph. *sibun*, seven.

Seean. Soon. Icel. *senn*, soon.

Seeves. Rushes. Icel. *sef*, Dan. *siv*, a rush. Called also in Scotland and on the border, *rash*, e. g. 'Green grow the rashes, O.'

Segg. A hard callous place on the hand. Icel. *sigg*, thick, hard skin.

Sel. An Icelandic word very frequent in *Landnáma*, meaning a shed on a mountain pasture, but within the landmarks of each farm, where the milk cows were kept in summer. In place-names in Lakeland, e. g. Sellafield, Selside, &c., we seem to retain this word.

Sett. To accompany so as to direct or place in the right way. Icel. *setja*, to place or set in the right direction.

> 'Aw *sett* Betty yem aw the way to Kurkbanton,
> An on the ole settle we coddlet aw neet.'—ANDERSON.

Settle. A long seat with a high back. 'The *settle* neist was thrown aseyde.'—Anderson.

Seyme-twiner. A small machine placed under the arm and used for twisting straw ropes for stacks. Cf. Icel. *síma*, n., rope and *tvinna*, to twine.

Seymie. Used of any ill-natured, twisted fellow. It occurs in this sense in the following verse of Anderson's *Kursmas Eve* :—

> 'Than wry-gobb'd *Seymie* neest meead a lang speech
> Bad them drop o' their fratchen and speyte yè tknaa
> "What neybers" said he "yud far better gree
> "Nor for lawyers and doctors thus feight yè tknaa."'

Shank. The lower or remaining part. Dan. *skank.*

Sheep-sime or **seyme.** A straw rope hung round a sheep's neck, including the foreleg, to prevent its leaping fences. Cf. seyme-twiner.

Shive. A slice. Icel. *skífa* ; Dan. *skive.*

Shive, *vb.* To slice.

Shrike. To shriek. Icel. *skrœkja.*

Side. A settlement. In place-names, as Arnside, Ormside, Ambleside, Swinside. Icel. *síða, side,* name of many settlements.

Sike or **Syke.** · A small stream or gutter. Icel. *síki.* Found also as part of place-name in Sykehouse, Syke-side, Sykehead. Also as surname, Sykes.

Sile. Used for straining milk, a sieve. In domestic language in the east of Iceland *síli,* for liquids only.

Sile, *vb.* To strain milk with a *sile.* East Icel. *síla.*

Sime or **Seyme.** The straw rope used for holding down the thatch or covering upon stacks. Icel. *síma,* a cord or rope.

Sin. Since. Icel. *síðan* ; Dan. *siden.*

Sine, *sb.* A strainer ; Icel. *síja* (Engl. in = Icel. *í,* in many cases), a sieve.

Sine, *vb.* To strain. Icel. *síja.*

Sipe, *vb.* To drip. Dan. *sive,* to drip.

Skarn. Dung. Icel. *skarn*, dung.

Skel. Shell. Icel. *skel*, a shell. ' " Here's five dozen o' eggs," sez she ".I wadn't give a *skell* o' them mair nor ten for sixpence." ' — *B. B. B.*

Skemmel. A long wooden bench used as a seat. Icel. *skemill*, a bench.

Skep. A circular basket made of rushes, a beehive. Icel. *skeppa*.

Skift. To shift. Icel. *skifta*.

Skill. To shell, as peas. Icel. *skilja*, to separate. Cf. however Dan. *skalle*, Swed. *skala*, to shell.

Skillings. The farinaceous portion of wheat or oats separated from the husks. Cf. Icel. *skilja*, to separate.

Skirl. To scream.

Skratti. The name of a hobgoblin or boggle. This name and idea were once very well known in Cumberland, and I remember having heard it often forty or fifty years ago. This name, as known in Cumberland, is evidently the Norse or Icelandic *skratti*, a wizard or warlock. The Swedish *skratti* refers to the strange noises with which wizards work ; also a goblin or monster, as *vatna-skratti*, a water sprite or monster. *Skratta sker*, the scar or rock by Karmt isle in Norway, on which certain wizards were exposed to die, reminds one of Scratchmere Scar, in Lakeland.

Skreek. To shriek. Icel. *skrœkja*.

Skufter. To run about hastily or in a confused manner. Icel. *skotta*, to veer, or hover about.

Skum. That which rises to the top when a liquid is boiled. Dan. *skum*.

Skŭn. To throw with a quick and hasty effort. Icel. *skunda*, to speed, *skynda*, to cause to speed, to throw.

Skut. The hind-end board of a farmer's cart, which can be taken out. Icel. *skutr*, the stern.

Slack. A hollow boggy place. Also as place-name, e. g. Nettleslack, Ashslack. Icel. *slakki* has the same meaning. Found in Cumberland as surname.

Slape. Slippery. Icel. *sleipr*, slippery.

Slape-clogs. A cheat.

Slatter. To spill. Icel. *sletta*, to dash.

Sleck. To quench. Icel. *slekka*, to slake.

Sled. A sledge shod with iron, and used for dragging slates or peats, where carts or wheel carriages could not be used. Icel. *sleði*, a sledge.

Slocken. To quench thirst. Icel. *slökkva*, to extinguish.

Smit, *vb. a.* To mark sheep with a distinctive mark, or smear them, as farmers do, with red or ruddle previous to sending them to the fell. Lambs are so smitted when first put upon the fell, and sheep at clipping time. Each farmer has his own distinct *smit* or brand, which are carefully noted in the shepherd's book. *Smeitan*, to smear, is found in the Bible of Ulphilas = Icel. *smyrja*, to smear or anoint, as of kings. There is an Icel. word, *smita*, of fatty humors oozing through the pores of the face.

Smit, *sb.* A farmer's mark upon sheep; from the above. With the 'smit' and the 'lug mark' there are, it is stated, about 600 varieties of sheep marking in Cumberland, Westmorland, and Furness.

Snarl. A string or rope is said to be in a *snarl* when it

is twisted and tied, so that it cannot easily be un-
fastened. Magnússon says, 'I have heard this expression
in Eastern Iceland "færið er alt i snerli"=the line
(a new fishing tackle) is all in a *snarl*, i. e. all twisted
into a knot.'

Sned. To cut, lop, or prune. Icel. *sníða.*

Snop snarl. An ill-natured person.

Soop. Old dialect for sweep. Icel. *sópa.*

Sotter (of porridge). To seethe, or simmer.

Soua! Soua! or **Swa!** *interj.* Don't! or cease! or fie! was
very common in the dialect with old people, but is now
fast dying out. Vigfusson gives almost the same word in
Icelandic, *svei*, fie, and he says that 'svei þér, svei, svei,
svei!' is the cry of the Icelandic shepherd to his dog if
he worries a sheep or barks at a stranger; and I have
heard almost the very same words, under the same
circumstances, used by a shepherd to his dog in Lakeland : 'Sooa, theer, sooa, sooa, sooa!'

Sour. Boggy and swampy land is called *sour* land. Icel.
saur, boggy or moorland. In *Landnáma*, 126, it is said of
the settlement of Steinolf: ' He saw a clearing in the dale,
and there he built his house (bæ), and called the whole
dale *Saurbœ*, the swampy dwelling, as there was much
sour land there.' Cf. Sowerby, Sowerby Castle, Temple
Sowerby.

Sowens. The husks of oatmeal were steeped in water,
and the farinaceous matter so extracted was served up
boiled in milk. So served it was called *sowens.*

> 'Sup good *sowens,*
> Sup good man,
> If thou issnt full
> Thou may lick o'ot t' pan.'—*Cumberland Old Saw.*

Spean. To wean. Icel. *speni*, a teat or dug of animals.

Speer. To ask. Icel. *spyrja*, to ask.

Spelk. A splinter. Icel. *spelkr*.

Stack. Pret. Icel. *stakk*, pret. of *stinga*, to stick.

Stag. A colt when first mounted to be broken in. *Stagg* is found in surname.

Staip. To overturn, as a cart. Icel. *steypa*, to make to stoop, to overturn.

Stang. A post pole, or shaft of a cart. Icel. *stöng*, gen. *stangar*.

Stangin. On the evenings of Christmas Day and New Year's Day the revellers were accustomed to mount those they met upon a *stang*, bear them so mounted to the public house, and compel them to 'stand drinks'; this was called *stangin*.

Sted. A place, as housested, fairsted; or abode, used in the sense of place in the Bible: 'And Abijam his son reigned in his stead,' 1 Kings xiv. 31. Icel. *staðr*, a place, from *steðja*, to place. We have it in Lakeland frequently in place-names, as Souterstead, Bowmanstead. The place where the Temple of Thor is said to have stood at Thursby, is called Kirksteads. There, possibly, a Christian Church had been built upon the site of the former temple of Thor.

Stee. A ladder. Icel. *stigi*, a ladder, *stigr*, a step, steep ascent. Dan. *stige*, a ladder, *sti*, a steep path or ascent. Stye Head Pass, Kidsty Pike, Stake Pass.

Steek. To shut or close. In domestic speech in East Iceland *stjaka dyr*, is to fasten the door of a sheep-pen by a pole, (stjaki) slantingly pressed against it.

Steel. A stile, from the same root. Dan. *steile*, Icel. *stagl*. As place-name, Steel Fell, High Steel, Steel Bank, Climb Steel. Cf. Icel. *Stagley*, an island so called.

Steg. A gander. Icel. *steggr*, a male bird.

Stoun. A sudden fit of pain. Icel. *stingr*, pl. *stingir*, shooting pains?

Stower. A stake, as 'dyke *stower*,' a hedge stake. Icel. *staurr*; Dan. and Sw. *stör*.

Sump or Sumph. The puddle about a midden. Dan. *sump*, mire, or puddle.

Swange. When hay is rolled into two ridges, leaving a hollow between them, it was in the dialect called a *swange*. In Icel. *svangi* means that hollow which shows between the vertebrae of the long back and the belly of a hungry cow. In Yorkshire, *swangs* are hollow places in high ground.

Sweel. To flare up and burn rapidly, as a candle. Cf. Icel. *svœla*, heat accompanied by smoke.

Sweltered. Overcome with heat. Icel. *svœldr*, Ulph. *swiltan*, to be overcome.

Swey. To swing. Dan. *svaje*. Cf. Icel. *sveigia*.

Swingle-tree. The splinter bar. Icel. *svingla*, to rotate.

Swipe. To drink off hastily. Icel. *svipa*, to swoop. Cf. the Icelandic phrase *drekka út í einum svip*, to quaff off in one gulp.

Taggy Bell. The curfew. So called near Penrith, where the custom of ringing the *taggy* is still kept up. Dan. *tœkke*, to cover.

Taistrill. Waistril or vagabond.

Tak. To take. Icel. *taka.*

Tanggal. Seaweed. Icel. *þöngull* (from older **þangall*), seaweed stalk (*þara-þöngull*). Cf. Dan. *tang.*

Tarn. A small mountain lake, e. g. Blea Tarn, Little Langdale Tarn, Easedale Tarn. Icel. *tjörn*, gen. *tjarnar*, a tarn. A tarn without visible outlet is called 'a blind *tarn.*'

Teem, *adj.* Empty. **Tūm,** *vb.* To empty. 'An theer *tum* thy brock skin-bag,' *Fray o' Sowport.* Icel. *tómr*, empty. 'Jörðin var eyði og tóm,' the earth was without form and void; *tœma*, to empty.

Tengs (C.), **Tangs** (W. and F.). Tongs. Icel. *töng*, pl. *tengr*, Dan. *tang.*

Thack, *sb.* Thatch. Icel. *þak* and *þekja*, to thatch or cover.

Thack, *vb.* To thatch. Icel. *þekja.*

Thivel or Thyvel. . The round stick still used for stirring the porridge. Cf. the unique passage in *Eyrbyggja-saga,* ed.Vigfusson 1864, p. 70, 9 : '*hann hafði þá enn eigi þafðan sinn graut*'=he had then still not stirred (done stirring) his porridge. This pp. *þafðr* must go back to an inf. *þefja,* to beat, stamp, stir, cf. *þœfa* ; once there doubtless existed an O. N. **þœfill*=thyvel.

Thole. To bear or endure. Icel. *þola*, to bear or endure. 'He that *tholes*, overcomes.'—*Scottish Border Proverb.*

Thor. In place-names. Thursby, pronounced Thorsby ; Thuston Water, former name of Coniston Lake.

Thrang. Busy. Icel. *þröngr*, close or tight. Proverb, '*Thang* as Throp's wife.' A rock very close to the margin of Coniston Lake is called Thrang Cragg.

Threep. To argue persistently. Icel. *þrefa*. There are lands in Cumberland called Threeplands or Threaplands, i. e. debateable lands or lands of disputed ownership.

Thum-sime or **-seyme.** A short rope made by twisting straw round the thumb.

Thur. These. Icel. *þeir*, they, these.

Thurm. Gut. Used of fiddle strings. Icel. *þarmr*, Dan.-Swed. *tarm.*

Thwaite. A piece of land cut off by a fence, or enclosed ; a fell or meadow. Icel. *þveit* or *þveiti.* The root is found in A.-S. *thwitan*, to chop or cut off [Chaucer]. *Thwíte*, Cumberland dialect, *to white*, q. v. *Thwaites* in Lakeland were originally fields or meadows fenced or cut off. In this acceptation we have *thwaites* used as a common noun of the *thwaites* or meadows on the margin of Coniston Lake. So in Icelandic, of a piece of land or paddock of land, in which language it seems to have been originally used of an outlying cottage with its paddock. ' Þær jarðir allar, bú ok þveiti,' all the estates, dwellings, and thwaites ; where *bú*, cottage, and *þveiti*, field, seem opposed to one another. The modern sense of *þveit* in Icelandic is the brim of dry meadowland that gradually inclines towards bogland. From being a field-name, thwaite gradually, in Cumberland and Westmorland, became applied to farms, and then to villages and parishes, as The Thwaite near Coniston, Seathwaite, Ormthwaite, Crossthwaite, Bassenthwaite. And in this sense it is of very frequent application in Norway and Denmark. *Tvæt*, Dan. *tvæde* ; or *thwaite*, a surname ; and the word *thwaite* is also found as a surname in High Furness. There are several names ending in *thwaite*, almost identical in Norway and Lakeland :

LAKELAND.	NORWAY.	LAKELAND.	NORWAY.
The Thwaite	Thveit / Thveitor	Branthwaite / Braithwaite	Brandsthvet
Applethwaite	Epelthvet	Micklethwaite	Mykelthvet
Birkthwaite	Birkethvet	Seathwaite	Sjothvet
Birthwaite	Borthvet	Ruthwaite	Rugthveit

Tike or **Tyke.** A dog; an unruly fellow. Icel. *tík*, Sw. *tík*. There is a tradition that a Curwen of Workington Hall shot a Howard of Corby in a duel on Carlisle Sands, during an assize meeting, for offensively using the word 'tyke' to him. *Tyke* is a trickster, especially in dealings in horses, and in this acceptation the word seems, like the character which it represents, to have come to us from Yorkshire. What *tyke* means in that county, and hence often in Lakeland also, may be made evident from the following description of 'A Yorkshire Tyke.'

'Bane ta Clapham town gate, liv'd an owd Yorksher tike
Who i dealing i horseflesh had ne'er met his like,
Twor his pride that ive au the hard bargains hede hit,
Hede bit a girt monny, bud nivver been bit.'

Nidderdale Almanac, 1873.

Til. To. O. N. and Dan., Swe. and Scotch, *til*, to.

Tite. Soon. Cf. Icel. *títt,* n. of *tíðr,* often, and *tíðla* (for *tíðlega*), early.

Titter. Sooner. Cf. Icel. *tiðar,* adv., oftener. '*Titter* an better,' Proverb.

Toft. A homestead. The farmhouse including the farm buildings. Icel. *toft* or *topt,* orig. the four roofless walls of a house, hence, in pl. homestead, in place-names. In the East of England this word is used as part of place-name, as Lowestoft. In Cumberland it is the most usual name for farmhouse, farm buildings, or homestead. E. g. 'That barn,' says Hyne, 'i' Palmer's *toft* e'll dea reet weel to keav in,' *The Upshot.* In a Court Book of the Manor of Derwentwater, Gawen Wren was fined ten shillings about the year 1640 for having two fires in one *toft* at the same time. The fuel then chiefly used was wood, and this was one of the various expedients for preventing its too rapid consumption. In the article upon Bloomeries it will be seen that an Act was passed in the reign of Elizabeth abolishing Bloomeries in High Furness, because they deprived the tenants of their proper wood and fuel. *Toft* is found as surname.

Top Sark. A loose overcoat of coarse grey wool, very commonly used by farmers and their men servants in the early part of this century. 'I set off i t' rain wid my basket an' t' things in't, anonder my *top sark*, to keep o' dry.'—*B. B. B.*

Trail. To go slowly. Icel. *tregligr*, indolent.
    'They were o' trailin away Varra slā.'—Gibson, *Folk-speech.*

Trinter. Sheep of three years or winters. An example of the method of reckoning by winters is found in the Bible of Ulphilas, where the girl of twelve years old is said to be ' twalib wintrus,' Luke viii. 42. The method of counting years by winters is almost invariably found in the *Landnáma*, e. g. ' At that time had passed from the beginning of the world 6073 winters ' (*Landnáma*, ch. vi. p. 33). The corresponding Icelandic word is *þrévetr* = a sheep of three winters or years old.

Trod. A footpath, called a fit *trod*. Cf. Icel. *tröð*.

Tuithwark. Toothache.

Tun or **Ton.** Originally a field or place surrounded by a hedge. In this sense Wycliffe translates Matt. xxii. 5 : ' But thei dispiseden, and wenten forth, oon to his *tūn* (field), another to his merchandise.' Cf. Icel. *tún*, an enclosed field round a homestead.

Twinter. A sheep of two years old (lit. two winters). Corresponding to Icelandic *tvævetr* = a sheep of two winters old.

Unco. Uncommon. Found on both the Cumberland and Scottish side of the Border as '*unco* gude,' very good. Icel. *einkar*, specially or greatly, prefixed to adjectives or adverbs, as '*einkar vel*,' very well.

Unket. Uncommon.

Upshot. A Cumberland festive gathering of general entertainment and merriment usually held upon Fassen's even, i. e. Shrove Tuesday evening, or the eve of the Feast before Lent. *The Upshot*, Mark Lonsdale's longest poem in the dialect, takes its title from being the description of such an upshot. The opening lines are as follows:

> 'Thur Worton lads an twea three mair
> Theer mud be six or seeven
> Tawk't of an *upshot* lang an sair,
> To keep up Fassen's even.'

It seems to have taken its name *upshot* from paying *up* the *shot* or expenses described in the following lines:

> 'At teyme when nwote bit teeth was gaun,
> An' aw by the chafts was tether'd
> Wull Brough an' Ritson tuik in haun,
> To see 'at *shot* was gether't.

Uptak. The taking up or finding of anything. Icel. *upp-tak*, a seizure or confiscation.

Waffle. To hesitate or vacillate. Icel. *væflast*.

Waffler. One who hesitates. In the slang of Iceland both *væfill* and *væflari*, in the same sense, occur.

> 'St. George the greet Champion o' fame an renown,
> Was nobbit a *waffler* to Matthew Macree.'—ANDERSON

Wale, *vb.* To select. Icel. *velja.* In the Bible of Ulphilas *waljan* is 'to choose,' and *walis* is 'chosen' or true. Professor Wilson calls the Old Man Mountain, 'The *wale* o' gude fellows, the king of old men.' The Old Man has probably in his time formed the subject of more comparisons than any other man. In a letter I have from Professor Ruskin, he says, 'I have more correspondence upon my table than the bulk of the Old Man. I mean the cairn upon the top, not the mountain.'

Wale, *sb.* A selection. Icel. *val,* choice, selection. Outweels or wales, from *wale,* to select, is used of small apples selected from the rest as worthless. Cf. Icel. *út-val,* selection, *út-valinn,* selected. 'There's no *wale* o wigs in the Tweed.'

Wanely. Quietly. Icel. *vanalega,* wontedly, in the usual way.

> 'He shuts the fold yett *wanely* to,
> Deuce tak that cwoley dog.'—ANDERSON.

Wankle. Feeble, tottering, failing in health. A.-S. *wancol.*

Wap. A truss or lap of straw. Cf. Icel. *vaf,* what is lapped together, and *vefja,* to roll or lap.

Warday. Every day, i. e. week-day, as distinguished from Sunday. Swed. *hvardag,* Dan. *hverdag,* cf. Icel. *hvárr dagr,* every day.

> 'Hes better in his *warday* duds
> Than udders drest in aw their best.'—ANDERSON.

Wark. To ache. Icel. *verkr,* an ache, *verkja,* to ache.

Wath. A ford. The word was formerly well known in the dialect, but has now in some measure fallen into disuse. It is still found, however, in place-names. The Wath in the Abbey Holme, How Wath, Holly Wath.

*F

Watendlath may be 'the lath or barn at the end of the wath.' Icel. *vað*, a ford.

Welt. To roll or roll over, to incline to one side. A cask or vessel is thus said to *welt* over. Icel. *velta*, to roll or roll over; Ulph. *valtjan* = κυλίνδειν, to roll.

Whang. A Shoelatchet. Icel. *þvengr*, Dan. *tvinge*. See Gen. xv. in Icelandic Bible.

Whelp. A pup. Icel. *hvelpr*.

Whidder. To tremble. Cf. Icel. *hviðra*, to move shudderingly, said of a spasmodic pain shooting through the intestines.

Whilk. Which. Dan. *hvilken*.

Whinge. To cry. Cf. Icel. *kveina*, to cry, to whimper; and *kveinka*, to whimper from pain or discomfort.

Whins. Furze.

White. To peel or cut with a knife. Chaucer, 'to thwite,' the same root as thwaite.

Whittle. A carving-knife.

Whittle Gate. The right of the schoolmaster to dine at each house in the parish in turn. In the last century this was in the rural parishes of Cumberland the usual method of providing the board of. the village schoolmaster; in some instances he staid a week at each farmhouse in turn. Wastdale Head, where it continued until about twenty years ago, was the last parish in which this custom prevailed.

Whye or **Quey.** A heifer of any age up to three years old. Icel. *kvíga*, a young cow before she has calved.

Whye Cofe. A female calf. Icel. *kvígu-kálfr*.

Wineberries. Red currants. Norweg. *vinbær*.

Wizzent. Withered. Often applied to small withered or shrivelled apples. Now wizened. Icel. *visnaðr*, withered, from *visna*, to wither or dry up.

Wrang. Wrong. Icel. *rangr* (anciently *vrangr*).

Wyke or **Wick.** A small bay. Icel. *vík*; the Norse sea-kings were called vikings, or creekers, from frequenting bays or creeks. *Pool Wyke* in Windermere and also in Bassenthwaite Lake = pool or deep-water bay.

Yammer. To talk or hum indistinctly. Icel. *jamla*, to grumble. I think I may say for certain that I have heard *jamra* used in the same sense.—E. M.

Yark. Old Cumbrian for ' beat' or ' belabour.' Icel. *þjarka*, to belabour.

Yek. Oak. Icel. *eik*.

Yek Cubbert. Oak cupboard.

Yule. Icel. *Jól*. Christmas. This was a great festival in heathen times, and afterwards applied to Christmas.

SUPPLEMENT

CHIEFLY OF DIALECT WORDS AS APPLIED TO SHEPHERDING,
OR USED IN LOCAL FOLK-LORE AND ANTIQUITIES.

Allans. The land in a stream or beck, partly or entirely
surrounded by water; an island in a river (as if from
'à,' a beck or stream, or river, and 'land'). The charter
of the Manor of Coniston describes 'Torver Beck and
Beck Allans,' for a stated distance, as belonging to the
adjoining Manor of Coniston. In a county division,
Westmorland claims 'the Beck and Beck Allans' from
Lancashire for the boundary extending from Windermere Lake to Little Langdale, i.e. for nearly the whole
course of the River Brathay.

Attermite (Westmorland). A family likeness; a chip of
the old block. Icel. *aettar-mot*, a family likeness. See
Cleasby, under the word, where it is said of two men
that they had a family likeness, in that both had an unsteady gait.

Bate. Applied in the Lake Country to the angle of the
cleavage of the rocks.

Batter. The angle of inclination in stone walls. In house
walls where the stone is exposed, it is the slope of
particular stones inwards from the face of the wall most
suitable for carrying off the rain water; in fence and dry

stone walls upon the fell, the bottom of the wall is
generally much broader than the top, and the *batter*
is the angle of inclination between them. ' Chock ' is
a square stone used to block the top ' cam ' in such walls ;
and ' a through ' is a large flat stone going quite *through*
the wall as a support.

Bell wether. The leader of a flock of sheep upon the
mountain or fell. A bell is attached to it, to guide the
other members of the flock at night or in misty weather,
and they are accustomed to follow it. Such a bell
wether is yet (1896) to be found in this parish in a flock
whose boundaries are the Walna Scar Mountain, approaching 2,000 ft. above the sea level.

Blanchard. A one-eyed cock ; a veteran. ' Stags ' are young
cocks.

Brash. The plunge of the brasher or dasher of a churn.
' Cursty ! Cum kurn a *brash*, butter's abuin.'—*Old
Cumberland Proverb.*

Carry. The *sett* or direction of the clouds.

Charms. The value of charms in connexion with the
dialect is that many of them were framed in the dialect,
e. g., a charm to be used to cure an attack of hiccough,
as :

> ' Hiccough, hiccough, gang away
> An cum ageean some udder day
> When aw brew an when aw beeake,
> An than awl mäk a hiccough ceeake.'

When one of the first set of teeth is extracted, a little
salt is to be placed upon it and it is then to be placed in
the fire with the following incantation :

> ' Fire fire ! burn beean, .
> God sen my tuith ageean.

Charr. A beautiful and palatable fish, belonging to the salmon and trout genus, Salmo, and differing from the true salmon only in a few particulars. British Charr are found chiefly, if not wholly, in Windermere and the neighbouring lakes. Coniston Lake and Gaits Water Tarn in Torver are amongst the most favoured resorts of the Charr. Francis Hoylake's *Latin Dictionary* (1640) has: 'A *Chare*, a fish so called, onely proper to Winandermeer in Lancashire.' The *New World of English Words* (1658) has: '*Chare*, a kinde of fish, which breeds peculiarly in Winandermere in Lancashire.' In Camden's *Britannia* it is said of Windermere that it 'breeds a peculiar kind of fish found nowhere else, which the inhabitants thereby call a *Chare*.'

Cinder. Icel. *sindr*, slag or dross. This word is applied to the slag or dross containing a large percentage of iron which is found on the margin of Wastwater, Coniston, and other lakes, also in the Duddon Valley. It indicates the sites of the Old Bloomaries, where iron was brought to be smelted: suppressed in the Hawkshead and Coniston district, in A.D. 1565, the seventh year of Queen Elizabeth, the tenants agreeing between themselves to pay an annual rent of £20 called Bloomsmithy Rent. Many field-names are derived from it, e. g., Cinder Hill, Cinder How, Cinder Knab, Cinder Beck, Cinder Barrow.

Claggeran. Holding to a rock with hands and feet, so as to climb it. 'Gaun up an' doon t' brant pleases, lowpen t' becks an' *claggeran* up t' craggs.'—Rev. T. Clarke's description of *Shippardan or Shepherd Life*.

Clay Daubin or **Dabbin.** In the North and East of Cumberland the cottages were usually built of clay, interspersed with layers of straw. It was necessary for the proper consolidation of the fabric that the whole of it should be built in one day. Hence there was a very general gathering of the neighbours to assist in such erections (often for a new married couple), and after the edifice was completed the day was concluded with festivities including music and dancing. Anderson's Dialect Poem, *The Clay Daubin*, gives a graphic description of such an occasion.

Cock drunks. The fruit or berries of the mountain ash. The name explains the superstitious idea connected with it.

Cock Loft. The attics in Cumberland farmhouses were formerly so called as being the out of the way places in which cocks were trained for battle.

> 'See dancing we'd hev on the *cock loft*,
> Bill Adams the fiddler sud play,'—ANDERSON.

Cock Main. Name of a contest in which several pairs of cocks were matched against each other. Thus, twenty pairs were called a ' forty-cock main.'

Cock-Penny. The fee paid by scholars to the master in Cumberland Parish Schools, to be staked upon the annual school cock fight, fought upon Fassen's Even or Fastings Eve, i.e. the eve of Lent.

Cock-walk. Farm yard where a cock was kept to be prepared for fighting.

Cocker. One who trains and fights game cocks. 'The *cocker* o' Dawston.'—Anderson.

Cocking. Cockfighting. 'At *cocking* the Dawstoners nivver were bet.' — Anderson. At present the crest of the Dalston School Board is a fighting cock.

Cowgate or **Cattlegate.** The right of pasturage upon a common or marsh.

Crock or **Crock Yow** = ewe. An old and powerless ewe. To crock is to become feeble and powerless through age.

Darrack, Dark, or **Dargue.** A day's work. 'Ive nit sea offen hed a harder *darrack* efter t'sheep owther at clippin time or soavin time, as a hed followin that ould gray heidit chap an carryin his ledder bags.'—Gibson's *Joe and the Geologist.* In the dialect this word was very generally used to denote measure or extent. For example, a field was said to be of so many *darrack* of shearing, that is, it would take a man so many days to reap it. A *darrack* of peats upon a moss was as much turf as a man could dig in one day.

Daub. To plaister, as with morter.

Dumb wife. An idea formerly prevailed in Cumberland that dumb people had the power of foretelling the future. Hence, any old dumb woman in a parish became a sort of wise woman, and as such was consulted in the case of stolen property, or future events, or telling fortunes: such wise women were not always dumb. I have known one remarkable for her volubility. See *Viss*, as applied to Guest in the *Landnáma.* Generally, however, they were dumb, and marked their predictions with initial letters upon a board with chalk, as in the following verse, from Anderson's popular song of *Sally Gray:*

> 'I caw'd to sup cruds wi' Dick Miller,
>   An hear aw his cracks an his jwokes,
> The *Dumb weyfe* was tellmg their fortunes—
>   What! I mud be leyke udder fwokes—
> Wi' chalk, on a pair o' auld bellows,
>   Twea letters she meeade in her way,
> S means Sally the wide warl' owre
>   And G stands for nwote else but Gray.'

Dwinnal. To pine or waste away by degrees. 'He *dwin-*

nalt awae ta nwote, an than deet.'—Rev. T. Clarke, *Johnny Shepherd.*

Dwine, as above.

Feeace o' clay.   A solid and inflexible countenance.

'Aw defy t' *feeace* o' clay.'—GIBSON, *Folk-Speech.*

Fell. A mountain. The Icelandic form is *fjall* ; Norwegian *fjeld*, pronounced *fiell*.   In the lake district it is applied to particular mountains, as Scawfell, Kirkfell, Bowfell, and is applied to a mountain district generally which is termed 'The Fell.' The unenclosed upland common is also called 'The Fell,' as in the following verse from Richardson :

> 'Ya winter neet, aw meynd it weel,
> Our fowk hed been at *fell* ;
> An beein tired went suin ta bëd,
> An aw sat be mesel.'

Fell seyde.   The mountain districts of Cumberland are so called.

> 'If they ax whoar aw cum fra
> Awl say the *fell seyde,*
> Whoar fadder and mudder,
> An honest fowk beyde.'—ANDERSON, *Croglin Watty.*

Fell seyders.   Cumbrian mountaineers are so called.

Fodder-gang (North Lancashire).   The narrow passage or *gangway* in front of cattle stalls, by which fodder was conveyed to them.

Fratch. A scolding match. 'The Cumberland Scold,' a poem which is the joint effort of two Cumberland poetesses (Miss Blamire of . Thackwood, from 1747 to 1794, and Miss Gilpin of Scaleby Castle, from 1738 to 1811) is the poetical reproduction of such a scolding which they had themselves heard. The following is the last verse:

> 'For thou was nowther gud nor rich,
> An temper'd leyke auld Scratch 'em
> The deil a day gangs owre me heed,
> But *fratch 'em* FRATCH 'EM FRATCH 'EM.

Frith. Land is said to be *frithed* when it is freed from tillage and devoted to pasturage, as grass land or wood land. The original idea seems to be to devote the land to *wood growing*, as *frith* means a *wood* in the old dialect, and it is still found in this sense in place-names, as High *Frith*, in Cartmel.

Geeàll. To ache with pain brought on by intense cold.

Git ower. A very common Cumbrian phrase, meaning to *get the better of* in a bargain or an argument. Richardson has a. poem founded upon the Cumbrian phrase of defiance, 'Git ower me 'at can.' The following is the concluding verse:

> Thinks I, its queer, an axt a man
> If t' reason he could tell:
> 'Aye weel eneùff I can,' he said,
> 'He's gitten ower his-sel;
> He's swallow'd aw his fadder left
> Aw t' hooses, brass, an lan,
> An twenty scwore o' sheep beside,
> Git ower that 'at can!'

Godspeed. A wooden screen or barrier against the wind, within the door, apparently called 'Godspeed[1],' because leave-takings or good-byes were said there. 'Betty com limpin by t' *Godspeed*.'—*B. B. B.*

Goods. Property. This word however has a very different meaning in Cumberland and in Furness. In Cumberland, goods = household furniture, 'goods and chattels'; in Furness, goods are the sheep and cattle belonging to a farm.

---

[1] To greet the coming, *speed* the parting guest.

Goose Grass or **Gūse Grass.** The right of depasturing a goose with its goslings upon the fell or common.

Harden. Very rough and coarse linen used in Cumberland in the last century for jackets and overcoats.

Harden Sark. An overcoat made of such linen. The total annual payments made to the preaching schoolmaster of the parish of Buttermere, in the last century, were— a *harden sark,* the right of Whittle Gate, a darrack of peats, and a gùse grass.

Hay Bay. A commotion or disturbance. At times used to signify a 'discussion with sticks,' as in the following lines from Anderson :

> 'The *Hay Bay*[1] now ceast
> For he späk leyke a Preest
> An cawt for a bottle o' rum ye tkna.'

Heaf, *sb.* The place where a mountain or fell sheep is born, and where it continues to live and pasture, is called its *Heaf.*

Heaf, *vb.* Of sheep, to cling to the same spot. Hence, people who cling to their home or birthplace, are said to *heaf* themselves to it.

Heaf-going Sheep. Sheep which remain as one flock upon a certain portion of the fell, and which are usually sold with the farm to which that portion of the fell is apportioned.

Hefted. Meaning as above, and used in dialect of North Cumberland.

Heronsue. The heron.

Hogg. A lamb for twelve months after weaning.

---

[1] The quotation is from Anderson's 'Kursmas Eve,' and the reader will know the kind of discussion implied in a *Hay Bay* if he read the three or four verses of that poem which precede the quotation.

Hogg-whooals. Holes made through the fence walls in Lakeland to allow the sheep to pass from one pasture to another : ' When aw gat him intult *hogg-whooals* wi' his heead in an his feet oot aw *dud switch him.*'—Gibson's *Betty Yewdale.*

Horsin stean. The stone (often formed into steps) near Cumberland farmhouses, from which horses were mounted. Horsin or horsing is here used as a verb, as it is also in the old popular Cumberland measure, ' Horse and away,' i.e. mount or *to horse* and away.

Hullet. The owl. ' The silence was broken by a skirling *hullet*; Sure nivver did hullet, heronsue, or miredrum mak sec a noise before.'—*A bran new Wark.*

Kurruck, Kirruck, Sunken Kirk, or **Kirk Sucken.** Words in the dialect used to describe the huge stone circles to be found in the districts of Lakeland. Examples : Long Meg and her daughters, near Little Salkeld, Cumberland ; Stone Circle, near Keswick; and Stone Circle at Swinside, near Broughton-in-Furness. For full description see vol. v, part i, article vii, ' On a group of Cumberland Megaliths in *Transactions of Cumberland and West-morland Antiquarian Society for* 1881.

Miredrum. The *bittern*, a bird frequenting swampy and miry wastes, in which it kept up a continuous *drumming* sound, hence its local name of miredrum or drummer. Several fields in the Lake district, which have apparently been the resort of this bird, have their place-name of Drummer Mire derived therefrom ; there is one so called in Troutbeck in Westmorland, and one at Coniston.

Need-fire. A fire first kindled by rubbing two pieces of wood together ; ignited by this, a fire of wood was piled up, through the smoke of which all the cattle upon the farm were made to pass, as a remedy against murrain or other infectious disease. From this fire a brand was passed on to light a similar fire on the next farm, where the process of passing the cattle through the smoke was repeated, and so on at other farms in succession. This process was formerly well known and believed in, in High Furness and also in Cumberland.

Pack Saddle Bell. A curious brass bell formed of a hollow globe, with a brass ball inside, and attached to pack saddle horses, to guide those that followed. The writer has such a bell formerly used on the pack saddle road between Kendal and Whitehaven, passing over Hard Knott and Wrynose.

Push Plu or **Plough.** A plough which was used by being pushed by the hand. It was generally used for taking off the surface or top sod from turf, and this top sod was used to bank up the surface of turf fires so that they might continue alight and smoulder for a long time. Such ploughs are still to be found in Lakeland, and are much sought after by collectors of local antiquities.

Rashbearing. The annual custom in northern parishes still kept up at Ambleside and elsewhere in Westmorland, of collecting flowers and rushes (rashes), and walking in procession to spread them on the floor of the parish church, where they remained as a covering for the whole year. The young girls generally took a part in this. *T' Resh Bearin* is one of the Rev. T. Clarke's best dialect pieces. In some parishes, *rushing* the church in this way was paid for, and in this (Torver) parish, in the early part of the last century, it is an annual item represented in the church accounts by one shilling a year. The object was to counteract the effect of the damp, unpaved church floor: an allusion is made to it in the hymn :

'Our fathers to the house of God,
   As yet a building nude,
Brought off'rings from the flowery sod,
   And fragrant rushes strewed.'

Rud. The red haematite used for marking or smitting sheep. Formerly obtained chiefly from the Wasdale Screes. Called also *Ruddle.* The smit marked upon the sheep with this Rud or Ruddle is generally the initial letter or letters of the owner's name, except in *sword* smit, resembling sword, *staple* smit, resembling staple.

Rushstand. Called *rashstand* in Central and N.-W. Cumberland, and *reshstand* in North Cumberland. The iron stand used for supporting rush lights, once the sole light used for domestic purposes. A great variety of these stands have been obtained by local collectors, some very complex and bearing several lights.

Saurin. *Vinegar.* See *Ann Wheeler's Dialogues.*

Scarrow. A name generally applied to small fish in the dialect of the Abbey Holme, seems to be from the Latin *scaurus*, a name brought there possibly by the monks of the Monastery or Abbey which gives its name to the parish.

Shepherd's Book, The. A book published at irregular intervals extending over several years, and containing the distinctive marks, ear mark and smit (see under the word) of the stocks of heaf-going sheep of the farms in the fell or mountain districts of Cumberland, West-morland, and North Lancashire. With the ear mark and smit together, the marks of upwards of 600 farms or estates are given therein. The ear mark is the most important, as being that which is generally sworn to in any legal suit. Each stock[1] is illustrated by the diagram of a sheep, nearly 1000 in all. These marks are interesting as being described in the technical dialect of the sheep farmers, e. g. :

Bitted. With a triangular piece cut out of the ear.

Cropped. A portion of the top of the ear cut off.

Cropping in both ears is conceded only to Hall farms, or such as belonged to the lord of the manor.

Forked. With a triangular piece cut out of the top of the ear.

Fold-bitted When the ear is folded and cut, leaving a triangular space.

Fold-bit. The ear mark so formed.

Halved. With half the ear cut off.

Key-bitted. With a rectangular piece cut out of the ear.

Punched. With a circular hole in the ear.

Ritted. With a rectangular piece cut out the whole length of the ear, dividing the ear into two parts.

Shear-bitted. Sheared or cut to a point at the end of the ear.

Sneck-bitted. The ear cut in resemblance of the *sneck* or latch of a gate.

In the stock of sheep belonging to Raven Cragg, Barton, Westmorland, is a curious connexion between the place-name and the smit, which for that farm is the figure of a raven, smitted or marked upon the side of the sheep.

Siddick. This word, which is found in many instances as place-name, and also as common noun on the Cumberland shore of the Solway, has been originally Sea dyke, corrupted to Siddick, and was applied to the sea dyke which, in the Abbey Holme and other parts of Cumber-

---

[1] In some cases there are two or more stocks with distinctive ear marks and smits belonging to the same farm named by the mountain or fell upon which they pasture, e.g. Downey Dale Farm in Wasdale Head has the following :—Greenhow Stock, Lingmel Stock, Yewbarrow Stock, and Mosedale Stock.

land, was reared and maintained to protect the flat agricultural country against the encroachment of the sea. In the Abbey Holme the rent of a large and valuable farm is assigned to a parish committee for the proper maintenance of this sea dyke.

Smiddy. A blacksmith's shop. Applied also as a nickname to the blacksmith, as in the following instance from Anderson : ' Treype Tom, *Smiddy* Dick, an Deef Reed, ye tkna.'

Snāpe, *vb.* To check or restrain. ' This wedder ell *snap't* grass.' Colloquial in High Furness.

Snape, *sb.* A check.

Stint or **Stent.** The Cumberland marshes adjoining the Solway and its tributaries, the Wampool and Waver, have their pastures limited or *stinted* as to the number of cattle for which they will afford grass. To define them thus is to stint them, and each cattle grass is called a stint or stent ; called also *Marsh Stint* or *Marsh Stent.*

Teanale. The basket used for cockling on the Arnside and Cartmel coasts of Morecambe Bay. ' He threw a *teanale* wi' cockles at me.'—*Ann Wheeler's Dialogues.*

Tether or **Tedder.** A rope to fasten sheep or cattle.

Tether Styak. The stake to which it was tied.—*Borrowdale Letter.*

The Borrowdale Letter. This is a somewhat unique production, as being much the earliest piece of prose extant in the Cumberland dialect [1]. It is by Isaac Ritson, and

---

[1] Dr. Gibson, in his introduction to his volume of *Folkspeech*, claims for the Borrowdale Letter, the merit of surpassing all productions in the Cumberland dialect (prose or poetry), because, to quote his own words, ' it is an exposition of the folkspeech in that part of the county where,

professes to be the letter of a Borrowdale shepherd to his friend, describing his voyage from Whitehaven to Dublin, and the wonderful sights he saw there. The peculiarity of the letter is not so much that the writer employs a dialect different from that of other Cumberland dialect writers, but that having had all his former experiences in a valley where he had heard nothing but what was connected with farming, and more especially with shepherding, he is put to great straits in relating his adventures at sea, and the wonders which he saw in the Irish metropolis. Thus he calls ships, sea nags; the harbours he calls 'girt foalds wi' out gates,' i. e. farm yards without gates; pulling up the anchor he calls 'slippin t' helter'; an anchor he terms a tedder styak, from the custom of fastening an unruly animal to a stake; sails are *wind clythes* like *blinder bridles*[1]. Trinity College, Dublin, which, with its museum, especially attracted his attention, he calls Collership hoos or scholarship house, and the river Liffy he terms Dublin Beck. The following is the language in which he records his appreciation of the music in St. Patrick's Cathedral; ' Summit they cawt rowargins (organs) began bealin like ea hundred mad bulls, an as menne lads i their sarks began a skreamin, murder.'

and where only, the unadulterated Old Norse rooted vernacular is spoken.' The other Cumbrian writers, in which he includes Stagg, Anderson, and Rayson, he calls *Scoto*-Cumbrian. In making this sweeping assertion Dr. Gibson is, I think, decidedly wrong Stagg, Anderson, and Rayson wrote as unmixed a form of the Cumberland dialect as Dr. Gibson himself, and the poetic productions of every one of them were singularly free from that Scottish intermixture which meets one in the dialect almost as soon as we cross Stanwix Bridge at Carlisle, or at any rate Gosling Syke, which is a little further on.

[1] Blinder bridles (called in Furness, gloppers) are horse bridles, with large eye shades to prevent the horses from becoming restive.

Twine t' tail ont. Used in the *Borrowdale Letter* for the steersman guiding the ship with the helm, which the writer compares with twining or twisting the tail of a cow, a method practised in Cumberland with the object of turning the cow in the required direction.

Watch Hill. The hill from which the outlook was kept against border freebooters; hence now frequent as Border place-name.

Whick. Alive or living.

Whicknin. Leven or yeast.

Whicks. Maggots.

Whicks. Young shoots of thorns transplanted.

Whickset Hedge. A growing or living fence.

All dialect forms of the old word *quick*, living, as found in 'Let them go down *quick* into the pit,' 'Judge the *quick* and the dead.'

Woo or **Oo** or **Ooa,** are all dialect names for wool in Cumberland, Westmorland, and North Lancashire. The following represents a dialect conversation which has been heard here :

> Wool-dealer (pointing to well-filled bag): 'Oo?'
> Farmer (owner of bag) : 'Aye, oo.'
> Wool-dealer : 'Aw oo?'
> Farmer : 'Aye, aw oo.'
> Wool-dealer : 'Aw, ya oo?'
> Farmer : 'Aye, aw ya oo.'

which being interpreted means :

> Wool-dealer : 'Wool?'
> Farmer : 'Yes, wool.'
> Wool-dealer : 'All wool?'
> Farmer : 'Yes, all wool.'
> Wool-dealer : 'All one wool?'
> Farmer : 'Yes, all one wool.'

By asking, Is it all one wool? is meant, Is it all the wool

of one season, and sheared or clipped at the same clipping time or shearing time. Such wool is, in the dialect, sometimes called the wool of ' one clip.'

Woo craggs or **oo craggs**. The names of rocks or craggs in Lakeland, over which sheep having passed, have left some of their wool cleaving to the craggs.

Yilp. To make a sound like the squeak or yelp of a mouse. ' *Yilp* leyke mice.'—*Borrowdale Letter.*

OXFORD : HORACE HART, PRINTER TO THE UNIVERSITY

A GLOSSARY

OF

WORDS USED IN EAST ANGLIA.

Oxford

HORACE HART, PRINTER TO THE UNIVERSITY

A Glossary of Words

USED IN

EAST ANGLIA.

FOUNDED ON THAT OF FORBY.

WITH NUMEROUS CORRECTIONS AND ADDITIONS

BY

WALTER RYE.

London:
PUBLISHED FOR THE ENGLISH DIALECT SOCIETY
BY HENRY FROWDE, OXFORD UNIVERSITY PRESS WAREHOUSE,
AMEN CORNER, LONDON, E.C.

——

1895.

PREFACE

In collecting the material for the following work I wish at once to state that I have none of the qualities necessary to be possessed by the editor of a Dialect Dictionary, and that I do not consider myself as having done anything more than to mechanically collect what others have recorded and add to certain words which I have noted myself.

In such collection I have been greatly helped by several correspondents, and especially by the Rev. M. C. H. Bird, of Brunstead, who has kindly helped me to read and correct the proofs, and also by Sir Hugh Beevor, Mr. P. B. Ficklin, the Rev. F. J. Braithwaite, the Rev. C. H. Evelyn White, and the other gentlemen mentioned in my list of abbreviations.

It may be as well to say a few words about what has been done heretofore about the dialect of East Anglia. A short account of the best-known works and articles I have noted later on; but speaking shortly, the first serious attempt to collect and print it, was that by the Rev. R. Forby. He collected with little discrimination, was very garrulous, and often indecent, but East Anglians owe him a great debt for having done what he did. Much of his work I have omitted from the following pages, for he included in it many such ordinary words as *aggravate*,

alley, age, ague, &c., and duplicated words for no reason,
e. g. :—

Minnock (S).   One who affects much delicacy.
Minnock (V).   To affect delicacy.

Nall's *Glossary* is a very good and careful one, and added
many new words and readings to our store, and so did
Broad Norfolk, which is very amusing reading, but only
consisted of various letters to a newspaper, was not 'edited'
or supervised, and contained many words of common use
which had no business in a local dialect book.

I cannot help thinking that many of the words included
in the following pages are only the imperfect remembrance
by an ignorant countryman of some 'good word' which
took his fancy.

Only two or three years ago, being in the company of
a little farmer who was extremely fond of using long and
fine words, I remember mischievously asking him whether
he did not think it fine 'feasible' weather for his crops, and
he jumped at the word, and soon after I heard him repeat
it to a friend.

Many of the amusing words and phrases given by
Fitzgerald in his *Sea Words* are manufactured. A good
example is when he makes a gamekeeper refer to a weasel
as a 'suckeggliest warmint,' the vermin most given to suck
eggs.

Pea-goosin, 'prying about like a peahen'; *cabobble* 'to
confuse'; *squackled, sploddin, quavery-mavery, ruffatory,
hammer-snouting, rumgumptious, undercumstumble, rum-
bustical, dardledum due,* and others, are words framed after
the fashion of Lewis Carroll, and in most cases are omitted
from these pages, as they are not dialect at all. One might
as well insert such words as *tootsicums, babsicums, coodli-
cums,* and *popsy wopsy.*

Very many are caused by nothing more or less than
transpositions of the initial. *Pulfer* for *fulfer* (fieldfare),
bunker for *funker, stuggy* for *pluggy, pample* for *trample,*

nigger for *snigger, doss* for *toss, jounce* for *bounce, himps*
for *limps, twilting* for *quilting, skive* for *dive, tunnel* for
funnel, cristle for *gristle, quaddle* for *coddle*, and *wewling*
for *mewling*, are a few which occur to me.

Many too are obvious corruptions, e. g. *sarn* for *concern,
sloven wood* for *southernwood*, and *grubbage* for *rubbish.*

If it were possible to divide the words into districts, we
should no doubt find a great difference between the dialect
of one part of a county from that of another. 'When
I left Strumpshaw for Ryburgh,' said my old skipper
Tungate, a very careful observer, 'the words fared very
strange to me.'   .

Occasionally one finds a trace of an old lost verb,
e. g. p. 92, 'She did fare to slov,' i. e. to become a sloven.

Except in well-known instances, I have not attempted to
give the dialect names, often widely varying, of the local
fauna and flora, and must refer my readers to the numerous
local works on natural history.

The following specimens of modern Norfolk have been
handed to me by correspondents :—

Wh' lor', bor, yow fare t' bee s' strange. Wh' darn ya' ole skull,
I now yow werry well. My fa' he now ya' fa'. Ya' fa' kep a dickey.
Hee one da' hult a stoon agin a guce, an' he kilt 'er ded, an' my fa'
he sez, sez hee, that he worn't t' kum ower hisn troshel agin. An' n'
moor he dint.

But my fa' hee arter'ards maade it op, an' axd ya' fa' t' goo t'
Kootch an' Hosses an' hev a glarss a aale an there tha tuk on, tha
did, lik a kupple a ole fules. An arter that there tha wuz frenz
agin.

I went for tree punner of trid (thread). I tumbled over the troshel
and cut my lip trow and trow (through).

Jack : Look there's some red Blackberries.
Bill : Ye fule, theyre allus red when they're green (meaning when
they are not ripe).

I wish you might live to be as gray as a dow and yar hair trape
arter ye yards.

Biller he went afoul on him, he did, and he rightsided him in a hurry; he gave him what for. Then there was a pretty how der yer du; his owd womman come out, and she went a foul o' Biller; she mobbed and went in wonnerful.

As I was jumping t' holl from Farmer Thirkettle's littl pightle inteu t' rhoed, she come up teu me and say:

'Can I get trew here?'

'Iss,' sed I, 'but it is no matter of a rhoed.'

'Whawt?' sed she.

'It's only a driftway like,' sed I.

'Eh?' sed she.

'Nobbut a packway,' sed I.

'Oh,' sed she; 'and which way deu I go?'

'Yew go as the rhoed go, for tew or tree hundred yard till yeu come teu a paryard,' sed I.

'Teu whawt?' sed she, &c., &c.

A bibliography of the Dialect would be difficult to compile, but a long list of all authors on this dialect will be found in the Appendix to the *Promptorium Parvulorum*, an Anglo-Latin Lexicon compiled by Brother Geoffrey of Lynn about the year 1440 (Harl. MSS. 221), printed by Pynson; also with Notes by Albert Way, Camden Society, p. lxxxii. The more important works on the subject are:—

(1.) Forby's *Vocabulary* (two vols. 8vo, 1830), with Supplementary Volume by the Rev. W. T. Spurdens (1858).

(2.) *Additions to Forby*, by the Rev. F. Gillett (*East Anglian*, iv. pp. 128, 156). *Norfolk Words not in Forby*, by the Rev. G. J. Chester, Transactions of the Norfolk and Norwich Archaeological Society, v. p. 188. Ditto by W. G. Waters, ib. viii. p. 167.

(3.) E. S. Taylor's interleaved copy of Forby is mentioned in *Notes and Queries* (2nd Ser. vii. p. 38), but I have been unable to trace this, nor the valuable dialect notes collected by the Rev. E. Gillett of Runham (E. G. R.).

(4.) J. G. Nall's *Etymological and Comparative Glossary*, in his Appendix for his *Guide to Yarmouth and Lowestoft*, 1866, 8vo.

(5.) *Sea Words and Phrases along the Suffolk Coast* (*East Anglian*, iii. p. 347; iv. p. 109); and

(6.) *A Capful of Sea Slang* (*East Anglian*, iv. p. 261). These two articles were by the late Edward Fitzgerald.

(7.) A reprint of Forby with additions, forming the basis of the present work, was published by the Author in volume iii. of the

Norfolk Antiquarian Miscellany, pp. 465-602 (A few copies were printed off and paged separately, and were sent round to all likely to help in getting together the present collection.)

(8.) *Broad Norfolk*, by Cozens-Hardy (reprinted from the *Norwich Daily Press*), Norwich, *Norfolk News* Office, 1st ed. (103 pp., 1893) ; 2nd ed. same, with Index added, Jarrolds, Norwich.

For MSS. and detached collections on East Anglian dialect the following references may be useful.

Glossaries of Words used in the Counties of Lincoln, Norfolk and Kent, 1779-1814, by Sarah Sophia Banks (Additional MSS. 32640).

Glossary of Provincial Words, collected by G. Nicol, 1789 (Additional MSS. 32640, fol. 237).

Peculiarities of the Norfolk Dialect, by G. Nicol, Eighteenth Century (Additional MSS. 32530, fol. 147 b).

Collections for the Dialect of Suffolk and Essex (*East Anglian*, New Series, i. pp. 84, 109, 132).

Arderon's *Collections* as to ditto (ib. p. 297).

An Old Specimen of Norfolk Dialect (in 1807), (*East Anglian*, New Series, iii. p. 17). Of Suffolk ditto (*East Anglian*, New Series, v. pp. 129, 152-155).

See also :—

Arderon's *Collections as to Norwich Dialect*, 1745-60 (Additional MSS. 27966, fols. 228-253). I have printed notes of some of these in the *East Anglian*.

The Song of Solomon in Twenty-four English Dialects, 1858-61 ; Prince Buonaparte (Norfolk : by the Rev. E. Gillett of Runham).

Catalogue of Local and Vulgar Words used in the County of Norfolk (folio, about 1780), by Anthony Norris. Was No. 345 in Dawson Turner's sale catalogue, but I cannot trace where it is.

Archaeologia, xix. p. 15.

For several articles on Norfolk Dialect, see *Notes and Queries*, 1st Ser. ii. pp. 217-365 ; vi. pp. 326 and 400 ; 5th Ser. ii. pp. 147, 353, 377, 397 ; iii. p. 166 ; xii. p. 174.

Glossary of Norfolk Provincialisms (17 pp.). Vol. ii. of Marshall's *Rural Economy of Norfolk*, 1837.

Kent's *General View of the Agriculture of Norfolk*, 1796.

Young's *Farmer's Tour through the East of England*, four vols. 1771.

Similarity of Norfolk Dialect with that of Cheshire (*Archaeologia*, xix. p. 15).

Norfolk Words, by Anne Gurney. (*Philological Society's Transactions*, 1855, p. 32.)

Of dialect ballads we have few. There is an amusing one telling how 'Giles Jolterhead, a joskin raw,' took his 'darter Dinah' to the Norwich Festival, printed in *East Anglian*, ii. p. 67; and the Norfolk version of the ballad of *Arthur O'Bradley* was recently printed by me in the *East Anglian*. The most readable of all the dialect stories of the present day are *Giles's Trip to London*, and the rest of the series, which are very clever and deservedly popular.

ABBREVIATIONS

———◆———

*Arderon=Arderon's *Collections for Norwich* (Addl. MSS. British Museum, 27, 966).

B. A.=Baret's *Alvearie.*

*P. B. F.=Mr. P. B. Ficklin of Tasburgh Hall, Norfolk.

B. G.=Barnes' *Glossary.*

B. Jon.=Ben Jonson.

Br. = Brockett's *Glossary.*

*C. H. E. W.=The Rev. C. H. Evelyn White, Editor of the *East Anglian.*

*C. D.=The Rev. Cecil Deedes, of Wickham St. Paul, Essex.

Cr. = *Craven Glossary.*

*C. S. P.=Mrs. Petre, of Cavendish Rectory, Suffolk.

*Cull. Haw.=Cullum's *Hawsted* (Suff.), 1813.

E. A.=*East Anglian.*

*E. F. G. = The late Edward Fitzgerald, *Sea Words and Phrases along the Suffolk Coast* (*East Anglian* iii. p. 347 and iv. p. 109), and *A Capful of Sea Slang* (*East Anglian* iv. p. 261).

*E. G. R.=The late Rev. E. Gillett, of Runham, Norfolk, *Additions to Forby's Vocabulary of East Anglia,* in *East Anglian,* Ser. iv. 128, 156.

Em.=Dr. Emerson.

*E. S. T.=The late Rev. E. S. Taylor, of Ormesby, Norfolk.

*F. J. B.=The Rev. F. J. Braithwaite, of Great Waldingfield, Suffolk.

*G. E.=George Ellis.

*G. J. C.=The Rev. G. J. Chester, *Norfolk Words not in Forby* (*Norfolk Arch.* v. p. 188, viii. p. 167).

Gr.=Grose's *Provincial Dict.*

*H. B. = Sir Hugh Beevor.

*H. C.=Mr. Hugh Clark, of Cavendish.

Jam.=Dr. Jamieson.

Jen.=Jennings' *Glossary.*

*J. G. N.=J. G. Nall's *Etymological and Comparative Glossary to the Dialect of East Anglia*, comprised in his *Guide to Yarmouth and Lowestoft*, 1866.

*J. H. G.=Mr. J. H. Gurney, of N. Repps, Norfolk.

L. Sc.=Lowland Scotch.

*Marsh.=Marshall's *Rural Economy.*

M. C. H. B.=The Rev. M. C. H. Bird, of Brunstead, Norfolk.

M. E.=Middle English.

Min.=Minsheu's *Dict.*

M. S.=Moor's *Suffolk Words.*

N. E.=Northern English.

N. G. Nares=Nares' *Glossary.*

N. & Q.=*Notes and Queries.*

O. E.=Old English.

O. V.=Ortus Vocabularum.

P. Pl.=*Piers Plowman.*

Pr. Pa.=*Promptorium Parvulorum.*

R. N. C.=Ray's *North Country Words.*

R. S. E. C.=Ray's *South and East Country Words* (reprinted by English Dialect Society, 1874).

S. D.=Hotten's *Slang Dictionary*, London, 1864.

Sk.=Skinner's *Etymol.*

Som. = Somner.

*Spur.=The Rev. W. T. Spurdens' Supplementary Vol. to Forby, 1858 (reprinted by English Dialect Society, 1879).

T.=Tusser.

T. B.=Tim Bobbin.

T. J. = Todd's *Johnson.*

*Tungate=The late J. Tungate, an old marsh and boating man (Strumpshaw, Norfolk).

W.=Wickliffe's *Translation of the Gospels.*

W. B.=Mr. William Bull, of Wickham, Essex (born near Bildeston, Suffolk).

W. C. = Wilbraham's *Cheshire Glossary.*

*W. G. W.=W. G. Waters' *Words not in Forby* (*Norfolk Arch.* viii. p. 167).

*W. R.=W. Rye.

W. W. R.=Willan's *West Riding Words* (*Archaeologia*).

*W. W. S.=W. W. Skeat.

VOCABULARY

About. Sometimes used thus :—'Is the horse worth forty pounds?' 'Nothing *about* it.' 'Is he a mile off?' 'No, nor *about* it.'

*Abroad. Out to sea [S. S.]. Outside the house [M. C. H. B.].

*Acknowledge. To tip [M. C. H. B.].

*Acre-spire, or Acre-spit. The sprouting or 'chicking' of barley in malting, or of stored potatoes [E. S. T., J. G. N.].

A-days. For 'nowadays.' Ex. 'Flour sells cheap *a-days.*' 'I seldom see Mr. Smith *a-days*' [O. E.]. Sed quere? [Spur.].

Addle, Aidle. (1) To grow, to thrive. Ex. 'That crop *addles.*' Also see Tusser. (2) To earn, to profit gradually. Ex. 'I have at last *addled* up a little money.' (3) Cropping, lopping, or pruning [E. S. T.]. Spurdens wrongly conjectures it to be 'to *huddle* up.'

*Aerigel. Earwig [Arderon]. See Erriwiggle.

*After. Sometimes used in a peculiar sense, for about, e.g. 'The hen is *after* laying.' 'The child is *after* the measles' [E. S. T.].

*Aftermath. The second crop of grass.

B

Again (pronounced AGIN). For against (AGINST) [Spur.]. Ex. 'I am not for it, but *again* it.' For near to. Ex. 'She stood *again* the door.' If she stood very near the door, it would be more correct to say 'close *again*,' or 'right *again*'; if facing it, at some little distance, 'over *again*.'

*Against. Close against thunder; i.e. thunder is in the air [M. C. H. B.].

Agone. For ago. Our word is the older of the two.

*Agraft. To lay in, of a tree put into the soil so as to just cover its roots [M. C. H. B.].

Ahuh. Awry, aslant. Better **Ahoe**, and sometimes **All-a-one-hoh** [Spur.]. *Vel* **All-of-a-hugh** [J. G. Nall].

*Ailing. To move listlessly [G. E.].

*Aint. To anoint, to beat [J. G. Nall, E. S. T.].

*Aker. A turbulent current, a commotion of a river [Pr. Pa.].

*A'lady. For Our Lady, Lady Day [E. S. T.].

*Alegar. Vinegar made from ale. Ale-aigre, as vin-aigre [E. S. T.].

Ale-stall. The stool or stand on which casks of ale or beer are placed in the cellar.

*Alexandra Plovers. Kentish plovers (*Aegialitis cantiana*) so called by Breydon gunners. E. T. Booth in *Rough Notes* [M. C. H. B.].

*All. 'I shall do it for "all" you' [M. C. H. B.].

Allen. Grass land lately broken up; **Ald-land**. It is synonymous with **Olland**, q. v.

*Alliwig. An earwig [Spur.]. See **Erriwiggle**.

*Allus. Always [E. S. T.].

*Alm. Chill. 'Just set the mug down to the fire, and take the cold "*aam*" off the beer' [Johnson].

*Almanacks. 'Making of *almanacks*,' forecasting the weather [Sea Slang].

*Alone. We have the odd phrase 'all-a-living-*alone*,' i.e. 'quite entirely *alone*,' spoken compassionately of a sick person left improperly in a helpless condition [Spur.].

Alp, Olp. The bullfinch. E. S T. says *alf* in Suffolk, and *ulf* in Norfolk, i.e. finch, as blood*ulf*, bullfinch. Nope in Ray, and Alp in the *Romaunt of the Rose*, l. 658 [W. W. S.].

*Amenden. A sort of oath. e.g. '*Amenden* take you.' 'Where *amenden* are you goin'?' [E. S. T.] (?).

Amper. A sort of inflamed swelling. Pustules [J. G. Nall].

Ampersand. The character &, representing the conjunction *and*. This is *and per se and*; by a little smoothing and elision in pronunciation becoming *Ampersand*.

An. (1) If. Ex. '*An* I do,' &c. (2) Than. Ex. 'Little more *an* a half.'

Anan! 'How! what say you?' It is often contracted to *A'an*, or *N'an*. The same as Shakespeare's Anon [W. W. S.]. [? W. R.]

*Anatomy. The skeleton [M. C. H. B.].

Anberry. (1) A small swelling, or pustule, to which horses are subject on the softest parts of their bodies. In books of farriery, and in the Dictt. the word is Ambury. (2) A [small] knob or excrescence, on turnips and other roots, caused by the punctures of insects, to deposit their eggs [Marshall].

Anchor. The part of a buckle commonly called the Chape, put into a slit in the strap; so called from some resemblance in shape to an anchor.

An-end. Onward, towards the end. It also signifies upright, rearing [M. E. *on ende*].

Angry. Painfully inflamed. Ex. 'My corn, or my kibe, is very *angry* to-night.'

†**Angry-water.** Discharge from any scorbutic or eruptive disease [Johnson].

Anpasty. Another name for **Ampersand.** In Jennings' *Glossary* it is **Anpassy**; and the author (rightly) supposes **Passy** a corruption of **Per se.**

*****Ans.** Awns [M. C. H. B.]

*****Antrums.** Used for tantrums [J. G. Nall, E. S. T.].

*****A'pieces.** For to pieces, e.g. 'Ta crumble all *a'pieces* [E. S. T.].

Apple-jack. A pastry, better known as **Apple-turnover, Flap-jack, Apple-hoglin,** and **Crab-lanthorn.**

Apple-john, John-apple. A species of apple.

Apron. (1) The caul or omentum of a hog, film of fat [Tungate]. (2) Also the fat skinny covering of the belly of a goose or duck. (3) The upper part of a chimney opening above the grate [Spur.].

Argufy. To import, to have weight as *argument.* Ex. 'What does that *argufy*?' [Jen.].

*****Arm.** A trowel [B. B. F.].

*****Armstrong.** Arm in arm [E. F. G.] Qy. Arm-strung [W. R.].

*****Arrawiggle.** The earwig [E. S. T.].

Arsle. (1) To move backwards. (2) To be unquiet, to fidget, to move frequently in any direction, particularly on a seat. In this secondary sense the adverb *about* is usually annexed.

Arselling-pole. The pole with which bakers spread the hot embers to all parts of the oven.

*****Arsy-farcy.** Vice versa [E. S. T.].

*****Arter.** After. Ex. 'What are you *arter*?' [M. C. H. B.].

*****Artful.** (1) In good sense. Ex. of our Lord in His mother's arms, 'How *artful* He do look!' [C. S. P.]. (2) Ingenuous, clever (N. Ess.) [C. D.].

Article. A poor creature! a wretched animal!

As. Who, which. Ex. 'Those *as* sleep.' 'He will come *as* (=as it were, not *who* nor *which*) to-morrow.'

*__Ashel.__ To cut bricks to form a joint in masonry [W. G. W.]. Coined from the sb. **Ashlar** [W. W. S.].

*__Ashentree.__ The ash [M. C. H. B.].

*__Asked.__ To have banns of marriage published [M.C.H.B.].

*__Asked-out,__ or **Out-asked.** To be 'asked' for the third time [M. C. H. B.].

*__Asleep.__ Sails are *asleep* when steadily filled with wind [Sea Slang].

Asosh, Ashosh. Awry, aslant. Compare **Ahuh.**

*__Ass-upping.__ Hand-hoeing (of wheat, e.g.) to turn the docks and thistles end upwards, or to cause the posterior to be the superior part of the body whilst stooping in the act of hoeing [M. C. H. B.].

*__Ast.__ Ask [M. C. H. B.].

*__Athort.__ Across, athwart [M. C. H. B.].

A'top of. Upon. Ex. 'I saw Mr. Brown *a'top of* his new horse yesterday.'

Atter. Pus, morbid matter.

Attery. Purulent.

*__A'twixt.__ Betwixt or between [E. S. T.]. There seems some difference, for a common expression is 'a'twixt and a'tween' [W. R.].

Aught. Another form of **Owed.** 'He *aught* me ten pounds.'

*__Aunt Hannah.__ White arabis [M. C. H. B.].

Ausier. The osier.

Avel. The awn or beard of barley.

*__Avellong Work.__ 'Mowing or reaping, lying out of the perpendicular' [J. G. Nall].

*__Avellong Workmen.__ Reapers or mowers approaching the side of an irregularly shaped field will have an unequal portion to do. The excess or deficiency is called *avellong work* [E. S. T.]. See **Avelong** in Murray.

*__Avelly.__ Barley is said to be *avelly*, if when dressed for market some of the awms (awns) stick to the grains [E. S. T.].

__Avised.__ Aware, informed. 'I am not *avized* of it,' I do not recollect about it [Johnson, Cull. Haw.]. The original M. E. form, of which Mod. E. *advised* is a corruption [W. W. S.].

__Awk.__ Inverted or confused. Bells are 'rung ˙*awk*' to give alarm of fire. This is the only connexion in which the word is used among us, without its adjunct *ward*. L'Estrange (who was a Norfolk man) uses it. In Pr. Pa. *awk* is rendered into Latin by *perversi*. Ray says that *awkward* is opposed to *toward* [R. S., E. C.].

*__Awms__ (for awns). The beard of barley; so pronounced in Suffolk [Moor]. In Norfolk usually **Aans** or **Harns**, i.e. awns. In Essex, **Ails**. See **Avel** [E. S. T.]. Sometimes **Haulms** [A. E. R.].

__Ax.__ To ask.

*__Axt-out,__ or **Out-axt**. Said of banns when asked for the last time.

__Bab.__ To fish by throwing into the water a bait on a line, without float or hook, with a small piece of lead to sink it, lifting it up from time to time, and dropping it again. It is the same as *bob*. The bait used for fishing in this manner is usually made of large worms, strung together on worsted which catches in the eels' teeth [Tungate], and tied in a bunch.

__Babs.__ Small prints to amuse children.

*__Bachelor.__ Elderly single men of a better rank are mostly so styled. Ex. 'Bachelor D.' [C. S. P.].

*__Back-stalk.__ The back of a low hearth [*B. N.* 27] (? corruption for back-stove [id. 87]).

*Backsticking. A way of ploughing in. The earth having been previously turned is turned back again. See Strike [E. S. T.].

*Back up. Angry. Ex. 'Tha' got his back up' [M. C. H. B.].

*Backus. The back kitchen or scullery [back-house; compare Wuddus, wood-house.—W. R.].

Badget. A badger.

Badly. In ill health. Sometimes sadly badly, and sometimes sad bad.

Baffle. (1) To gull, to cheat, or make a fool of. (2) To manage capriciously or wantonly, as in the case of children or cattle. Ex. 'He was sadly baffled in his bringing up.' (3) To beat and twist irregularly together, as 'growing corn or grass is baffled by wind and rain.'

Bag. The dug of a cow.

*Bag Harvest. A harvest when the men board themselves, carrying their food in bags [Johnson].

*Bahangs. Hanging down untidily, said of clothes [J. G. Nall].

*Bahd. A bird [J. G. Nall].

Bail. The handle of a pail, bucket, or kettle. Also the bow of a scythe. See Bale. Sometimes Bile [B. N. 83].

Bain. Pliant, limber.

*Bait. Bundle. In Suffolk, hemp, when pulled, was tied up in small 'baits,' to cart home [C. D.].

*Balaam Sunday. The Sunday in which the lesson relates to Balaam and his ass, on which, says Spurdens, though I cannot see why, 'the Norfolk housewife is reminded of the approach of the mackerel season.'

*Balaam's Smite. The mark on a donkey's back [B. N. 54].

Balder. To use coarse language. See Bawda.

Balderdash. Not 'frothy and confused' as the Dictt. have it, but filthy or obscene talk.

*Baldrick, or Balderick, or Balderdick. A girdle made of horse's hide placed round a bell [M. C. H. B.].

*Bale (pronounced BILE). A slight withy stick or rod, bent so as to form a bow, and attached to the scythe stick [Johnson, and see *B. N.* 83]. See Bail and Rifle.

Balk. (1) A ridge of land left unploughed, to serve as a boundary, either between two contiguous occupations, or two divisions of the same farm, in an unenclosed cornfield [*vide* Merebalk]. (2) A ridge so left in the body of the land, at certain intervals, in a particular mode of ploughing called *balk-ploughing*. (3) A beam in a building, supporting an upper floor or roof; or any piece of timber, squared, and ready for any purpose in building. (4) The failure of an expectation. (5) A piece of machinery used in the dairy district of Suffolk, into which the cow's head is put when she is milked. It allows her to move her head freely up and down, but when she attempts to withdraw it, she finds herself *balked*, and that she must stand still till the dairymaid dismisses her. (6) Straight young trees after they are felled; but before they are hewn, it should seem, for then they would become *balks* in the *third* sense. (7) Applied to preventing animals from the chance or opportunity of propagating their species. (8) Earth turned up to the plough-ridges or ringes [M. C. H. B.].

Balker. A great beam. An augmentation of Balk.

Bamble. To shamble, to walk unsteadily and weakly. To tread one's shoes awry, 'How yew dew *bamble* your shoes.'

Bandy. (1) The curved stick with which the ball is struck at sundry games. (2) Any game so played is called by the general name. (3) A hare, from the curvature of her hind legs.

Bandy-hoshoe. The game of ball played with a *bandy*.

The *hoshoe* may be from the resemblance of the lower end of the *bandy* to a *horseshoe*.

Bandy-wicket. The game of cricket.

Bang. Cheese made, in Suffolk, of milk several times skimmed; therefore very hard and tough, and with which a hard knock or *bang* might be given. Otherwise Suffolk Thump; possibly from its being impossible to make any impression on it by *banging*.

*****Bange** (pronounced BANJ). Light rain [J. G. Nall].

Banging. Huge; beating or excelling in size other things of the same kind.

Bangled. (1) When cocked hats were worn, one of the sides was sometimes let down to protect the face of the wearer. The hat was said to be *bangled*. Also said of a round hat with a broad and loose brim, such as is worn by Quakers. (2) Also applied to the young shoots, or more particularly the broad leaves of plants, when they droop under heavy rain or strong sunshine. Teut. *abbangen*, dependere.

*****Bangy** (pronounced BANJ-I). Dull, gloomy [J. G. Nall].

*****Bank.** Generally used for beach [Miss Gurney].

*****Bannock.** A cake baked in a French oven [*B. N.* p. 85]. [I greatly doubt this.—W. R.]

Bargain. An indefinite number or quantity of anything; not necessarily conveying the idea of purchase and sale. Ex. 'Two good tidy *bargains* of hay from an acre,' meaning something less than wagon loads. 'A poor *bargain* of wool from three score hoggets.' 'A sad *bargain* of lazy chaps.' [A wagon load according to J. G. Nall and E. M.].

*****Bargander.** The sheldrake [E. S. T.], the solan goose (?) [Moor]. Probably the same as 'Garganer,' a bird sometimes called 'Garner.' Tungate used to talk of shooting (what I thought was) gardeners in the most cold-blooded way [W. R.] (*Tadorna cornuta*) [M. C. H. B.].

Bargood. Yeast; the flower or cream of it. It is sometimes corrupted into Burgood, and even Bulgood. In Suffolk, Bulgard [Spur.]. Moor (Suff.) says he never heard the word, and E. S. Taylor says it is not in use in Norfolk. Formerly Beer-good, as noted by Ray in his Preface [W. W. S.]

Bark. The tartar deposited by bottled wine or other liquor, encrusting the bottle.

*****Barksel.** The season for barking trees [M. C. H. B.].

Barley-bird. The nightingale, which comes to us in the season of sowing barley.

Barley-mung. Barley meal mixed with water or milk, to fatten fowls or pigs.

Barley-sele. (1) The time for sowing barley. (2) It is time to set barley when a man in leather breeches can feel the earth warm whilst sitting on the ground [M. C. H. B.].

*****Barm.** Yeast; called Rising or Raising in Essex.

*****Barney Bee,** or **Burney Bee,** quasi Burnis Bee, i.e. Fiery Beetle, the May Fly [? W. R.] or Lady-bird [Spur.]. *Vide* Bishop Barnabee.

Barrow-pig. The least pig of the litter. The Pitman has the same meaning, and perhaps is more general; also called a Dodman. In [Jen.] a *barrow-pig* is a gelded pig.

Barsele, Barksele. The time for stripping bark. See Sele.

Barth. A shelter for cattle, &c.; cf. seamen's berth; but see Murray.

Barton. Formerly the demesne land of the lord of the manor; not let out on lease, but held by the lord, in his own hands, for the sustenance of his household. Now used for a farm-yard, a rick-yard, or even a poultry-yard.

Basking. (1) A drenching in a heavy shower. (2) A sound drubbing [Forby, E. S. T.]. Basting [J. G. Nall].

*****Bass, Base, or Bast.** Matting made from the inner bark of a tree (*the* tree, viz. lime) [E. S. T.]. A hassock.

*****Baste.** (1) To stitch together slightly and loosely before hemming [E. S. T.]. (2) To beat [Johnson].

Batch. A bout; as of drinking, card-playing, &c. Properly it means a quantity of bread, or other things, baked at the same time. This is a dictionary sense.

Batlins. The loppings or stowin of trees [J. G. Nall]. *Vel* Battlings, toppings and loppings of trees. An unhewn rail is also called a *battling* [Forby]. Croppings of trees larger than faggot sticks, yet less than timber [Cull. Haw.].

*****Batter.** A slope. 'I'll have that ditch made 5 ft. deep on the *batter*' [Johnson].

*****Battors.** Strong broad fencing-rails [Marshall].

*****Battry.** A tea-kettle.

*****Bauley Boats.** Harwich fishing-smacks [*B. N.* 77].

Bavin. A light, loose faggot.

Bavish. To drive away. Corruption of *banish* (?).

*****Bawda.** To abuse grossly [J. G. Nall, quoting Moor].

*****Bawley.** A fishing-smack.

Bawnd. Swollen [Sir Thomas Browne]. Now obsolete. See Ray's *Gl.*, ed. Skeat, p. 16.

Bay. (1) The space in a building between two main beams. We speak of a barn, or a cart-lodge, of so many *bays*. Sometimes, but not so correctly, the whole space between the threshing-floor and the end of the barn is so called ; cf. bays of a window. (2) The nest of a squirrel; [but this is probably an error for 'dray.'—W. W. S.]. (3) A division or compartment, a window. Also **Day** [Spur.]. (4) A dray [Moor].

Bay-duck. The shell-duck; from its bright colour, like that of a *bay* horse. Sometimes the 'May duck [W. R.] or gargander.'

*****Bayn.** Pliant, limber [Pr. Pa.].

Beaker. A drinking-glass.

*****Beam-bird** [or **Wall-bird**]. Spotted fly-catcher [J. H. G.].

*****Bear.** 'To *bear* a bob,' to make one among many; to lend a helping hand, at the risk, as it should seem, of receiving a bob, or blow. From ringers, who have several sorts of bob, all, of course, involving the idea of a blow. (2) An instrument used to cut sedge [Johnson]. Also a surname common in S. Suffolk [F. J. B.].

*****Bear 'em.** As much wood from fencing as can be tied up and carried off at the end of work time. Taken as a right in old times, now often by consent [W. B.].

*****Beargood.** Yeast [Arderon]. See **Bargood** and **Burgard**.

Bearn. A barn.

*****Bears' Ears.** The auricula [F. C. H. in *N. and Q.* 4th Ser. vii. p. 350].

Beast. An animal of the beeve kind in a fatting state. [I doubt this. Why do we speak of a fat beast if this is so?]

Beastlings. The first milk drawn after a cow has calved. Pronounced BIESTINGS, from the A. S. *bysting* [Spur.]. See **Beezlins**.

Beat. To repair, to supply the gradual waste of anything. We seem to apply it only to mending the broken meshes of a net. See **Beet**.

*****Beath.** To place green wood by the fire, to set out or straighten it by heat [J. G. Nall].

Beatout. Puzzled [J. G. Nall]=beat out.

*****Beatworld.** Beyond control [J. G. Nall] (?).

Beck. A brook or rivulet.

*Becket. A spade used in cutting turf [J. G. Nall].

*Becket. A sheath, e.g. 'knife *becket*' [E. F. G.].

*Becomes. One's best clothes [J. G. Nall].

Bed. (1) The uterus of an animal. (2) A fleshy piece of beef cut from the upper part of the leg and bottom of the belly.

*Bedded. Bedridden [C. D.].

Bed-faggot. A contemptuous name for a *bedfellow*, as it were, a wretched substitute, no better than a faggot in the muster of a regiment.

*Bedrepes. Days of harvesting formerly performed by customary tenants for their lord [J. G. Nall].

*Bee-bird. Great-tit (*Parus major*); also oxeye [M.C.H.B.].

Bee-bread. A brownish opaque substance, with which some of the cells in a honeycomb are filled, for the food of the insect in its larva state.

Bee-drove. A great confluence of men, or of any other creatures, as it were a swarm of them.

Beein. A home, a place to be in [J. G. Nall, quoting Moor].

*Beergood, Bergard, Bargood. Yeast [M. C. H. B.].

*Beever. A slight repast in the intervals of regular meals, a luncheon; used in the southern parts of Suffolk and [in] Essex [Spur.]. An afternoon snack about 4 p.m. [E. S. T.].

Beet. Bet up, to mend nets [J. G. Nall and E. F. G.]. See Beat.

*Beetsel. The time for sowing beet [M. C. H. B.].

*Beetster. A net-mender [J. G. Nall and E. F. G.].

*Beezlins. The milk of the third or fourth 'meal' or milking after calving [E. S. T.]. See Beastlings.

Beggar's Velvet. The light particles of down shaken from a feather-bed.

Beggary. (1) The copious and various growth of weeds in a field. (2) The name of a specific plant [Spur.].

Begone. Decayed, worn out.

Being. (1) An abode, particularly a lodging. (2) Because. Ex. 'I could not meet you yesterday, *being* I was ill a-bed.'

Belike. (1) Likely. Ex. '*Belike* we may have snow.' (2) As it is said. Ex. 'I hear Mr. A. is to be married to Miss B.' 'Aye, so *belike.*'

*****Belking.** Lounging at full length [J. G. Nall].

Belliborion. A variety of apple.

Bell-soller. The loft on which ringers stand.

*****Below.** Downstairs, North of England. Ex. 'He ha' gone below'=He has gone to the North [M. C. H. B.].

Belsize. Bulky, of good size.

*****Ben.** A figure put in front on the last load of the harvest, intended to represent Ceres [Johnson].

*****Benane.** Beneath [Spur.].

Ben-joltram. A brown bread soaked in skimmed milk; the ploughboy's usual breakfast.

*****Bentles.** The low sandy flattish land on parts of the Suffolk coast [E. S. T.].

Bents. (1) Dry stalks of grass remaining in pastures after summer feeding [Forby]. (2) Benten, Benting, or Bentles, coarse reedy grass [E. S. T. and J. G. N.][1].

*****Bequixt.** Betwixt [Spur.].

*****Bergard.** Vide Bargood.

---

[1] When the wild dove finds all other food fail she has to betake herself to the seeding bentles, hence these sayings:—

> 'The dove she do no sorrow know
> Until she do *a-benting* go.'

And

> 'When the pigeons go *a-benting*
> Then the farmers lie lamenting' [E. S. T.].

*Besom. A broom made of birch twigs cut and dried for the purpose, and then tied up in a bunch. In some parts of Suffolk called Birch-broom. In some parts of Norfolk called Ling-broom or besom [H. C.].

Bess o' Bedlam. A sort of vagrant, once very common in this country, who were wont to announce themselves as inmates of Bedlam, allowed in some lucid interval to range the country, and return at a stated time to their confinement.

*Best. Used as a verb. Ex. ' I bested him in the bargain.'

Bestow. (1) To deliver a woman, otherwise, to ' put her to bed.' (2) To lay up, to put out of the way. It is equivalent to the seamen's phrase, ' to *stow* away.'

*Bet. To beat. Mispronunciation [H. B.].

*Betty. (1) The nickname for the kettle [W. G. W.] (2) To dawdle or waste time [F. J. B.].

*Betty-tit. The titmouse [J. G. Nall].

Bezzle. (1) To blunt or turn the edge of a tool in the process of whetting or grinding [Forby]. (2) To drink greedily [E. S. T. and J. G. N.].

Bibble. To eat like a duck, gathering its food from water, and taking up both together. Johnson says that ducks bibble when they put their beaks in the mud.

*Bick. A wooden bottle or cask in which beer is carried to the field, E. Norf. [Johnson].

*Biddies. Young chickens [Spur.].

Bide-owe. Interpreted by Ray '*paenas dare.*' It may be so. It is impossible to assent or gainsay, as it is totally extinct. It is one of Sir Thomas Browne's words.

*Bies. See Bighes. ' He is in his *bies,*' he is according to his fancy or desire (bias ?) [Arderon]. Tungate used this when referring to my boat being at her *best*, when sailing on one wind [W. R.]. See *B. N. 12.* But probably ' at its best.'

*Biests. The wen-like protuberances on growing trees [E. S. T., J. G. N., Suff.].

*Biffin. A half-dried or preserved, apple. [Beef'un, the name of an apple with red skin.]

Bigg. (1) A species of barley; called also Barley-big. (*Hordeum hexastichon*, Lin.) (2) A pap or teat [J. G. Nall].

*Biggoty. Overbearing [G. E.].

Bighes. Ex. 'She is all in her *bighes* to-day,' q.d. best humour, best graces, &c. See Bies. [Spelt *bighes*, and explained (wrongly) by Forby as 'jewels' in order to force a false etymology.—W. W. S.]

*Bile. See Bale.

*Biler. Boiler [M. C. H. B.].

*Billows of Snow. Snow-drifts [*N. and Q.*, 3rd Ser. vol. ii. p. 371].

*Billy-boy. A sea boat [M. C. H. B.].

Billy-wix. An owl.

*Bind. Anything to tie up a bundle with. Cobbler's sewing thread is called wax-bind, or wax-bonds ends [E. S. T.].

*Bind, Bellbind. Bindweed. (*Convolvulus*) [M. C. H. B.].

Bing. A bin for corn, flour, wine, &c. The proper word.

*Binne. By-and-by [?].

Bird of the Eye. The pupil, or rather, perhaps, the little refracted image on the retina, or that of a very near spectator reflected from the cornea.

*Bishimer. An ant [*B. N.* 62] (obviously a corruption of pismire).

Bishop. To confirm.

Bishop-barnabee. The pretty insect more generally called

the **Lady-bird**, or **May-bug** [? W. R.], *Coccinella septem punctata*, Lin.

'Bishop, Bishop Barnabee,
Tell me when your wedding be.
If it is to-morrow day,
Take your wings and fly away.'

Bushy barnabee [E. S. T.]. A variorum reading on the Norfolk coast is—'Busk ye, busk ye, all hands on deck.' 'Co', busk ye, mates, ta' grow late, and time to go' [E. S. T.]. It is sometimes called **Bishop Benebee**, which may possibly (?) have been intended to mean the blessed bee; sometimes **Bishop Benetree**, of which it seems not possible to make anything. Moor gives this for Suffolk :—

'Gowden bug, gowden bug, fly awah home,
Yar house is bahnt down, an' yar children all gone.'

*****Bit.** The chief difficulty in an affair. Ex. 'Ay, ay, that will be the bit' [C. S. P.].

Bitch. A trull; the female companion of a vagrant. Our tinkers do not keep *bitches*, but trulls.

*****Bitterly.** Excessively. 'It is odd enough that sweetly is used in the same way' [Spur.].

*****Bittore.** The bittern [E. S. T.]. M. E. *bitoure* [and correct, W. W. S.].

*****Blabber.** To talk idly, or chatter [E. S. T.].

*****Black-cap.** Marsh-tit (*Parus palustris*) [M. C. H. B.].

Black-sap. Very advanced jaundice.

*****Black Meat.** Cured bacon [E. F. G.], or ham smoked [W. R.].

*****Black Squire.** A clerical squire, squarson [M. C. H. B.].

*****Black Weed.** *Sparganium ramosum* [M. C. H. B.].

*****Blains.** Ulceration at the roots of the tongues of cattle [Johnson].

Blame. An evasion of **Damn**. Ex. '*Blame* me,' or 'I will be *blamed* if,' &c.

Blar. Calves, sheep, asses, and children all *blar*, or *blare* in their several natural modes. (2) A mixture of pitch and tar [E. F. G.].

*Blare. A loud cry [G. E.].

*Blarm. Blame. Ex. 'Blarm me if you baint' [M. C. H. B.].

Blaunch. A blain.

Blauthy. Bloated.

*Bleach. A drying-ground [M. C. H. B.].

Blee. General resemblance, not 'colour and complexion.' Ex. 'That boy has a strong *blee* of his father' [Ch., P. G.].

Bleek. Pale, sickly, sheepish.

*Bleff. Turbulent, noisy [J. G. Nall].

*Blether. A bladder [Johnson].

Blind. Abortive. When blossoms fade away without forming the fruit, we say they are *blind*. It seems to be particularly said of strawberries and other small summer fruits.

Blind-hob, Blind-sim. Blind-man's buff.

Blinked Beer. Not with acidity, but an ill flavour peculiar to itself; said to be occasioned by too long delay of fermentation, until the wort is too cool to ferment with proper activity. Others account for it from insufficient stirring of the mash, so as not to wet all the malt.

*Bloated. Puffed. Ex. 'A fond mother, looking at her poor little boy's swollen cheek, observed sorrowfully, " He was a bloaty little cousan and no mistake "' [C. S. P.].

Blob. (1) A small lump of anything thick, viscid, or dirty, as of tallow, dregs of ink, &c. [Forby]. (2) To shake [G. J. C.]

Block-horse. A strong wooden frame with four handles, commonly called a hand-barrow, for the purpose of carrying blocks.

*Bloifin. A kind of blowing cough [G. E.].

Blood-fallen. Chilblained.

Blood-olf. The bullfinch. Pronounced ULF [E. S. T.]. See **Alp.**

*****Bloom.** (1) Plumage. Ex. 'Cock teal in full bloom.' (2) Full plumage, or breeding plumage [M. C. H. B.].

Blore. (1) To bellow like a bull. The same as **Blare.** (2) Used of a cow moaning after a weaned calf [E. S. T.].

*****Blossom.** (1) An ewe, when 'maris appetens'; a sow is said to look 'proud' [E. S. T., also Johnson]. (2) The state of cream in the operation of churning, when it seems to be in a state of fermentation, and will not coagulate and become butter [Johnson].

*****Blossomed.** Said of cream whilst churning becoming full of air [J. G. Nall].

Blouze. (1) A woman with hair or head-dress loose and disordered, or decorated with vulgar finery. (2) A woman's bonnet; more properly that sort which is otherwise called a **Slouch.** (3) All of a *blouze*, red in the face from heat and exertion [Spur.]. (4) When the growth of one plant is hindered by the over-growth of another, it is said to be *blouzed* by that plant [Spur.].

Blow. Blossoms. Ex. 'There is a fine *blow* of apples this year' [B. R.].

*****Blown, to be.** To be detected [Arderon]. This is modern London slang, e.g. 'To be *blown* upon' [W. R.].

Blown-herring. A herring slightly cured, for speedy use and home consumption, and smoked but once, which has the effect of plumping them, without discharging the fat, somewhat like the baking or roasting of apples. On some parts of our coasts a *blown-herring* is called a **Tow-bowen.** Why? They are also called **Bloaters.**

*****Blowzin.** 'Flowers comin' on a *blowzin*' [W. R.].

Blubber. A bubble, from *blob*.

Blubber-grass. Different species of *bromus*, from their soft inflated glumes; in particular *mollis*, which infests barren pastures.

*Blunk. Squally, tempestuous [J. G. Nall and Marshall].

*Blunt. A blunt of snow, a heavy fall of snow [M.C.H.B.].

*Bluster-wood. Shoots of fruit-trees, or shrubs that require pruning [E. S. T. and J. G. Nall].

Bluther. (1) To blot in writing. (2) To disfigure the face with weeping.

*Boak. A definite quantity, *quasi* bulk [Spur.]. See Boke.

Boar-thistle. The *Carduus lanceolatus*, Lin.

Board-cloth. A tablecloth.

*Board you! When one harvester wants to drink after another, he calls *board you*, which means, give the bottle to me when you have drunk [Johnson].

Bob. (1) To cheat. (2) A plummet [E. S. T.]. (3) A blow or smack, e.g. ' a *bob* i' the chops.'

Bode. (1) To board. Ex. ' He *bodes* and lodges there.' (2) Past tense of bid, to offer, ' He *bode* me 2s.' [E. S. T.]

Bode-cloth. A tablecloth. See Board-cloth.

Bodge. (1) To patch clumsily; the same as *botch*. (2) To *boggle*, to fail.

*Body. For belly [M. C. H. B.].

*Body of. Large quantity. Ex. ' A *body* of rain ' [C. H. B.].

Bog *vel* Boggy. Sturdy, self-sufficient, petulant [Forby]. Malapert, consequential, saucy, impertinent [Johnson].

Boist. A swelling. A sore or blain [E. S. T.].

Boke. (1) Bulk. Ex. 'There is more *boke* than corn in that goaf' [Forby]. See Boak. A large quantity, an abundant crop [Johnson]. (2) To nauseate, to be ready to vomit. (3) Part of a cart [M. C. H. B.].

*Boke-load. A load of hay or straw, or of corn in the straw [Johnson]. A large top-heavy bulky load [Marshall].

Boke out. To swell, to gain bulk and prominence.

*****Boky.** Proud, conceited, saucy [Spur.]. Vide **Bog** [W. R.].

*****Bolders.** (1) Bulrushes [W. R.]. (2) *Scirpus lacustris* [M. C. H. B.].

*****Bolter, Bolted.** Applied to a bump, raised [M. C. H. B.].

*****Bolted.** Of plants run to seed [M. C. H. B.].

*****Bolling.** A pollard tree (N. Ess.). See Murray's Dict. for instances [C. D.].

Bombaze. To confound, bewilder, perplex; as if a veil were thrown before the eyes, to hinder one from seeing what he is about.

*****Bone-cart.** To carry on one's shoulder. Ex. 'I coudn't av a horse, so I was forst to *bone-cart* 'em' [J. G. Nall]. Also used for the human body. 'I'll baste your *bone-cart*' [Johnson].

Bone lazy, Bone sore, Bone tired. So lazy, sore, or tired, that the laziness, the soreness, or the fatigue, seem to have penetrated the very bones.

*****Bones.** It is said to be unlucky to burn bones, and that it gives the burner the bone ache (Brunstead, 1890) [M. C. H. B.].

*****Bonker, or Bonka.** Strapping, bouncing. Applied to young women [E. S. T. and J. G. Nall].

Bonny. Brisk, cheerful, in good health and spirits. We do not include in it the idea of 'comeliness' [? W. R.].

*****Bonx.** To beat batter for puddings, Essex [J. G. Nall].

*****Boodle.** The corn marigold [J. G. Nall].

*****Boots on.** Died with his *boots on*, viz. died a violent death [M. C. H. B.].

Bop. To dip or duck suddenly [Forby]. Come to stoop or squat down, coming with the idea of secreting [Johnson]. (2) *Bopped*, said of a baby when its long clothes are exchanged for short ones. (3) To drop a curtsy [M. C. H. B.].

Bor. A term of very familiar address, generally [mis]-understood to be a coarse pronunciation of the word *boy*, but applied indiscriminately to persons of both sexes and of all ages. A part of the word neighbour (A. S. *néah*, prope, and *búr*); and why may it not exist in the simple as well as in a compound form? If this explanation be admitted, one old woman may, without absurdity, say to another (as often happens), 'Co', *bor*, let's go a-sticking in the squire's plantations.' And the other may answer, 'Aye, *bor*, so we will.' See **Bor** in Murray, Part III.

*__Border.__ To use coarse language [Spur., E. S. T.].

Bosh. To 'cut a *bosh*' is something stronger than the more usual expression to 'cut a dash'; something more showy and expensive.

*__Bosky.__ Tipsy [E. S. T. and J. G. Nall].

*__Bosom.__ The join in a grain of wheat is called the bosom. 'If you put some wheat into water the bosom will open' [M. C. H. B.]

Boss. A hod for mortar, carried on the shoulders like a hump.

Bossock. To toss and tumble clumsily, as it were to throw all the limbs together into one heap [W. R.].

Bottle. (1) By a 'bottle of hay' is now understood such a moderate bundle as may serve for one feed, twisted somewhat into the shape of a bottle. (2) *Barley-bottles.* These were little bundles of barley in the straw, given to farm horses. This wasteful mode of giving feeds of corn is probably now quite disused. (3) The dug of a cow is called her *bottle*, as well as her *bag.*

Bottle Bird. An apple rolled up and baked in a crust.

Bottle Bump. The bittern, anciently called bittour, or buttour.

Bottle-nose. The common porpoise.

Bottle Tom. Long-tailed tit (*P. caudatus*) [M. C. H. B.].

***Bottomfy.** To throw out the bottoms of marsh ditches, as opposed to 'pulling' or drawing the weeds with a crome only [M. C. H. B.].

***Botty.** Proud [J. G. Nall]. For boggy; see **Bog** [W. W. S.]. Impertinent [B. N. J.].·

Bouds. Weevils in malt.

Bouge. (1) 'To make a *bouge*,' to commit a gross blunder, to get a heavy fall by taking an awkward false step. (2) To bulge or swell out.

***Bough-load.** The last load of the harvest, so called because dressed with boughs [W. B.].

***Boulders.** (1) Bulrushes [*Eastern England*, by W. White, vol. i. p. 175]. (2) Stubs [C. H. B.].

***Bout.** A furrow [E. S. T., J. G. Nall]. Rather, a double furrow; to go to the end and come back [W. B., H. C.].

Bout-hammer. The heavy two-handed hammer used by blacksmiths.

***Bown.** A swelling or lump [G. J. C., quoting J. Steele].

***Bownd.** Swollen [Ray]. See **Baund.**

Bowry. A bower or arbour. The word was anciently written *bowre*, and signified a room, particularly a woman's apartment. A bed-chamber [E. S. T.].

***Boxing Harry.** Going without food all day [Johnson].

***Brabble.** A ruffle on the surface of the sea [Spur., E. F. G., and E. S. T.].

***Bracing-down.** Third time of turnip-hoeing, drawing down the ridges [M. C. H. B.].

Brackly. Brittle. Particularly applied to standing corn, some ears of which are so quickly ripened as to snap off short [M. S.].

***Bradocks.** Young turbots [J. G. Nall].

Braid. (1) A culinary term; to beat and blend soft

substances or mixtures; particularly to press them with a spoon through a colander or sieve. It is probably different from Bray, to pound in a mortar. (2) To half cut, then interlace quick or other hedge stuff [M. C. H. B.].

*Braiding. Applied to net-making [J. G. Nall].

*Bramble. A blackberry-bush [G. E.].

Bramish. To flourish, gesticulate, and assume affected airs, to boast [Forby]. A boasting showy coxcomb, one who spreads himself and appears of great importance; more particularly so called if his face is red from drinking or from standing by the fire [Johnson].[1]

Brand. The smut in wheat, making it look as if a hot iron had passed over it.

*Brandy Bottles. The yellow water-lilies [J. G. Nall].

*Brandice Fashion. Planting in a triangle.

Brank. Buckwheat; *Polygonum fagopyrum.*

Brash. (1) An acid and watery rising from the stomach into the mouth. (2) Refuse boughs, clippings of hedges, &c.

Brashy. Applied to land overgrown with faint grass, rushes, or twigs [Forby]. Wet, cold, and coarse meadows, especially if rushy, are said to be *brashy* [Johnson].

Brattle. To lop the branches of trees after they are felled.

Brattlings. Loppings from felled trees.

Bravely. Very much recovered from sickness.

Brawn. A boar.

*Braze. To deny, contradict [G. E.].

*Bread, Diss Bread. A kind of cake or gingerbread made at Diss [M. C. H. B.].

Breck. A large division of an open corn-field, q.d. Break. But query from bracken, cf. the breck district.

Bred. A board to press curd for cheese, somewhat less

---

[1] A marvellously comprehensive word this!

in circumference than the vat. A. S. *bred*, a board [W. W. S.].

Bred-sore, Breeder. A whitlow, or any sore coming without wound or other visible cause. A whitlow only [Spur.].

*Breeder. (1) A weather breeder—an unseasonably fine day. (2) To breed for—when a woman enceinte is in good health, whilst her husband is ill, he is said to breed for her (1891) [M. C. H. B.].

*Brenner. A sharp gust of wind on the water [E. F. G.].

*Brew. The field side of a ditch, its brim, brow, or berm [E. S. T. and J. G. N.].

*Bridleway. A way with gates, where riders can go but not carts [C. D.]. Also a Spurway.

Brief. Any written or printed petition, or begging paper.

Brig. A bridge.

*Bright. The appearance of marshes when flooded, 'the marshes are *bright* to-day' [W. R.].

Brim. Commonly, but erroneously, supposed to be another name for a boar. We say, indeed, the 'sow goes to *brim*'; but we never call the boar a *brim*. In Cheshire, the sow is said to be *brimming*, which is exactly the A. S. *brem-mende*, fremens. E. S. Taylor says *brim* is said of a sow when she is 'maris appetens,' and that 'proud' or 'salt' is used for the same thing.

Brim. The past of to broom or to sweep with a broom, 'I *brim* up all the muck I could' [E. S. T.].

*Bring up. To stop, to bring to a standstill, to assume a threatening attitude; e.g. 'He brought up before me' = 'he drew his guard at me'; also 'he brought up' = 'he stopped his cart' [M. C. H. B.].

Brink-ware. Small faggots, generally made of whitethorn, to repair the banks of rivers.

Broaches, Brauches, Brotchwood. Rods of sallow, hazel,

or other tough and pliant wood, split, sharpened at each end, and bent in the middle like an old-fashioned hairpin; used by thatchers to pierce and fix their work. A fell of such wood is divided into hurdle-wood and *broach*-wood; the stouter and the slenderer. M. E. *broche.*

Broad. A lake formed by the expansion of a river in a flat country.

Broad-best. The best suit of apparel. Perhaps because understood to be made of broadcloth.

Broak, Brock. To belch, to break wind [W. R.].

*****Brogues.** Breeches, Suff. [J. G. Nall].

*****Brooches.** Sores [M. C. H. B.].

*****Broomstick Marriages.** Marriages contracted to save the legitimacy of a child, or to father the child on another parish; otherwise **Hop-pole marriages.**

*****Brow.** To clear away rough grass and brambles; the clearings are called **Browings** [W. G. W.].

Bruckled, Brucket. Grimy, speckled and ingrained with dirt. Ex. ' That child's hands are all over *bruckled.'*

Bruff. Hearty, jolly, healthy, in good case.

*****Brum.** A broom [Spur., E. S. T.].

*****Brumble.** A bramble.

*****Brumble gelder.** A farmer [J. G. Nall]. Lit. bramble cutter.

Brump. To lop trees in the night (?).

Brun. Bran.

*****Brush.** (1) To cut down weeds, &c. [E. S. T., J. G. Nall]. (2) To beat a covert; ' a day's brushing with the governor' [H. B.].

Brustle. A bristle.

*****Brut.** To browse, Suff. [Bailey].

Buck. That part of a cart or waggon which may be very

properly called its belly [Forby]. The body of a cart [Cull. Haw.].

Buck. To spring or bound with agility. A horse bucks [F. J. B.].

Bucker. (1) A horse's hind leg. (2) A bent piece of wood somewhat like it in shape; particularly that on which a slaughtered animal is hung up, more generally called a Gambrel. It has been guessed that this is the origin of 'kicking the bucket.' (3) A bucket.

Bucker-ham. The hock joint of a horse.

Buck-head, Buck-stall. To cut down a quickset hedge to the height of two or three feet, with a view of renovating its growth [Forby]. Sometimes called a thorn boll or bull [Johnson.]

Bud. A calf of which the horns are beginning to shoot. But the name is equally applied to those of the same age, of the polled breed [Forby.] A heifer, steer, or bull at a year old, not two [Johnson]. Yearling cattle [Marshall].

Buddle. A noxious weed among corn. *Chrysanthemum segetum*, Lin.

*Buetiful. Beautiful.

Buffer. A fool, a buffoon.

*Buffet. A corner cupboard, used for the display of glass or ' chany ' [E. S. T.].

Buffet Stool. A four-legged stool set on a frame like a table. It is the poor man's sideboard, table, or stool, as occasion requires.

Buffle. (1) To handle clumsily, as if the fingers were stuffed or blown up. (2) To speak thick and inarticulately, as if the mouth were stuffed. (3) To baffle [Spur.]. (4) To be buffled, to be confused [E. S. T.]. ' That 'll hull him in a buffle '—put him into a difficulty [*B. N.* p. 85]. (5) To warm one's hands in pockets, &c., N. Ess. [C. D.].

Bulk. To throb.

*Bull. Is always pronounced as in mull or hull [Spur.].

Bull-feist. The common puff-ball.

*Bullakin. Low vulgar abuse [Johnson].

*Buller. To bellow ; a noise [G. E.].

*Bullkin. A bull calf [E. S. T.].

Bullock. (1) To bully. (2) To bellow or lament vociferously. Ex. 'Sobbing and bullocking.'

*Bulls. The stems of hedge thorns [Marshall, and *B. N.* 66].

Bull's Noon. Midnight. The inhabitants of dairy counties can feelingly vouch for the propriety of this term. Their repose is often broken in the dead of night by the loud bellowing of the lord of the herd, who, rising vigorous from his evening rumination, rushes forth on his adventures, as if it were broad noonday.

Bully-mung. (1) A mixture of the meal of oats, peas, and vetches [Forby]. (2) Scurrilous and abusive language [E. S. T.].

Bully-rag. To revile in vulgar and opprobrious terms.

*Bulmong. Peas and oats sown together [Cull. Haw.].

Bulver. To increase in bulk by being rolled over and over, like snow. The word is often applied to hay or corn collecting into increasing heaps.

*Bulver-head. One whose brains are a thick confused mass [Johnson]. [Bull-headed? Tungate].

*Bulvering. Sticking out [Johnson]. Cumbersome [*B. N.* 100].

Bumbaste. To beat or baste severely, particularly to inflict school discipline.

*Bumble. A hoarding in front of a building being rebuilt [W. R.].

*Bumbled. Blinded as with a handkerchie [Arderon].

*Bummaree. To run up a score at a newly opened public-house [Hotten's *Slang Dictionary*]. Not known [W. R.].

*Bumbay. In Suffolk a quagmire from stagnating water, dung, &c. [Cull. Haw.]. See Bumby.

Bumble. (1) To muffle. Ex. 'The bells were *bumbled* at his burial.' (2) A cover of a vessel [Spur.].

Bumble-bee. The Humble-bee. Bumbler [Em.]. ⟋

Bumble-footed. Having a thick lumpish foot; which moves as if it were made whole, without articulations.

Bumbles. Coverings for the eyes of a horse, obstructing his vision more effectually than common blinkers.

Bumby. Any collection of stagnant filth, into which the drain from some dirty place runs. See Bumbay.

Bun. A dried stalk [Halliwell].

*Bunch. (1) To beat hemp [Spur.]. Also, 'bunch' of plovers, as we say a 'skein of wild duck' [W. R.]. (2) A small flock [M. C. H. B.].

Bund-weed, Bunds. Different species of wild centaureae, particularly *nigra*, Lin., which much infests grass land; and some species of scabiosa (*succisa*, Lin., for instance). It is quasi *bum-weed*, from the roundness and plumpness of the parts of fructification in the plants above-mentioned [sed quaere *bind*-weed—W. R.].

Bundle. An opprobrious term applied to females, equivalent to baggage, which perhaps means strictly a follower of the camp. Bunch is used in the same sense.

Bungay Play. A simple straightforward way of playing the game at whist, by leading all winning cards in succession, without any plan to make the best of the hand. From Bungay, Suffolk.

Bung-tail. The tail of a draught-horse, docked and pared down to the shape and size of a *bung* [? bangtail—W. R.].

*Bunkas. A crowd collecting together confusedly, Suff. [E. S. T. and J. G. N.].

*Bunker.   Any large rank-growing weed [M. C. H. B.].

*Bunkers.   Strong growing bunches (e. g. *Carex caespitosa*) [M. C. H. B.].

Bunks.   (1) The wild succory, *Chichoreum intybus*, Lin. (2) A rabbit [E. S. T.].

Bunny.   A small swelling caused by a fall or blow. Allied to E. *bunion* [W. W. S.].

*Bunt.   To strike with the head, to gore [G. J. C.].

Bunting, Bunty.   Miserably mean and shabby.

Burbles.   Small tingling pimples, such as are caused by the stinging of nettles or of some minute insects. Minsh. calls them Barbles. Qu. because they have been produced by puncturing the skin with little *barbed* points?

*Burgard.   Yeast [E. S. T. and J. G. N.].   See Beargood and Bargood.

Burr.   (1) A mistiness over and around the moon ; E. S. T. quotes the proverb, ‘ Near *burr*—far rain.’   (2) The wart-like excrescence on trees, Norf. ; the same as the Suffolk Biest [E. S. T.].   (3) The rough edge of wood left by the tool on the lathe [E. S. T.].

*Burrow Duck.   Sheldrake (*Tadorna cornuta*) [J. H. G.].

Burthen.   To charge closely and pressingly. Ex. ‘ I *burthened* him with it as strong as I could, but he would not confess.’

*Bush.   (1) Reeds. When a wounded fowl swims from the open water into the reeds, it is said to have got into the *bush*.   (2) Reed-bed [M. C. H. B.].

Busk.   (1) Particularly applied to domestic fowls exposing themselves to the sun on a hot day, lying in the most dusty place they can find, and scratching up the dust among their feathers, to rid themselves, it is said, of the vermin with which they are infested.   (2) To prepare, to get ready to go [E. S. T.].   (3) The piece of wood or iron that confines the bung of a churn [H. B.].   See Bishop-barnabee.

*Buskings. Gaiters [C. S. P.].

*Buss. A fishing-boat [J. G. Nall].

*Bussen-billy. Ruptured [J. G. Nall]. Busten-belly, *Id.* [E. S. T.].

Butes = Crotch-boots, the boot of boots. Ex. ' You won't take no harm, you ha' got your butes on ' [M. C. H. B.].

*Butlands, or Buttles. Land set apart for butts at which to practise archery [Spur.].

*Butt. A flounder [J. G. Nall].

Butter Teeth. Broad and yellow teeth.

*Buttery. A pantry [Spur.]. All colleges have butteries [F. J. B.].

Buttle. (1) Another name for the Bottle Bump, Butter Bump, or Bittern. (2) Archery grounds, as in Butlands.

Buttress. An implement used by blacksmiths for paring hoofs of horses [B. N. 56].

Buzzle Head. B. N. p. 68. Probably a corruption for puzzle head [W. R.].

*Bybler. A great Bible reader [E. S. T.].

*Bylders. A kind of watercress [J. G. Nall].

Caddow, or Cadder. A jackdaw. ' A *caddus'* nist.'

*Cade. A measure for herrings, not now used; 2 *Henry VI*, iv. 2. 36. A cade of sprats at Aldborough is a thousand [E. F. G.].

*Cadpig. The smallest pig in the litter [W. B.]. Vide Petman.

*Caffling. Hesitating, shilly-shallying; cheapening an article or shifting a bargain [Johnson].

Cail. (1) To throw weakly and wide of the mark. A boy throws a stone, a *mauther cails* it [or Shails, Johnson.] (2) To move with a wavering and irregular gait. (3) To gambol and throw out the heels like a skittish colt, 'kicking and *cailing.*'

*Cakey. Soft or silly [F. C. Husenbeth in *N. and Q.* 4th Ser. vol. iv. p. 127].

*Calder, or **Caulder,** or **Chalder, Chauldron.** The husk of wheat [M. C. H. B.].

Call. (1) To use abusive language; to call names, not particularizing any. Ex. 'How she did *call* me!' Jen. **Becall.** Br. **Call.** (2) Need, occasion. Ex. 'There was no *call* for your doing so'; i. e. you were not called upon.

Callow. (1) The stratum of vegetable earth lying above gravel, sand, limestone, &c. [Forby]. (2.) The surface of the land removed to dig for stones [E. S. T.].

Calm. The concreted scum of bottled liquors.

Calmy. Mothery.

Cambuck. The dry stalk of dead plants, as of hemlock, or other umbelliferae.

Camp. An ancient athletic game at ball (football), now superseded by cricket, a less hardy and dangerous sport [and by football, a more dangerous one].

Canch. (1) A small quantity of corn in the straw put into a corner of the barn or an out-house. (2) A short turn or spell at a job of hoeing, ditching, &c. (3) A trench, cut sloping to a very narrow bottom, or an angle. See **Cansh.**

*Cand. To adhere 'It *cands* together' [Johnson]; i. e. candies.

*Canker. Seed-pods of the wild dog-rose [C. D.].

Cankerfret. Verdigris. The rust of copper or brass. When the tinning is worn off from kitchen utensils, they are said to be *canker-fretted.* It is not used for the rust of any other metals.

Canker Rose. The common red field-poppy, otherwise called **Copper Rose,** and **Headache.**

*Cankers. Caterpillars [Marshall].

Canker Weed. The *Senecio Jacobaea*, or common ragwort.

*Cansey. Causeway. See Carnsey. In Suff. pron. CAISEY [H. C.].

*Cansh. A small mow [Marshall]. See Canch.

Cant. (1) To set up on edge. (2) To throw upwards with a jerk [Forby]. (3) To turn, or slew round as an anchored vessel with the tide [E. F. G.].

Cant Rail. A triangular rail; of which two are cut from a square piece of timber sawn diagonally.

*Capped. Land is capped when beaten down hard by heavy rain [F. J. B.].

*Cappel. (1) The iron fixed to the end of the horsetree, and to which the traces are hooked when at plough or harrow [Johnson]. (2) The revolving wooden loop on the top of a flail, by which the 'swingel' is attached to the 'handstaff' [W. G. W.].

*Capper [Suff.]. A hardish crust, formed on recently harrowed land by heavy rain [E. S. T.].

Cappered. Usually applied to cream wrinkled on the surface by standing in a brisk current of air; sometimes to the surface of land suddenly dried after rain.

*Cappers. Setting 'cappers,' a schoolboy's game of following the leader over hedge or ditch [M. C. H. B.].

Car. A wood or grove on a moist soil, generally of alders or osiers; a plantation by a river.

*Carnser. Causeway, e. g. 'Heigham *Carnser*,' for 'Heigham *Causeway*' [W. R.].

*Carnsey or Causey, *id.* [E. S. T.]. Johnson says Cantsa, a raised footway, and the side of a horse or carriage way. Browne (Letters to Dugdale) has Cawsing. See Caunsey.

*Carpeted. Had up for a fault before one's master 'onto the carpet, into the room' [M. C. H. B.].

D

*Carr. Alder carr, a wood or spinney of Alder Trees, which if composed of Osiers and Willows would be called a 'bed' [M. C. H. B.].

*Carre. A stoat [*N. and Q.*].

*Carrying the Blacksmith. A horse does when his hinder shoes knock against his fore ones [Johnson].

*Car Stone. A peculiar stone found principally near Swaffham [Spur.].

Cart. Crab. The carapace of a crab [Hotten's *Slang Dictionary*].   .

*Carwo. The word used by boys to scare rooks and crows from the corn. The Norfolk boys say—

> 'Bird a bird, a wooh,
> Here come the clappers,
> To knock ye down back'ards,
> Carwo l Carwoo—oh !'

Case. Cause. We whimsically transpose these two words. Ex. 'He did it without any *case* whatsomever.' 'Oh, if that be the Cause, indeed!' We may say Becase for Because.

Caseworm. The caddis.

Cast. (1) Warped, thrown on one side as it were, from a straight form [Forby]. (2) To vomit [E. S. T.].

Cast. (1) Yield, produce. Ex. 'How did your wheat *cast*?' In Suffolk the question would be, 'How did it rise?' (2) Of rabbits: they are not counted per head, but two or three for one according to size and quality. Rabbits that 'cast' twelve to the dozen are called 'full' rabbits [M. C. H. B.].

Casualty. The flesh of an animal that dies by chance. Ex. 'Gipsies feed on *casualties*.' 'This mutton is so pale and flabby, it looks like a *casualty*.' 'He gave a bullock to the poor at Christmas, little better than a *casualty*.' But to be correct, pronounce it Cazzlety.

Cat. (1) A mass of coarse meal, clay, and some other ingredients, with a large proportion of salt, placed in dovecotes to prevent the pigeons from leaving them, and to allure others to come. Called also a Salt Cat; meaning, no doubt, a Salt Cate. (2) A ferret. A coped cat is a muzzled ferret [W. R.].

Catch Land. Border land, of which the tithe was disputable, and taken by the first of the claimants who would *catch* it.

*Cauf or Cawf. A floating perforated box to keep lobsters in [E. S. T.]. See Corf.

Caulk. Calcareous earth in general; any sort of limestone. The same as E. *chalk.*

Caunsey. A causey, a raised and paved way. [By no means necessarily paved, Spur.]. See Carnser. In Pr. Pa. also spelt ' Cawcewey ' [C. D.].

Cause. Case, q. v.

*Cave. To fall in, a grave begins to cave [M. C. H. B.].

*Caven. Coarse chaff, &c., raked off the barn floor, Essex. See Colder.

Caving. The chaff and broken ears of corn, swept from the threshing-floor.

Cess. A layer or stratum; when successive quantities of things of the same kind are regularly placed one over another [Forby]. Johnson has Ceace.

Chaam. To chew or nibble into small pieces. Books and papers are too often *chaamed* by mice, if they can get at them. [M. E. *chammen,* to chew (Sir T. More's Works, p. 241); Mod. E. *champ.*—W. W. S.]

Chads. Dry husky fragments among food. This bread is *chaddy.*

*Chaffy. Thirsty [Johnson].

Chaits. Fragments or leavings on plates or trenchers, or of the food of animals, as turnip chaits. To which may be added Chats, as Ash Chats, Sycamore Chats, Maple Chats (what are otherwise called the Kegs (keys!) of those several trees). Blackthorn Chats are the young shoots or suckers of the blackthorn on rough borders, where they are occasionally cut and faggotted, but the roots left in the ground. All different forms of the same word, and of connected meaning; also Chanks [Spur.]. Chating stuff is soft grass grown among rushes [M. C. H. B.]. See Chats, Chites.

Chalder. (1) To crumble and fall away, as the surface of cawk, gravel, &c., by the action of moist air. Otherwise Cholder and Cholter. (2) A chaldron.

*Chamber. The room over any other room, e. g. the bed-room over the parlour is the parlour *chamber* [W. R.].

Chamble. To chew minutely. Frequentative of Cham, old form of Champ.

Chamblings. Husks of corn, or other very small scraps of what has been gnawed by vermin. Sometimes called Chankings [G. E.].

*Chanks. The same as Chaits [Spur.].

*Char. For chair [Johnson].

*Charhole. The place in the roof of the stack in which stands the harvestman, who takes the corn from the man below him [W. G. W.].

*Chase. A green lane [C. D., C. S. P.].

*Chats or Chatters. Protruding bushes of blackthorn, &c., running into a field from the fence [E. S. T.]. See Chaits. Otherwise Sprawls.

Chatter-pie. A magpie.

*Chatty. Well or neatly finished, natty [M. C. H. B.]

*Cheary. Careful, sparing [Marshall]. Chary? [W. R.]

Check. (1) To taunt, to reproach. Ex. ' He *checked* him

with the favours he had done him.' (2) Shutters are *checked* when put half to for mourning [W. R.].

*Cheese. One meal cheese = cheese made from one milking [M. C. H. B.].

*Cheese Braid. A dairy utensil, into which the curd is put and pressed [Johnson]. See Bred.

*Chest. An oak coffin [E. T. Booth, M. C. H. B.].

Chick. (1) A flaw, as in earthenware. (2) To begin to germinate; as seeds in the earth, leaves from their buds, or barley on the couch in the malt-house. (3) To crack, chap, chop; as the skin in frosty weather.

Chicken's Meat. (1) The herb chickweed, *Alsine media*, Lin. (2) Also dross corn, only fit to feed fowls.

Child-age. Childhood. Intended as a term of contradistinction to old age.

*Children's Shoes, to make. To suffer oneself to be made sport of [E. S. T.]. See Little Shoes.

Chine. The part of a cask into which the head is fixed.

Chine-hoop. The extreme hoop which keeps the end of the staves together, and is commonly of iron.

Chingle. (1) Loose gravel, shingle. (2) Lump sugar [W. R.].

Chink. (1) To cause a sprain on the back or loins, seeming to imply a slight separation of the vertebrae. Ex. 'The fall *chinked* his back.' (2) To cut into minute pieces.

Chipper. To chirp.

*Chirm. The noise of birds, children, and sometimes of women [Spur.].

*Chist. Chest [*N. and Q.*].

*Chites. The bottoms of turnips, the tops of which have been eaten by sheep [Johnson]. See Chaits.

*Chitlings. The small gut of pigs [C. H. B.].

*Chittled.   Sprouted, vegetated [Johnson].

Chitty, Chitty-faced.   Baby-faced.

Chizzly.   Harsh and dry under the teeth.

Chobbins.   Unripened grains, not coming out of the husks under the flail, but beaten off by it, quasi Choppings.

Chobby.   Abounding in chobbins.

Chomp.   To chew loudly and greedily, to champ.

*Chop.   Half a sweath [Spur].

Chop-loggerhead.   An intense blockhead. One who has a head to all appearance thick and stout enough to bear a blow of a hatchet.

Chout.   A jolly frolic ; a rustic merry-making.

Chovee, Chovy.   A small beetle.

*Chow.   To chew [E. S. T.].

Christian.   A man as distinguished from a brute beast.

*Christmas.   Technical term for holly.

Chubby.   Surly.

*Chubbock.   A thick, short lump of wood, fit only for the fire [Johnson].

*Chuck.   (1) Food or provision for an entertainment [*Hotten's Slang Dictionary*]. (2) A term of endearment for girls [E. S. T.]. (3) To throw or jerk [M. C. H. B.].

*Chuckle.   To submit, cringe, play the sycophant [Johnson].

Chuffy.   Fat and fleshy, particularly in the cheeks.

Chump.   (1) A small thick log of wood [Forby]. (2) The thick end of a tree [E. S. T.]. (3) Wooden. Ex. 'Don't be a *chump*.' (4) Head. Ex. 'He is going off his *chump*.'

Church Clerk.   The parish clerk. Long in use.

*Churched.   Returned thanks in church [M. C. H. B.].

*Church Hole.   A grave [*B. N.* 83].

Churching. The Church Service. To one of the offices in particular this name is given in the Book of Common Prayer. But we say in general, 'We have *churching* twice on a Sunday.'

Churchman. An officiating minister. He is a good, bad, or indifferent *churchman*, as he acquits himself in the desk or pulpit.

*****Churn Milk.** Milk that has been churned [Spur.].

*****Cinder Pit.** The ash pit [G. E.].

*****Cla, Cley.** The claw of a bird, crab, or lobster [Spur.]. See **Cleas.**

*****Clack.** To clatter [E. S. T.].

*****Claggings.** Refuse wool shorn from the breech of the sheep [Johnson].

Claggy. Clogged with moisture, as roads and footpaths are after moderate rain [Br.].

Clag-locks. Locks of wool matted or clogged together by the natural moisture of the animal, or wet and dirt.

Clam. (1) Clamminess. Ex. 'The meat has been kept too long, and has got a *clam*,' begins to decay. (2) A slut, so excessively dirty that her skin looks *clammy*. (3) To stick together by some viscid matter. (4) To emaciate, to starve with hunger ; the juices of the body being supposed to be thickened and gradually dried up. Cf. the north country 'clemmed.'

*****Clammed, or Clemmed.** To kill or 'do for' [West Rudham, May 27, 1887, M. C. H. B.].

Clamp. (1) An extempore brick-kiln, in which bricks are burned when there is not earth enough near the spot to answer the expense of erecting a regular kiln. Also used for burning lime for manure [Spur.]. (2) A mound of earth lined with straw to keep potatoes or mangold wurzel through the winter. Now called a pie [Spur.].

Clamper. To make a noisy trampling in walking, as men do whose shoe soles are guarded with iron, women in iron pattens, &c.

*Clams. Wooden pliers or nippers by which the harness-maker holds leathers while he sews them [Johnson].

*Clapgate. A small swing gate between two posts [G. E.].

*Clapping-post. The post on which the gate shuts or closes. The other is the hanging-post [E. S. T.].

Clart. To daub with syrup, juice of fruit, or the like.

Clarty. Daubed with syrup, &c., sticking to the fingers.

*Clates. Pieces of iron in the shape of the heel and toe of the shoe, fastened to these parts to make the shoes more durable [Johnson].

*Clating. To choose sides by measuring with the feet. Cf. 'cleated shoes.' See Clepe, Clip, and Cleat.

Claumb, Clomb. To clamber in a heavy and awkward manner. Intens. of *climb*.

Claunch. To walk in a lounging manner, as if the feet were dragged along in the dirt, to save the trouble of lifting them up. Ex. 'Yinder go Black Betty, *claunching* along in her creepers.' Also used for to catch hold [Spur.].

*Claver, Clever. Generally used as inferring goodness of heart or benevolence. Also pretty or neat; as 'a *claver* mauther,' a pretty or neat girl (Acle, Norf.) [W. W. S.].

*Claw, or Clay. To claw hold on anything = to take hold of it with one's hands, generally, roughly or suddenly [M. C. H. B].

*Clay Lump. Bricks of sun-dried clay. Vide Dauber [H. B.].

Clay-salve. Common cerate; from its colour.

Clead. To clothe. Cf. Du. *kleed*, clothing.

Cleading. Clothing [O. E.].

Cleas, Cleyes. Claws; as of a lobster or crab. Ex. 'Crack the *cleas* in the hinge of the door.' See **Cla.**

Cleat. To strengthen with thin plates of metal. Shoe-heels are often *cleated* with iron; and kitchen utensils worn thin, with copper. See **Clates.**

*Cleat. Pleat, in nautical phraseology [M. C. H. B.].

Clepe. To call. The word is used by our boys at play, who *clepe* (or, as they commonly pronounce it, *clip*) sides, or opposite parties at ball, &c. [A. S.]. See **Clip.**

*Clevers, or Cluvers. Tussocks or tufts of coarse grass, or roots of rushes with earth adhering to them, turned up by the plough [E. S. T.].

*Click, or Clock. A blow [E. S. T.].

Clicket. To chatter. Dim. of *clack* [T.].

Clicket. Voluble.

*Clift. A cliff [E. S. T.].

Clim. A sort of imp which inhabits the chimneys of nurseries, and is sometimes called down to take away naughty children.

Climp. (1) To touch a polished surface with dirty or greasy fingers, and leave marks upon it. (2) It is a sort of cant term for steal.

Clink. A smart slap.

Clinks. Long nails used for fixing irons on gates, &c., where they are wanted to take strong hold.

Clinkers. Bricks of a smaller size than usual, burned very hard, and set up on edge to pave stables, or other places where there is trampling of heavy cattle.

*Clip. (1) To choose sides [E. S. T.]. (2) To embrace [E. S. T.] (3) A blow [B. N. 5]. (Common all over England, W. R.) See **Clepe.**

*Clitchy. Clammy, gummy, &c.

Cliver. (1) A chopping-knife. (2) Goose-grass (*Galium aparine*) [M. C. H. B.].

Clod. To clothe.

Clodding. Clothing. A pauper solicits *clodding* for her children; the overseer tells her they were *clodden* but a little while ago.

Clodger. The cover of a book. See Clozzier.

Clogsome. Dull, heavy, tiresome.

Clog-wheat. A bearded species.

*Clomed. Caught. 'He *clomed* hold of me' [Johnson]. Also, climbed.

*Close. Dusky, a close evening, day closes in [M. C. H. B.].

*Closen. Enclosed fields; plural of close [Spur.].

*Closes. Fields with footpaths through them [B. N. 26, ? W. R.].

Clotch. To tread heavily, and move awkwardly.

*Clote. Colt'sfoot [Marshall].

Clough. (1) A ravine between two precipitous banks, having a run of water at its bottom; Forby only cites one case at Lynn. (2) A sluice with one door, drawn up like a portcullis; a Stanch has a pair of doors; a Lock, two pairs of doors [E. S. T.].

Clow. , (1) The clove pink. Fr. *clou de girofle*. (2) A slice of bread, cheese, &c. [E. S. T.].

*Clozzier. The binding or covering of a book [Johnson]. See Clodger.

*Club. To jump, keeping both feet together [Johnson].

Clue. Three skeins of hempen thread.

Clunch. Close-grained hard limestone, fit to be used in building, but soft when first taken from the quarry.

Clunchy. Short, thick, and clumsy.

Clung. (1) Tough, juiceless; land hard to work [Forby]. (2) Rather shrunk, shrivelled, or collapsed [E. S. T.].

*Clutch. A brood of chickens or ducks [M. C. H. B.].

Clutter. (1) Confusion, disorder. (2) To make a noise or hurly-burly by talking [E. S. T.].

*Co! Exclamation; abbreviation of come. 'Co! bor' [H. B.]

*Coach. A four-wheeled perambulator [M. C. H. B.].

Coal-hod. An utensil of metal or wood, to hold the coals to be thrown on the fire; otherwise called the Coal-scuttle, -shoot, or -shoe.

Coal-shoot. A coal-scuttle [H. B.].

Coarse. Opposed to fine, as applied to weather. 'It is a *coarse* morning.'

*Coat. A petticoat [C. S. P.].

Cob. (1) A sea-gull. (2) The stony kernel of fruit. (3) In Suffolk, a basket for seed corn, the same as the seed-leap or seedlip [E. S. T.]. (4) Husk or chaff [Johnson]. (5) Loam or clay [*Id.*]. (6) The boast, pride, or crack [*Id.*]. 'He was the *cob* of all this county for fishing.' (7) A pile of herring. (8) A roe herring.

*Cob-baker. Anything unusually large [Johnson].

Cobble. (1) The round stones with which most country towns are paved. (2) The stone of fruit. (3) Any small, hard, pebbly substance. Also the small lumps of earth raked off garden beds [Spur.]. (4) A fishing-boat; formerly *coble*, as in Johnson's Dict.; Welsh *ceubal*, a ferry-boat, a skiff.

*Cob-boy. One who is between boy and man [W. B.].

Cob Irons. (1) The andirons on which wood is burned on the hearth. (2) The irons hung upon the bars of the kitchen range on which the spit is supported.

*Cob Loaf. The outside loaf of a batch [Johnson].

Cock-brumble. The hawk's-bill bramble, as it is otherwise called, from its curved spines. *Rubus fructicosus*, Lin.

*Cocker. To fondle, to indulge [Johnson].

*Cockerell. A young cock of the first year [J. W. G.].

*Cockey. A sewer; London Street, Norwich, was originally called Cockey Lane [W. R.]. The trap leading to a drain [A. E. R.].

Cock Farthing. A term of endearment used to a little boy.

Cock's Egg. An abortive egg, without a yolk.

*Cock's Heads. Plantain, ribwort, or ribgrass [Marshall].

*Cockshot. A passage cut through a wood for woodcocks to fly through, in which a net was placed to catch them. In an old Act of Parliament it was Latinized 'volatile woodcoccorum.'

*Cockshut Time. The time of fowls going to rest [Johnson].

*Cod. The pocket of a net.

*Coding Comber. A woolcomber who went his rounds on foot [Johnson].

Coffer. A chest to keep clothes in.

Cofin. (1) A coffin. (2) A basket which preceded the use of coffins [Spur].

*Coil. A company. Ex. 'A coil of teal' [M. C. H. B.].

*Coiled up. Curled up. Of ferrets, cats, or dogs [M. C. H. B.].

*Coipy. Haughty, assuming airs of consequence, coupled, of course, with ignorance [Johnson].

Coit. To toss up the head. Of a proud and affected minx it is said she '*coits* up her head above her betters.'

*Cokered. Unsound, as applied to timber [Cull. Haw.].

Cold-chill. A ridiculous pleonasm, meaning an ague fit, on the first access of a fever.

Colder. Broken ears of corn mixed with short fragments of straw, beaten off by the flail. Rubbish; as 'Colder (sometimes cholder) may be shot here.' See Cavon.

*Colderskep. A large basket for chaff, &c. [G. E.].

*Cole. Money [Johnson]. Also used in London slang [W. W. S.].

*Coll, or Call. A brood of wild ducks [Johnson]. See Coil.

Collar. To sully with soot or coal-dust.

Collar, Collar-coal. Black smut from the chimney or bars. We distinctly pronounce it thus. Sed vide Colly. Shakespeare has *collied*, i. e. black, *Mid. Nt. Dr.* i. 1. 145. *Collie dog* was formerly *coaley dog*: it is a Gallic word. Gallic *cuilean*, a puppy.

Collar Ball. A light ball with which children play.

Collar Beam. The highest and shortest beam in a building, which is thought perhaps to hold together and secure the roof, as the garments are held by the *collar*. Also Wind Beam, q.v.

Collogue. To confer together for some mischievous purpose.

*Colly-ball, Colly-coal. The collar-ball and collar-coal of Forby are better pronounced thus [Spur.].

*Colly-coal. A sort of charcoal [Johnson].

*Column of wild duck. A string or skein of them [W. R.].

*Comb. 'Comb your hair,' viz. 'put you to rights, set you straight.' 'Mob,' or even to 'pay' [M. C. H. B.].

Come. Intruded into several phrases, awkwardly and vulgarly perhaps, but not without meaning. Ex. 'To-morrow - come - se'nnight.' 'Tuesday - come - fortnight.' Meaning, no doubt, when to-morrow se'nnight, or Tuesday fortnight shall come; or, let them come, and then the thing will happen. A more facetious phrase is, 'to-morrow-come-never,' i. e. Ad Graecas calendas. To this may also be referred Miscomfortune and Misconhap; words very injuriously reputed corruptions. Come hardy, Come hether, Cope harby, or Cope a holt—horse language for come to the left. See Weesh away for the right [E. M.].

*Come-along. Suff. and N. Essex. ' I fetched him a come-along,' i. e. gave him a good knock-down blow [W. B.].

Come-back. A guinea-fowl. Its harsh cry is supposed to resemble the pronunciation of those two words.

*Comepted. Facetious [C. S. P.].

*Comforter. A thick neck-wrap [M. C. H. B.].

Compass. An outline ; as of carpenters' work, of laying out ground, &c., with a sweep, approaching to a circular form. A bow-window was anciently called a *compass-window*. Shakes. *Troilus and Cressida*.

Compassing. In a roundish or circular form.

*Compo'. Composition, cement [M. C. H. B.].

*Conceit. Fancy [M. C. H. B.].

*Coney-chuck. The wheat-ear [J. H. G.].

*Conge. A road or way [*N. and Q*, 2nd Ser. x. pp. 67–137].

*Conkers. Shells of the small variegated snail [W. B.].

*Conquer. A chrysalis, like a snail [G. E.].

Contain. For detain [E. M.].

Cookeel. A sort of cross-bun, made and eaten in Norfolk during Lent. They are sold cheap, and may be from Fr. Coquille. The last remnant with us of the Romish Carnival [Spur.]. Sugar'd loaves stained yellow [Arderon]. A sort of simnel or cross-bun, made and eaten during Lent. Query, similar to Kichel in Chaucer [Johnson]. Certainly not [W. W. S.].

*Coomb. Four bushels or half a quarter [M. C. H. B.].

Cooms. The high ridges in ill-kept roads, between the ruts and the horse-path [Forby]. Cullum says the ridge which is raised between the horse-path and the rut. Literally, *combs*.

*Coop. To muzzle ferrets [H. B.].

Cop. To throw something upwards, in order to reach a mark at some moderate distance ; also to throw right away [Spur.]. To throw underhand [Johnson]. To toss lightly, in Cambridgeshire [W. W. S.].

Cope. (1) A large quantity or great number [Forby]. (2) To exchange or chop [Ray]. (3) To fasten up or muzzle the mouths of ferrets [W. R.].

*Copper Jack, or Copper-hole Jack. A scullion [M. C. H. B.].

Copper Rose. The wild red poppy.

Copple-crown. A tuft of feathers on the head of a fowl, not such as can be depressed at pleasure, like the crests of many birds, but permanently erect. It is sometimes called a Topple-crown, which is strictly synonymous. Cop means a Top.

Coppling. Unsteady, in danger of falling. Ex. 'It stands coppling,' i. e. toppling, unsteady. Copply [M. C. H. B.].

Cop-web. A cob-web. The old form.

*Cord. A triplet of faggots [M. C. H. B.].

Corder. For Colder or Cholder, q. v.

Corf. (1) A floating cage or basket to keep lobsters. See Cauf. Used on the Suffolk coast [Forby]. (2) To untwist a rope or line from its kinks [E. F. G.].

Corn. A particle, a very minute portion, as it were a grain. We also apply it to salt, and to many other things.

Corny. (1) Abounding in corn. Ex. 'These sheaves are heavy and corny.' (2) Tasting well of malt. Ex. 'The ale is corny.' (3) Tipsy.

*Corroborate. To match. Ex. 'You don't call those a pair, do you? Why now, bor, I don't think they do fare to corroborate.' [M. C. H. B.].

Cosh. (1) The glume of corn, particularly wheat. 'White wheat in a red cosh,' is a favourite variety [Forby]. (2) A husk of wheat containing grain [Johnson]. (3) A stick. 'Let us cut a cosh.'

*Coshie. A small sweetmeat [W. R.].

Cosset. (1) To fondle. (2) A pet, something fondly caressed.

Cosset-lamb. Cade or tame lamb [Arderon]. A lamb reared without the ewe. Cot-lamb, a Cade-lamb [Johnson].

Cost or **Coast.** The ribs of cooked meat, particularly roast lamb. ' Do you choose *shoulder* or *coast* ? '[E. S. T.].

Costly. Costive. Frugal.

Cot. (1) A case for a wounded finger [Spur.]; a finger-stall. (2) The open part of a spade or shovel, into which the hand goes [Johnson]. (3) A lamb brought up by hand [Marshall].

Cothe. To faint.

Cothish, Cothy. (1) Faint, sickly, ailing. (2) Morose [Kennett's *MS. Glossary, Lansdowne MS.* 1033]. This is the meaning also given by Sir Thomas Browne.

Cotterlin. *Vide* Cossett.

Cotterling. Tame, docile, gentle [Johnson].

Cotterly. A tame docile animal is said to be cotterly [Spur.].

Couch, Couch-handed. Left-handed.

Count. To guess, to suppose, to opine. Ex. ' I *count* you farm three hundred acres.' Similar to the Yankee, ' I reckon ' [W. R.].

Counter. The cutting knife of a plough [G. E.]

Couples or **Couplings.** A passage left through a fence, so that a man may pass, but not a cow, horse, ass, or large beast; also a Turn-stile [Spur.].

Cousin. (1) Nephew or niece [O. E.]. (2) Hardly to know the queen's cousin = to be haughty [M. C. H. B.].

Cousin Betty, Cousin Tom. A bedlamite, or rather an impudent vagrant pretending to be such; who used to enter the sitting-room of a family, having first ascertained that there was nobody in it but women and children, with whom he or she claimed kindred. *Vide* **Bess o' Bedlam.**

*Covey. Lifeless, listless [M. C. H. B.]. See Cothey.

*Cow. (1) Cowl of a chimney [C. D.]. (2) A turned or faced quoit [M. C. H. B.].

*Cowgrass, or Cocksfoot. (*Dactylis glomerata*) [M. C. H. B.].

*Cowl. (1) The top of a malt-kiln. (2) Also a cask with one end out, carried by a pole on the shoulders of two men, for the conveyance of water [Spur.]. (3) A tub [Ray.]. (4) A cart [F. J. B.].

Cowlick. A twist or wreathing in the hair of the forehead, which, in a calf, might be supposed to have been licked by the cow out of its natural position.

Cow-mumble. A wild plant, more commonly called Cow Parsnip.

Cowslop. A cowslip. The old form.

Cow-tongued. Having a tongue smooth one way and rough the other, like that of a cow. Expressively applied to one who gives fair or foul language, as may best suit his purpose.

Coy. (1) A decoy for ducks. (2) A coop for lobsters.

Coy-duck. A duck trained to entice others into the tunnel in a decoy.

Coxy-roxy. Merrily and fantastically tipsy.

Cra. A crow.

Crab Grass. The common sandwort [W. G. W.].

Crab-harrow. A large heavy harrow used on strong adhesive soils [Johnson].

Crab-lanthorn. A sort of pastry.

*Crabs, Cromer crabs. Two hundred go to one hundred at wholesale price [M. C. H. B.].

Crack, Crake. To brag.

Crack. (1) Something to boast of. Ex. 'She is the *crack* of the village.' (2) A very short time. Ex. 'It was done in a *crack*.'

Crag. The craw. Ex. 'He has stuffed his *crag* well.'

Crag. A deposit of fossil sea shells (?). The Norfolk crag consists of incoherent sand, loam, and gravel, and contains a mixture of marine, land, and fresh-water shells, accumulated at the bottom of the sea, near the mouth of a river. Tate's *Hist. Geology* (1875), p. 215 [C. D.].

*Cramp-bone. The patella of a sheep or lamb, carried about as near the skin as possible as a charm against cramp [E. S. T.].

*Cramp-rings. Rings made of sixpences subscribed for (unasked) for a person afflicted by fits, by nine young men [E. S. T.].

Crample. To move with pain and stiffness, as if affected by cramps.

Crample-hamm'd. Stiffened in the lower joints.

*Cratch. An old Suffolk word for a manger [E. S. T.].

*Craunchlings. Small apples of any kind having an uneven surface [Johnson]. See **Crinchlings** and **Crumplings**.

Crawly-mawly. In a weakly and ailing state.

*Craw-water, Water-craw. The water-ouzel (*Cinclus aquaticus*), water-crow. Craw = crawl [M. C. H. B.].

Creepers. (1) Low pattens mounted on short iron stumps, instead of rings. (2) Grapnels to bring up anything from the bottom of a well, pond, or river. Used to recover dead bodies.

*Creeple. To squeeze.

Crevet. A cruet.

*Crewel. A fine sort of worsted work [E. S. T.].

*Crib. A manger [M. C. H. B.].

Crible. A finer sort of bran. When the broad bran has been separated from the meal, a second sifting through a finer sieve brings off *crible*.

*Crick. The teal (*Querquedula crecca*), probably from their note [J. H. G.].

Crickle, Cruckle. To bend under a weight, to sink down through pain or weakness.

*Crid. Crowded, carted, or pushed (of a wheelbarrow) [M. C. H. B.].

Crimble. To creep about privily, to sneak, to wind along unperceived.

Crinch. To crush with the teeth some harsh and brittle substance, as unripe fruit. In Suffolk more frequently pronounced CRANCH.

Crinchling, Chringlings. A small apple. See **Craunchlings.**

*Cringe, Curl. All cringed up, all crinkled or curled up [M. C. H. B.].

*Cringle. A withe or rope for fastening up a gate [Marshall].

Crinkle, Crunkle. To wrinkle, twist, plait, or rumple irregularly.

Crish, Crush. Cartilage, or soft bones of young animals, easily crushed by the teeth.

Crock. (1) Smut, dust of soot or coal. (2) In Suffolk, the bricks or plate of a fire back, called in Norfolk the back-stock [E. S. T.].

*Crod. Occurs in the *Paston Letters* [M. C. H. B.].

*Crolter, or **Krolter.** The front board of a wagon or tumbrel [M. C. H. Bird.]

Crome, or **Croom.** A crook ; a staff with a hook at the end of it, to pull down the boughs of a tree, to draw weeds out of ditches, and for a variety of other useful purposes. [We have muck-*crooms*, fire-*crooms*, and mud-*crooms* — Spur.]

Croodle. To lie close and snug, as pigs or puppies in their straw [Forby], as chickens do under the hen. Also sometimes of various liquors, which are said to be ' very pretty *croodle* ' [Johnson].

Crop. (1) Annual produce, as well animal as vegetable. We talk of *crops* of lambs, turkeys, geese, &c. (2) The craw of birds, metaphorically applied to other animals. (3) A joint of pork, commonly called the spare-rib.

Crope. To creep slowly and heavily.

*Cropfull. (1) Vexed, sorrowful [Spur.]. *Sed quaere.* (2) Satisfied [M. C. H. B.].

Crotch. (1) The meeting of two arms of a tree ; or of an arm with the trunk ; or of the limbs of the human body, below the waist. (2) A staff under the arm to support the lame ; a crutch.

*Crotch-boots. Water-boots that come up to one's crotch [M. C. H. B.].

Crotched. Cross, peevish, perverse. Perhaps for crouched, q. d. crossed

Crotch-room. Length of the lower limbs. It is said of one who has long legs that he has plenty of *crotch-room.*

Crotch-trolling. A method of trolling or angling for pike, used in the broads and rivers in Norfolk. The fisherman has no rod, but has the usual reel, and, by the help of a *crotch-stick*, i.e. forked stick, throws his bait to a considerable distance from him into the water, and then draws it gently towards him. It is much practised by poachers, as there is no rod, or ' pole,' to betray their intention.

Crouse. To caterwaul. A cat is said to *crouse* when she is ' maris appetens ' [Johnson].

Crowd. (1) With us, one individual can crowd another. No doubt the origin of the American word. (2) To drive or wheel a handbarrow [E. S. T. and Marshall]. This occurs in the *Paston Letters*, Dec. 18, 1477. In Suffolk a wheelbarrow is a crowding-barrow. See Crud.

Crow-keeper. A boy employed to scare crows from new-sown land.

*Cruckle. (1) To sink down through faintness or exhaustion [Spur.]. (2) To bend or nearly break [G. E.].

Crud-barrow, Crudden-barrow. A common wheelbarrow, to be shoved forward. In *P. L.* we find the phrase crowding a barrow; *crud* is the part. See Crowd.

Crumbles. Crumbs, dimin.

*Crummy. Short and fat.

Crump. To eat anything brittle or crimp.

Crump, Crumpy. Brittle; dry baked; easily breaking under the teeth.

Crumplin. (1) A diminutive and misshapen apple. (2) Met. a diminutive and deformed person. See Craunchling.

Crunkle. To rumple.

*Cruse. A pitcher [C. S. P.].

Crush, Crustle. Gristle.

Cuckoo-ball. A light ball made of parti-coloured rags, for young children.

Cuckoo-flower. *Orchis mascula*.

*Cuckoo-pint. (*Arum maculatum*) [M. C. H. B.].

*Cuckoo's mate. The wryneck, which comes with the *cuckoo* [Tungate].

Cuff. A lie, or rather a hoax or deceit; ' don't *cuff* us,' i.e. don't try to take us in [Johnson].

Culch. Thick dregs or sediment.

*Culls. Refuse cattle [W. G. W.].

Culp. A hard and heavy blow.

Culpit. A large lump of anything. This should rather be Culpin, a large thick slice. Culpon occurs in Pulham

Town Accounts, 1570, and Chaucer has the same word [Johnson].

Culver. To beat and throb in the flesh. As a sore advances towards suppuration it ' bulks and *culvers.*' In Suffolk it is pronounced gelver.

Culver-headed. Soft-headed, harmless.

Cumbled, or Cumbly-cold. Oppressed, cramped, stiffened with cold. ' *Accomeled* for coulde' [Pr. Pa.].

*Cums. When the wetted and sprouting barley has been malted, by screening the small sprouts are knocked off, and they bear this name among maltsters.

Cupboard-head. A most expressive designation of a head both wooden and hollow.

*Cupboard-love. Arising from stomach rather than heart (cook and policeman) [C. H. B.].

*Cur, Cuth. Quoth. Ex. ' Cur Bob, you are a liar' [M. C. H. B.].

*Curb. A fire-guard [M. C. H. B.].

*Currel. A rill or drain. A diminutive run of water. Drindle is nearly the same, and is also the bed of such, a *currel* or small furrow [E. S. T.].

*Currie. The long narrow Yarmouth cart, adapted to go up the rows [Johnson]. They are said to have been invented in the reign of Henry VIII, and called Harry carriers. But for years they have been called Trollies.

Cushion-man. The chairman at the Quarter Sessions, or at any other public meeting, where there is the same distinguishing mark of presidency.

*Cussy. A rap on the head [*B. N.* 85]. See Custard.

Custard. The schoolmaster's ferula, or a slap on the flat hand with it.

Cute. Shrewd, quick in apprehension. The origin, no doubt, of the American word.

*Cuts. To draw, to draw lots. The *cut* is the shortest straw, or that which has been cut short [E. S. T.].

*Cuttering. Confused hasty talking, in rather a hasty whisper [Johnson].

*Cutting goods. Drapery is so called in village shops [Johnson].

*Cutting-out. First time of turnip-hoeing. Thinning out the young plants with the hoe [M. C. H. B.].

*Cyprus cat. Tabby cat [C. S. P.].

*Dab chick. Didapper, Dive-an-dop, Divy duck ; the little grebe [J. H. G.].

Dabs. Dibbles, instruments for dibbling (pron. Debs), knucklestones.

Daddle. To walk unsteadily, as a child.

*Daffadowndilly. The common daffodil [M. C. H. B.].

*Daft. Cracked, crazy [M. C. H. B. and *B. N.* 84].

Dafter. A daughter.

Dag. Dew.

Dag of rain. A slight misty shower.

*Daibles. Scrapes, convictions, notions, dibles [M. C. H. B.].

*Dakeshead. A spiritless, moping, stupid fellow [Johnson].

*Dale. Devil; e. g. 'Dale me if I don't,' Devil take me if I don't [M. C. H. B.].

Dallop, or Dollop. (1) A patch of ground among growing corn where the plough has missed [T.]. (2) Rank tufts of growing corn where heaps of manure have lain. (3) A parcel of smuggled tea, varying in quantity from six to sixteen pounds, and perhaps more or less. (4) A slattern, synonymous with Trollop. (5) A clumsy and shapeless lump of anything tumbled about in the hands. (6) To paw, toss, and tumble about carelessly.

Dame. Once an honourable designation of females of high rank ; now applied only to those of the lowest. It is almost obsolete even there.

*__Dams.__ Drained marshes [*B. N.* 77 (? W. R.)].

*__Dander.__ Temper. 'He ha' got his dander up' [M. C. H. B.].

*__Dandy.__ A conical-shaped contrivance for warming beer [Johnson].

*__Dandying,__ or __Danning.__ Plastering a wall or studwork [Johnson].

Dangerous. Endangered. Ex. 'Mr. Smith is sadly badly ; quite *dangerous.*' .

*__Danish Crow, Norway Crow.__ The hooded crow [J. H. G.].

*__Danks.__ Tea-leaves [*B. N.* 54].

*__Dannies.__ Hands [E. M.] ; but query an error for *dannocks.*

*__Dannock.__ A small loaf of bread. A piece of dough left over not large enough for a loaf, put into the oven and eaten hot [W. B.].

*__Dapter.__ One who is clever at anything (pronunciation DAPSTER). See *Hotten's Slang Dict.* [W. B.].

*__Dar,__ or __Daw.__ The tern (*Sterna*), blue daw, black tern (*Hydro chelidon nigra*), in immature plumage, the adult being black dar [M. C. H. B.].

*__Dare.__ To dare one's eyes = to try one's eyes [M. C. H. B.].

Dark Hour. The evening twilight. The interval between the time of sufficient light to work or read by and the lighting of candles ; a time of social domestic chat. Ex. 'We will talk over that at the *dark hour.*'

Darnocks, Dannocks. Hedger's gloves ; that for the left hand being made whole to grasp the thorns, and for the right, with fingers to handle the hedging-bill. __Darnic__ [Johnson].

*__Dart.__ An eel-spear [M. C. H. B.].

Dash. To abash.

Dauber. A builder of walls with clay or mud, mixed with stubble or short straw, well beaten and incorporated, and so becoming pretty durable. The mixture is used, particularly in Suffolk, to make fences for farmyards, &c., and even walls for mean cottages.

*__Dauling.__ 'The markets are very *dauling* to-day'; no spirit in purchasing [Johnson]. Dawdling? [W. R.].

Daunt. To stun, to knock down.

Dauzy, Dauzy-headed. Dizzy; either literally or metaphorically, as if confused, bewildered. [Now Duzzy, W.R.]

*__Davying.__ Marl is got up the cliff by a winch, which is called *davying* it up [Marshall].

*__Dawds.__ Rags [Johnson]. Duds? [W. R.].

*__Dawzle,__ or **Dorsle.** To stun. S. Suff. and N. Essex [W. B.].

*__Daxt.__ Confused, nonplussed [Johnson].

*__Dead, to.__ To whip him to *dead,* to whip him to DEATH [W. R.].

*__Deadman.__ A piece of timber buried in the earth to secure posts, &c. [Spur].

*__Deadman's Day.__ St. Edmund's day, Nov. 20 [Spur.].

Deal Apples. The conical fruit of the fir-tree.

Deal Tree. A fir-tree.

Deathsmear. A disease fatal to children.

*__Debbles.__ Tools to make holes for grain [G. E.].

Dee. A die or dice.

Deen. See **Dene** or **Din.**

Deke, Dike. A ditch. Properly a ditch, but sometimes used for the bank of earth thrown out of the ditch. . **Deeke** is very often used for the ditch and bank together, but a fen **deeke** has in general no bank [Spur.].

Deke-holl, Dike-holl. A hollow or dry ditch. Not necessarily a dry ditch [Spur].

Delf. A deep ditch or drain.

Delk. A small cavity, in the soil, in the flesh of the body,
or in any surface which ought to be quite level.

*****Delph**-holes. Deep holes in the broads, over springy
ground. *E. D. Press*, Feb. 2, 1891 [M. C. H. B.].

Dene. (1) Din. (2) Slightest noise. Ex. 'I don't hear
a *dene*' [M. C. H. B.].

*****Dent.** The worst of anything, the pinch [M. C. H. B.].

Dere. Dire, sad [Sir Thomas Browne].

Derely. (1) (Really) direly, lamentably, extremely. Ex.
'I am *derely* ill'; '*derely* tired,' &c. (2) Thoroughly,
dearly [M. C. H. B.].

*****Destitute.** This curious expression was used quite recently
in advertisements, when a man was leaving a farm and
had no other to go into. 'Mr. A. B., who is destitute of
a farm, will sell,' &c. [W. R.].

Deusan. A hard-sort of apple which keeps a long time,
but turns pale and shrivels. Hence the simile, 'pale as
a *deusan.*'

Deve. To dive.

Devilin. The swift (*Hirundo apus*).

Deving Pond. A pond from which water is drawn for
domestic use, by dipping a pail.

Dew Drink. The first allowance of beer to harvest men
before they begin their day's work.

*****Dibbler, Dib,** or **Deb.** An (iron) tool for dibbling wheat,
beans, &c. [M. C. H. B.].

Dibles. Difficulties, embarrassments, scrapes.

*****Dick.** (1) Very poor Suffolk cheese [Johnson]. (2) A
ditch (deke) [Marshall].

Dick-a-dilver. The herb periwinkle.

Dicky. An ass, male or female.

Dicky Ass. A male ass; the female being usually called a Jenny ass or a Betty ass.

***Didall.** A triangular spade, very sharp, used for cutting roots of sedges or rushes [Johnson]. The Rev. J. Gunn says a small net for cleaning the bottom of ditches. To clean out rivers and dykes [W. R.]. See **Didle**.

***Didapper.** (1) A kind of water-fowl; applied to a Baptist [Spur]. (2) Dabchick, dob-chicken (*Podiceps minor*) [M. C. H. B.].

Didder. (1) To have a quivering of the chin through cold [Forby]. (2) To tremble or shake generally, as 'a bog *didders*' [Johnson].

Diddle. To waste time in the merest trifling. An extreme dimin. of *dawdle*.

Diddles, Diddlings. Young ducks, or sucking-pigs.

Didle. (1) To clean the bottom of a river with a scoop or dredge. (2) Also an expression used in marble-playing, to denote inanimate movement, supposed to give some unfair advantage [C. H. E. W.].

***Dier.** One likely to die. Ex. 'He don't look like a *dier*' [M. C. H. B.].

Dills. The paps of a sow.

Dilver. To weary with labour or exercise; from *delving*?

***Dindle.** (1) The plant dandelion [Spur]. Sow-thistles, hawk-weeds [Marshall]. (2) To dawdle over [M. C. H. B.].

Ding. (1) To throw with a quick and hasty motion. Ex. 'I *dung* it at him.' (2) To beat or knock repeatedly. Ex. 'I could not *ding* it into him' [R. S., E. C.] (3) To fell or knock down [E. S. T. and Johnson]. (4) A smart slap; particularly with the back of the hand.

Dinge. · (1) To rain mistily, to drizzle. (2) Dark colour or hue. 'He has got a *dinge*,' a blot on his character.

*Dingey.   Dull, faded [M. C. H. B.].

*Dingling about.   (1) Hanging or swinging about [W. R.].
(2) To loiter about, hesitate, &c.   'He is *dingling* away
his time after that young woman' [Johnson].

Dip.   A sauce for dumplings, composed of melted butter,
vinegar, and brown sugar.

*Dip-ears.   The common Tern [J. H. G.].

Dirt Weed.   *Chenopodium viride,* Lin.

*Disannul.   To disturb or do away with.   Ex. 'Pray now,
don't *disannul* the primrose roots' [C. S. P.].

Discomfrontle.   Seems to be a compound of **Discomfit** and
Affront in sense as well as in sound.

*Dishabille.   In working dress [C. S. P.].

*Dish Ladle.   A tadpole, from its shape [Spur.].

*Disimprove.   To get worse, not to improve [W. R.].

Disoblige.   To stain or sully.

Do.   'To do for.'   (1) To take care of, provide for.   Ex. 'The
children have lost their mother, but their aunt will *do for*
them.'   (2) To kill [M. C. H. B.].

Doated.   Decayed, rotten ; chiefly applied to old trees.

Dobble.   (1) To dawb.   (2) Snow or earth which balls on
the feet [W. B.].

Dock.   The broad nether end of a felled tree, or of the
human body.

Docksy.   A very gentle softening or dimin. of the foregoing in its second acceptation.

*Docky.   The labourer's dinner he carries with him [H. B.].

Doctor.   An apothecary, who is invariably addressed and
mentioned under this title.

Doctor of Skill.   A physician, who never receives his proper
title, but is as invariably styled *Mister*.   It is fruitless
to attempt to explain this commutation.

*Doddie-wren. The common wren (*Troglodytes vulgaris*) [M. C. H. B.].

*Doddles. Pollards [M. C. H. B.].

Doddy. Low in stature, diminutive in person. Probably from the common vulgarism Hoddy-doddy.

Dodge. A small lump of something moist and thick.

Dodman. A snail.

Doer. An agent or manager for another.

Dogs. Andirons on the hearth where wood is the fuel. Carpenters also use *dogs* to support some of their heavy work. Probably formerly made in the form of a dog sitting [Spur.].

*Doke. (1) A dint or impression, an indentation [Johnson]. See Dooke. (2) A dimple [G. E.].

*Doker. A diminutive used with respect to young animals [W. G. W.].

*Dole. A number or quantity [Spur.].

*Dole, or Dool. A boundary stone or mark in an uninclosed field. It is very often a low post; thence called a *dool* post. A subsidiary meaning, as in *turf dole*, which means a place where turf is being cut, and has nothing to do with *dole* allotments to the poor [W. R.]. Marshall says a *dole* is a place off which only one particular person has a right to cut turf.

Dolk, Doke. A larger and deeper Delk, q. v. See Doke and Dooke.

Dollop. See Dallop.

Dollor. To moan [F. J. B.].

*Dolly. A beetle used in bunching hemp [Spur.].

Dome, Doom, or Dum. Down; as of a rabbit, a young fowl, &c.

*Doney, or Downy. A shepherd [Johnson].

*Dooblus. Doubtful, suspicious [Johnson].

*Dooke. The impression of a body in a bed, &c.; the indentation from a blow upon anything soft; the depression in a cushion, pillow, soft earth, &c. [Spur.].

*Door. 'It's up to the door,' or 'up to the knocker' = It's well finished, up to dick [M. C. H. B.].

Door Stall. A door-post. The very Saxon word.

Dop. A short quick curtsy.

Dop-a-low. Very short in stature. Dopperlowly [Johnson].

*Dopler, or Dopper. A thick woollen jersey for outside wear [M. C. H. B.].

Dor. A cockchaffer.

Dore Apple. A firm winter apple of a bright yellow colour.

Dormer. A large beam.

Doss. (1) To attack with the horns, as a bull, a ram, or a he-goat. 'No more ear for music than Farmer Ball's bull, as dossed the fiddler over the bridge' [W. R.]. So it cannot be, as some suppose, the same as Toss; because, though bulls can do so, the other two horned animals cannot. Has it any connexion with Dowse? (2) A hassock to kneel upon at church.

*Dossekin. To drop a curtsy [G. E.].

*Dotts. The roe of a female herring, the male being Milts [*B. N.* 56].

*Double-dweller. Semi-detached houses [M. C. H. B.].

*Double-swath. Marsh grass cut once in two years only [M. C. H. B.].

Dough up. To stick together, as if with paste.

Dow. (1) A dove. (2) To mend, in health. Of a sick man continuing in the same state, it is said that he 'neither dies or *dows.*'

*Dowelled. Dovetailed [M. C. H. B.].

*Dowfulfer. The mistle-thrush [M. C. H. B.].

Dow Fulter [Fulfer? W. R.]. The fieldfare [G. J. C.].

Dowler. A sort of coarse dumpling.

Down bout. A hard set-to; a tough battle.

Down-lying. A lying-in.

Downpins. Those who in a jolly carousal are dead drunk. Metaphor from ninepins. Also a ruined man, see Borrow's *Lavengro.*

Downy. Low-spirited. [*Sed quaere,* W. R.]

*Dow-pollar. Dove-house; pronounced ' duff-huss' [M. C. H. B.].

*Dowshie. A large hoe for scraping roads [*B. N.* 28].

Doxy. An old wife [Spur.].

Drabble. To draggle, to soil.

*Drabbletail. A slattern [Pr. Pa.].

Dragging Time. The evening of the fair day, when the young fellows pull the wenches about.

*Drain. A rivulet or running ditch. Also the channels that run through the Breydon mudflats [M. C. H. B.]

Drains. Grains from the mash-tub, through which the wort has been *drained* off.

Drant. (1) To drawl in speaking or reading; more properly, perhaps, spelled *draunt* (pronounced like aunt). (2) A droning or drawling tone. Ex. ' He reads with a *drant.*'

Draps. Fruit in an orchard dropping before it is fit to be gathered.

*Draw (verb). To picture to oneself [M. C. H. B.].

*Drawed. Drawn. Ex. ' Them ditches was *drawed* last year'; i. e. they had the weeds pulled out of them with a crome [M. C. H. B.].

Drawk. The common darnel-grass.

Drawlatch. A tedious dawdling loiterer. Minshew explains *drawlatchet,* a sort of nightly thief, from his drawing the latchets, or latches, of doors. A sneaking fellow; an eavesdropper [Spur.].

*Drawquarters. To keep alongside of. To be on equal terms with. To give a *quid pro quo* [M. C. H. B.].

*Drawts. (N. Ess.) Draughts (Suff.), or sharves, the shafts of a wagon.

*Draw water. The goldfinch [M. C. H. B.].

*Dreening-wet. Draining or dripping wet [M. C. H. B.].

Drepe. To drip or dribble. See Drope.

Drift-way. A driving-way, a cart-way along an enclosed slip of land.

Drindle. A small channel to carry off water; a very neat diminutive of Drain.

Dringle. To waste time in a lazy lingering manner.

Dringling pains. Premonition of labour in women [W. G. W.].

*Driving. Longshoring for herring (*E. D. Press*, May 8, 1891) [M. C. H. B.].

Droll. To put off, to amuse with excuses. Pronounced like DOLL.

*Drop. To stoop or curtsy [G. E.].

Drope. (1) To run down like wax or tallow from the candle, or perspiration down the face in violent heat. (2) To have a downward inclination [E. F. G.]. See Drepe.

*Dropper. A woman or child who goes behind the dibbler.

*Drove. A wide path or way over flat or open lands [W. R.].

Drovy. Itchy, scabby, lousy, or all three; a word of supreme contempt, or rather loathing.

Droze. To beat very severely.

Drozings. A hearty drubbing.

Drug. A strong carriage with four wheels for conveying

heavy loads of timber. [This is, I think, wrong—a drug has two wheels, a jill four.

Drugster. A druggist.

*Dubbing. (1) A coat of clay plastered immediately upon the splints and rizzors of a studwork building. (2) A part of a bullock or piece of beef [Johnson]. The same as the 'bed' [W. G. W.].

*Dubstand. A term used at marbles [G. E.].

*Duck. To bop, bob, drop or dodge or duck the head to escape being hit. In allusion to the habit of ducks when bobbing their heads, the why and the wherefore of which habit I have never seen or heard discussed [M. C. H. B.].

*Dudder. To shiver with cold or fear [Spur.].

Duddle. Commonly used with the addition of 'up.' 'To *duddle* up' is to cover up closely and warmly with an unnecessary quantity of clothes. Ex. 'How he do *duddle* hisself up.'

*Duddle. A bird-snare made of hair [*E. Daily Press*, Dec. 4, 1894].

Duels. Pegs or pins, used by coopers to fasten the heads of casks [Johnson].

*Duffer. A cross-bred pigeon. Supposed by some to be contracted from dovehouse.

*Duffhus. A dove-cote [M. C. H. B.].

*Duffle. A duffle coat [M. C. H. B.].

Duffy Dows. Young pigeons not fully fledged. **Dovies?** [Spur.].

Duggle. (1) To lie snug and close together, like pigs or puppies. (2) To cuddle or caress [Em.]. (3) To rain heavily [M. C. H. B.].

*Dug Udder. 'She begins to dug,' of a cow. A sign she is near calving, as her udder begins to fill out [M. C. H. B.].

*Dukes, or Dukes-headed. A stupid fool [*B. N.* 85–94].

Dullor. A dull and moaning noise, or the tune of some doleful ditty. Nothing more likely to produce moaning than *dolour.* Loud speech [Spur.]. A noise or shindy [W. R.].

*Dumpling. Dough boiled [G. E.].

*Dumpy. Sullen [Johnson].

Dundy. Of a dull colour, as *dundy-grey,* or whatsoever other colour is to be coupled with it.

Dunk-horn. The short blunt horn of a beast.

Dunk-horned. Sneaking, shabby.

Dunt. (1) Stupid, or dizzy. A dizzy calf with water in the head is said to be *dunt.* (2) To stupefy.

*Dust. A dust of coal=just a very little coal (or tea, or seed) [M. C. H. B.].

*Dutch Nightingale. A frog [Spur.].

Dutfin. The bridle in cart-harness. A Suffolk word only [Spur.].

Duzzy. Dizzy; an easy change of letters. Not dizzy, but foolish, stupid, crazy [Spur.]. ‘Yew mucka duzzy fule.’

Dwain, Dwainy. Faint, sickly.

Dwile. (1) A refuse lock of wool. (2) A mop made of them. (3) Any coarse rubbing or cleansing rag.

Dwinge. To shrivel and dwindle. Apples are *dwinged* by over-keeping.

Ea. Water. Popham’s *ea,* and St. John’s *ea,* are water-courses cut for the drainage of different parts of the Bedford level into the Ouse above Lynn. *Ea* brink is the beginning of a very sudden curvature of that river, from which point a new cut was made at a prodigious expense, and finished in the year 1820, to improve the outfall of the fen waters into Lynn harbour, by giving them a straight direction. It is commonly written and printed, and generally pronounced by strangers *eau,* as if the word had been borrowed from the French, which it certainly was not.

Eachon. In speaking of two individuals we commonly say *eachon* (each one), as in speaking of more than two *every one.* In common pronunciation it may sound like eachin, or even itchin. Ex. ' I gave *eachon* of them half a crown.' [I doubt. It should be ' each on 'em.']

Eager, or Eagre. A peculiarly impetuous and dangerous aggravation of the tide in some rivers ; caused, as it would seem, either by vehement confluence of two streams, or by the channel becoming narrower, shallower, or both. We have an *eager* in our river Ouse, many miles above Lynn, near Downham Bridge, where the waters seem to ' stand on a heap ' along each bank [Forby]. But is it not the tide running up a narrow river ?

*Eave Boards. Boards put upon dung-carts to make them carry more [Johnson].

Eavelong. Oblique, sidelong ; along the edges, skirts, or *eaves,* as we often call them, of inclosed grounds, particularly when they deviate from straight lines. Hence, ' *eavelong* work ' is mowing or reaping those irregular parts in which the corn or grass cannot be laid in exact parallel lines.

Ebble. The asp-tree.

Eccles-tree. An axle-tree.

Eddish. Aftermath.

*Eelset. Snare to catch eels.

*Eft, Effet. *Vide* Swift [M. C. H. B.].

*Eldern. Elder-tree [*Pr. Pa.*].

*Election. In election, likely. ' We are in election to have a bad harvest this year ' [Cull. Haw.].

*Ellus. Ale-house [*N. and Q.*].

Elvish. Peevish ; wantonly mischievous.

End. (1) Part, division. Ex. 'He has the best *end* of the staff.' 'It cost me the best *end* of an hundred pounds.' (2) The stems of a growing crop. Ex. 'Here is a plenty of *ends*, however it may fill the bushel.'

*Enddish. A second crop of grass [Pr. Pa.].

Endless. Intestinum caecum ; blind gut.

Enemis. Of very obscure and doubtful meaning, like most of Sir Thomas Browne's words. Hickes says it means Lest (ne forté). A note in Bohn's edition says the word is still used in the sense of Lest, but rather pronounced **Enammons.** 'Spar the door ennemis he come,' is the example given in Ray. [Obsolete.]

*Enow. Enough [M. C. H. B.].

*Envy. 'Not to envy a dish,' not to care about eating it [C. S. P.].

Erriwiggle. An earwig. See **Aerigel.**

E'ry. Every. A very common elision.

Esh. The ash-tree.

Ether. To wattle, or intertwine, in making a staked hedge. Otherwise to 'Bond a hedge,' meaning, particularly, the finishing part at top, of stouter materials, which is to confine all the rest.

Even-flavoured. Unmixed, unvaried, uniform. 'An *even-flavoured* day of rain,' meaning a day of incessant rain.

Every-each. Alternate, every other.

*Every futen non. Every now and then [Johnson].

Ewe. For 'owed.' 'He *ewe* me sixpence' [W. R.].

Exe. An axe.

*Eye. (1) As in Trowse Eye ; for **Hythe** [W. R.]. (2) Also applied to a brood of pheasants, as covey would be to partridges [J. H. G.].

*Eyes. Spectacles [Em.].

*Eynd. The water-smoke [W. R.].

Fadge. (1) To suit or fit. Two persons, two things, or two parts of the same thing fadge well or ill together. (2) To succeed, to answer expectation. ' We will have, an this fadge not, an antic.' (3) A bundle or parcel [Johnson].

*Fadom. (1) Full growth, applied to plants, sometimes to young stock. ' It has not yet got its *fadom.*' It is not yet fully grown [Spur.]. (2) A *fadom* of bullrushes is six shows (sheaves), measuring six feet round, not high. [W. R.].

Fagot. A contemptuous appellation of a woman. Ex. ' A lazy *fagot.*'

*Fag out, To. To fray out, as a rope's end [E. F. G.].

*Fain. Contented. Davis in *Swan and her Crew* [M. C. H. B.].

*Fairies' Loaves. Petrified Echini. Yarrell, *Brit. Birds,* 4th ed. vol. iii. p. 203 [M. C. H. B.].

Fairy Butter. A species of *tremella,* of yellowish colour and gelatinous substance, not very rarely found on furze and broom.

*Faite. Well made, well proportioned, thriving [M. C. H. B.].

*Faithful, To be. To tell an unpleasant truth. Ex. ' How like you poor John's grave ? ' ' Well, Jane, to be faithful with you, it similars nothing in the world but a pig's grave ' [G. S. P.].

Fall. For ' fell.' ' I shall *fall* that tree next spring.'

*Fal-lals. Finery [M. C. H. B.].

*False. He is a *false* man : he is telling lies. *Halst. Gazette,* Mar. 15. '88 [C. D.].

Famble Crop. The first stomach in ruminating animals.

*Fan. A large basket [W. G. W.].

Fang. (1) A fin. (2) A finger. (3) To lay hold of. 'He *fanged* hold of him.' (4) To clutch; e. g. 'He fanged her by the throat and nearly quackled her' [*B. N.* 27.].

Fangast. A marriageable maid [Sir Thomas Browne]. The word is not now known, and is therefore given with Ray's interpretation and etymol.

Fapes. Green gooseberries. Variously called also **Feaps,** **Feabs, Fabes,** and **Thapes**; all abbreviations of **Feaberries**. But these names are with us applicable in the immature state of the fruit only. Nobody ever talks of a ripe *fape*.

Fare. (1) To seem. Ex. 'She *fared* sick'; 'they *fare* to be angry.' To be, to feel; e.g. 'How do you *fare*?' 'I *fare* pretty well.' (2) A litter of pigs. Farrow is commonly used in this sense, but *fare* is the better word.

Farmer. A term of distinction commonly applied, in Suffolk, to the eldest son of the occupier of a farm. He is addressed and spoken of by the labourers as 'the *farmer*.' The occupier himself is called master. A labourer speaking to the son would say, 'Pray, *farmer*, do you know where my master is?' Or one labourer would ask another, 'Did my master set out that job?' And would be answered, 'No, my master didn't, but the *farmer* did.'

***Farr.** A fair. 'Ar you ar goin' to thah far?' [Johnson, Spurden].

Farrer, or **Farrow.** Barren. A cow not producing a calf is for that year called a *farrow cow*. In Suffolk she would be called **Ghast** [Forby, Johnson].

***Farthing-weed.** Marsh penny-wort (*Hydrocotyle vulgs.*) [M. C. H. B.].

Fasguntide. Shrovetide, which is interpreted fasting-time. This is given by Blount, in his *Dictionary of Hard Words*, 1680, as a Norfolk word. If it were so then, it is, like many of Sir Thomas Browne's words of nearly the same

age, very little if at all known now.   Perhaps Blount was
misinformed. The word, however, to do it justice, has
somewhat of a Saxon air, and may have been in use;
indeed, may be so still, though inquiry has not detected
it. [Obsolete.]

*Fasking about.   Bothering or bustling [M. C. H. B.].

*Fassal.   For ' vessel ' [Spur.].

*Fast.   In use, occupied [M. C. H. B.].

Fat Hen.   A wild pot-herb, very well worth cultivation.
It is as good as spinach if its grittiness be well washed
off, and it be dressed in the same way.   *Chenopodium
album,* Lin.

*Fathom.   Growth, whether in length, size, or maturity;
but generally used to growing corn ready for harvest.
' That field has nearly got its fathom ' [Johnson].   See
Fadom.

*Fawny.   A ring [B. N. 27] (? slang, W. R.).

*Fearful.   Timid, or timorous [E. S. T.].

*Feat, or Fate.   (1) Excellent, choice, very good [Spur.].
(2) Pretty [Arderon].   (3) Nice, clever.   ' A *fate* little
mawther ' [E. T. S.].

Feather Pie.   A hole in the ground, filled with feathers
fixed on strings, and kept in motion by the wind.   An
excellent device to scare birds.

*Feeding.   A pasture.   Almost obsolete in Norfolk, but
more usual in Suffolk.

Feft.   To persuade, or endeavour to persuade.   It is one of
Sir Thomas Browne's words become obsolete.

Feist, Feistiness.   Fustiness.   Ex. ' This cask has a *feist*
in it.'

Feisty.   Fusty ; but *fusty* is the corruption.   *Feisty* is the
original, and a most expressive word.

*Felfoot, or Fulfit.   The fieldfare (N. Ess.) [C. D.].

Felt. (1) A thick matted growth of weeds, spreading by their roots, as couch-grass. Ex. 'This land is all a *felt.*' (2) A fieldfare.

***Fendeek.** A dyke or drain [G. E.]

Fen Nightingale. A frog; otherwise called a March bird.

***Ferridge.** A common sort of gingerbread, made very thick, and generally with some figures imprinted on it before baking [Johnson].

***Ferry fake.** To pry impudently [*B. N. 56*].

Few. Little. It is a plural adjective, used with a singular substantive in two instances only. We talk of 'a *few* broth' and 'a *few* gruel.' In all other cases we use the word like other people. This use of *few* is peculiar to Norfolk, and I believe to the eastern part' [Spur.]. E. F. G. correctly points out that it sometimes means 'quantity' only. 'We brought in a good *few* of sprats.' [Clearly the origin of the Americanism.]

Fewty. Trifling, of no worth [Johnson]. Down south 'footy' [W. R.].

***Fie, or Fye.** To cleanse out a ditch, a pond, or any other receptacle of mud or filth.

***Fierce.** 'Don't fare fierce,' don't feel bright, up to the mark [W. R.].

***Fifering.** Shooting; a 'fifering' pain [M. C. H. B.].

Fifers. The fibrous roots of a plant [Spur.].

Fighting Cocks. The spikes of the different species of plantain, with which boys play a game so called [Br.].

Filands. Field lands, or rather *filde* lands. Tracts of un-inclosed arable land.

File. (1) To foil. (2) To defile; the simple for the compound, as in 'stry' for destroy, and some others.

Fill Bells. The chain-tugs to the collar of a cart-horse, by which he draws.

Filler. (1) To go behind. (2) To draw back.

Fill-horse, Filler. The horse which goes in the shafts. In a regular team, the order is, the fore-horse, the lark-horse, the pin-horse, the *fill-horse*. Perhaps more correctly the Thill-horse, or the Thiller. But *f* is very commonly substituted in pronunciation for *th*, as we sometimes call a thistle a fistle. In Suffolk the horses in a team are distinguished by the names of fore-horse, fore-lash, hand-horse, and *filler*.

Fimble. (1) To touch lightly and frequently with the ends of the fingers. A gentle diminutive of *fumble*. (2) To pass through without cutting. Ex. ' My scythe *fimbles* the grass.'

*Finder. An obsolete term in coursing [J. H. G.].

*Finify. To be over-nice in doing anything [Johnson].

*Fintum. (1) A sudden freak of the mind. ' Well, there! what *fintum* now?' (2) A piece of wood fastened by a girdle or cord round the waist of a reaper to carry his reaping-hook [Johnson].

Firepan. A fire-shovel. The word is in Johnson, but not in this sense, in which it seems provincial.

*Fishimer. *B. N.* 62. [Corruption of pismire.]

Fit. Ready. Ex. ' Come, stir, make yourself *fit*.' Compare the racing term.

Fitter. To shift from one foot to the other [W. C.].

*Five Finger. The common starfish [M. C. H. B.].

Five Fingers. Oxlips.

Fizmer. To fidget unquietly, and make a great stir about some trifle, making little or no progress. Formed, perhaps, from the slight rustling noise produced by these petty agitations.

*Fiz'n. First-rate. Ex. ' How does that colt get on?' ' Oh! fiz'n' [W. B.].

Flack. (1) To hang loose. Akin to **Flake.** (2) A blow, particularly with something loose and pliant. (3) ' Hurry, John is always in a flack ' [W. B.].

Flacket. A tall flaunting wench, whose apparel seems to hang loose about her.

Flag. (1) A portion of the surface of heathy land turned up by the spade, and heaped to dry for fuel. The more it abounds in roots of *ericae*, &c., the better fuel it makes. (2) The surface of a clover lay of the second year turned up by the plough. The wheat for the next year's crop is dibbled into the *flag*. (3) The top spit of a marshy meadow, which is skinned off the top ; in contradistinction to a ' turf ' which is cut *down* after the *flag* is taken off [W. R.]. Also a level piece of grass fit for athletic sports. See advertisement of the **Aylsham Derby.**

Flagelute. A very small rent or hole in a garment. Perhaps from resemblance to the small perforations in a flageolet.

***Flail-basket.** Frail basket, or squeeze basket [M. C. H. B.].

***Flaking.** Boughs or branches laid crossways on the rafters of a shed before thatching over [Johnson].

***Flang.** To slap [G. E.].

Flap. A slight stroke or touch. Ex. ' I have got a *flap* of cold,' the cold has touched or struck me. ' A *flap* of wind,' a cold caught by exposure to a current of air [Spur.].

Flap-jack. (1) A broad flat piece of pastry. *Vide* **Apple-jack.** (2) A flat thin joint of meat, as the breast of a lean sheep or calf [Jen.].

Flapper. A young wild duck which has just taken wing, but is unable to fly far.

Flaps. Large broad mushrooms.

***Flaregee.** A kind of candlestick [G. E.].

Flarnecking. Flaunting with vulgar ostentation. Intensive of *flare*.

Flash. To flash a hedge is to cut off the lower parts of the bushes which overhang the bank or ditch.

Flazzard. A stout broad-faced woman dressed in a loose and flaring manner.

Fleaches. The portions into which timber is cut by the saw. Another form of **Flitch**.

Fleck. The down of hares or rabbits torn off by thè dogs. Dryden has **flix** in the same sense. A. S. *flex*, linum.

Flecked, Fleckered. Dappled, speckled with differences of colour.

*Flee. To flay.

Fleet. (1) To skim the cream from the milk. (2) A channel filled by the tide, but left very shallow and narrow at low water. This seems to be the proper sense, and the word is thus used at Lynn. (3) Shallow; a dish or a basin, a ditch or a pond, or anything else of little depth, is said to be *fleet*, e.g. ' We ploughed the field as *fleet* as may be ' [W. R.]. ' *Fleet* of herring-nets,' five or six score [E. F. G.].

*Fleeting, Fleeter. A system which has grown up on the E. Anglian coast in the place of the old method of smack fishing. ' Four or five or more smacks have gone out together and stayed during several weeks upon the deep sea fishing ground, tended by a steam vessel which has travelled backwards and forwards, taking fish home and bringing stores out ' (*Suff. and Ess. Press*, March 14, 1886) [C. D.].

Fleeting Dish. A skimming-dish to take off the cream from the milk.

Flegged, Fligged. Fledged.

Flet Cheese. Cheese made of skimmed milk. This is the name by which the celebrated Suffolk cheese is universally called in its native county.

Fletches. Green pods of peas ; from some resemblance

they are supposed to bear to an arrow. Fletcherds, the very young pods; query from their flatness [Spur.].

Flet Milk. The skimmed milk from which the cream has been taken by a fleet or shallow wooden skimming-dish [Johnson].

*****Flew.** Down. The dirt under a featherbed is *bed-flew* [Spur.]. See **Fluff.**

Flick. (1) A smart stinging slap. (2) The outer fat of the hog, which is cured for bacon. In Suffolk this is called '*the flick*,' and the rest of the carcass '*the bones.*' (3) A flitch, either of bacon, or of sawn plank; and a better form of it. (4) Hare's or rabbit's down [Spur.].

*****Fligged.** Fledged [*Pr. Pa.*].

Fligger. To quiver with convulsive motion. The shaking of the flesh of an animal after its death, while the butcher dresses it [Johnson].

Fliggers. The common flag, so called from the motion of its leaves by the slightest impulse of the air.

*****Flight.** The course wild ducks take on their homeward evening journey. A marshman will tell you that they come over the river night after night, within a yard or two of the same place; naturally that is the spot to wait for them [W. R.]. Boys also say they have the *flight* of pigeons, when they come home after having been let out the first time.

*****Flight.** (1) Of bees, a swarm of bees [Marshall]. (2) A second swarm [W. B.].

*****Flight Oats.** Oats grown on the poorest sand and in the fen districts [C. D.].

Flit. (1) To remove from one house to another. (2) Midnight-flit, to run away [M. C. H. B.].

*****Flitch.** To move from place to place, as from farm to farm [Marshall]. But this was probably his mistake for to *flit* [W. R.].

*Flits, or Flites. Chaff [Spur.]. Johnson has it Flight.

Flizzoms. Flying particles, or very small flakes in bottled liquors. The bee's wings, by which some persons of fine taste prove the age of their port, are nothing but *flizzoms.*

*Flocklet. The *flock* mark put on sheep [Johnson].

*Florch. To spread the mouth from affectation. To display dress or finery [Johnson].

*Flote. A dam in a stream.

Flue. (1) Shallow [Forby]. (2) The coping of a gable or end wall of a house [Marshall].

*Fluff. See Flew.

*Flukers. The external extremities of angles of mouths of pikes [M. C. H. B.].

*Flummox, Flummocks. To embarrass [M. C. H. B.].

*Fobby. Soft, no substance [G. E.].

*Fod. A pet animal.

*Fodder. Litter, and again nonsense. 'Thank goodness, there is no fodder in his letter' [C. S. P.]

Fog. Long grass, growing in pastures in late summer or autumn; not fed down, but allowed to stand through the winter, and yielding early spring feed. By its length and thickness the outer part forms a cover or sort of thatch for the lower, which is kept fresh and juicy, at least through a mild winter.

Fogger. A huckster, a petty chapman carrying small wares from village to village.

*Fog-off. Of plants: to damp off [M. C. H. B.].

Foison. Succulency, natural nutritive moisture, as in herbage. Ex. 'There is no *foison* in this hay.'

Foisonless. Devoid of foison [Sc. N.]. See the Scotch fusionless [W. R.].

*Foisty. Stale [Tusser]. See Fosey.

Foky. Bloated, unsound, soft and woolly. Ex. 'a *foky* turnip.'

Fold-pritch, or Pitch. A heavy pointed iron, to make holes in the ground to receive the toes-of hurdles.

***Follow - the - sea** (or **the - plough**). A fisherman, &c. [M. C. H. B.]

Fond. (1) Luscious, fulsome, disagreeably sweet in taste or in smell. (2) For 'found'; 'I have *fond* it' [Johnson].

***Foot anon.** 'Every *foot anon.*' Every now and then [Cull. Haw.].

Footing-time. The time of recovery from a lying-in, of getting on *foot* again [R. S. E. C.].

***Foot-lace.** To repair a wall just above its foundation [W. G. W.].

***Foot-locks.** The corn or grass collected upon the feet of mowers [Johnson].

Force. A strange sort of neutro-passive. Ex. 'I *forced* to go.' I was obliged, I could not help.

Forecast. To think before. It is an excellent quality in a servant to '*forecast* his work,' to think what he is to do next.

***Foreigner.** Any one who does not belong to the district. All the shire men are foreigners [F. J. B., C. D.].

Fore-summers. The forepart of a cart. This kind of cart was some years ago much used in Norfolk, but is now wearing out. A sort of platform projecting over the shafts was called 'the *fore-summers*, or *fore-stool.*' Now almost driven out by the introduction of the tumbrel [Johnson].

Forgive. To begin to thaw.

Forhinder. To prevent.

Forlorn. Worthless, reprobate, abandoned. Ex. 'A *forlorn* fellow' is one with whom nobody would have any concern.

*Fosey. Over-ripe [*B. N.* 3]. See Foisty.

Foulty. Paltry, trumpery, despicable.

Four-eyed. Applied to dogs which have a distinct mark over each eye, of a different colour; for the most part tan upon black. One who wears spectacles is also said to be *four-eyed.*

Fourses. The afternoon refreshment of labourers in harvest, at four o'clock. Fourings [Marshall].

Foy. A supper given by the owners of a fishing-vessel at Yarmouth to the crew, in the beginning of the season. It is otherwise called a Bending foy, from the bending of the sails or nets, as a ratification of the bargain.

Fozy. Very nearly, if not exactly, the same as *foky.*

Frack. To abound, to swarm, to be thronged, or crowded together. Ex. ' The church was *fracking* full'; ' My apple-trees are as full as they can *frack.*'

Frail. (1) A wicker [rush] basket. (2) To fret or wear out cloth.

Frame. To speak or behave affectedly; to shape the language and demeanour to an occasion of ceremony. ' *Framed* manners' is Low Sc.

Frampled. Cross, ill-humoured.

*Frank. A heron [E. F. G. and W. R.].

*Fraps. Entanglements [M. C. H. B.].

*Frary or Pharisee Rings. Green circles seen in pastures. No doubt a corruption from *fairy rings.*

*Frase. To break [Ray and J. Steele].

Frazle. To unravel or rend cloth. In the north, a Frize of paper is half-a-quarter of a sheet.

*Frazled. In confusion, entangled [Johnson].

Frazlings. Threads of cloth, torn or unravelled.

Freckens. Freckles.

Freeli - frailies.   Light, unsubstantial delicacies for the table; frothy compliments, empty prate, frippery ornaments; almost any sort of trumpery meant for finery.

*Freemartin.   A barren heifer [W. G. W.].

Frenchman.   Any man, of any country, who cannot speak English; as any one who does not understand East Anglian is a shireman.

Fresh.   (1) Home-brewed table beer, drawn from the tap. (2) Hence, tipsy.   (3) Store sheep, cattle, &c., when in condition [Johnson].

Fresher.   A small frog.   Frosher, a frog [Spur.].

*Fretful.   Overwhelmed with grief [C. S. P.].

*Frettened.   Pock-marked [Johnson].

*Frewer.   A sirreverence [Johnson].

*Fribble.   To fuss about [G. E.].

Frightful.   Apt to take fright.   Certainly more expressive than fearful, which would be generally used, yet the effect of substitution is very ludicrous.   Ex. 'Lauk! Miss, how *frightful* you are!' says a homely wench, when Miss screams at the sight of a toad or a spider.

Frimicate.   To play the fribble, to affect delicacy.

*Frimmicating.   Particular as to dress [B. N. 92].

*Frimmock.   To assume affected airs [Spur.].

Frize.   To freeze.

Frog-spit.   See Cuckoo-spit.

Froise, Froyse.   (1) A pancake.   (2) To fry.

*Frolic.   Water-frolic, a gala, regatta, or water-picnic [M. C. H. B.].

*Frorn.   Frozen [N. and Q.].

*Froschy.   [B. N. 7. 30, 38].

Frouzy.   Blouzy, with disordered and uncombed hair.

***Frown, Froan.** Frozen [W. B.].

Frowy. Stale ; on the point of turning sour from being over kept.

Frugal. The reverse of costive or 'costly,' q. v. 'Good woman,' quoth the village doctress, 'is your child *costive?*' '*Costly!* ma'am, no, quite the contrary, sadly *frugal* indeed!'

***Frummety for firmety.** Boiled wheat in milk.

Frump. A sour, ill-humoured person ; more particularly an old woman.

Frumple. To rumple, crease, or wrinkle.

***Fule for Fool.**

***Fulfer.** The missel-thrush.

Full due. Final acquittance. Ex. 'I shall soon have done with Mr. A., or I shall go away from B., for a *full due*,' for good and all.

Full flopper. A young bird sufficiently feathered to leave the nest.

Funk. (1) Touchwood. (2) Also a term used in marble-playing [C. H. E. W.]. (3) A verb. Ex. 'The soot funked up in my face' [M. C. H. B.].

Furlong. A division of an uninclosed corn-field, of which the several subdivisions are numbered in the map, and registered in the field-book.

***Furrin or Gone-furrin.** Gone foreign, abroad ; emigrated to furrin parts [M C. H. B.], i. e. out of England.

***Fursick, Fussick.** To potter over one's work [*B. N.* 14].

Further. A word which can only be explained by examples of its use, which is very common. Ex. 'If I do so I will be *further*,' meaning 'I will never do it.' 'I wish that fellow *further*,' i. e. 'I would I were well rid of him.'

*Fussle or Fusk. To bustle. Ex. 'The partridges fussled or fusked up right under my feet' [M. C. H. B.].

*Fut it. Move your feet, move on, be off [M. C. H. B.].

*Fuzhacker. The whinchat, stonechat, or wheatear generally (*Pratincola rubicola*) [M. C. H. B.].

Fuzzy. Rough and shaggy.

Fye. To clean or purify. To *fye* out the pond ; to *fye* up the corn [Spur.]. See Fie.

*Fyesty. Foisty, fusty [Spur.].

*Gad. A guide, a long stick [G. E.].

*Gaddy-wentin. Gossiping [*B. N.* 94].

*Gadge. To mark out the dimensions of a ditch or drain by cutting out a small quantity of the soil by a line or cord [Johnson].

Gag. (1) To nauseate ; to reject with loathing, as if the throat were closed against the admission of what is offered. (2) To make an unsuccessful effort to vomit.

Gage. A bowl or tub to receive the cream as it is successively skimmed off.

*Gaggles or 'skeins.' Cf. Geese [*B. N.* 87].

Gain. Handy and dextrous, as Johnson explains it. But it is of more extensive sense, and by no means out of use, as he supposed it to be. On the contrary, it is very frequently used, and means convenient, desirable ; just as may be wished. Ex. 'The land lies very *gain* for me.' 'I bought this horse very *gain*' (cheap) [W. R.]. Br., as a qualifying term used with other words ; '*gain* quiet,' pretty quiet.

Galdeb. To prate in a coarse, vulgar, noisy manner.

Gall. A vein of sand in a stiff soil, through which water is drained off, and oozes at soft places on the surface ; otherwise Sand Galls. [? Gault.]

Gallopped Beer. Small beer for present drinking, made by simple boiling, or, as it is called, *galloping* small quantities of malt and hops together in a kettle.

Gallow Balk. The *balk* or strong bar of iron to which the pothooks, or hakes, as we call them, are appended in the open kitchen chimney ; so called because it resembles the upper part of the gallows. **Gally Balk** [Johnson].

Gamakin, or **Gamalkin.** Said of an awkward, gaping, staring, and vacant person, walking about, having no idea or object in mind. ' What are you *gamalkin* arter ? ' [Johnson].

*****Game Hawk.** The peregrine (*F. peregrinus*) [M. C. H. B.].

*****Gan,** or **Garn.** (1) For 'grin ' [Johnson]. (2) For 'gave.' Ex. ' He *gan* me it' [M. C. H. B.].

Gander. To gad, to ramble.

Ganger. (1) A goer, a speedy horse. (2) The overlooker of a gang of workmen' [M. C. H. B.].

*****Ganging.** (1) Going [W. R.]. (2) ' To go *ganging*,' to beat the parish bounds [C. S. P.].

*****Gangle.** Ganway. *Vide* Cromer Manor [W. R.].

Gant. A village fair or wake. There are probably few instances of the use of it. But in those few it is not likely to be lost. Mattishall *Gant* is in no danger of losing its ancient name while it retains any portion of its attraction and celebrity in the neighbourhood.

Ganty Gutted. Gaunt ; lean and lanky.

Gape Stick, Garpe Stick. (1) A large wooden spoon, to which it is necessary to open the mouth wide. (2) Also to feed young fowl [W. R.]. (3) To stare and gape. (4) To go garping about, to wander listlessly [M. C. H. B.].

*****Gardene.** Guardian (N. Essex) [C. D.].

*****Garget.** (1) A distemper affecting the throats and udders of cattle or pigs [F. J. B.] [Johnson]. A disease incident to. calves [Marshall]. (2) Pigeon berry [M. C. H. B.].

*Gargut Root. The root of hellebore [Marshall].

Garle. To mar butter in the making, by handling in summer with hot hands. This turns it to a curd-like substance, with spots and streaks of paler colour, instead of
the uniformly smooth consistency and golden hue which
it ought to have. Johnson says 'mottled or streaked
from mismanagement.'

Gartle-head. A thoughtless person.

Gartless. Heedless, thoughtless, regardless.

*Gashful, Gastly. Frightful (East, Halliwell).

Gast, or Gast Cow. A cow which does not produce a calf
in the season. Otherwise a Farrow Cow, q. v. Also
applied to mares [F. J. B.].

Gast Bird. A single partridge in the shooting season
(Suff., Halliwell).

Gat. An opening in the great sand-bank which lies at the
back of the Yarmouth Roads. There are several, distinguished by names, as Fisherman's *gat*, &c.

*Gatless. Half-witted, shiftless [*B. N. 5*].

Gatter Bush, Gattridge. The wild guelder-rose, *Vibur-
num opulus*, or the wild dogwood, *Cornus sanguinea*,
Lin.

Gault. (1) Brick earth. Occasionally any sort of heavy
and adhesive earth. (2) A cavern. (3) A cavity caused
by a sudden subsidence of earth or soil [M. C. H. B.].

Gavel, Gavin. (1) A sheaf of corn before it is tied up.
(2) To collect mown corn into heaps in order to its
being loaded. (3) A bundle of hay ready for cutting
[*B. N.* 40].

Gawp. To gape very wide, to stare with a sort of idiotic
wonder.

*Gay. (1) Many-coloured. 'My leg is *gay*' is said of an
inflamed leg [C. S. P.]. (2) Also applied to animals in
the sense of pied [J. H. G.].

Gay Cards. The cards in a pack which are painted with figures.

Gays. Prints to ornament books. The word is in Johnson on the sole authority of L'Estrange, who was a Norfolk man, and not infrequently betrays it. Frequently applied to coarse engravings pasted on cottage walls [Spur.].

Ge. To go [? W. R.]. Ex. 'This does not *ge* well with that.' 'He and she will never *ge* together,' meaning it is an ill-suited match [W. C., Jen.]. It may be added here that when to make our draught-horses go on we call indifferently *ge-ho* or *ge-wo!* This is sad confusion, and we ought to know better; for *ge-ho*, being interpreted, means *go stop*, and *ge-wo* is *go go*. We express ourselves with much more propriety when we say *woochwo* and *wo*, q. v.

*Gear-stuff. Doctors' gear, medicine [M. C. H. B.].

*Gedless. Thoughtless [C. S. P.].

Generals. The Archdeacon's Visitation. The diocese of Norwich seems to be the only one in which this popular name is used. It is to be presumed that everywhere the Visitation is officially called the Archdeacon's *General* Court.

*Gere. Unintelligible stuff [Arderon]; or a confused heap.

Get. 'To *get* over the left shoulder,' to be a loser.

Giffle. To be restless, unquiet, fidgetty. It ought to be spelled with *g*, not *j*, as the Dictt. have it. 'Jiffling and jaffling' is still a phrase.

Gig. A trifling, silly, flighty fellow.

*Giglot. Occurs in W. White's *Eastern England* as the feminine of the last word [W. R.].

*Gill. A pair of timber wheels [Marshall]. A vehicle for conveying timber, consisting of two wheels, a strong axle-tree supporting a very stout bar, on which the timber is slung, and shafts.

Gilver. To ache, to throb. Possibly a softening of Culver.

*Gim and Gin. For 'give' and 'gave.' 'Tom, will you *gim* me that there ball?' 'Tom, he *gin* it to me' [Johnson].

Gim, Gimmy. Spruce, neat, smart. But probably the common slang word 'jimmy' [W. R.].

Gimble. To grin or smile. Johnson has Gimling, Giggling.

Gimmers [sometimes Gimmels, W. R.]. Small hinges; as those of a box or cabinet; or even of the parlour door. Leather hinges [C. W. B.].

*Gimption. Brittle, of a machine or toy [Spur].

*Gimsering. Carving or making any small things in brass, wood, iron, &c. [Arderon].

Gimson. A gimcrack.

*Gin or Jin. The entrails of a calf preserved with raisins, currants, lemon-peel, &c., and made into a pie called a *gin* pie; 'all gone, skin and *gin*' [Johnson].

*Girn. To sneer, to make faces [Johnson].

Give. (1) 'To *give* one white-foot,' to coax him. The phrase is certainly allusive to the fawning of a dog. (2) 'To *give* one the seal of the day,' to greet civilly with a salutation suitable to the hour of meeting, as 'good morning,' or 'good evening.' Our phrase is general, and exactly equivalent to '*give* you good time of day,' in Shaks. (3) 'To *give* grant,' to allow authoritatively. The Justice, the overseer, or anybody else in authority, is often solicited to '*give* grant,' that such or such a thing may be done.

*Gladden. (1) Or gladden bushes, bulrushes [W. R.]. Marshall says large and small catstail. (2) *Typha latifolia* [M. C. H. B.].

*Glaze-worm. Glow-worm [M. C. H. B.].

*Gleave. An eel-spear [W. G. W.].

Glemth, Glent, Glint. A glimpse, a short and slight view.

*Gloat, or Glot. A species of eel [*B. N. 77*].

Glouse. A strong gleam of heat, from sunshine or a blazing fire; also Scot. spong [Johnson].

*Glowsy. Heavy, oppressive. 'The day fare so *glowsy* like' [Em.].

Glusky. Sulky in aspect.

*Glut Wedge. A quoin or wedge of hard wood, to widen the cleft made by the iron wedge [Johnson].

Gly-halter. A halter or bridle with blinkers, as those of draught-horses.

*Glys. Blinkers.

*Gnatling. Very much engaged about trifles, busy doing nothing [Johnson].

Goaf. A rick of corn in the straw laid up in a barn : if in the open air it is a Stack. Johnson says the corn at the bay or end of the barn.

*Goafe, or Gofe. A corn mow [Arderon and Cull. Haw.].

Goaf-flap. A wooden beater to knock the ends of the sheaves, and make the *goaf* or stack more compact and flat. In Suffolk the *goaf-flap* is seldom or never used ; but it is a standing joke on the 1st of April to send a boy, or a silly fellow, to borrow a *goaf-flap*, and the messenger invariably 'runs the gauntlet' of all the servants and labourers at the farm-house to which he is sent.

*Goaf-horse. The horse ridden upon corn deposited in a barn so as to compress it [Spur.].

Goaf-stead. Every division of a barn in which a *goaf* is placed. A large barn has four or more. The threshing-floor is called the Middle-stead.

Goave. To stow corn in a barn [Pe.]. Ex. 'Do you intend to stack this wheat, or to *goave* it ? '

Gob. (1) The mouth. Ex. 'Shut your *gob*' [Br.]. A great talker is said 'to have the gift of the *gob*' [*gab* ?]. (2) A large mouth-filling morsel, particularly of something greasy. Ex. 'A *gob* of fat, suet, bacon, pudding, or dumpling, well soaked in dripping, which will easily slip down.' (3) Metaph. A considerable lump of something not eatable. By 'such a *gob* of money,' our countryman must have meant, as we still mean, by the very same phrase, a good round sum. (4) To expectorate [M. C. H. B.].

*Go, a. To ride, run away [Arderon].

*Go, to. To follow a business or calling, e. g. 'my son *go* by water,' gets his living on the water [Spur].

*Gobbity. Pleasant to the taste [J. H. G.].

Gobble. Noisy talk.

Gobbler. A turkey-cock.

*Goer. Thick mire or dirt, such as are in the kennels [Arderon]. See Gore.

Golden-knop. The lady fly, otherwise golden bug.

*Golder. A chat [M. C. H. B.].

Goles, Gosh, Goms. Foolish and very vulgar evasions of profane oaths, all including the Sacred Name, combined with some other word or words.

*Gollder. Low vulgar language, loud and vociferous [Johnson].

*Gollop Ale. Ale made in a copper from malt and water simply boiled [M. C. H. B.].

Golls. (1) Fat chops; or ridges of fat on the fleshy parts of a corpulent person. It is in Johnson, with authorities, as used contemptuously for hands; paws. It is not known to us in that sense. (2) Pendent matter hanging from children's noses, sometimes called lambs' legs [Johnson].

*Gommerel. A fool [M. C. H. B.].

*Gon. For given. 'It was *gon* me' [Spur.].

*Gong. The ringe or rickles of corn or hay collected in the field by a horse or other rake [Johnson].

Good-doing. (1) Charitable in various modes. Ex. 'The parson's daughters are very *good-doing* young women.' (2).To put flesh or fat on rapidly. (3) Of land in good working order. (4) Of roads in good state for walking [M. C. H. B.].

Good Mind, Good Skin. Many combinations of the adjective *good*, with different substantives, are detailed in Johnson; but these two are not among them. They both express good humour. Ex. 'He is not in a *good mind*,' or 'he is in a *bad skin* to-day.'

Good'n, Goody. Contractions of **Good Man** and **Good Wife** (the first sometimes farther contracted to **Go'on**).

Good Tidily. Reasonably, pretty well. Tolerably, pretty middling [Spur.].

Good Tidy. The adverb *good*, in its sense of 'reasonably,' or 'not amiss,' as given by Johnson, does not satisfy us without the addition of *tidy*, which in strictness means **Timely**, from A. S. *tid*. Ex. 'She stayed a *good tidy* stound,' i. e. 'a good while.' It has not, however, always a perceptible connexion with time. Ex. 'This is a *good tidy* crop,' i. e. a pretty good one. 'He slapped him *good-tidily*.'

*Goolie, or Guler. The yellowhammer (*Emberiza citrinella*) [M. C. H. B.].

*Gophering Irons. For crimping linen [M. C. H. B.].

Gore. (1) Mire. 'Slush and *gore*' are generally mentioned together. The former expresses the thin, the latter the thick part of the mire. See **Goer**. (2) The same as scoot.

Gore Blood. Clotted, congealed blood. 'All of a *gore*,' or 'all of a *gore of blood*.'

Gosgood. Yeast [Sir T. Browne]. Ray says that in his time it was in use also in Kent. The word is now utterly extinct.

Goslin. The male catkin of different species of *Salix*.

Gotch. (1) A large coarse ewer or pitcher. (2) Also a disease to which rabbits are liable [M. C. H. B.].

Gotch-belly. A fair round belly, much resembling the protuberance of a *gotch*.

Go-to bed-at-noon. The apposite name of the common goatsbeard.

*Gouch, Gush, Gulch. ' It came down gulch,' swop, flop, all of a heap [M. C. H. B.].

*Gour. Voracious [M. C. H. B.].

Gow. Let us go ; an abbreviation of Go we, the plural imperf. of the verb to go. It implies, ' but let us all go together.' A farmer in Suffolk, speaking of the difference between the old farmers' wives and the modern ones, observed that ' when his mother called the maids at milking-time, she never said go, but *gow.*'

*Grabble. To resist, to contend, to grapple with [Johnson].

Grain. To gripe the throat ; to strangle. Grane [Spur.]. Greened [*B. N. 6*]

*Grainer. A vat used in tanning—in the second operation. It is filled with a strong solution of pigeons' dung to destroy the effects of the lime on the hide [Johnson].

*Graned. A sheep whose wool is a mixture of black and white, or speckled, is called a *graned* sheep [Johnson].

*Grassing. The grassing requires about five weeks, and if there are showers constantly turning thrice a week, if not twice. This is always on grass land [C. D.].

Grattan. Stubble [Johnson].

*Graycoat. An epithet applied to an agent employed to collect tithes [J. H. G.].

Graze. To become covered with the growth of grass.

Grease. A faint and dim suffusion over the sky, not amounting to positive cloudiness, and supposed to indicate approaching rain.

Greenolf. (1) The greenfinch, or, more properly, green grosbeak, *Parus viridus*, Lin. (2) *Loxia chloris* [M. C. H. B.].

*****Green Way.** A road over turf between hedges, usually without gates [W. R.].

Green Weed. The dyer's broom, *Genista tinctoria*, Lin.

Greft, Grift. To graft.

Grewin. A greyhound.

Grey-backs. Scaup ducks (*Fuligula marila*) [M. C. H. B.].

*****Grey-bird.** An English partridge [M. C. H. B.].

*****Grey-coat Parson.** An impropriator ; or, the tenant who hires the tithes.

*****Grey-duck** or **Hearth-duck.** Gadwell (Stevenson) [M. C. H. B.].

*****Grey-gulls.** Immature herring- and saddle-back gulls [M. C. H. B.]

Grigs. Small eels.

Grimble. To begrime. **Grumbled** in the same sense is stronger, implying a thicker coat of dirt.

Grimmer. A pond or mere, of considerable extent, but of such moderate depth as to have much of its surface covered with weeds, appearing to the eye a *green mere*.

Grindle. A small and narrow drain for water. But **Drindle** is a better word, q.v.

*****Grip.** A shallow drain [Cull. Haw.]. **Grup** [Em. and B. N. 28, 36].

*****Gripple.** A small drain, stream, or beck [Johnson]. Surely a diminution of 'grip' [W. R.].

Grissens. Stairs or staircase.

*****Grit.** To take work by contract=great [F. J. B.].

*****Grittle.** Corn just broken or cracked. Oatmeal so done is called **Grits** or **Grots** [Johnson].

Groaning. A lying-in.

Groaning Cake. A cake made on such occasions, with which about as many superstitious tricks are played as with bride-cake.

*Ground. Go to ground, to defecate [M. C. H. B.].

Ground Firing. Roots of trees and bushes, taken as a sort of perquisite by the labourers who stub them, and used for fuel.

Ground Gudgeon. A small fish, adhering by its mouth to stones at the. bottom of brooks and shallow rivulets; the loche, otherwise called ground-bait, being used to catch pike or perch. It is *Cobitis barbatula*, Lin.

Ground Lark. (1) What species of lark is meant is not easy to determine, for all our indigenous species build their nests on the ground. Any, rather than the sky-lark, which soars to a vast height from the ground, or the woodlark, which perches and sings on boughs. (2) Meadow Pipit [M. C. H. B.].

Ground Rain. A plentiful but gradual fall of rain, which works its way deep into the ground.

Grout. A sort of thin mortar poured into the interstices of building materials, as flints or other substances of small size and irregular shape, which cannot be laid even. They are confined with a wooden frame till the *grout* is incorporated with them, and fixed. Then the frame is removed, and another portion of wall formed in like manner.

Grub. (1) Idle, nonsensical talk. (2) Food. (3) To pick up a living in mean haphazard ways.

Grubblings. Phr. ' To lie *grubblings*,' i. e. grovelling, with the face downwards.

Grub Felling. Felling of trees by undermining them, and cutting away all their roots.

*Grub Stubbling. Half chop off, half stub a tree [H. B.].

Gruffle. To make a sort of growling noise in the throat, as men are wont to do in sleep or in drink. In fact, it is a diminutive of **Growl.**

Grunny. The snout of a hog.

Grup, Groop. A trench, not amounting in breadth to a ditch. If narrower still, it is a **Grip**; if extremely narrow, a **Gripple.**

Grutch. To grudge. An old word with us, and occurs in the Lynn Guild Certificate, temp. Richard II [W. R.].

*Guards. 'Drawing the *guards.*' Just ready to fight [W. R.].

*Gudgeon. A small axle [G. E.].

*Guler. Gulefinch or yellowhammer [E. S. T.].

Gull. (1) To sweep away by force of running water. Ex. 'The bank has been *gulled* down by the freshes,' q. v. (2) A breach or hole made by the force of a torrent. (3) Also a brook thickly overgrown with underwood or brushwood [H. C.].

Gulp. (1) The young of any animal in its softest and tenderest state. Can the meaning be (hyperbolically) that it looks as if it might be swallowed, taken down at a *gulp?* *Gulp*-o'-the-nest, the smallest of the brood. (2) A very short, squabby, diminutive person. (3) A very severe blow or fall; enough to beat the sufferer to a mummy. Here is enough of association. But in this sense it must be taken as a variation of **Culp,** which we use in its proper sense, and q. v.

Gulsh. (1) Mud. (2) A heavy fall. (3) Plump, souse, &c., applied to the fall.

Gulsher. A heavy fall [*B. N.* 56].

Gulsky. Corpulent and gross.

Gumption. Understanding.

Gurn. To grin like a dog.

Gush. A gust of wind.

Gussock. A strong and sudden gush of wind.

*__*Guy.__* A feint or trick [Johnson].

Gye. A name of different weeds growing among corn. In some places *Ranunculus arvensis*, Lin. is so called, and in others, different species of *Galium*; sufficient diversity. And see *N. and Q.*, 4th Ser. viii. p. 108.

Gyle. Wort.

*__*Gyp.__* (1) To cheat, to trick [Johnson]. (2) Cambridge college-servants. So called from their vulture-like propensities [M. C. H. B.].

*__*Hack.__* (1) Probably havock, e. g. a flock of sheep playing hack [W. B.]. (2) Birds play hack with fruit-trees [F. J. B.].

Hack, Half-hack. A hatch, a door divided across.

Hack. (1) To stammer, to cut words in pieces. (2) To cough faintly and frequently.

Hackering. Stuttering [*B. N.* 88].

Hackle. To shackle, or tether beasts, to prevent their running away.

Hack Slavering. Stammering and sputtering, like a dunce at his lesson.

Haggy. Applied to the broken and even surface of the soil, when in a moist state. Were it dried and hardened by sun or frost, it would be **Hobbly.** Rough, uneven as a road having large stones laid upon it, or deep uneven ruts [Johnson].

Haifer. To toil.

Hain. To heighten [W. R.]. To rise in price.

*__*Hainer.__* The master who holds or sustains the expenses of the feast [Johnson].

Hait-wo! A word of command to horses in a team, meaning, 'go to the left'; for *wo*, in this case, is not stop, but go, by the commutability of *w* and *g* in A. S. words. This was horse language in the fourteenth century. *Ch.* '*Heit* Scot! *Heit*, Broc!' which, by the way, are names still given to cart-horses.

Hake. (1) A pothook. The progress is hook, hoke, *hake*. But this is inverted order. (2) Now chiefly used for a kind of gate which hangs over the kitchen fire, or another utensil which hangs down the chimney, both used for suspending pots and boilers [Spur.]. A horse is said to *hake* at plough when he works heartily, doing more than his share [Johnson]. (3) Hooks generally [W. R.]. (4) To toil, particularly in walking. There is an obvious connexion in sense with *hack* and *hackney*. It is often joined with Hatter, q. v. Ex. 'He has been *haking* and *hattering* all day long.'

*****Hale.** (1) A long range or pile of bricks set out to dry in the open air before being burned [Johnson]. (2) Mangold clamp [M. C. H. B.]. (3) A heap of anything [Em.].

*****Half Fowl.** Any wild fowl other than mallard [M. C. H. B.].

*****Half-hack.** A hatch, a door divided into two parts.

Half-hammer. The game of 'hop, step, and jump.'

Half-rocked. Oafish, silly. It seems to imply that a poor creature's education as a simpleton was begun even in his cradle by his careless nurse.

*****Haller.** To halloo. To 'haller hold yer,' is to warn the man on the top of the wagon to hold tight whilst the wagon is being moved from shock to shock in loading up corn in the harvest field. A boy rides the horse and 'hallers hold'yer' [M. C. H. B.].

*****Hallorin.** To shout, loud call [G. E.].

Hallowday. A holiday.

*****Hamper.** To impede [M. C. H. B.]. 'I 'ont be *hampered* up along o' you.'

***Hample Trees.** The bars by which horses draw a plough, &c. [Spur.]. Hames or Hameltrees [Johnson].

***Hancer.** The heron [G. E.].

Hand. To sign. Ex. ' They made me *hand* a paper.' (2) Performance. It is the eleventh sense of the word in Johnson, and nothing is commoner than to speak of making a good or a bad hand of any undertaking. With us the phrase, in the latter sense, admits no qualifying epithet. To ' make a *hand* on,' is to make waste of, to spoil or destroy. Ex. ' He has made a *hand* of all he had, he has wasted his whole property.

***Handhawk.** A plasterer's tool on which he lays the plaster [Johnson].

Hand-over-head. (1) Thoughtlessly extravagant. (2) Hemp is said to be dressed ' *hand-over-head*,' when the coarse part is not separated from the fine.

***Handsel.** A helping hand [M. C. H. B.]. A start [*B. N.* 71].

***Handsel.** To inaugurate, to begin. To put the first coin into a collection [M. C. H. B.].

Hand-smooth. Uninterruptedly, without obstacle. Also, entirely. Ex. ' He ate it up *hand-smooth*.'

Handstaff. The handle of a flail. See **Swingel**.

***Handstaff-cap.** The swivel that joins handle and swingel [W. B.].

Hang. (1) A crop of fruit. ' A good tidy *hang* of apples.' (2) A declivity.

***Hangy.** A clayey soil when wet is *hangy* [Spur.].

Hanging Level. A regular and uninterrupted declivity, an inclined plane.

***Hang on to.** To scold. ' I'll hang on to him properly when I catch him ' [C. S. P.].

Hang Sleeve. A dangler, an officious but unmeaning suitor.

Hang Such. A worthless fellow, a fit candidate for a halter.

Hank. (1) A fastening for a door or gate. (2) A small quantity of twine, yarn, &c., not rolled in a ball, but doubled over in lengths, is called a hank.

Hap. To cover or wrap up.

Happing. Covering, wrappers, warm clothing.

Hap Harlot. A coarse coverlit.

Harber. The hornbeam or hardbeam.

Hards. (1) Coarse flax, otherwise **Tow-hards.** (2) The very hard cinders commonly called iron cinders. The calx of pit coal imperfectly vitrified by intense heat [M. S.].

*Harkany. A job. Ex. 'I have finished my harkany' [M. C. H. B.].

*Harness. Leathern defences for the hands and legs of hedgers, to protect them from the thorns [Spur.].

Harnsey. A heron. See **Hornsey**, a young heron [E. S. T.].

Harnsey Gutted. Lank and lean, like a harnsey.

Harren. (1) Made of hair, q. d. *hairen.* 'A *harren* brum' is a hair broom. (2) Herring is so pronounced [M. C. H. B.].

Harriage. Confusion. The *i* is to be sunk in pronunciation, as in carriage and marriage. Ex. 'They are all up at *harriage.*' I think I have heard that, in the south part of Suffolk, the phrase, 'He is gone to *Harwich*' (alike in pronunciation), means he is gone to rack and ruin. Johnson has it **Harridge.**

*Harry Denchman. The Danish crow [W. G. W.].

*Hartree. The vertical part of a gate which claps against the gatepost [Spur.]. Johnson has it, the upright wood at that end of a gate to which the irons are fixed, and spells it **Heart-tree.**

Harvest Lord. The principal reaper, who goes first, and whose motions regulate those of his followers.

Harvest Lady. The second reaper in the row, who supplies, or supplied, my lord's place on his occasional absence, but does not seem to have been ever so regularly greeted by the title, except on the day of harvest-home.

Hase. The heart, liver, &c., of a hog, seasoned, wrapped up in the omentum and roasted.

*Hasel. See **Haysele.**

Hassock. Coarse grass growing in rank tufts in boggy ground.

Hassock Head. A shock-head, a bushy and entangled growth of coarse hair.

*Hatch. A gate. A half *hatch*, where a horse may go but a cart cannot [E. S. T.].

Hatter. To harass and exhaust with fatigue.

*Haughty Weather. Windy weather [Marshall].

Havel. (1) The beard of barley. (2) The slough of a snake.

*Havel and Slaie. Parts of the fittings of a weaver's loom [W. R.].

Haw. The ear of oats. Johnson spells it **Haugh.**

Hawkey or **Horkey.** The feast at harvest-home.

Hawkey-load. The last load of the crop, which, in simpler and ruder times, was always led home on the evening of the *hawkey*, with much rustic pageantry.

Hay. (1) A hedge, more particularly a clipped quickset hedge. It is most commonly pronounced as if it were in the Pl. N., or ather as if it were spelled *haze*. In Suffolk it is always pronounced **Hay** [Forby]. (2) A rabbit-net [Cull. Haw.].

Hay-crome. No rustic implement is now literally called by this name, but a metaphorical use of the word is very

common. The characters scrawled by an awkward pen-
man are likened to ' *hay-cromes* and pitchforks,' as they
more generally are to ' pot-hooks.'

*Hay-goaf. Hay mow.

Hay-jack. (1) The lesser reedsparrow, or sedgebird of
Penn. (2) The Whitethroat (*Sylvia cinerea*) [M. C. H. B.].

Hay Net. (1) A hedge net. A long low net, to prevent
hares or rabbits from escaping to covert in or through
hedges. (2) Hang net [M. C. H. B.].

Haysele. The season of making hay.

Haze. To dry linen, &c., by hanging it up in the fresh
air, properly on a hedge. But that circumstance is not
essential. Indeed, anything so exposed is said to be
hazed, as rows of corn or hay, when a brisk breeze
follows a shower.

Hazle. To grow dry at top. Dim.

Head. (1) Face. We say ' I told him so to his *head*,' as
old as Sh. [Forby]. (2) Bullocks are said to go at *head*
when they have the first bite, in distinction to those who
follow [Marshall].

Headache. The wild field-poppy.

Head Man. The chief hind on a farm.

Headswoman. A midwife.

Heads and Holls, Humps and Holls. Pell-mell, and topsy-
turvy. Prominences and hollows tumbled confusedly
together ; promiscuous confusion. Hills and Holls [W. R.].

Heap. A great number or quantity.

Heart. The stomach. ' A pain at the *heart*' means the
stomach-ache.

*Hearth. The island on Scoulton Mere is so called
[M. C. H. B.].

*Heart Spoon. The pit of the stomach. It is, no doubt, so
called from the little hollow, or depression, near the point
of the sternum.

*Heater. The fork of a road [*B. N.* 88].

*Heavels. Plain work in weaving [Arderon].

*Heck. A half-door or latch [Marshall].

*Heckfor. A heifer [Marshall].

Hedge Accentor. The hedgesparrow.

*Hedge-betty. A hedgesparrow [W. B.].

*Hedge-pig. A hedgehog [W. R.].

*Heel. 'You have got me by the *heel.*' You have out-reached me [Arderon].

*Heft. A handle of a knife, &c. [G. E.].

*Heft or Hift. A lift or a push [M. C. H. B.].

*Hefty. Blusterous weather [M. C. H. B.].

Heifker. A heifer.

Heigh'n. To heighten. See **Hain.**

Heir. To inherit. Ex. ' His son will *heir* his estate.

Help up. To assist or support. It is commonly used ironically. Ex. ' I am finely HOLP UP.' O. E.,' A man is well *holp up* that trusts in you.'

Helve. The handle of an axe.

*Hempland. A little field or pightle attached to a cottage, so called from being used to grow hemp on [Spur.].

Hen Poller. A loft for poultry to roost. Sometimes simply *poller.*

Hen's nose full. A very minute quantity.

*Herbage. The right of feeding or pasturage [M. C. H. B.].

Hereaways. Hereabouts.

Herne. A nook of land, projecting into another district, parish, or field. See **Hyrne.**

*Herring Spink. (1) A bird often seen during the herring fishery. The golden-crested wren [E. F. G.]. (2) (*Regalus cristatus*) C. T. Booth [M. C. H. B.].

***Hess.** A quantity of yarn containing fourteen leas, or two skeins [Johnson].

***Het.** Past imp. of heat. Ex. ' I ha het the kittle.'

***Hey.** A hedge. See **Hay.**

***Heyhowing.** Thieving of yarn from the master weaver [Arderon].

Hick. To hop or spring.

Hickle, Heckle. (1) To dress flax ; to break it into its finest fibres. (2) A comb to dress flax.

Hickler. A dresser of flax or hemp.

Hide. (1) To thresh ; ' to curry the hide.' (2) Abdominal skin, e. g. ' Suck that into your hide ' [M. C. H. B.].

***Hides.** Entrails prepared to make sausages in [Spur.].

Hiding. A beating.

***Hidlings.** At random [Spur.].

Higgle. (1) To be nice and tedious in bargaining. It is dimin. from **Haggle,** with a sense of contempt. It implies the most petty chaffering. (2) To effect by slow degrees, and by minute sparing and saving. The poor often talk of *higgling* up a pig, i. e. buying and fattening it up in that way.

***High.** Aristocratic, whilst **Low** = short in stature [M. C. H. B.].

***High Learned.** University-taught [C. S. P.].

***Highlows.** Half-boots [M. C. H. B.].

***High Surprizes.** High spirits ; hoity toity [Spur.].

Hike. To go away. It is generally used in a contemptuous sense. Ex. ' Come, *hike,*' i. e. take yourself off ; begone. Probably local pronunciation for ' hook ' it [W. R.]. Johnson gives its meaning as to seek, search, or find ; ' go, *hike* him up.'

Hild. The sediment of beer ; sometimes used as an imperfect substitute for yeast. Better *hilds* [Spur.].

*Hilding. Leaning or tilting, as a cask [Spur.].

*Hill. A floating hover or piece of high ground entirely surrounded by water on the Broads [M. C. H. B.].

Himp. To limp. ·A variety rather than a corruption.

*Hinder. Yonder [Spur. and Cull. Haw.].

Hingin. A hinge. Belg. *hengene*, cardo.

Hingle. (1) A small hinge. (2) A snare of wire; moving easily, and closing like a hinge. (3) To snare. Poachers *hingle* hares and rabbits.

*Hingling is the term used for a snare for pheasants, made with one or with two wires [W. B.].

Hippany. A part of the swaddling-clothes of an infant; a wrapper for the hips.

*Hipstrap. A strap which passes down near the hips of the horse, to support and hold up the trace [Johnson].

Hire. To borrow. We speak of 'hiring money' for taking it up at interest. And why not money as well as house or land? The interest is rent.

*Hirn. A narrow line overhung with bushes [Johnson]. But I doubt this, and fancy Johnson merely noticed a place at the corner of the hyrne, q. v., which answered this description [W. R.].

*Hisen. (1) To raise or advance the price of anything [Johnson]. This, too, I doubt. We always say 'hain' [W. R.]. (2) His. Ex.—
    'He who takes what isn't his'n,
    When he's cotched is sent to prison' [M. C. H. B.].

Hitch. (1) To change place. (2) To stop at [*N. and Q.*, 3rd Ser. iv. p. 363]. (3) To make room [Pr. Pa.]. (4) To jerk. (5) To twist, of rope. (6) Nautical phrase, 'half hitch' [M. C. H. B.].

*Hitchel or Hickel. A hemp-dresser's comb [Spur.].

*Hitchel. A kind of halter, for hitching a pony to a fence [W. B.].

*Hitcheler, or Hickler. A hemp-dresser [Spur.].

Hithe. A small port.

Hithertoward. Towards this time, or place.

Hitty-missy. At random ; hit or miss.

Hob, Hub. (1) The nave of a wheel. (2) The flat ends of a kitchen range, or of a bath-stove ; not the back. (3) The mark to be thrown at in quoits and some other games. (4) The hilt or guard of a weapon. In general ' up to the *hub* ' means as far as possible.

Hobbles. Roughness on a road or path, which causes passengers to hobble in their gait.

Hobble-de-poise. (1) Evenly balanced, so that any slight wavering is immediately recovered. If we had rocking stones in our country, we should describe them among ourselves as standing exactly *hobble - de - poise.* (2) Metaph., wavering in mind, unable to come to a determination.

*Hobbly. Rough, rugged, stony [M. C. H. B.].

Hobby. A small horse ; synonymous with Pony.

Hobby-lanthorn. A will-o'-the-wisp ; from its motion, as if it were a lanthorn ambling and curvetting on the back of a *hobby.*

*Hocket. To romp about foolishly [C. S. P.].

Hocs and Hoes. The feet and leg bones of swine.

*Hodman Hob. A snail-shell [Spur.]. ? Dodman [W. R.].

*Hod. A shell or skin, potato hod, bean hod. ' Hodding peas,' shelling peas [M. C. H. B.]

*Hodmedod. A small snail [G. E.].

Hodding Spade. A sort of spade principally used in the fens, so shaped as to take up a considerable portion of earth entire, somewhat like a *hod.*

Hoddy. Pretty well in health and spirits, in tolerably good case. May it not be a corruption of Hardy ?

*Hoffle. To shuffle or hobble.

Hogget, Hog. A sheep a year old, before its first shearing [W. B.].

Hoglin. A homely article of pastry.

Hog-over-high. The game of leap-frog.

*Hogweed. (1) Knotgrass. (2) Scarlet poppy and also sowthistle, thus called [M. C. H. B.].

Hoist. (1) A cough. (2) To cough. (3) To raise. Ex. 'The river is hoisted' or risen [M. C. H. B.].

Hoit-a-poit. Assuming airs of importance unsuitable to years or station.

Holie Verd. Holly used in the Christmas decoration of churches [Spur.].

Holl. (1) A ditch, particularly a dry one. This is the simple form; we also use the compounds **Deke-holl** and **Dike-holl**, i. e. a hollow or empty ditch. By no means necessarily a dry one [Spur.]. (2) Hollow, which, in strictness, is a compound of two adjectives.

*Holls. The groin, legs, &c. 'Head and *holls*,' heads or tails [Spur.].

*Holped. Helped [H. B.].

Holt. A small grove or plantation.

Holymas. All Saints' Day.

*Homer. A very short plump skate [W. R.].

*Hommer. A hammer [G. E.].

Honey Crach. A small plum, of luscious sweetness but little flavour.

*Hoogo. A kind of taint in meat, &c., from too long keeping [Spur.]. *Haut gaut?*

*Hop and go one, or **Dot and go one.** A lame man, a one-legged one who uses a crutch, which makes the dot or impression like a dot [M. C. H. B.].

Hop Crease. The game among boys, more commonly called Hop Scotch.

Hop-pole Marriage. A marriage just in time to save the legitimacy of a child. Also a Broomstick Marriage.

Hopping Giles. A common appellation of any one who limps. St. Giles was reputed the especial patron of cripples.

*Hoppintoad. A toad [G. E.]. I think natterjack toads . are so called [M. C. H. B.].

Hopple. A tether to confine the legs of beasts to prevent their escape, or to make them stand still. A beast tethered by having a fore foot tied to the opposite foot behind, is said to be *cross-hoppled*.

Hoppling. Tottering, moving weakly and unsteadily ; frequently applied to children. All these words are nearly allied to Hobble, and have certainly the same origin, q. v.

*Horder. To hoard or lay up [G. E.].

*Horkey. Better thus than Hawkey, for which see Spur.

*Horkey Load. The last load of the harvest [F. C. H. in *N. and Q.*, 4th Ser. vi. p. 487].

Hornen. Made of horn. Ex. ' The *hornen* book.' ' A *hornen* spoon ' [Jen.].

Hornpie. The lapwing.

Horns. The awns of barley. Though a corruption, not an unmeaning one.

*Hornsey. A crane [Arderon]. This is an error for hern-saw or heron [W. R.].

Horse. (1) A seed or straw introduced into a cask, by means of which the liquor is stolen [Johnson]. (2) To work on a dead horse = to draw money on account before work is finished. (3) A dead freight = vacant space in chartered ship. (4) That is a horse of a very different colour = that is a different matter altogether [M. C. H. B.].

***Horse Brambles.** Briars, wild rose [Marshall].

***Horsetree.** The whipple or swingle tree [Marshall].

Horse-ma-gog. Boisterously frolicsome.

Hose. The sheath or spathe of an ear of corn.

***Hose-in-hose.** A primrose or polyanthus with one corolla within another [M. C. H. B.].

***Hotkin.** A case for a sore finger [Arderon].

***Hotness.** Very hot. Ex. 'That makes some *hotness*' [Pr. Pa.].

Hot Pot. A mixture of warm ale and spirits.

***Houghses.** Feet or shoes of any one [Johnson]. I have often heard ' Huffs ' used, but have thought it a corruption of ' Hoofs.' 'Take your clumsy *huffs* off the chair ' [W. R.]. See Houss.

Hounce, or Houncer. The ornament of red and yellow worsted spread over the collars of horses in a team.

Houncings. Housings [Spur.].

***Houndings.** The housings of the harness [W. R.]. Covering the collar (Suff.) [E. S. T.].

House. (1) The family sitting-room, as distinguished from the other apartments [Gr.]. (2) To grow thick and compact, as corn does. If this have any relation to a house at all, it must be to the roof.

***House Dowly.** A tenderly brought up person [Johnson].

***Housen.** For houses [W. R.].

Houss. A contemptuous name for feet, as being like those of a beast's hoofs. [I cannot help thinking this is a transcriber's error for ' houffs ' (hoofs). See Houghses — W. R.]. Miss Matthews, howe er, has ' Howshies or hoishies ' for boots or feet.

Hoven. Swollen. Cattle are *hoven* by eating too much

green clover in a moist state, or other flatulent and suc-
culent food. Turnips are *hoven* by rank and rapid growth
in a strong wet soil.

*Hover. A floating reed-bed [M. C. H. B.].

*Hover Spade. A tongue-shaped spade for cutting turf
for burning [M. C. H. B.].

*Hovvers, or Huvvers. Dried flags for fuel, differing from
Howes in being the upper cut, with the grass, reeds, &c.
[Spur.].

*How-do-ye-do, Hullabaloo. To make a pretty piece of
work = to kick up a hullabaloo [M. C. H. B.].

*Hubs. Hoofs [Spur.].

*Huckering. To stammer [G. E.].

*Huckle. To bend down with pain [Spur.].

*Huckle Bone. The hip bone [Spur.].

Huckles. The hips.

Hudderin. A well-grown lad. If a Suffolk farmer (in
East Suffolk at least) be asked how many male servants
he keeps, his answer may probably be 'Two men and
a *hudderin*.' (2) Large and loutish [G. E.].

*Huddle me-close. The side-bone of birds, not the merry-
thought [M. C. H. B.].

Huff. (1) A dry, scurfy, or scaly incrustation on the skin.
Also Hoof [Spur.]. (2) To scold, rate, or take to task.
In O. E. a *huff*-cap is a swaggering blade. (3) In a
temper. 'He is in a huff.'

Huffle, Huffles, Hufflins. A rattling in the throat in
breathing. 'The death-ruffle' [Spur.].

*Huffs, Hoofs. Men's feet [W. R.].

Huggy-me-close. The clavicle of a fowl; more commonly
called the Merry-thought.

*Hugger-mugger. Stingy [Pr. Pa.].

Hulk. (1) A lout, a lubber; one who, in vulgar phrase, seems to have 'more guts than brains.' (2) A gross overgrown fat fellow. (3) To pull out the entrails of a hare or rabbit. It does not appear to be applied to the exenteration of any other animal.

Hull. (1) To throw. It is pretty plainly a corruption of **Hurl**, and is therefore not to be spelled **Holl**, e. g. 'He *hulled* it into the holl'=He threw it into the ditch. (2) To take off the husks. 'To hull the banes'='To shill the paas' [Spur.].

*****Hullett.** A brook with woody banks [C. S. P.].

Hulls. The husks of peas, pulse, beans, &c. [Spur.]. Gooseberries [Em.].

Hull and **Hullchin.** A broad, thick piece of bread and meat or other victual [Johnson]. Often **Hunchin** [A. E. R.].

*****Hullpoke.** A bed made with oat flites [C. W. B.].

Hullup. To vomit, viz. to hurl up your food.

*****Hullyly.** Wholly. 'That du *hullyly* stam me'=That puts me to a nonplus [M. C. H. B.].

Hulver. Holly.

Hulver-headed. Stupid, muddled, confused, as if the head were enveloped in a *hulver* bush.

Hume. A hymn. This word is curiously puzzling.

Hummer. (1) To begin to neigh. The gentle and pleasing sound which a horse utters when he hears the corn shaken in the sieve, or when he perceives the approach of his companion, or groom. (2) Frequentative of hum [M. C. H. B.].

Hump. (1) A contemptible quantity, a poor pittance. (2) Ill-temper. Ex. 'He has got the *hump*.'

Hunch. (1) A lift, or shove. 'Give me a *hunch*, Tom,' said an elderly East Anglian matron, somewhat corpulent, to her stout footman, who stood grinning behind her, while she was endeavouring to climb into her carriage. (2) A thick slice of bread and cheese [C. H. E. W.].

*Hunchin. See Hull.

Hunch Weather. Cold weather, which makes men hunch up their shoulders, and animals contract their limbs, and look as if they were *hunch*-backed.

Hunger Poisoned. Famished, unhealthy from want of sufficient nourishment. In Suffolk, *hunger-poisoned* is applied solely to misers.

*Hurdle, Hox, or Huddle. To thread the hind legs of rabbits [M. C. H. B.].

Hurry. A small load of corn or hay got up in haste, from apprehension of rain.

*Hutch. (1) A chest [C. S. P.]. (2) An iron chest in which the registers are kept [C. D.].

Hutkin. A case or sheath for a sore finger. Otherwise and generally called a Cot. See Hotkin. Hoodkin, a little hood [Spur.].

Hnvel or Hoofel. The feet. Hence Huvelling, leaving dirty marks. 'I've just cleaned the place, and you've come *huvelling* about' [W. B.].

*Hyrne. A corner, the portion of the village situated in an angle or corner [E. S. T.].

*Hyter Sprite. A beneficent fairy, not a ghost. Also antics, 'high surprizes' [Em.].

Ice Bone. A part of the rump of beef. The Aitch- or Edge-bone [E. S. T.].

Ichon. Each one. Ex. '*Ichon* on'em.'

*Iller. More, 'more *iller* ' is worse [Arderon].

*Imber. Numbers [Arderon].

Imitate. To attempt, to endeavour, to make as if. Ex. A child or a sick person *imitated* to walk, or to do something else, which he proves unable to accomplish.

*Imp. A child. Ex. 'I was afraid the poor *imp* would have been frizzled.'

*Inards. Inwards, entrails, the inward part [M. C. H. B.].

Inder. A great number or quantity of valuable things. Ex. 'He is worth an *inder* of money.' India?

Indifferent. Not merely middling, neuter, neither good nor bad, but positively bad.

*Ing. A common pasture or meadow [Ray].

*Ingain. Profit in buying and selling [W. B.].

*In general. Generally, in a general way [M. C. H. B.].

*Innocent. Rather half-witted, not by any means the same as harmless; e. g. 'He's a rare simple *innocent.*'

Inward-maid. The housemaid in a farm-house, who has no work in the dairy, &c.

Iron-sided. Hardy, rough, unmanageable. A boy who fears nobody, and plays all sorts of mischievous tricks, is called an *iron-sided* dog.

*Ivory. Ivy (N. Ess.) [C. D.].

*Jack. A farthing [Johnson].

*Jack-o'lantern. *Ignis fatuus*, Will-o'-the-wisp. One seen at East Ruston, 1890. Also called lantern-man [M. C. H. B.].

*Jacky Breezer. (1) A dragon-fly [Spur.]. (2) More usually Tom Breezer, plural Breezes [M. C. H. B.].

*Jacob. A small frog [C. S. P.].

Jade. (1) A horse. We do not always use it in a contemptuous sense, as it is in general use. (2) A horse that will not work well up to the collar [M. C. H. B.].

*Jaffling. Jiffling.

Jag. An indefinite quantity, but less than a load, of hay or corn in the straw. Johnson says 'a quantity of hay or corn in the straw, or thorns, faggots, &c., any of which is three courses upon a waggon and topping up. As Major Moor observes, a *jag* and a bargain are as one.' And as to the meaning (of this sentence) it's what you please [W. R.].

*Jam. Of clay. *Vide* Webster [H. B.].

Jamb. (1) A mass of masonry in a building, or of stone or other mineral in a quarry or pit, standing upright, and more or less distinct from neighbouring or adjoining parts. (2) To squeeze or to walk, e. g. Some one has been jambing here afore us = Some one has walked on these ronds before us, looking for snipe. (Jacks lay till you almost jamb on to them.) (3) 'To jamb the ronds,' to hunt them for eggs or snipe, &c. [M. C. H. B.].

Jammock. (1) To beat, squeeze, crush, pummel, or trample into a soft mass. Intens. of **Jam**. (2) A soft, pulpy substance.

*Jannock. (1) Fair, honourable, or straightforward [W. R.]. (2) A cake baked on the hearth [Spur.].

Jatter. (1) To split into shivers. (2) To jolt [Johnson].

*Jaffle. Idle discourse of an indecent or malicious character [E. S. T.]. *Sed quaere.* See **Jiffling**.

Jay-fulfer or **Felt.** The fieldfare (*S. pilaris*) [M. C. H. B.].

*Jeldered up. Severely bruised [Johnson].

Jeroboam. A capacious bowl or goblet, otherwise and more generally called a **Joram**.

Jet. (1) A very large ladle to empty a cistern. (2) To jet, to take out with a jot [F. J. B.].

Jib. The under lip. Of a whimpering child it is said 'he hangs his *jib*.'

Jibbet. To put a toad or a hedgehog to a cruel death, by placing it on one end of a balanced plank, and striking the other smartly, so as to send the poor animal high into the air, and of course to kill it by the fall. In some counties it is called **Fillipping**.

Jibby. A frisky, gadding, flaunting wench, full of fantastical and affected airs, and dressed in flashy finery.

Jibby Horse. A showman's horse decorated with particoloured trappings, plumes, streamers, &c. It is sometimes transferred to a human subject.

*****Jibe, Gibe.** To make a fool of, to turn, nautically of the boat-sail or bowsprit [M. C. H. B.].

*****Jib Fork.** A two-pronged fork of the length used in harvest [Johnson].

*****Jiccop.** To move or disturb a seat [G. E.].

*****Jiffling.** Fidgety [W. R.].

Jiggs. Small dregs or sediment, as in a pot of coffee or a bottle of physic [M. S.].

Jig-by-jowl. Phr., close together. Apparently a corruption of a phrase more general, 'Cheek-by-jowl.' But Jun. admits, and we use it.

Jill-hooter, Jilly-hooter. An owl. Jill is a female name, formerly very common. Madge is another familiar appellative of the same animal. Billy-wix is a third, which should belong to the male bird; but it does not appear that difference of sex is at all regarded.

Jill or Jim. A machine with two wheels for carrying timber; otherwise, and in Norfolk most frequently, called a *Jill*. The Drug, q. v., is in many parts called a Timber-jill [a drug is a two-wheeled carriage]. See Gill.

*****Jimmer Hinges.** Leathern hinges [C. W. B.].

*****Jip.** To trick, cheat, or impose upon [Johnson].

*****Joalies.** Young herrings [E. F. G.].

· **Joan's Silver Pin.** A single article of finery, produced occasionally and ostentatiously, among dirt and sluttery.

*****Job.** To peck with a sharp strong beak [Pr. Pa.].

Jogging. A protuberance in sawn wood, probably where

the saw was *joggled* and thrown out of the line, by a knot or some accident.

*Joist. Joist cattle are those of other persons taken in to pasture [Cull. Haw.]. Possibly a corruption of Agist [W. R.].

*Joll. (1) To peck [W. G. W.]. (2) To jolt.

*Jollick, or Jonniok. Right. 'That's not *jollick*' [Johnson]. This is another example of the interchanging of *ll* for *nn*. No doubt it is the same word as Jannock, q. v.

*Jolly. A jolly man = a stout man [F. J. B.].

Joram. Br., &c. *Vide* Jeroboam.

Joseph. A very old-fashioned riding-coat for women, scarcely now to be seen or heard of.

Joss, Jostle. To make room by standing or sitting close.

Jostling Block, Jossing Block. A horse-block, to which the horse must be made to *joss* as close as possible, and to stand quite still for the convenience of mounting.

Jot. Plump, downright. Ex. 'He came down *jot* upon his rump.' Also for the paunch ; sometimes the breech [Spur.].

Jot, Jotter. To jolt roughly. The latter, indeed, is somewhat stronger than the former, and a sort of frequentative.

Jot, Jot-cart, is properly a cart of which the body is set flat, or *jot*, on the axle, in immediate contact, without anything to give it play. It is used, however, with some latitude, for any cart of very rough motion.

Jot-gut. The intestinum rectum, in which the largest and finest hog's puddings are made.

Jottee. A delicate dimin. or softening of jot, or jot-cart, meaning a vehicle approaching to a gig, or park chair, as nearly as the statutable price of a taxed cart will admit.

Jounce. To bounce, thump, and jolt, as rough riders are wont to do.

Journey. The time a man is at plough, generally about six hours. Properly it means a day's work. Sometimes, however, the plough is at work nine hours, and then two *journeys* in the day are taken.

Jower. To exhaust with fatigue, as from a day's labour, or travel. Ex. 'She came home right on *jowered* out.'

*Jowiney. The time a man is at plough [Pr. Pa.].

Jowl. (1) To peck furiously, or strike hard with a pointless instrument. 'Them old crows hev been rarely a jowlin o' them turnips' [Em.]. To strike with a sharp one is to *job*, q. v. (2) The head or skull [Spur.].

Jub. The slow heavy trot of a sluggish horse [M. S.].

Jug. To squat, and nestle close together, as partridges at night.

Julk. To give a sound like liquor shaken in a cask not quite full. Otherwise *yulk*. No doubt a word fabricated from sound.

Jum. A sudden jolt or concussion, from encountering an obstacle unnoticed; for instance, driving a carriage against a large stone, or taking a post in brisk motion; also a heavy loss in cattle or money [Johnson].

*Jumper, Dopper or Dopler. A thick jersey [M. C. H. B.].

*Jump it. To understand it [Johnson].

*Kane. Water at low tide between the outer sandbank and the beach. 'I shall bathe in the *kane*' [*B. N.* 26].

*Karma. 'Mother,' a fungoid growth on jam, vinegar, &c. [M. C. H. B.].

*Ka-there, or Kith-there, or Karinder. An expression calling or requiring the attention of others to something, e. g. 'Ka there, if hare beent John Thompson cum to that far' [Johnson].

Kedge. Brisk, active. This is Sir Thomas Browne's spelling. We pronounce it **Kidge** or **Kidgy**, and apply it exclusively, or nearly so, to hale and cheerful old persons.

*Keel. A kind of boat chiefly employed on the Yare [Spur.]. Compare the Newcastle *keels.* Now very rare; they differ from wherries by their mast being stepped amidships [W. R.].

*Keeler. A shallow tub. See **Killer.**

Keep. (1) To associate, to keep company with. (2) To lodge, to keep residence, or abode. For this we have academical authority. Inquire of anybody you meet in the court of a college at Cambridge your way to Mr. A.'s room, you will be told that he *keeps* on such a staircase, up so many pairs of stairs, doors to the right or left. (3) To persevere [Spur.].

Keep. Food for cattle. Ex. 'I am short of *keep* for my cows.'

Keeping-room. The general sitting-room of the family, the common parlour.

*Keesle, or Schisle. A boy's taw, formed from a schistus kind of stone found in the clay [Johnson]. Boys talk of *chiselling* at marbles, by which they mean swindling, taking unfair advantage. It is frequently heard in that sense. 'You are an old *chiseller.*' 'He *chiselled* me out of it' [A. E. R.].

Kell. (1) The omentum or caul of a slaughtered beast. (2) A kiln [Spur.].

Kelter. (1) Condition; order. Ex. 'My farm is in pretty good *kelter.*' 'The mauther have slumped into the slush, and is in a nasty forlorn *kelter.*' (2) Applied to a plough; which is said to *kelter* well or ill, as it works in a slope or curvature.

*Kelks. The testicles.

Kemp. [Sir Thomas Browne.] *Vide* Camp.

*Kench, or Kinch. The part of a haystack in use or cutting down. ' Shall I begin another cut of the stack, Sir, the last *kinch* is getting very low ' [Johnson].

Kernel. A grain. Ex. ' A *kernel* of wheat ' ; ' a *kernel* of salt.'

Kett. Carrion. ' A *ketty* cur ' is a nasty stinking fellow. Our word includes any kind of garbage.

Kett Pole. A carrion pole.

Key Beer. Beer of the better sort, kept under lock and key ; or having a lock-cock in the cask.

Kibbage. Small refuse and rubbish ; riff-raff.

*Kibe. *Quasi* chilblain, discharging matter.

Kick. (1) A novelty ; a dash. It seems an abbreviation of kick-shaw, or kick-shoe. (2) The extreme of fashion, ' all upon *kick*, like Tom Turner's wife's coffin ' [E. S. T.].

Kickel. A sort of flat cake with sugar and currants strewn on the top. Coquille. [Kichell, *B. N.* 78.]

Kicky. Showy.

*Kid-faggot. A double *faggot,* one tied with a withe at each end [E. S. T.].

Kiddier, Kidger. One who buys up fowls, eggs, pork, &c., at farmhouses, or rears them himself, and carries them to market. He is the same person with Ray's Cadger. [Kiderer, *B. N.* 92.]

*Kidder. This has much the meaning of the French *charcutier* in the Norman province. A pork-butcher, sausage-maker, a low dealer in poultry and provisions.

Kiddle. (1) To embrace, caress, fondle. A more delicate form of Cuddle, q. v. (2) Synonymous with Higgle in the second sense, q.v.

*Kidge. See Kedge.

Killer. A shallow tub, particularly a wash-tub. Cooler (?) [W. R.]. Often **Keeler** [A. E. R.].

Kilver. A mincing pronunciation of **Culver**, q. v.

*****Kinder.** Somewhat, in a slight degree [Spur.]. Clearly the origin of the American expression [W. R.]. See **Kind o'.**

Kindful, Kindly. In the same sense which that word bears in the Litany—'The *kindly* fruits of the earth.' The fruits in their several *kinds*.

*****Kinderlike.** As it were, *quasi*. Saxon *kyndelich* [Spur.].

*****Kindle.** A rising of the wind [Johnson].

*****Kindling.** Firewood [M. C. H. B.].

Kind o'. In a manner, as it were; a sort of qualifying expression; often, as if on recollection of having gone too far, thrown in at the end of the sentence or clause; but its place is of no importance, it makes equally good grammar anywhere. Ex. 'He fared *kind o'* sorry to hear it.' 'She made game on it, *kind o'*.' It was a kind of sorrow or of merriment which was shown. This no doubt is the American ' kinder,' imported by our East Anglian colonists [W. R.]. See **Kinder.** Sometimes **Kindly** [Em.].

Kiner. A flannel wrapper used by nurses for infant children, to cover a certain part of their bodies.

King Harry. A popular name of two common singing-birds. (1) King Harry redcap is the goldfinch, the *Fringilla carduelis*, Lin. (2) King Harry blackcap is the bird which is commonly called simply the blackcap, *Motacilla atricapilla*, Lin.

*****Kings and Queens.** Herrings with coloured fins [M.C.H.B.].

Kink. (1) To be entangled, set fast, or stopped. The thread or yarn *kinks* in winding. Bailey uses the same verb to express the stoppage of breath in children in violent fits of crying or coughing. (2) To be disentangled, to be set free. This is not a solitary instance of the same word being made to express opposite or correlative ideas. But we are concerned with no other at present. We use it in both senses, of stoppage and of relief. Of the first an instance has been given ; of the second, we have more than one equally common. In an alarming fit of sickness, whether cough or anything else, when slight but progressive symptoms of amendment appear, it is prognosticated that the patient ' will *kink* up again.' When the fire seems extinct, a latent spark may remain which will ' *kink* up,' not by stirring or blowing the coals, but by laying the poker over them, and setting up the fire shovel in front, in other words, by having patience with it.

Kinsman, Kinswoman. Not a relation in general, but a *cousin german* in particular. Ex. ' What relation is Tom Smith to you, good woman ? ' ' He is my *kinsman*, Sir.' Sometimes, indeed, it is, ' my *own* cousin.' In Suffolk there is a different usage of the word. There a nephew is generally called *kinsman*.

*Kip. The skin of a calf after it is weaned, before it arrives at a year old [Johnson].

Kiplin. The palates, gullets, sounds, or other perishable parts of the cod-fish, cured separately from the body, which they would taint and putrefy. The ruddy-hard parts obviously [W. R.].

*Kirt. An abbreviation of **Kirtle** ; in Suffolk sometimes **Skirt** [Spur.].

Kirtle. An outer petticoat to protect the other garments from dust, &c., in riding. Such was our sense of the word, which is scarcely, if ever, heard of now that pillions are so gone out of use.

Kisk. Anything perfectly dry and husky. Johnson has ' the act or noise of pigs in eating peas or barley when thrown among straw.' Which seems to me very absurd [W. R.].

Kiss-me-at-the-garden-gate. A fanciful yet rather a pretty name of the several beautiful varieties of the garden pansy, or *Viola tricolor*, Lin.

*Kiss-me-quick. The curl of hair growing on a woman's head at the nape of the neck [M. C. H. B.].

*Kisses. The pansy, heartsease [Spur.].

*Kissey. As adj. thirsty, dry [W. B.].

*Kissing. In fashion whenever you can find a piece of furze in bloom [M. C. H. B.].

Kit. (1) A wooden utensil, with two handles, and a cover fitted in between them, as a flour *kit*, a salt *kit*, &c. Sometimes, but less properly, (2) the flesh of animals for dogs [Johnson]. Often spelt Kid [A. E. R.].

Kit Cat. A game played by three or more players [M. S.]. The *cat* is shaped like a double cone. Tip Cat [W. R.].

Kit-cat Roll. A bellied roller for land, the horse going in the furrow, and the roller acting on the sloping surface of the ridge on each side.

Kitling. A young cat or kitten.

Kittle. (1) To tickle. (2) Uncertain. '*Kittlish* weather.' (3) To bring forth young, especially of rabbits [G. J. C.].

Kitty Witch. (1) A small species of crab on our coasts, with fringed claws. (2) A species of seafowl, probably more than one, certainly including that which is called by Pennant the *kitty-wake*. (3) A female spectre, arrayed in white, of course. (4) A woman dressed in a grotesque and frightful manner; otherwise called a *kitch witch*, probably for the sake of a jingle. It was customary, many years ago, at Yarmouth, for women of the lowest order to go in troops from house to house to levy con-tributions at some season of the year, and on some pretence, which nobody now seems to recollect, having

men's shirts over their own apparel and their faces smeared
with blood. These hideous beldames have long discon-
tinned their perambulations, but, in memory of them, one
of the many rows in that town is called *Kitty Witch* Row.
(5) A buffoon [Arderon].

Kiver. To cover.

Knacker. (1) A saddler and harness-maker. (2) A husband who is not able to procreate. Also called a Burglar
[Johnson].

Knacker's Brandy. A sound strappado.

*Knape or **Knave.** The frame which contains the straw
which is carried up the ladder to the thatcher [Johnson].

Knap Knees. Knock-knees. *Knap* is a gentle knock.
Also used thus, 'My knees *knapped* together' = knocked
together.

Knobble Tree. The head. It is of course implied that
the head is wooden. See **Knubble.**

*Knob-stock Wedding. A compulsory marriage owing to
the interference of the parish officer, the lady being in
the family way and likely to be actually chargeable
[Johnson]. The same as **Hop-pole Wedding** [W. R.].

Knock. To stir or to work briskly. Ex. 'He came
knocking along the road in a great hurry.'

*Knock Salt. A great heavy stupid awkward fellow
[Johnson].

Knoppit. (1) A little clod; or, indeed, a small lump of
almost anything. Dimin. of **Knop** or **Knob.** (2) A child
[Spur.].

Know. Knowledge. Ex. 'Poor fellow! he has but little
know.' 'My *know* is better than yow thowt.'

Knub. A knob.

Knubble. (1) A small knob, as at the end of a walking-
stick, a poker, the handle of a door, &c. (2) To handle

-clumsily; using thumbs and knuckles, as in kneading dough. See **Knobble**.

*Laash or **Leaish**. Wet, cold, chilly, uncomfortable [Spur.]. Spurdens regards this word as the shibboleth of East Norfolk; all these vowels to be distinctly separately sounded so as to leave the word a monosyllable. *Vide* **Leasty**.

*Lab Dab. A profuse perspiration with a filthy habit. ' The wench is all of a *lab dab*' [Johnson].

Lace. To beat. In Lowl. Sc. and N. E. it still means also to mix with spirits [Jam., Br.].

Laced Mutton. A prostitute.

*Lack. (1) To lack anything is to have an indifferent opinion of it [Johnson]. (2) A goose is said to *lack* or *lag* to her nest from repeatedly coming to it and continuing some time. Said to be a sign of her desiring incubation [Johnson].

Ladle. To dawdle.

Lad's Love. The herb southernwood, *Artemisia abrotanum*, Lin. **Boy's Love** [Jen.].

*Lafter or **Latter**. The number of eggs laid by a fowl before she sits [Johnson].

Lagarag. A lazy fellow who will do no more work than he is forced to.

*Lagtail. A loiterer [Johnson].

*Laid. (1) ' The river is *laid*'=the river is frozen at the bottom [Arderon and also E. S. T.]. Marshall, however, says just or slightly frozen. (2) She is laid, i. e. lying down [C. S. P.], [in the day time, M. C. H. B.]. (3) Frozen at the top, not bottom. Also **Just Set** [M. C. H. B.]. (4) Gone to bed [W. R.]

Laldrum. An egregious simpleton, ' a fool and a half.'

Certainly it implies something more than an ordinary every-day fool.

Lall. (1) To lounge, to loiter. Perhaps a contraction of **Ladle**, q. v. Perhaps another form of **Loll.** (2) A lounger, with the idea of silliness annexed. Perhaps a familiar abbreviation of **Laldrum.**

Lam. To beat unmercifully.

Lamb Storms. Stormy weather near the vernal equinox, often hurtful to the new-yeaned lambs.

*****Lamb, Summer Lamb.** The common snipe (*Scolopax gallinago*), from the noise it makes lambing in spring [M. C. H. B.].

*****Lamming for eels.** Thrashing the water to make the eels go into a net [W. R.].

Lammock. (1) To lounge with such an excess of laziness as if it were actual lameness [Forby]. (2) A large quantity. 'A good tidy *lammock* of grass' [Johnson].

*****Lam Net.** A net into which fish are driven by beating the water [E. S. T.]. 'Lamming for eels' [W. R.].

*****Lamper along, to.** To take big strides [*B. N.* 34].

Lamper Eel. The lamprey.

*****Lampit.** A field name in N. Ess.＝Loampit, says Mr. H. Round [C. D.].

*****Lanarkin.** 'They was lanarkin' an' golderin' together,' ? larking [Em.].

*****Landstroke.** The iron which is fixed on the side of the head of the plough [Johnson].

Land Whin. The rest-harrow, *Ononis spinosa*, Lin.

Langle. To saunter slowly, as if it were difficult to advance one foot before the other.

Lanner, Lanyer. The lash of a whip. In Suffolk, 'the *lanner*' is only used for the leathern lash, and does not include the whipcord attached to it [Forby]. Johnson has it **Lanierd.**

*Lantern-man. *Ignis fatuus,* Syleham Lights [M. C. H. B.].

Lap. Thin broth or porridge, weak tea, &c. ' Poor *lap*!'

*Lape. A large skep or basket used in a farmyard for carrying chaff or colder [Johnson].

Lap-sided. Deformed on one side, as if the protuberance were caused by wrapping or *lapping* folds of cloth over the part. [Lopsided.]

Largess.· A gift to reapers in harvest. When they have received it, they shout thrice the words 'halloo *largess*'; an obvious corruption of the words, '*à la largesse,*' a very ancient form of soliciting bounty from the great, not of thanking them for it. But whatever may be the irregularity in performing the ceremony, or the ignorance of the performers, it is unquestionably a remnant of high feudal antiquity. It is called 'hallowing a *largess,*' and is generally a harsh and discordant yell, but might be much otherwise if the fellows had good ears and tuneable voices. Indeed, sometimes, when mellowed by distance, it may be reckoned among pleasing 'rural sounds.'

Larrup. To beat.

Lash, Lashy. (1) Soft and watery, as applied to fruits, &c. See Laash. (2) Also cold and raw as applied to weather [E. S. T.].

Lash Egg. An egg without a full-formed shell, covered only with a tough film.

*Last. (1) Of corn, in Norfolk was twenty-one coombs. (2) Of herrings, ten thousand [E. F. G.]. (3) Thirteen thousand two hundred. Six score and twelve go to a hundred herring [M. C. H. B.].

*' Lat, dat [dirt], and lumber '= great nonsense [Em.].

Latch. (1) To catch what falls; also to alight. Ex. 'He will always *latch* on his legs.' (2) To throw from below so as to lie or lodge upon some projection or branch above [Spur.]. (3) A thong of leather [Spur.]. (4) A string of anything, e. g. a *latch* of links = a string of sausages.

Latch-on. To put more water on the mash when the first wort has run off.

Latch Pan. The pan placed under the joint while it is roasting, to *latch* the dripping.

*__Latch of Links.__ A string of sausages. Johnson says a *latch* is the number contained in a skin or hide, but this seems wrong.

*__Lather.__ To flog or pay. 'Yer father'll *lather* you' [M. C. H. B.].

*__Latten.__ We do not mean any mixed metal, but give the name to common tin plate.

Latter. The number of eggs a hen lays before she begins to sit. We do not talk of setting her upon her *latter*, but upon a Clutch of eggs, generally thirteen or fifteen, but always an odd number for luck's sake.

Laugh and lay down. A childish game at cards, in which the player, who holds a certain combination of cards, lays them down on the table and is supposed to *laugh* at his success in winning the stake.

Launch. A long stride (diphth. pron. broad).

*__Law.__ 'To follow the law on yer' is to 'pull yer,' to follow it up, or pull you up before the magistrates to prosecute [M. C. H. B.].

*__Law or Layer.__ Young plants, such as whitethorn, crab, and brier [Johnson].

Lawnd. A lawn.

Lay. (1) A very large pond. Seemingly connected with Lake. Always *lays* in the plural; ponds in the midst of copse and timber [Spur.]. (2) Pools of sea water left along the beach at the ebb of the tide [E. S. T.].

Lay. (1) To intend, to lay out, to lay a plan. Ex. 'I *lay* to plough for turnips to-morrow.' (2) Gain or profit. 'What sort of a *lay* did you make of him?' [Johnson].

*Layer. Arable land in grass and clover [H. B.].

Layer of Wind. A dead calm in which the miller cannot grind.

Layer Over. (1) A gentle term for some instrument of chastisement. See *N. and Q.* 2nd Ser. vii. p. 38. (2) A meddler [E. S. T.].

*Lay on to. To beat, to lay the hand or stick on [M. C. H. B.].

*Lay-out. Of a ferret when on heat [M. C. H. B.].

Laze. To be lazy. In fact, the adjective seems derived from the verb; not the verb from the adjective.

*Lazy-bed. A system of potato-planting [M. C. H. B.].

Lea. (1) Forty threads of hemp yarn [Forby]. (2) Eighty yards of yarn [Johnson].

*Leach. A perforated tub used for making lye from wood ashes [Spur.].

*Lead. 'Star leading the moon.' When the evening star is in front of the moon, that is on the right-hand side, or west of it, a sign of bad weather [M. C. H. B.].

*Leaders. Sinews [M. C. H. B.].

*Leads. Pencils. Cedar as opposed to slate [M. C. H. B.].

Learn. To teach. Pronounced 'larn.' 'I'll *larn* you tew be a hedgepig,' as a keeper once said when he shot a hedgehog [W. R.].

*Lease. To glean, Suff.

*Leastways. Leastwise, at least [M. C. H. B.].

Leasty. Dull, wet, and dirty; applied to weather. *Vide* Laash or Leaish.

*Leave, Lief. As lief. 'I had as *lief* have one as the other.' I would just as soon have one as the other [M. C. H. B.].

Lecking Time. Showery weather, rain with short intervals of sunshine. 'This is a *lecking time* for hay' [Johnson].

Leck on. (1) To put water on [Johnson]. (2) To add more liquor, as in brewing [Marshall].

Lection. In election, in likelihood. Ex. ' 'Tis *'lection* to rain.' The phrase in proper form is very common.

Ledge. A bar of a gate or stile, of a chair, table, &c.

*****Ledged.** The tool used by thatchers for driving or cleaning reed [Johnson].

Led Will. An odd, ungrammatical person. It means '*led by will*,' i. e. by a will-o'-the-wisp, and it is metaphorically applied to one who is in any way puzzled and bewildered by following false lights.

*****Ledwilled.** Bewildered [*N. and Q.*].

*****Leech.** *Medicus*; as in horse leech, cow leech, &c. [Spur.].

*****Leer.** To grin, or sneer, or look with eager eye [M.C.H.B.].

*****Leet.** (1) A meeting of three cross-roads as ' three a-*leet*.' (2) A place where three cross-ways meet [E. S. T.]. In Surrey this would be a **Three went way.** Was the village court : the court leet was held at the cross-roads? [W. R.].

*****Length of foot.** 'He has got the length of yer foot'= He has measured and reckoned you up, and knows how far he can trust you or presume upon you [M. C. H. B.].

*****Length of** tongue. To give one the length of your tongue, to slang [M. C. H. B.].

Lep, Lepe, Lip. A large deep basket, e. g. a seed-*lip*.

*****Lessest.** For ' least ' [Spur.].

*****Lether or Latther.** A ladder [*B. N. 63*].

*****Let** out. To scold [Em.].

Level. To assess. Ex. ' I will pay whatever you *level* upon me.' It is implied in the very word that the assessment is a fair and equal one.

*****Levenses.** The reapers' repast at eleven o'clock [Spur.]. See **Noonings.**

Lewer, Lower. A lever. The first an obvious variation of that word; the second a very common change of the diphthongs *ew* and *ow*.

Lick-up. (1) A miserably small pittance of anything, as if it were no more than the cat can take up by one stroke of her tongue. (2) Leavings, orts [M. C. H. B.].

*Lie. Sleep. 'Where does he *lie* to-night?' [C. S. P.].

*Lie-by-the-wall. To be dead and laid out [C. S. P.].

*Liefer. Sooner, rather [M. C. H. B.].

Lie Latch. A wooden vessel filled with wood ashes, on which water is poured, and the *lye* which runs through holes in the bottom is caught or *latched* in another vessel below. Some call it a *letch*.

Lift. A sort of coarse rough gate of sawn wood, not hung, but driven into the ground by pointed stakes, like a hurdle, used for the same purposes of sub-dividing lands, stopping gaps in fences, &c., and deriving its name from the necessity of *lifting* it up for the purpose of passing through. In Suffolk, however, a *lift* differs from a gate principally in not being hung on hinges, but in having the projecting ends of the back and lower bar let in to mortice holes in the posts, into and out of which it must be *lifted*.

*Lig. To lie [Spur. and W. R.].

Ligger. (1) A line with a float and bait for catching pike, thrown into the water and allowed to *lie* there some time before it is examined. (2) A plank bridge over a ditch [W. R.]. (3) A pole nailed horizontally from stud to stud to support the splints before receiving a coat of clay or loam, the same as Rizzor [Johnson].

Lig, Liggle. To carry something too heavy to be carried with ease, as a child *liggles* a puppy about. Both the words are dimin. of *lug*.

***Light.** To shut up a light in a cellar, e. g. is a sign of a death in the house [M. C. H. B.].

***Lights.** The lungs [M. C. H. B.].

Light-timbered. Light limbed, active and alert.

Like. One mode of forming adjectives in the Saxon language was by adding *lic* or *lice* to substantives or verbs. In English this termination is softened into *ly*; often, but not always, conveying the original idea of *likeness*. To effect this, we are in the habit of annexing our own word *like* in propriâ formâ, not so as to form one compound word, nor to affect any word, verb, or substantive in particular, but the whole phrase or clause in which either occurs. Ex. ' She was in a passion *like*.' ' She fare to be angry *like*.' ' She scolded me *like*.' The usage may be said to be awkward enough, but it is after the antique. It means, ' in a manner,' or ' as it were.' It may be added that in our use of the common anomalous colloquial phrase, ' had *like*,' we generally use the Saxon word pure and unchanged. Ex. ' He had *lic* to have broken his head.'

Like of. (1) To approve. Ex. ' My master will not *like of* it.' (2) ' The likes of us '—people of our station [M.C.H.B.].

Limb. A determined sensualist; [a limb of the devil] one who eats, drinks, &c., with peculiar glee and zest.

Limmock. Intens. of **Limp**, q. v.

Limp, Limpsy. (1) Flaccid. Apparently a contraction of **Limber**. (2) A loose lazy fellow is said to be a *limpsy* rascal [Johnson].

***Lim to.** To suck [*B. N. 3*].

Line. To beat; from the implement of chastisement, a rope's end.

***Linger.** To long after. Sick people ' linger ' for food they fancy [C. S. P.].

Link. A sausage. From the usual mode of forming sausages, it should seem that a single one was only half a *link* of the savoury hain. We call two (several?) together a **Latch of Links.** In some other counties a far more correct expression is used, 'a *link* of sausages.'

*Link Hides.** Sausage skins, the intestines of a pig prepared and stuffed [Spur.].

*Link-meat.** Mince-meat. A boy quarrelling with another was heard to say, 'I'll cut you into *link*-meat' [W. B.].

Link Pin. Why not as good as **Linch Pin**?

*Lint.** A net [S. Abbs, W. R.].

List or Listly. Quick of hearing. Ex. 'I am very *listly* of hearing.' Sometimes **Lest.**

Listly. Easily, distinctly. Ex. 'I heard it very *listly*.' Ch. has the verb **Lisse**, to make easy. This is an adverb, formed from the participle of that verb.

*Lit.** A stain [*B. N. 3*].

*Lithy.** Supple, pliant: a merry Andrew is said to be a '*lithy* fullah' [Johnson].

*Litter.** Fodder, straw or rushes [M. C. H. B.].

*Little-est.** Smallest [M. C. H. B].

*Little Shoes, making.** Said of a labourer when he has no regular employment, but only odd days [Em.].

Little Silver. A low price. Ex. 'The stover in my low meadows have been so 'nationally damnified by this slattering weather (said an old farmer) that 'tw'ont be worth but *little silver*.'

*Little Stands.** A loke [Johnson].

*Livelong.** The head of the dandelion [Johnson].

Live under. It strongly expresses the close connexion between landlord and tenant: the latter looking up to the former as his patron, and being desirous of showing him every mark of attention and respect, and being

K

in his turn considered as under protection. I *live under* Lord A., Sir B. C., Squire D., are expressions seldom heard in the present state of things, and never with all their old meaning.

*Living. 'Very good living, very pleasant living'; not only good pay but nice surroundings. 'To dream of the dead is to see the living,' betokens the unexpected meeting of friends or relatives [M. C. H. B.].

*Loaders. Herring of specially beautiful tints [*B. N.* 77].

Lob. To kick on the seat of honour [Spur.].

Lobcock, Lubbock. A lout, a lubber. Not only a northern word but an eastern one.

Loblolly. Neither water-gruel nor any particular seafaring dish. With us, as in Exmoor, it means 'any odd mixture of spoon meat,' provided only that it be very thick. We have a simile founded upon it, 'as thick as *loblolly*.' Though what *loblolly* exactly is we do not pretend to define [J. H. G.].

*Lobspound. To be in any difficulty or perplexed state [Johnson].

*Lobster. The smallest of the tribe Stoat [J. H. G.].

*Lock. A bunch [*B. N.* 40].

*Locked. Cards when faced are said to be *locked* [Johnson].

Lock Spit. A small cut with a spade to show the direction in which a piece of land is to be divided by a new fence. We also commonly narrow the word 'spade' to *spid* or *spit*, in talking of the depth to which labourers are required to dig. Ex. 'Go three *spid* deep.'

Lode. An artificial watercourse. In the fens in the south-west angle of Norfolk are several *lodes* to aid the drainage; as Salter's *lode*, &c. But the term is not confined to fen drainage. At Fincham, the common watercourse, which intersects the lower part of the parish from west to east, to the outfall into the river Wissey, is called at present, and in all old writings, the *lode ditch*. It is often corruptly called the low ditch; so easy is it to lose ancient names by confounding them with more modern and familiar words.

*Loggats. Short sticks used for throwing at a stake in the game of Trunket [M. C. H. B.].

Logger. To shake as a wheel which has been loosened, and does not perform its motion correctly.

Loke. An inclosed footway, a short narrow turn-again lane [Forby]. Generally a private green road leading tielden [Spur.]. An inclosed footway, not a driftway [W. R.]. Johnson says a close or enclosed lane, the branches forming almost a canopy.

Lollop. To lounge and saunter heavily.

Loll poop. A sluggish sedentary lounger. Literally one who is sluggish in the stern.

Lolly Sweet. Lusciously sweet, without any flavour to relieve the sweetness.

Lond. (1) Land in the abstract. Arable, as distinguished from pasture [Spur.]. (2) A division of an uninclosed field. Rather, indeed, a subdivision; for in the old maps of uninclosed parishes, each field is divided into furlongs, and each furlong into *londs*. (3) To clog with mire. Ex. 'He came walking over the ploughed field, and was *londed* up to the knees.'

*Lonesome. Lonely, applied to people and animals [M. C. H. B.].

Lone Woman. A woman unmarried, or without a male protector.

Long. (1) To forward to a distance, from one hand to another, in succession. (2) Great. Ex. 'He asks a *long* price.' (3) Tough to the palate. Its opposite, *short*, means easy to masticate, as pie-crust, &c. (4) To think. Ex. 'I think *long* to hear from him' [W. B.].

Longful. Very long; full long. Ex. 'He was gone a *longful* while.'

*Lookem. A window in an attic or upper room of a house, generally in the roof [Johnson]. *Vide* Lucam.

*Look over. To forgive [C. D.].

*Loomy. Meat that has got rancid and mouldy [Johnson].

*Loon. The great crested grebe [J. H. G.].

Loop. The part of a pale-fence between one post and another. Otherwise a length or lift of paling.

Loose-ended. Lewd. Ex. 'She is a *loose-ended* baggage.' Generally used for the opposite of costive [W. R.].

*Loose twisted. Lewd [Spur.].

Lop. To hang loosely. ' A *lop*-eared rabbit,' a rabbit whose ears hang down.

Lope. To take long strides ; particularly with long legs.

*Lopeway. A foot and bridleway not adapted for carriages [Johnson]. Probably a mispronunciation of Lokeway [W. R.].

Lopper. To turn sour and coagulate by too long standing. *Loppered* milk has been explained *du lait pourri*.

*Lord. In Suffolk, the labourer who goes foremost through the harvest [E. S. T.].

Lords and Ladies. The flowering stems of the *Arum maculatum*, Lin.

*Low. A salt lake left by the retiring tide [M. C. H. B.].

*Low. Short of stature [M. C. H. B.].

Lowen. (1) To fall in price. Very analogically opposed to Heigh'n or Hain, q.v. (2) To depress anything [Spur.].

*Lower. A lever [Johnson].

Lueam. A window in the roof of a house. Sir Thomas Browne spells it Leucomb. *Vide* Lookem. A garret window [*B. N.* 84].

Lucks. Small portions of wool twisted on the finger of a spinner at the wheel or distaff. The same word as **Lock**, when applied to hair, &c., but in form nearer to the original.

*Lug. (1) To hang loosely, dangling heavily [Spur.]. (2) The ear [M. C. H. B.].

Lugsome. Heavy. Either to be borne as a burden, or when applied to a road, causing a wearisome drag to cattle.

*Lug Worm. The sand worm used as bait [M. C. H. B.].

*Luller. 'The nightingales luller so that I cannot get to sleep' [M. C. H. B.].

Lumber. Coarse, dirty, or foolish talk.

Lummox. A fat unwieldy person, and very stupid to boot; heavy in mind and body, as if made of loam or unctuous earth. Ex. 'Look o' yin great *lummox*, lazing and lolloping about.'

Lump. (1) To drub with heavy blows. (2) Lump of fowl, a large bunch of wild fowl [M. C. H. B.].

Lumps. (1) Bricks of the common length and breadth, but half as thick again, and harder. (2) Clay lumps, cottages built of clay [M. C. H. B.].

Lunge. To lean forward, to throw one's whole weight on anything.

Lunt. Short, crusty, surly in speech or in manners.

Lure. To make a loud and shrill cry. Ex. ' They halloo'd and *lured* to one another.' It has no less authority than that of the great Bacon. It is an old term in falconry, meaning, not only to hold out an enticement, but to utter a particular call to bring the hawk back.

Lurry. To daub by rolling in mire. Ex. ' His clothes were *lurried* all over.'

Lust. To incline. Metaph. from inclination of mind. Ex.

' This wall *lust* o' one side.'   B. gives it as a sea term.
' The ship *lusts.*'

***Lute.**   Bent, curved [E. F. G.].

***Luthur.**   A ladder [Johnson].   I usually note it ' lather '
[W. R.].

Macaroon [or **Macaroony**, Spur.], a fop.   All sexagenarians
must well remember the time when the jackanapes,
who are now called dandies [mashers], were denominated
macaronies.

***Maekly.**   Exactly alike, fitting nicely [Pr. Pa.].

Madam.   A term of respect to gentlewomen, below *lady* but
above *mistress.*   In a village, the esquire's wife, if she be
not literally a lady, must have *madam* prefixed to her
surname.   The parson's wife, if he be a doctor, or a man
of considerable preferment and genteel figure, must be
madam too.   The wife of the humble vicar, the curate,
the farmer, and the tradesman, must be content with the
style of *mistress.*

Madgetin.   The Margaret apple.   Margaret being familiarly
reduced to Madge.

***Madgin** or **Mudgin.**   The ·lime and clay rubbish of old
buildings or the refuse of limekilns used for manure
[Spur.].

***Maffle.**   See **Moffle.**

Mag.   To chatter.   It implies somewhat of displeasure, not
amounting to wrath.

Magot.   A whimsy, odd fancy, freak, monkey trick.

***Magoting.**   Pron. marketing [W. B].

***Maid.**   The contrivance by which a smith sprinkles water
on the fire.   Also an iron (trivet) to be placed on the fire
on which to stand a kettle [Johnson].

Main. (1) That part of the meat which is least dressed. Ex. 'Give me a slice in the *main*.' (2) Very. 'This is a *main* cold place' [*B. N.* 70].

Make. (1) ' To *make* count,' to intend, to reckon upon. Ex. ' I *make* count to go to the fair to-morrow.' (2) To *make* on, to caress, to distinguish by particular attention. (3) To *make* a hand on, to waste, to destroy; to *make* a good, bad, or indifferent hand of an undertaking, are phrases common enough. With us a bad sense is always understood, when no qualifying epithet is used. Ex. ' He has *made* a hand of all his property.' ' That dog is mad, I must *make* a hand on him.' (4) To *make* a noise, to scold, or rate severely. (5) To *make* a die on 't, to die after long sickness or decline. Ex. ' So Will Young is like to *make* a die on 't at last.' (6) An instrument of husbandry with a long handle and a crooked iron at the end, chiefly used to pull up peas. Tusser calls it a *meake*. We pronounce it *make*, and talk of *making* the crop of peas. Indeed, every crop, howsoever severed from the soil, and left upon it to dry, is said to be *made* when it is in a fit state to be carried. We say, ' in this cloudy weather there is no *make* for the hay,' &c. In Suffolk the instrument is always called a *peas-make*. (7) A short-bladed long-handled scythe, used to cut reeds [W. Wright's *Eastern England*, i. p. 100]. (8) To *make* as if = to pretend [M. C. H. B.].

*Maker. Making. Ex. ' It will be the *maker* of the boy' [C. S. P.].

Malahack. A word ludicrously fabricated, which means to cut or carve in an awkward and slovenly manner [Forby]. G. J. C. has *malahank*, to twist up in an awkward manner as an eel *malahanks* a fishing-line.

Malan Tree. The beam across an open chimney, in front of which the mantelpiece or shelf is fixed.

Male Pillion. A stuffed leathern cushion to carry luggage

upon, behind a servant attending his master on a journey.
A mode of travelling and of conveyance gone out of use
in our own times, since the universal adoption of gigs,
whiskies, tilburies, dennetts, &c.

*Malkin. See Maukin.

*Malt. Sweat, malting hot [M. C. H. B.].

Malt Cumbs. Malt dust. The little sprouts and roots of
malted barley, withered, turned dry, and separated by the
screen. Qu., are they so called because produced upon
the *couch*?

*Malted. Heating, perspiring.

*Mam. 'All beat to a *mam.*' Severely bruised by repeated
blows [Johnson].

Mamble. To eat with seeming indifference as if from want
of appetite or disrelish of food. A dimin. of Mumble, by
change of vowel.

Mammocks. Leavings, wasted fragments. Ex. 'Eat up
your *mammocks*, child.' Sometimes, indeed, we talk of
tearing a thing 'all to *mammocks*.'

*Mand of Sprats. About a thousand [E. F. G.].

*Mander. To meander, stroll [M. C. H. B.].

*Manment. (N. Ess.)=manure. 'That field wants plenty
of *manment*' [W. B.].

*Manner. So pron. Earth dug out of ditches and put as
dressing on fields. Yard-manure is called 'muck' [W. B.].

*Mantle. A full apron, used when doing any dirty work
[Johnson]. Also Mentle [*B. N.* 58].

*Mantle Tree. The beam across and in front of the chimney
[Johnson].

Mara-balk, Mere-balk, Mire-balk, Mere. A *balk* or narrow
slip of land, unploughed, separating properties in a common
field.

March Bird. A frog. Clearly an error for Marsh Bird.

Marchpane. A favourite delicacy in old times: the principal ingredients were almonds and sugar, much like our macaroons, but made broad and flat, cut into slices, and so distributed to the guests at desserts or tea-tables.

Mardle. (1) A pond near the house, in the yard, or on the neighbouring green, or by the road side, convenient for watering cattle. Exactly the Fr. *mardelle*. (2) A jolly meeting, *compotatio* [Spur.]. (3) To gossip [W. R.]. The last is the only sense in which the word is now used. *Vide* **Maudle.**

***Mardlens.** Small duck, a week on ponds. ' That pond 's full of *mardlens*' [W. B.].

Mare's Fat. *Inula dysentrica*, Lin.

Mare's Tails. Long narrow clouds irregularly floating below the general mass, and of a darker colour; reckoned a strong indication of continued rainy weather.

Margent. A margin.

***Marram.** See **Reed grass.**

Marshalsea-money. The county rate.

***Martin Snipe.** The green sandpiper [J. H. G.].

***Marvels.** Marbles [Johnson].

***Mash Butes.** Marsh boots [Spur.].

***Mash tea.** To make tea [C. S. P.].

***Mash Tub.** The brew tub [M. C. H. B.].

***Masterful.** Spiteful [M. C. H. B.].

***Masterfule.** A champion ass [B. B. F.].

***Masterpiece.** Anything wonderful or surprising.

***Mat.** A tool for stubbing furze, ling, &c. [Johnson]. **Mattock** ?

Matchly. Exactly alike, fitting nicely. Another of Sir Thomas Browne's words, happily explained by modern pronunciation **Mackly.**

*Math. Mowing [Pr. Pa.].

Matter. Number or quantity. 'There was a *matter* of 'em.' Generally used as expressing something surprising, wonderful, &c. [Johnson]. 'No *matter* of a road' [W. R.].

*Mattock. A kind of pick and adze [G. E.].

*Maudle. To gossip [Spur.]. *Vide* Mardle.

Maukin. (1) A dirty, ragged, blowzy wench. A dimin. of Mary or Moll, anciently written Mall. (2) A scarecrow; a figure of shreds and patches, imitating humanity abominably, in old ragged apparel, male or female, and set up in a garden or on new-sown land.

Maul. Clayey or marly soil, adhering to the spade or ploughshare.

Maulmy. Clammy, adhesive, sticking to whatever comes in contact with it.

*Maundering. Querulous, complaining [Spur.].

Mauther or Mawther. A girl. When addressing a girl you say 'maw' [*B. N. 5*].

Mavis or Mavish. A thrush. The missel thrush or storm cock is never so called, only the smaller thrush.

*Maw. Abbreviation of Mauther.

*Mawbish. Drunk [*Eastern England*, i. p. 97].

Mawskin. The maw of a calf, cleaned and salted, to produce the liquor called runnett, used for curdling milk.

*Mawth-dog. The phantom of a dog in Norfolk [Pr. Pa. (Shuck ? W. R.)].

*Mawther. See Mauth.

May. The flowers of *Crataegus oxyacantha* and of *Prunus spinosa*, Lin., are respectively called whitethorn and blackthorn *may*.

*May-bird. The whimtrel, also called Half-bird and Half-curlew [J. H. G.].

May Bush. Either of the shrubs which bear those flowers. In Suffolk, however, the ' *May bush* ' is always the white-thorn.

*Mazy. Sickly. Herrings about to shoot the roe are said to have the *maze* [E. F. G.].

*Mazzard. The face and jaws [Johnson].

*Meadows. Low, boggy, rotten grass land [Marshall].

Meal. As much milk as is taken from a cow at one milking.

*Meals. Sand-banks [Pr. Pa.].

Meal's Victuals or Meal's Meat. Food taken at one meal.

Meaning. An intimation; hint; likelihood; slight symptom. Ex. 'I felt some little *meaning* of ˏfever this morning.'

*Mear Balk. A ridge left unploughed in a field.

*Measlings. The measles.

*Meat for Manners. To keep a horse belonging to some one else but to use it as an equivalent for its keep, i. e. the cost of feeding and tending it [M. C. H. B.].

Meddle and Make. To interfere, to intrude into business in which one has no particular concern.

*Meesy. Tainted or unsavoury [M. C. H. B.].

Meetinger. A dissenter [M. C. H. B.].

Mell. To swing or wheel round, to turn anything slowly about; from resemblance to the motion of a mill.

Mending the Muck Heap. A coarse vulgar romping bout. If one falls down, others fall over till there is a promiscuous heap, of either or of both sexes, tumbling together, as they would express it themselves, 'heads and holls,' of course indelicately and seldom decently.

Mentel-piece. A cornice or mantle [G. E.].

Mentle. A woman's coarse woollen apron. Apparently a misapplication of **Mantle.**

***Meowun.**   Mown [Pr. Pa.].

***Mere Balks.**   Earth or sand boundaries [Stevenson].

***Mergin.**   The mortar and cement of old buildings [Marshall].   No doubt identical with **Merjin**, a sort of white marl, the refuse of a lime-pit [Johnson].   *Vide* **Mudgin.**

***Merry-may.**   The dragon-fly (N. Ess.) [C. D.].

Meslin.   A mixture of the flour or meal of different sorts of grain.

Meslin Bread.   Bread made of mixed flour or meal. · Fifty years ago, on the light soils of both our counties, thousands of acres produced only rye, which now yield an abundance of wheat.   At that time the household bread of the common farm-houses in those districts was made of rye.   *Meslin bread,* made with equal quantities of wheat and rye, was for the master's table only.

Mess.   A gang, a crew, a scrape.   Ex. 'It is well I was not in the *mess.*'

***Met.**   A customary measure of coals at Lynn, containing five pecks [Johnson]=two bushels [*Further Rep. of Charity Comm* p. 348].

***Mett.**   To measure [Spur.].

***Mettock.**   A mattock [Pr. Pa.].

Meve.   To move.

***Mice,** plural **Meece.**   Fried mice are given to children for whooping-cough, and the children are told that they are little 'bads,' i. e. birds [M. C. H. B.].

Middlestead.   The compartment of a barn which contains the threshing-floor; generally in the middle of the building.   But the same name serves, should it be, as in small barns it sometimes is, at one end.

***Middle Tree.**   The upright. shaft to which the doors of a barn fold, and to which they are made fast and locked when necessary [Johnson].

*Midsummer Men. Mandrake [Johnson].

Mile. An abbreviated pronunciation of Michael, which was anciently written Mihil or Mihel.

*Milk. A woman who wishes to wean her child burns her milk to make the remainder waste. I have heard of this within the last four years [M. C. H. B.].

Milk Broth. Gruel made with milk, and grits [groats] or oatmeal.

*Miller or Mellar. A moth [M. C. H. B.].

Million. A pumpkin. So called on account of its many seeds [M. C. H. B.].

*Milt. The roe of herring. See also Round [W. R.].

Mim. Primly silent; with lips closed lest a stray word should escape.

*Minchin or Mingin. A small piece of food [Johnson].

Mind. To notice. Ex. 'I never *minded* it'=I did not notice it [M. C. H. B.].

Mine. This and other possessive pronouns are used with the ellipsis of house. Ex. 'I wish you would come to *mine.*' 'I shall go to-morrow to *yours.*' 'We are invited to *his.*'

Ming. To knead; to mix the ingredients of bread. Not in general use in Norfolk, though its dimin. Mingle is, but very common in Suffolk. A. S. *mengean,* miscere. In Suffolk to *ming* is confined to kneading of dough for bread [Spur.].

*Minge, or Bange. To drizzle [M. C. H. B.].

*Mingins. Midges, small gnats [A. E. R.].

*Mingle-cum-pur. A mixture of ingredients or matters unpleasant to the sight as well as the palate [Johnson].

Minifer. The white stoat or ermine.

*Minify. Make less [M. C. H. B.].

*Miniver or Minifer. The weasel [M. C. H. B.].

Mink, Mint. To attempt, to aim at. It is not the only instance in which we change the consonants *k* and *t*.

Mink-meat. Meat for fowls, &c., *minged* with bran or barley-meal. *Vide* **Mung.**

Minnock. One who affects much delicacy, to affect delicacy, to play the fribble.

Mint. A great number [Spur.]. *Vide* **Mink.**

Misbeholding. Offensive, affronting. It is applied solely to words. Ex. 'I never gave her one *misbeholding* word.'

Miscasualty. An unlucky accident.

*****Mischief.** To happen with a mischief, to meet with an accident.

Miscomfortune, Miscomhap. Misfortune, mishap. The insertion of the syllable *com* is by no means without signification. Fortune or hap *comes amiss.*

*****Miseraled.** Pitied, commiserated [M. C. H. B.].

*****Miserated.** Rendered miserable [Spur.].

Misery. Acute pain in any part of the body. *Misery* in the head means a violent headache.

Mislin-bush. The mistletoe.

*****Misvigured.** Disfigured [Johnson].

*****Mitchpool.** A whirlpool [G. E.].

*****Mob.** To rail at. Ex. 'She *mobbed* me shameful' [C. S. P., C. D.].

*****Mob-cap** or **Mop-cap.** A tartar, hasty-tongued. Also a kind of Tam-o'Shanter hat [M. C. H. B.].

Mock-beggar Hall. A house with an inviting external aspect, but within poor and bare, dirty and disorderly, and disappointing those who beg alms at the door.

*****Mockbrawn.** See **Brawn.**

*****Mocking.** Alternate.

*Moderate, or Middling. In a fair state of health only [M. C. H. B.].

Moffle, Muffle. To speak thick and inarticulately. In East Norfolk more usually pronounced Maffle [E. S. T.].

Moil. (1) To labour. (2) To be fatigued or perplexed in body or mind is to be *moiled* [Johnson].

Moise. (1) To mend. improve, increase, &c. Old Fr. *moison*, not *moisson*. (2) To increase in growth as plants [S͵ur.]. (3) To thrive [Arderon and Marshall].

*Molberries. Skuas (*Lesteidae*) [M. C. H. B.].

Mold or Molt. A profuse perspiration.

*Moll, Mole. Dead; e. g. 'He's gone to the *moll* country;' viz. is dead [H. B.].

*Moll. Straw beaten small [M. C. H. B.].

*Mollified. Melted [M. C. H. B.].

*Moltlong. A sore or disease between or rather above the clees of cattle [Johnson].

Molt-water. Clear exudation. Ex. 'His face was all of a *molt-water*.' The discharge from a blister is likewise so called.

Month's-mind. An eager wish or longing. A very ancient phrase, many centuries old, in very general use in a different sense, perhaps now equally general in this. It was a feast in memory of the dead, held by surviving friends at the end of a month from the decease.

*Moon. 'The moon on her back holds water.' A sign of rain [M. C. H. B.].

*Mopsy. A slatternly mawther.

*Mor. A female [G. E.].

*Morcan. An effigy [G. E.].

*Moreish. Something so good that one would like to have more [Spur.].

Moreover than that. Besides, over and above that. It is equivalent to the common phrase, ' what is *more than that* ' [T.].

***Morfery.** A farmer's cart [G. E.]. A corruption of hermaphrodite [W. R.].

Mork-shriek. A mockery, a humbug, a foolish old wife's tale. Literally, it means a *shriek* in the dark.

Morris. (1) An ancient game in very common modern use. (2) To go away. 'He is *morris'd*,' he has taken French leave [Johnson].

Mort. A very great number or quantity.

Mortal. Very great, exceeding.

Mortation, Mortations. Used as adjectives, and with the addition of *ly*, as adverbs. Thus eked out with additional syllables, they may be understood as intensives of mortal and mortally; but are very vulgar words, of course.

***Morte.** A corpse, a dead body [J. H. G.].

Mortice, Morth. A corpse (mors) [M. C. H. B.].

***Mother Home.** The keeper at Scoulton, where the little gulls congregate annually, told me that the mere was like a *mother home* to them [W. R.].

Moultry. Spoken of earth when mellow, and neither too wet nor too dry [Spur.]. Surely from **Mould** [W. R.]. *Vide* **Muldry**?

Mouse-hunt. The weasel [J. H. G.].

Mowing. For mewing. 'It was *mowin* the bitterest,' said of a cat [Em.].

Mozy. Shaggy, covered with hair. The clown, who shaves but once a week, is of course very *mozy* when he comes under the barber's hands. It is a common nickname of itinerant Jews, whether bearded or not. In this case it may be meant for Moses, as we call a sailor Jack.

***Muck.** A term of disparagement, e. g. ' You young *muck* you ' [H. B.].

Muck Grubber. A hunks; a sordid saver of money, who delves for it, as it were, in the mire.

Muck of Sweat, Muck Wash. Excessive perspiration.

Muck Spout. One who is at once very loquacious and very foul-mouthed. A most expressive term.

Mucky. Dirty.

*****Muddle.** Fatigue, not necessarily from drinking. To muddle time away, muddle about [F. J. B.].

Mudgin. Rubbish of chalk and ruined buildings, mixed with lumps of clay, broken straw, &c., with which hovels or low walls for farmyards are sometimes built. See **Mergin.**

Muffitee. A covering for the wrists, of cotton, wool, or fur. A very small muff [Br.].

*****Muffle.** To bumble the bells [Spur.].

*****Muir-heart.** Faint-hearted [*B. N.* 99]. See **Mure.**

Mulder. To crumble into dust.

*****Muldry.** Said of earth greatly affected by the frost, finely pulverized [Johnson]. *Vide* **Moultry?**

Mull. (1) Soft, breaking soil; 'putris gleba.' The broken and dusty relics of turf-heaps are called *turf mull*, or *mool*. (2) A mill [Spur.]. (3) To make a mess of any undertaking [C. H. E. W.].

*****Muller.** Miller [C. S. P.].

Mulligrubs. A fit of the sullens. We do not use it for gripes.

*****Mullok.** A medlar [*N. and Q.* 2nd Ser. ii. p. 338].

Mully. To make a sort of sullen half-suppressed growling, like a dog before he barks, or a bull before he roars.

Mulp. To be sulky, to pout.

*****Mumby.** A kind of pear, a roussellette [Spur.].

Mump. A hop and a jump [Johnson].

Mumper. A beggar. Commonly used in Norwich for the waits [A. E. R.].

Mun? (1) A particle of interrogation, used in much the same manner as **Ah'n?** or **Anan?** q. v. (2) A low term of address, rather expressive of extreme familiarity than of contempt, as Jen. explains **Min**, which is used in the same manner in the West. Ex. ' 'Tis all true, *mun* '; corr. perhaps of **Man**. [I never heard it—W. R.]

Mung. A mixture of coarse meal with milk or pot liquor for the food of dogs, pigs, or poultry. From **Ming**, q. v. In Norfolk used for barleymeal only [Johnson]. From **Ming**, kneaded, mixed up.

*Munge. The human mouth [Johnson].

Mure-hearted. Soft-hearted, meek-spirited, easily moved to pity or tears.

Mure-mouthed. Using soft words.

Mush. Guardedly silent. 'As *mush* as a mackerel' [E. S. T.].

*Na (NAY). Offer or refusal. 'When you want to sell that horse I wish you would give me the *na* of him' [Johnson].

Nab. To catch, as a bird catches insects in its bill.

Nabbity. Short in stature, but full grown. Said of a diminutive female. A ludicrous derivative from **Nab**, as if the little creature might be taken up between one's finger and thumb.

Nabble. To gnaw. A stronger word than **Nibble**, by change of vowel. Mice *nibble* and rats *nabble* our victuals, and hares and rabbits our growing vegetables.

Nab-nanny. A louse.

*Nacker. A collar or harness maker [Johnson].

Naggle. To pace and toss the head in a stiff and affected manner, like a young nag bitted and reined to be shewn at a fair. Particularly applied to affected females.

Name or Half-name. To privately baptize [C. H. B.].

Nancy. A small lobster.

*****Nape.** In laying a hedge, to *nape* is to cut the branch partly through so that it can be bent down [Johnson].

*****Nares.** The kidneys of any animal [Johnson]. *Vide* **Near.**

*****Narn ?** An interrogation; as if to say, ' I did not hear or understand what you said' [Johnson].

*****Narnbut** Used in the sense of an excuse. ' I can't, sir'; ' I *narnbut* must go to-morrow' [Johnson]. **Nobbut** [W. R.].

Narrow-wriggle. Apparently a corrupt form of **Erriwiggle**, q. v.

*****Nasen.** Plural of nests [Spur.].

*****Nasty.** Disagreeable, bad tempered, easily offended. Ex. ' He was very *nasty* about it'=angry or uncompromising [M. C. H. B.].

Nation. Very, extreme.

Native. Pronounced na-tive, but as the word is in its nature an adjective, place must necessarily be understood. Ex. ' Norwich is my *native*.'

Nattle. To be bustling and stirring about trifles, or very busy in doing nothing at all.

Nature. (1) Natural feeling or affection. A simple old woman, as a reason for loving one of her daughters more than the others, said she had more *nature* in her. (2) Kinsfolk [Spur.].

Naughty-back. A term of gentle reproof, for the most part used to children.

Nay, Nay-say. Right or opportunity of refusal. Ex. ' Give me the *nay-say*, or the *nay*, of it' means ' Let me have the first choice, so that I may refuse it, if I think proper.'

Nayword. (1) A watchword, password, private token. Whosoever cannot give it must not be admitted or trusted, as the case may be. (2) A byeword, a laughing-stock.

Nazle, Nazzle. A ludicrous dim. of ass.

Near. The fat of the kidneys. In Suffolk it is pronounced 'nyre.' *Vide* **Nares.**

Near Now. A little while ago. Pegge imputes this word to us. But where did he hear it?

Neck-break. (1) Complete ruin. Ex. 'The fall of prices was his *neck-break.*' (2) A game for children, with two short splines having a third between them, fixed so as to move in a curious way on a ceiling, which makes the neck ache to look up long at them [Spur.].

Necking, Neckinger. A cravat or any other covering for the neck.

Neck Weed. A common ludicrous name of hemp.

*****Need.** Parturitio [Spur.].

Needle. A piece of wood put down by the side of a post to strengthen it, a spur.

Needles. (1) A common weed among corn, só called from its long and sharp seeds. (2) Shepherds' needles (*Scandix pecten veneris*). Shepherds' purse (*Capsella bursa pastoris*) [M. C. H. B.].

*****Needs' End.** In difficulties, on short commons [Johnson].

*****Neesen.** Plural of nest [*B. N.* 7—? W. R.].

*****Neffy.** Nephew [*N. and Q.*].

*****Neither nigh nor by.** Nowhere near, without one's leave [M. C. H. B.].

Nep, Nip. The herb cat-mint, which being covered with

a fine white down, has given rise to a common simile, 'as white as *nip*.'

Nervish. Affected with weakness of nerves.

*Nesing. For nesting, or rather looking after nests. Boys said to play truant after birds-*nesing* [W. B.].

Nest Gulp. The smallest and weakest of a brood of nestlings.

*Nestletripe. The worst of a litter of pigs [*N. and Q.* 2nd Ser. i. p. 75].

Nettle Springe. What is more generally called **Nettle Rash.** A small tingling and itching eruption, looking and feeling as if it had *sprung* up from the stinging of nettles.

*Nettus. A neat-house [Spur.].

Newdicle. Something new, just as a miracle is something wonderful. A fanciful and licentious fabrication, perhaps never used at all seriously.

News. To tell as news. Ex. 'It was *newsed* at market yesterday.'

*Newsed. Mentioned in the newspaper [M. C. H. B.].

Nexing, Nexting. Very near, coming *next* to.

Nicked. Exactly hit, in the very *nick*, at the precise point. Another of Sir Thomas Browne's words.

Nickled. Beaten down and intricately entangled, as growing corn or grass by rain and wind.

Nidget. (1) To assist a woman in her travail. See **Need** =travail. Johnson says it is only used when a woman gives the help. (2) A cowardly coxcomb or pretender. See *Norfolk Drollery*, 1673, 12mo, p. 40.

Niffle, Niffle-naffle. To trifle, to play with one's work [Forby]. **Niffy-naffy** [Spur.]. To walk daintily [G. E.].

*Nigeting. To call women to one in labour [Arderon].

Nigger. (1) A short half-suppressed neigh ; and a diminutive of that word. (2) A sneering contemptuous giggle. **Snigger** ?

Niggle. (1) To eke out with extreme care. (2) To cheat dexterously. Ex. 'He *niggled* him of his money' [Forby]. (3) To cuddle [G. J. C.].

Nildy Wildy. Whether one would or not ; *nilled he, willed he.*

Nine Holes. (1) A rustic game ; or, indeed, more than one. In one of them, nine round holes are made in the ground, and a ball aimed at them from a certain distance. This is supposed in N. G. to be the modern form (whether subject to the same rules or not) of 'Nine men's morris.' We have that game, and it is different, being played on a flat surface. In our other game of *nine-holes*, the holes are made in a board with a number over each, through one of which the ball is to pass. (2) A fish of the lamprey kind, not uncommon in our fen ditches.

Ninnie or **Ninny.** Soft, sawny, silly, or shannie [M.C.H.B.].

Nip. (1) To pinch close in domestic management. (2) A parsimonious housewife. Br. **Nip Cheese.** See **Nep.**

Nipper. A young nipper. *Vide* **Yipper.** To nip about. To stir nimbly, slightly [M. C. H. B.].

Nipt. Pinched. 'He lies *nipt*,' he is hard run.

Nishany. Very positive [G. E.].

Nisy. A very poor simpleton.

Nittle. Not a corruption or mispronunciation of *little* ; in addition to the import of that word, it includes the idea of neatness or prettiness.

***Nittled.** Entangled [Spur.].

***Noah.** The foot or swing plough [Johnson].

Noah's Ark. A cloud appearing when the sky is for the most part clear; much resembling, or at least supposed to resemble, a large boat turned bottom upwards. It is considered as a sure prognostic of rain.

Nobbut. Only, or except.´ It is a confused jumble of *none but*, or *nothing but*. Ex. ' I keep *nobbut* two cows.' ' Mr. Smith is a good master, *nobbut* he is too strict.'

Nobby. A fool; also a very young fool.

Noble. The navel.

***Nooky.** A ninny [Spur.].

Nog. A sort of strong heady ale. It seems to be peculiar to Norwich. Sir Robert Walpole's predilection to ' Norfolk *nog*' is well known. Nuttall's Dict., edited by a Norwich man, gives *nog*, a measure, a little pot.

Nogging. (1) Courses of brickwork, between or below upright posts or studs in the construction of some walls. (2) A small measure or pot of ale [C. H. E. W.].

No'hn. An awkward syncopated form of the word nothing. Ex. ' I don't know *no'hn* about it.' [? **None.**]

Noils. Coarse refuse locks of wool, of which mops and dwiles are made. Nolled, knotted or matted.

***'Noint.** (1) To beat [Johnson]. (2) A rogue, a good-for-nothing [H. B.].

***Noising.** A term given by Norfolk marshmen to several species of birds frequenting their native swamps. They apply it particularly to the song of the Nightjar, Grasshopper, ˙Reed and Sedge Warblers (E. T. Booth) [M. C. H. B.].

***Nolt.** A dunce or blockhead [Johnson].

No Matters. But moderate, nothing to boast of. Ex. ' The squire is *no matters* of a shot.' ' Is the parson a clever churchman ?' ' *No great matters*.'

Nonce. ' He did that for the *nonce*.' It always means something offensive [Forby]. Spurdens disagrees with this, and says, ' for the *nonce* or *noonst*' has its natural sense only.

Noneare. Not till now [Ray]. Sir Thomas Browne has it in the sense of presently. The *Paston Letters* has **Non er,** for not earlier or no sooner. G. J. C. says 'a little while.'

Nonekin. Playing nonsensical [G. E.].

*****N**one of both neither. [C. S. P.]

*****N**onnecking. Full of apish monkey tricks [Johnson].

Nonnock. (1) An idle whim ; a childish fancy. Connected no doubt with the following. (2) To imitate, to resemble (?) [Johnson]. (3) To play the fool [Spur.].

Nonny. To trifle ; to play the fool. Chiefly applied to the fondling and toying of sweethearts, and when the fair one is coy, and cries 'be quiet,' 'you shan't,' &c.

Nonplunge. Nonplus.

Noonings. The dinners of reapers, &c., still taken at noon. See **Levenses.**

*****N**ope. A bullfinch [Ray.].

*****N**oppet. A bunch of wood or straw [Johnson].

Nor. Than.

Noration. A loud rumour, or, as it were, a roaring general publication of what was meant to be kept secret.

*****N**orbor. Neighbour [M. C. H. B.].

*****N**orn. Nothing [Spur.].

*****N**ose. A smell. In use generally of hay, e. g. 'That hay have a buetiful *nose*' [H. B.].

*****N**ot but what. Nevertheless, or it was not because I did not [M. C. H. B.].

*****N**otch. To dock. 'He *notched* me half a day,' viz. deducted so much from my wages [W. B.].

Notchet. A notable feat, something that deserves to be marked, recorded, noted, *notched.*

*****N**oteless. Not taking notice, of old people with failing powers [W. B.].

*****N**othing. Not at all, not nearly, e. g. 'so large?' 'Nothing so large' [H. B.].

*Notified. Noted [Johnson].

Nowl, Noble. The navel. The *newell stone* of a circular staircase would seem to come from this [W. R.].

*Noyles. Refuse wool in combing [Johnson].

Nuddle. To hold down the head. Johnson has Nuddling or Nuzzling, hiding the face in the bosom to prevent being recognized.

*Nudge. To touch with the elbow [M. C. H. B.].

*Nudging. Cheerless, solitary, living in obscurity from penurious habits [Johnson].

Num. Stupid. Ex. 'As *num* as a post.' Compare Numskull.

*Numbchance. 'She niver offered to do a hand's tu'n, but stood garpin an' starin' just like *numbchance*' [Em.].

Numpost. An imposthume. This dreadful malady in the head must of course produce stupor. We should say, it makes a man 'as *num* as a *post*.' [What rubbish!— W. R.]

*Nunting. Sullenly angry [Johnson].

Nunty. Very plain and old-fashioned. Applicable to female dress only. Most probably clumsily formed from the word *nun*.

Nut-crome. A stick, with a crook at the end of it, to pull the boughs of filberts, or hazels, in order to gather the fruit.

*Oaf. Silly, stupid. You silly oaf, or oof [M. C. H. B.].

*Oamy. Light, porous, floury; spoken of ‚ploughed land [Marshall]. See Omy.

Oatflight. The chaff of oats, much lighter than that of any other sort of grain, and which may most properly be said to fly.

*Oiley. An oiled smock or canvas jersey [M. C. H. B.].

Old. Customary; what has commonly happened in like case [O. E.]. We should say, 'If we are found out, we shall have *old* scolding and storming.' 'There will be *old* cramming and tipling at the hawkey.'

Old Shock. A mischievous goblin, in the shape of a great dog, or of a calf, haunting highways and footpaths in the dark. Those who are so foolhardy as to encounter him, are sure to be at least thrown down and severely bruised, and it is well if they do not get their ancles sprained or broken; of which instances are recorded and believed. See **Shuck**.

Old Sows. Millepedes, woodlice. Used as pills, they are believed to have much medicinal virtue in scrofulous cases, especially if they be gathered from the roots of aromatic potherbs, mint, marjoram, &c.

Old Witch. The cockchafer.

Olf. *Vide* **Blood-olf** and **Green-olf** [Ulph]. In Suffolk more often pronounced **Olp** [Spur.].

*Olget Hole. A hole left in the side of a barn for light [W. G. W.].

Olland. Arable land which has been laid down in grass more than two years, q. d. **Old Land**.

*Ollost. For always [W. R.].

*Omy Land. Open, light, puffy soil. Land just brought into cultivation, and requiring clay or marl to give it firmness [Johnson]. See **Oamy**.

*On. (1) Of. 'I ha' read some on it.' (2) Setten on, sat upon. Of incubated eggs. (3) Tell on. 'I ha' never heard tell on' [M. C. H. B.].

One-and-thirty. A game at cards, much resembling vingt-et-un, but of very venerable antiquity, assuredly, for it is alluded to by Bishop Latimer in one of his sermons. It was, many years ago, called *one-and-thirty* turntail, and *one-and-thirty* bone-ace. The first name was from

turning up the last-drawn card, to show whether the
number was exactly made up, or exceeded; the second,
from the fortunate contingency of drawing an ace after
two tens; the ace, counted for eleven, made up the
game, and was certainly a good ace. It is still played
by children.

*One-eyed Steak. A Yarmouth bloater [M. C. H. B.].

Onto. Upon. Ex. ' I will lay my stick *onto* you' [T.]

*Open. Not spayed, spoken of a heifer or a sow [Marshall].

Opinion. To opine.

*Orts. Leavings, scraps, fragments, Suff. [E. S. T.]. Kings-
ley uses this word for pieces of a broken stick [W. R.].

*Othersome. Some other [*N. and Q.*].

Out Holl. To scour a ditch, and make it as it was at first,
completely *holl* [Forby]. A vile practice of scouring
out the ditch for manure, without returning any part of
the soil to the root of the hedgewood [Marshall].

*Out of one's hundred. To feel strange, out of one's
element [M. C. H. B.].

Outs. *Vide* Make.

Outshifts. The skirts, boundaries, extreme and least regarded parts of a town, parish, farm, or garden. Ex.
' He lives somewhere in the *outshifts* of the town.'

Oven Bird. The long-tailed titmouse. The bird itself is,
indeed, seldom called by this name, but most commonly
the long-tailed Pick-cheese. The allusion is to the nest,
which is otherwise, and more descriptively at least,
called a Pudding-poke's nest. Sometimes called a Ground
Oven [A. E. R.].

*Over. The Coroner is said to go ' over ' a corpse [M.C.H.B.].

*Overday-goods. Refuse stock. Goods whose day is over
[M. C. H. B.].

Over-flush. Superfluity.

Overgive. To thaw.

Overhew. To overgrow and overpower; as strong and luxuriant plants *overhew* those of humbler growths.

*****Overlay.** Overreach [M. C. H. B.].

*****Overlooked.** Bewitched [M. C. H. B.].

*****Overly.** Arbitrary, tyrannical [Johnson].

Overwhart. Across. To plough *overwhart* is to plough at right angles to the former furrows. **Overthwart** [W. R.]. **Overwort** [*B. N.* 22].

Overworn. Apparel worn as long as is thought fit, thrown aside, and given to servants or the poor, is called ' *overworn* clothes.'

*****Owdacious, Outdacious, Oudacious, Alldacious.** Audacious; 'An owdacious liar or scoundrel' [M. C. H. B.].

Owe. To possess by right. Ex. ' Mr. Brown *owes* that farm.' This seems to me a misunderstanding of our Norfolk phrase, ' Mr. B. *own* that farm,' for *owns* [W. R.].

*****Owl's Crown.** The wood cudweed [Marshall].

Pack Gate. A gate on a packway, which often lies through inclosed grounds. Many of such ways and gates still retain their names and use in high Suffolk.

Packman. A hawker, one who travels about the country with packs of goods [L. Sc., Br.].

Pack-rag Day. Old Michaelmas day, on which servants in the country pack up their tatters and go to new services.

Packway. A narrow way by which goods could be conveyed only on pack-horses; now a foot and bridle way with gates.

Pad. (1) To make a path by walking on a surface before untracked, as in new fallen snow, or land lately ploughed

[·Forby]. (2) Dried cow-dung, formerly collected for fuel [Johnson]. (3) A pannier [Marshall].

Paddle. To trample, applied principally to children [Forby]. Only when in water [Spur.].

*Padling. Trifling, 'peddling.' 'My small *padling* debts.' Will of James Poley of Little Hedingham, yeoman, 1679 [C. D.].

Page. The lad attending on a shepherd.

Paigle. A cowslip. The flowers are dried by some rustic simplers, and an infusion of them, under the name of *paigle* tea, is administered as a very mild and wholesome soporific. Certainly it has that effect ; and so, in different cases, has *paigle* wine, which is by far the more palatable medicine. The word '*paigle*' is, in Suffolk, applied to the crowfoot, *Ranunculus bulbosus*, Lin.

*Pake. To poke about. 'He *pake* about like a turkey arter dark.' He moons about [Em.].

*Pakenose. An inquisitive person [*B. N.* 27].

*Paking. ·Poking about. See **Peaking.**

*Pal. Two courses or rounds in stocking knitting [Johnson].

*Palky, Polky. Always of potatoes diseased.

Pamment. A square paving brick. Contracted from pavement.

Pample. To trample lightly. A child *pamples* about. A heavy-heeled fellow *slods*. Johnson has, 'to walk as if the feet were tender.'

*Pampling. Fidgety [M. C. H. B.].

Pan. (1) The hard earth below that which is moved by the plough. (2) To be hardened, as the surface of some soil is, by strong sunshine suddenly succeeding heavy rain. It seems a comparison (parvis magna) with the operation of fire in a pottery. Johnson has, 'to ·bind firmly, as a barn floor of clay.'

Panchion. A large broad pan. Augm. of Pan.

Pane. A regular division of some sorts of husbandry work, as digging, sowing, weeding, &c. It seems to have been figuratively taken from *panes*, or stripes of cloth. Indeed, that old sense is still in use among us. *Puned* curtains are made of long and narrow stripes of different patterns or colours sewed together [Forby]. The quantity of clay or brick between the studs [Johnson].

*****Pangle.** In the parish of Wereham is one of those fenny badly-drained pieces of land, which are usually called 'labours in vain,' from all attempts to turn them to profitable uses being ineffectual; this is called the *Pangle* [E. S. T.].

Panhin, Panchin. A small pan. Pannikin?

*****Paper.** 'A piece of paper,' a summons. 'I'll get a piece o' paper for you' [M. C. H. B.].

*****Papish.** A decayed pollard tree, showing white [Johnson].

Par [Yard?]. An inclosed place for domestic animals, for calves, perhaps, in particular.

*****Parcel.** A piece or quantity. 'A parcel of grub'—a pack of nonsense.

Parfit. Perfect. 'Noe was a just man and a *parfite*' [*Capgrave's Chronicle*, E. S. T.].

*****Parlour Chamber.** The room *over* the parlour, just as the porch chamber is the room over the porch [W. R.].

*****Parsley Breakstone.** The common saxifrage [W. G. W.].

*****Part.** Half [M. C. H. B.].

Partless. In part, partly. Perhaps the syllable *less* might be thought to express the intended idea more strongly.

Par-yard. The farm-yard. [Rather the manure-yard.]

Pash. To beat anything brittle into small fragments.

Pass. To '*pass* the bell' is to toll it for the purpose of announcing a death. On the day of the funeral the bell is not said to be *passed*, but tolled or rung.

Patch upon. To impute blame rashly or wrongfully. Ex. 'He *patched* it upon me, who knew nothing of the matter.'

***Paulk.** To climb, to stand high [G. E.].

***Paupusses.** Paupers. Suff. [Halliwell].

Paved. (1) Turned hard, as a clayey soil in dry weather [Forby]. Spoken of dirty clay lanes which have become passable [Cull. Haw.].

***Pawk.** To throw about awkwardly. Suff. Hence **Pawky,** an awkward fellow [Halliwell].

***Pawk.** To search [*B. N.* 26].

Pawts. Flat boards fastened on the feet to enable men to walk safely on mud or ooze.

Pax-wax. The strong tendon in the neck of animals [Sir Thomas Browne's list and *B. N.* 35].

Pay. To beat.

Peagoose. One who has an aspect both sickly and silly. It is a compound of *peak* and *goose*.

***Peaking.** (1) Secretly looking or prying about [Johnson]. (2) Also of a young chicken or pheasant that is not well and will not eat. Phonetic from the noise the latter makes [M. C. H. B.]. (3) Or peagoosing. 'How he do go a pea-goosin' about' [E. M.].

***Pearl.** The common tern (*Sterna fluviatilis*) and the lesser tern (*Sterna minnuta*) [J. H. G.]. This is called 'Chit' perle [M. C. H. B.].

***Pearwhelp.** A scion or offset from the root of a pear-tree [Johnson].

Peckish. Hungry, disposed to be pecking.

Pecurious. Very minutely and scrupulously exact. It

seems to be fantastically fabricated from *peak* and *curious;* importing a prying curiosity to see that all is quite right.

Ped. A pannier, a large wicker basket with a lid. Two are commonly used, and called a 'pair of *peds*,' one on each side of a horse, in which pork, fowls, butter, and eggs are carried to market, and fish hawked about the country.

Pedder. One who carries wares in a *ped*, pitches it in open market, and sells from it. But probably any foot-man, whether trader or pilgrim [W. R.].

Pedder's Way. In the old maps of Norfolk a road is laid down, under this name, from the north-west extremity, called St. Edmund's Point, over the champaign part of the county to the interior and central parts. It was much frequented of old, and goods of more value and importance conveyed along it than are now wont to be carried in peds. Some few reaches of it here and there still retain the old name; but the whole of its ancient course cannot be made out, being of course lost in the inclosures which have taken place in modern times.

*Pedware. For podware. Pulse, beans, peas, or any kind of pods [Johnson].

*Peel. A long-handed sort of shovel used for putting bread into the old-fashioned brick ovens [M. C. H. B.].

Pee-wee. (1) Peaking and pining; whining and whimpering. (2) To micturate, especially of children; pittle = the same. Ex. 'He ha' pittled his britches' [M. C. H. B.].

Pee-wic. To peak and pine, &c.

Peg. To thump with sharp knuckles.

Peg Trantum. A galloping, rantipole girl; a hoydenish mauther.

Pelt. (1) A sheep's skin with the wool on. In R. N. C. it is a raw skin or hide without the hair or wool. (2) A game at cards somewhat like whist, but played by three only. (3) The act of plucking feathers from live geese [Johnson].

Pelt Wool. The wool which is shorn from the hide after the animal's death.

Pend. (1) To press or pinch. Commonly said of apparel which does not fit. Ex. ' The shoe *pends* here.' A phrase sometimes used figuratively for ' that is the tender point,' or the like. (2) To incline or lean. ' The wall *pends* this way.'

Pense. To be fretful.

*Pent. Short of anything. '*Pent* for time.' '*Pent* for rume ' [W. R.].

Perceivance. Faculty of perception; aptitude to learn. Ex. ' The boy is a dunce, and has no *perceivance*.'

Perish. To destroy. Ex. ' The frost has *perished* all my tender plants.'

Perk. (1) To perch. (2) A perch. A legitimate noun substantive. (3) A wooden frame against which sawn timber is set up to dry. So called from its resemblance in form to a perch in a bird-cage. (4) Brisk, lively, proud. '*Perk* as a peacock.'

Perry Dancers. The Northern lights. The *peries* or *perries* are the fairies. There is fancy and elegance in this word. It is corrupted, it seems, in L. Sc. to *merry dancers* or *pretty dancers*.

*Perry Wind. Half a gale [W. White's *Eastern England*, i. p. 92; also E. F. G. and J. G. N.].

*Pesket (Peascod). A pod [M. C. H. B.].

Pess. A hassock to kneel on at church.

Peterman. A fisherman; in use on the Suffolk coast.

Petition. An adjuration. Ex. ' He took strong *petitions* that he was innocent.'

M

Petman or **Pedman.** The smallest pig in the litter. Sometimes Dodman of a litter, though this is properly used for a snail only [W. R.].

*Petty. House of commons, garden-house [M. C. H. B.].

Pheesy. Fretful, querulous, irritable, sore.

*Phossy or Phooky. Applied to fruits when unsound, soft and woolly [Spur.].

*Pick. The bar-tail godwit [J. H. G.].

*Pick or Bang. A way of deciding which side is to go in first at any game. A stick is thrown up, and if it falls upright it is *pick*, and *bang* if it falls flatling [Johnson].

*Pick. An eel-spear [M. C. H. B.].

Pickcheese. (1) The titmouse, or yellowhammer [W. B.]. (2) In the plural in general use by school-children for the seeds of *Malva sylvestris.* [H. B.]. (3) The blue tit (*P. cœruleus*) [M. C. H. B.].

Pickerel Weed. Most likely a species of *Potomogeton*, Lin. The pike, and other fresh-water fish, deposits its spawn in narrow stripes upon the stalks and leaves of the *Potomogeton* and other water plants.

*Pickings. A dirty, slovenly, ragged woman, is said to be ' a lump of *pickings* ' [Johnson].

Pickle. To glean a field a second time, when, of course, very little can be found. It can surely be nothing more than a mere dimin. of pick.

Picklin. A sort of very coarse linen, of which seedsmen make their bags, dairymaids their aprons, &c.

*Pickpurse or Sandweed. The common spurrey [Marshall].

*Pidgeon-pair. A male and female, used of human beings [F. J. B.].

Pie. (1) The heap of earth and straw piled over potatoes to protect them from the frost [Forby]. (2) A kind of gull or Scoulton *pie* (*Larus ridibundus*) [M. C. H. B.].

Piece or Pieces. Fields arable [M. C. H. B.].

*****Pie-wipe.** The pewit or common lapwing [also Arderon].

*****Pieyard = Paryard.** The bullock-yard [M. C. H. B.].

*****Pifler (Pipefiller).** A child who, in weaving, fills or winds the thread on the pipe ready for the weaver [Johnson].

*****Pigeon-pair.** A boy and a girl, not necessarily twins. When a man has two children one of each sex [M. C. H. B.].

*****Piggle.** To be nice with one's food, turning it over like a pig [G. J. C.].

*****Pightle.** See Pitle.

*****Pigmire, Pishmire, Pishemire, or Pishemeer.** The ant.

Pike off! Begone! 'Shoulder your *pike* and march.'

*****Pilch.** (1) A flannel wrapper for an infant [Forby]. (2) A thick shoulder shawl [Johnson].

*****Pile.** The head side or obverse of a coin [Johnson].

Pilger. A fish-spear.

Pimgenet. (1) A very delicate and mincing diminutive of *piemgenet* for *pomegranate*. (2) A small red pimple. Possibly a hyperbolically figurative application of the first sense.

*****Pin.** To fasten upon. As of a ferret and rabbit [M. C. H. B.].

Pin Basket. The youngest child in a family.

Pingle. To pick one's food, to eat squeamishly.

*****Pin Horse.** (1) The horse next before the shaft-horse or 'thiller' [Bevan]. Those in front of him are Lash Horse and Fore Horse [W. G. W.].

Pinning. The low masonry which supports a frame of stud-work.

Pin of the Throat. The uvula.

Pin-patches, Pin-paunches.   The small shell-fish called periwinkles, of which vast multitudes are found on our coasts.   They are commonly drawn out of their shells with a pin.

Pin Wing.   The pinion of a fowl.

*Pipe.   The narrow entrance to a wild-fowl decoy [W. R.].

*Pipes.   Channels in the human anatomy [C. D.] (N. Ess.).

Pipperidge.   The barberry-tree.   But the fruit is always called by its proper name.

Piss Bed.   The common dandelion.   So universally is its diuretic effect known, that it is said to have a name equivalent to this in every language in Europe.

*Pit.   Pond.   The word in Norfolk generally implies water [H. B.].

Pit Hole.   The grave.

Pitle, Pickle.   A small piece of inclosed ground, generally pronounced in the first, but not unfrequently in the second form.   [Never to my knowledge, W. R.]   See **Pightle**, always pronounced ' pytle.'

Pitter.   To grieve piteously.   ' *Pittering* and *pining*.'

*Pivet.   Privet [M. C. H. B.].

Placket.   A pocket.

*Plain.   A level place surrounded by houses in a town, as in Norwich and Yarmouth.

Plancher.   A boarded or *planked* floor.

Planets.   The phrase ' by *planets* ' means irregularly, capriciously, upon no intelligible principle.   In changeable weather the rain and sunshine come and go by *planets*.   A man of unsteady mind acts by *planets*; meaning much the same as by fits and starts [Forby].   The word *planet* is used as a horoscope [Spur.].

Planting.   A plantation.

*Plash. A shallow pool [E. S. T.]. Probably the same as **Splash** in Surrey [W. R.].

Plaw. A slight boiling. If the meat seems likely to be tainted before it can be dressed, the cook must ' give it a *plaw*' to check the progress of decay, and, if possible, keep it a little while at a stand.

*Plenna. To lose flesh, decline [Johnson]. No doubt the same as the next.

Plenny. To complain fretfully. Sick children are said to *plenny.*

Plounce. (1) To plunge with a loud noise [Forby]. (2) To nonplus [Johnson].

*Pluck. (1) A slight tear. E. g. ' That bromble gon my gown a rare *pluck*' [H. B.]. (2) Liver and lights, edible in'ards [M. C. H. B.].

Pluggy. Short, thick, and sturdy.

*Plump. Bread broken or cut, with salt sprinkled and water poured over it [Johnson].

Plunky. Short, thick, and heavy.

*Poach. To tread soft land by cattle [Spur.].

Pock-fretten, Pock-broken. Marked with the smallpox.

Pod. A fat protuberant belly.

Podge. To stir and mix together. The same as **Poach.**

Poit. Something stronger than **Pert,** in farther assuming an air of importance.

*Poke. A small sack [G. E.].

Poke Cart, Poking Cart, Poker. The miller's cart, which is laden with the *pokes* or flour-bags belonging to his customers.

Poke Day. The day on which the allowance of corn is made to labourers, who, in some places, receive a part of their wages in that form.

***Poker.** The red-headed pochard (*F. ferina*) and tufted duck (*F. cristata*), called respectively red pokers and black pokers [M. C. H. B.].

***Pokey Hokey.** A bugbear to frighten children [Spur.]. Hokey Pokey is now cheap fruit ice in Norwich [W. R.].

***Polke.** A pit full of mud [Pr. Pa.].

***Pollar.** (1) An upper apartment in a house for fowls, in which they roost [Johnson]. (2) A roosting-place [Spur]. Hen's Polly, a roost [*B. N.* 27]. Possibly from 'pillar' [W. R.].

***Pollard.** The best kind of bran, sharps the second quality, middlings third do. [F. J. B.].

Poller, Pollen, Pollinger. A pollard tree.

Polliwigs. *Vide* **Purwiggy.**

***Polly Washdish.** The common wagtail [M. C. H. B.].

Polt. A hard driving blow.

***Poltens.** Crutches [Johnson].

***Polter, Poulter.** To shoot with a cross-bow [M. C. H. B.].

***Poople.** The poplar-tree [Spur.].

Popinjay. A parrot; now obsolete [J. H. G.].

Poppin. A puppet. It is the French *popin*, which Cotgrave interprets 'spruce, brisk, quaint.'

Poppin Show. A puppet-show.

Popple. (1) A poplar-tree. (2) To tumble about with a quick motion, as dumplings, for instance, when the pot boils briskly.

***Poppling.** Talking nonsense [Johnson].

***Pork Cheese.** Brawn [M. C. H. B.].

***Porking.** To go. To go picking up small pieces of wood, coal, or other fuel at the seaside [Spur.].

Porkling. A small porker.

Pose. A catarrh, or cold in the head.

Potladles. Tadpoles, from their shape.

*Pottens. Crutches for the lame [Spur.].

Potter. To poke, pry, rummage.

Power. A great number. Ex. ' There was a vast *power* of gentlefolk at the music.'

*Poys. Pies [M. C. H. B.].

*Prate, Crake. The noise a hen makes, usually supposed to be a sign she is near laying [M. C. H. B.].

*Prayed for. Banns asked. Ex. ' Mr. Hunnard was *prayed for* in church to-day ' [H. B.].

Prest. Ready. In its common application it seems to be understood as an abbreviation of the adverb *presently.* Ex. ' I will be with you *prest.*'

*Pretty. The ornamented part of a wine-glass. ' Fill it up to the *pretty* ' [M. C. H. B.].

*Prey. The head of cattle driven from the common pasture, and impounded if any among them belong to adjoining parishes [Johnson].

*Prick. See **Pritch.**

Prim. Very small smelts. The fry of smelts. So called at Lynn, where the smelts are remarkably fine.

Prime. To trim up the stems of trees, to give them the first dressing or training, in order to make them grow shapely.

*Prink. To show out of the ground. ' The barley is just *prinking* out of the ground ' [Johnson].

Prise. A lever used for the purpose of forcing. This instrument is sometimes called a **Pry.**

Pritch. A strong sharp-pointed instrument of iron for various purposes. (1) A fold *pritch* is that with which holes are made in the ground to receive fold stakes, or what are called the toes of hurdles. (2) An eel *pritch* is a spear for taking eels. (3) Probably Prick, as an eel *prick* [Spur.].

*Pritchel. The iron with which the smith makes the holes in the shoes [Johnson]. A kind of hard chisel for millstones [W. B.].

Proctor. To hector, swagger, or bully. From the proctors, who were licensed collectors of alms [W. R.].

Prog. (1) To pry or poke into holes and corners. (2) A curved spike or prong, to drag what is seized by it. (3) Food. (4) Begging for food, or money to buy it with. Ex. ' He is on the *prog*.'

*Progue. To prick with a sharp stick [G. E.].

Proter. A poker.

*Proud. A sow is said to look *proud* when *maris appetens* [E. S. T.].

*Pucker. To draw up or gather [G. E.].

Pudding. A stuffed cushion put upon a child's forehead, when it is first trusted to walk alone.

Pudding Pie. A piece of meat plunged in batter and baked in a deep dish, thus partaking of the nature of both pudding and pie. Sometimes called a Toad in a hole.

Pudding Poke. *Vide* Oven and Poke.

*Puddle. The implement with which thistles and other weeds are cut below the surface [Johnson]. Spud ?

*Pulfer. The fieldfare [W. G. W.].

Pulk. (1) A hole full of mud, or a small muddy pond. Otherwise a Pulk Hole. Sir Thomas Browne speaks of them as shallow pools left at the ebb of the tide, but I think a *pulk* is rather a deep hole [W. R.]. Johnson says, ' a place whence water is drawn by a lever.' (2) A thick, chubby, fat figure, of low stature.

Pulky. Thick, fat, chubby, and short.

*Pull. To haul, to prosecute, e.g. to bring before the bench [C. H. B.].

*Pull. Of ditches; to draw out the weeds [M. C. H. B.].

*Pullen. Poultry [Pr. Pa.].

Pulling - time. The evening of the fair-day, when the wenches are pulled about.

*Pulling-trees. The part to which the horses are attached to plough [G. E.]. *Vide* Pundle-tree.

Pull-tow, Pull-tow Knots. The coarse and knotty parts of the tow, which are carefully pulled out and thrown aside before it is fit to be spun into yarn.

*Pulthy. Filthy [G. J. C.].

Pummace. The mass of apples mashed under a stone roller before they are placed between layers of straw or the cider press. The word is figuratively used for any soft pulpy substance, like rotten or mashed fruit. Ex. 'I will beat you to a *pummace.*'

*Punch it! Be off! [Johnson].

Punder. To be exactly on an equipoise.

Pundle Tree. The wooden cross-bar to which the horses are fastened to draw ploughs or harrows. *Tree* means *wood*, as has been before explained; and the compound word literally means, the *balanced wood*, which is descriptive of it. The *pundle tree* is thicker than the *whipple tree.*

Pungled. Shrivelled and become tough, as winter fruit overkept, but not turned rotten; also grain shrivelled with heat or disease.

Puppy. A puppet.

*Puppy-dogs. Small dogfish [M. C. H. B.].

Pur. A poker [also Arderon].

Purdy. Surly, ill-humoured, self-important. [This is not correct at Aylsham.]

Purely. Much improved in health. Ex. 'I am *purely* to-day.'

*__Purely.__ (Suff.) Only in connexion with a confinement. (N. Ess.) More generally [W. B.].

*__Purl.__ Advertised at beer-houses as a morning drink, is warm beer with a sprig of wormwood placed in it [A. E. R.].

Purle. (1) A term in knitting. It means an inversion of the stitches, which gives to the work, in those parts in which it is used, a different appearance from the general surface. The seams of stockings, the alternate ribs, and what are called the clocks, are *purled*. (2) A narrow list, border, fringe, or edging. The top of a knitted stocking may, perhaps, serve as an instance, and thus point out the connexion with the preceding word. It is a contraction of **Purfle.**

Purwiggy. A tadpole.

*__Push.__ A sore [Spur.]. Not all sores, but rather an abscess [A. E. R.]. A boil or sore swelling [C. D.].

*__Pushmire.__ For pismire or ant [Em.].

*__Pusket__ or **Puskit.** A peapod [G. E.].

Pussle, Puzzle. A very dirty drab ; a filthy slut.

*__Put his muck up.__ Raised his temper [W. R.].

*__Put out.__ To put out the bell = to toll the bell [M. C. H. B.].

*__Putty.__ The mud of a river. Probably only yachtsmen's slang [W. R.].

*__Puy.__ Johnson says the 'quant' used to be so called. It is now obsolete [W. R.].

*__Pye Wipe.__ See **Pie Wipe.**

Quackle. To interrupt breathing. Formed to express the inarticulate sound then uttered. 'My cough *quackles* me' [F. J. B.].

*Quackled. Choked, suffocated [Cull. Haw.]. 'He fanged her by the throat and nearly *quackled* her.'

Quaddle, Quoddle. To coddle; to boil gently.

Quaddling, Quoddling. Codling; a well - known soft summer apple.

Quaddy. Very broad, short, and thick in person.

Quaggy. Soft and tremulous. Primarily and particularly applied to soil, but not confined to it ; sometimes extended to great obesity and flabbiness of flesh.

*Quail. To curdle.

*Quake. In very common use. 'First time as ever I see the train I lay hold on the railings and lor' I *quaked* properly' [C. S. P.].

*Quant. See Quont.

Quarrel. Any four-cornered pane of glass; more particularly the ancient lozenge-shaped pane.

*Quarter. To quarter the road, to make a fresh track [M. C. H. B.].

Quavery Mavery. Undecided, and hesitating how to decide ; not on an even balance ; meaning to determine, but fearful of taking a wrong step.

Queach. A plot of ground adjoining arable land, and left unploughed, because full of bushes or roots of trees.

Quest. To yelp as a dog when he scents his game.

Questing. Barking. A '*questing* spaniel' is one who opens upon the scent of his game, in contradistinction to one who runs mute.

Quezzen. (1) To suffocate with noxious vapour. (2) To smother away without flame. If the fuel be damp, the fire *quezzens* out. Johnson says Quessomed.

*Quick. Dog's grass [Sir T. Browne]. Is this our south country Twitch or Couch, accursed of all gardeners ? [W. R.].

Quicks. Roots of grass, harrowed out of a foul soil long neglected, principally *Triticum repens*, Lin. They are commonly collected in heaps, and burned on the land. The process is called 'burning of *quicks.*' Couch, Quick, Twitch, are other common names of these rapidly rooting and stubbornly vivacious grasses.

Quons. A hand-mill for grinding mustard-seed. It may be suspected of being no other than a coarse corruption of *quern.*

Quont. A pole to push a boat onwards. Johnson says the pole is called ' puy.' There is an extraordinary variation in the way this word is pronounced. Some watermen say *quànt*, others *quont* [W. R.]. Similarly Rànd and Rond.

*Quotted. Squatted; e. g. of partridges, ' They've *quotted* ' [M. C. H. B.].

Rab. A wooden beater, to bray and incorporate the ingredients of mortar.

Rack. (1) A rut. We say a cart *rack* [Forby]. (2) Weeds and other rubbish growing among corn [Johnson].

*Rafe Board. A part of a wagon [*B. N.* 84]. See Rave Boards. Wings or side boards [M. C. H. B.].

Raff. Refuse, rubbish, worthless fragments. In T. J. it is assigned to Norfolk, in the sense of a ' low fellow.'

Raffling. Idle, unsteady, unthinking. Ex. ' A *raffling* fellow,' one who seems to act at random, hit or miss.

Raffling Pole. The pole with which the embers are spread to all parts of the oven.

Raft. A fusty and damp smell, such as often proceeds from what has been closely shut up.

Rafty. (1) Fusty, stale. A cask emptied of its contents is apt to become *rafty*, if there be not sufficient access of air ; and provisions, if the larder be not well ventilated.

(2) The air is said to be *rafty* when it is misty, with an unpleasant smell. If it be moreover cold, it is said to be 'raw and *rafty*.' Rather Rasty, q.v. [W. R.].

Raft, Raftiness. (1) A stinking mist. (2) Fustiness in a cask.

Rag. To rail; revile in outrageous and opprobrious terms.

*Raise. Of the act of expectoration. 'What I *raize* is wonderful' (N. Ess.) [C. D.].

Rally. (1) A projecting ledge in a wall built thicker below than above, serving the purpose of a shelf. (2) A coarse sieve, to sift peas or horse-beans. (3) To sift.

*Ram. The keel of a boat [M. C. H. B.].

Ramp. (1) To prance, to romp. L. Sc. Rampage. (2) To grow rapidly and luxuriantly. It is applied to the rank growth of plants supporting themselves. In the case of those which have tendrils or claspers, by which they lay hold on other supports, it is an admitted word.

*Ramper. A public road or highway [Johnson].

*Rampered. A road is said to be *rampered* when its sides are pared down and suitable material laid on the middle to raise it [Johnson].

*Ramprow Goose. A Yarmouth herring [*Eastern England*, i. p. 133].

Ramshackled. Confused and obstructed in motion, action, or intention, like a ram when his head is fastened to his fore leg. Sometimes used as tumbledown, all to pieces.

Ranch. To scratch deeply and severely, as with a nail or some more sharply pointed instrument.

Rand. (1) A joint of beef; or rather a piece than a joint. It does not seem to admit of any precise definition, but to signify any fleshy piece from the edges of the larger divisions of the hind quarter, the rump, loin, or leg. (2) A strip of leather in the heel of a shoe, turned over the edge, and firmly stitched down to strengthen it. In both senses from Teut. *rand*, margo. (3) The boggy space between embankments and stream of rivers [*N. and Q.* 2nd Ser. i. p. 522]. See **Rond**. I never heard it called *rand* [W. R.].

Randan. The produce of a second sifting of meal. *Vide* **Crible**.

*****Rannock.** Womack Broad is so called [M. C. H. B.].

Ranny. The shrew-mouse. The short-tailed field-mouse, abounding in moist meadows, is not unfrequently called by the same name, but sometimes distinguished as the water *ranny*.

Ranter. (1) A tin or copper can, in which beer is brought from ·the cellar, and poured out into drinking vessels. (2) To pour liquor from a large into smaller vessels. (3) To sew up a rent in a garment, or to apply a patch over it, so neatly as that the new stitches are not discernible.

*****Rap.** To exchange, to swop [Johnson].

Rap and Rend. To seize and apply to his own use whatever a man can lay hands on.

Rape and Scrape. Much the same in import as the foregoing phrase, but implying less violence.

*****Rape (REAP) Hook.** A sharpened sickle. A true sickle should have a slightly toothed or ragged edge [W. R.].

Rase. To cut or scratch superficially; to wound or abrade skin deep.

Rasp, Resp. To belch.

*****Rasty.** *Rāsty* meat is nasty, strong-smelling, though not quite stinking meat [W. R.]. See **Reasty**.

Rath Ripe. Coming early to maturity.

*****Ratified.** Scolded, lectured [Johnson]. **Rated?** [W. R.].

*****Rattlewing.** The golden-eyed duck [J. H. G.].

*Rattling. Scolding. 'I gon him a good *rattling*' [Johnson].

Rattock. A great noise. Rattacking [Johnson].

Raum. To sprawl; to move with arms and legs on full stretch.

*Ravary. A violent mad fit of passion, attended with loud vociferation [Johnson].

*Rave Boards. Eave-boards [Johnson]. See Rafe Board.

*Ravelings. The same as Frazelings.

Rawings. After-grass. *Vide* Eddish. Pronounced Rawrin [Johnson].

*Rawn. A second growth of meadow grass [H. B.].

Razor. A small pole, used to confine faggots [Forby]. More usually Rizzer [E. S. T.]. A long cleft pole, used to confine the splints in a building of stud and clay [Johnson].

*Razor Grinder. The night-jar [J. H. G.].

*Reach. A stretch of paling [H. B.].

Reast, Reastiness. Restiveness or rancidity. Indeed the two senses seem to be sometimes strangely confounded. Some talk of a horse 'taking *reast* or *rust*,' or 'running *rusty*,' meaning that he becomes *restive*, not *rancid* [Br.].

Reasty. (1) See Rasty. (2) Restive. A corruption, no doubt. (3) Rancid; and probably so is this of Rusty, from the appearance of things turned rancid, as of bacon, to which it is particularly applied.

*Reave. To unroof or disturb the roof [Marshall].

*Red Head. The common pochard (*F. ferina*), also called Dunbird.

*Red Leg. The redshank, not the French partridge [M. C. H. B.].

*Red Tail, Fire Tail. The redstart [J. H. G.].

Red Weed. Any of the species of field poppy with scarlet flowers.

Reed Pheasant. The bearded tit [M. C. H. B.].

Reed Roll. A thicket of reeds on the borders or shallow parts of a river.

*****Reign-upon-you.** To take violent hold. To get the mastery [F. J. B.].

Rein. (1) To droop the head, as ripe corn. (2) To bear the head in a stiff and constrained posture, through affectation, like that of a horse sharply bitted.

Releet. The meeting of different roads in the same point, as a three *releet,* a four *releet,* &c.

Render. To give a finishing coat of plaster to a wall [Forby]. To melt lard or other fat [Spur.].

*****Rennable.** Plain, easy to be understood. 'That boy reads very *rennable*' [Johnson].

Rere. Raw, insufficiently cooked.

Ret. (1) To soak, to macerate in water. (2) A wart [E. S. T. and Bevan].

Retting Pit. A pond used for soaking hemp. In the fens there are two different modes of *retting* : dew *retting,* which is spreading the crop on the grass, and turning it now and then to receive the dew ; and water *retting,* which is laying it in a pond or ditch, covered with turf.

*****Rice.** Pea straw [Johnson].

*****Rickles.** The 'ringes' or 'gongs.' Scattered corn or hay collected into ranks by means of large rakes, commonly called drag-rakes [Johnson].

*****Rickstavel.** A frame of wood placed on stones or piers [Johnson].

Ricky. Masterly.

Rid. (1) To remove litter or incumbrance ; to put in order. Ex. '*Rid* up the room, or *rid* yourself, before the company come.' (2) To dispatch. Ex. 'To *rid* work,' 'to *rid* ground,' &c.

Riddle. A coarse sieve; as a corn *riddle*, a cinder *riddle*, &c.

Ride. (1) 'To *ride* grub,' to be out of humour, sulkily silent and pouting [Forby]. (2) The quantity of wood growing from one stub [Johnson]. (3) A saddle-horse [Marshall].

*Ridgeband. That part of the harness that crosses the back of the horse. In use in 1775 [C. D.].

*Ridgewith(e). A tumbril. One was sold in an overseers' distraint at Great Waldingfield, Suff., in 1724 [C. D.].

Rie. The raised border on the top of a stocking.

*Riest. An iron which is fastened below the breast of a plough [Johnson].

*Riffle. To plough lightly [*B. N.* 14].

Rig. (1) A ridge in ploughed land, as much as lies between one furrow and another. (2) A rib in a stocking [Forby]. (3) A trick or hoax [Johnson]. (4) A sheep having one testicle [Johnson].

Right. (1) To set to rights; to put into order; frequently used with 'up.' Ex. '*Right* up the room, company is coming.' (2) Obligation. Ex. 'I have no *right* to pay so much,' q. d. I am not obliged to pay it.

Right on. (1) Positively. Ex. 'I am *right on* determined.' 'He is a plain *right on* sort of man.' (2) Straight forward. Ex. 'Go *right on*, and you cannot miss the way.' (3) 'I am *right on* jowered out' [W. R.].

Right out. (1) Directly, uninterruptedly, completely. (2) Put out, excited. Ex. 'He was *right out* about it' [M. C. H. B.].

Right side. (1) To state and balance an account. (2) To set in order, replace [*Eastern England*, i. p. 46]. (3) To put to rights in an offensive or punching way.

N

Right up. Upright. Ex. 'Stand *right up*, boy!' It is figuratively said of one who lives on his own means, without trade or profession, that he ' lives *right up.*'

Right-up-eared. Prick-eared, pert, saucy.

*****Rigsby.** A wanton romping girl [Johnson].

Rile. (1) To stir up water or liquor and make it turbid, by moving the sediment [Br.]. (2) It is figuratively applied both to the temper and to the complexion. A man is *riled* when he is provoked to anger. This is one of the numerous American words which came from the East of England.

Rim of the body. The membrane lining the abdomen, and covering the bowels.

*****Rime.** Fog (N. Ess.) [C. D.].

Rimple. A wrinkle.

*****Rine, Rin.** Brine [Marshall].

Ringe. (1) The border or trimming of a cap, kerchief, or other article of female dress. (2) A row of plants, or anything else [Forby]. (3) Corn or hay collected in a row [Johnson].

Ringle. A ring as used in the nose of a bull or in snouts of swine, or any sort of iron ring used on the farm [J. H. G.].

*****Riot.** Noise, a quarrel between two people only [M. C. H. B.].

Rip. (1) To swear profanely, and in anger. It is intended, perhaps, to intimate that the outrageous blasphemer, to whom it is applied, would, if he could, *rip* and tear the object of his wrath. Or peradventure it may be only a cant abbreviation of *reprobate*. (2) To be very violent and outrageous. (3) An outrageous profane swearer. (4) Any person or thing completely worn out and worthless. (5) Playful; 'you young *rip*,' said of children [M. C. H. B.].

*Rippier. One who brings fish from the coast to sell inland [J. G. N.]. But E. F. G. queries this, and so do I.

*Ripple. (1) To *ripple* or ribble land is to plough it in small wavy ridges [Bevan]. (2) A particular way of ploughing, laying the land two furrows together [Johnson].

Rising. Yeast, or whatever may be used as a substitute for it, to make the dough. *rise* in fermentation.

Risps. (1) The stems of climbing plants generally. (2) The fruit-bearing stems of raspberries; sometimes, perhaps, applied to other plants somewhat like them.

*Rissling. Beating walnuts off the branches with a pole [Johnson].

Rist. A rising or elevation of the ground.

*Rixy. (1) A half-castrated horse, having a testicle in its body not descending into the scrotum [Johnson]. See Rig [W. R.]. (2) The smallest sea-gull [E. F. G.].

*Rizzer. See Razor.

*Rizzers. Hurdle stakes [M. C. H. B.].

*Roaches. Sweets [*B. N.* 72].

Road. To force or jostle one off the road by riding or driving against him.

*Roading. Running races with teams upon the road [Marshall].

*Roarers. Wooden baskets to carry salt herrings [E. F. G.].

Roblet. A large chicken, or young cock.

Rock, Rock-staff. A distaff, from which, as we are told, the wool *was* spun by twirling a ball below. ' An old woman's *rockstaff* ' is a contemptuous expression for a silly superstitious fancy.

Rocket. A row of holes made by dibbles, the whole length of the Stetch, q. v.

*Rode. To spawn [W. R., E. F. G.]. Usually Roud or Rowd.

Roger's Blast. A sudden and local motion of the air, not otherwise perceptible but by its whirling up the dust on a dry road in perfectly calm weather, somewhat in the manner of a waterspout. It is reckoned a sign of approaching rain [see *N. and Q.*, 4th Ser., vol. vi. p. 502]. Usually now for a violent and sudden whirlwind, not uncommon in the summer on the broads; often of force enough to lift haycocks and dismast yachts [W. R.].

*Roil'd. Disturbed [Arderon].

Roke. A fog.

*Roker. A young skate [W. R.]. *Vide* Homer.

Roky. Foggy. Generally applied to the fog and mist rising in the evening off the marshes and water meadows [W. R.].

*Rolling Barley. Collecting it into heaps ready to pitch into the wagon [Johnson].

Rollipoke. Hempen cloth of very coarse texture. Perhaps so named because only fit to be used as bags or wrappers for *rolls* or bales of finer goods.

*Rolypoly, or Rollypolly. Rolled pastry and jam pudding served up boiled. A rolled pole, from its shape and make [M. C. H. B.].

*Rome. A candle is said to *rome* (roam?) when the tallow runs down wasting in a draught [Johnson].

*Roment. To raise a report or falsehood [Johnson]. [From Romaunt? W. R.]

Rommock. To romp or gambol boisterously. Apparently an intens. of Romp or Roam.

*Rond. (1) The slip of marshy land which lies between the natural river bank and the artificial embankment, which usually runs parallel to it [W. R.].

*Roof Raising. House-warming [M. C. H. B.].

Rosil. Rosin.

Rosilly. Like rosin. It is applied to a soil both sandy and clayey.

*Rouding Time. Spawning time [W. R.].

*Round. The roe or 'milt' of herring [W. R.].

Rove. (1) A scab [Forby]. (2) Half a ploughing, two furrows instead of four [Cull. Haw.].

Row. (1) A hedge. Probably an abbreviation of Hedgerow. (2) A narrow passage [M. C. H. B.].

Rowy. Of uneven texture, having some threads stouter than others.

*Rüd-burrow. A wheelbarrow.

*Rudder. The instrument used for stirring the mash in brewing [Johnson].

*Rume. A room [N. and Q.].

*Runaway. At Wisby there is an open ditch across the green where the water runs across, called the *runaway* [H. C.].

*Rundle, Rundall, or Roundle. A round field or marsh, or a field that lies round or adjoins a person's property or house. 'Johnson's *rundle*' [M. C. H. B.].

Runnably. Currently; smoothly; without hesitation. Ex. 'The boy reads pretty *runnably*.' Often Renably in Suffolk.

*Runner. (1) The water-rail (*Rallus aquaticus*). (2) Also of eggs when incubation has caused the yolk to change its appearance [M. C. H. B.].

*Running-calf. A calf brought up on the cow and not artificially [J. H. G.].

Runty. Crusty, surly, ill-humoured. 'To run *runty*' is to take affront and resent.

*Russel. A low, prickly plant, bearing a blue flower ; also called **Banerth** [Johnson].

Ruttle. To make a harsh and rough noise in breathing; as when the action of the lungs is impeded, or the passage through the trachea obstructed. The ' death *ruttle* ' [Spur.].

*Ryvers. Those who open the gills of herring to make way for the stick or ' speet ' on which they hang while being dried [*East. England*, i. p. 146].

Sad Bad, Sadly Bad, Sadly Badly. Very ill.

*Sad Bread. Soppy, heavy, unbaked bread [M. C. H. B.].

*Sag. Sedge, as sweet *sedge (Acarus calamus)* [W. R.].

Sag. To fail, or give way, from weakness in itself, or overloading; as the bars of a gate, beams, rafters, or the like. In nautical language, is when, from overloads, the middle of a ship lies lower than its extreme ends. If the reverse, it is said to **Log** [E. S. T.]. We also use it figuratively. Of a man who droops in the decline of life, we say, ' he begins to *sag.*'

*Sagging, Soughing. Of the wind in the reeds [M. C. H. B.].

Sag Ledge. A crossbar or brace to a gate, to prevent the *ledges* from *sagging.*

*Salad. Any green vegetables [M. C. H. B.].

Sale. The iron or wooden part of the collar of a cart-horse [Forby]. The same as **Hames** [Johnson].

*Sales. See **Seles.** Part of harness [G. E.]. **Harnes** [*B. N.* 90].

Sally. (1) To pitch forward. (2) An old hare [W. G. W.].

*Salt. When a sow is ' maris appetens ' [E. S. T.].

Salt Cat. *Vide* Cat.

*Salt Eel. A punishment by giving the rope's end [Johnson].

*Saltings. Meadows occasionally covered by salt water [Spur.].

*Same as. In N. Ess. a common interpolation, as e. g. 'I should have sent it down, *same as* to-morrow.' It seems to imply a slight indefiniteness [C. D.].

Sammen Bricks. Bricks insufficiently burned; soft and friable. They are commonly understood to be Salmon bricks, and to be so called, because, from lying near the outsides of the kiln, they get more smoke than heat, and assume a reddish hue, supposed to be something like that of the flesh of the salmon, to be properly salmon-coloured bricks. Sammel Brick [Johnson].

Sammodithee. This uncouth cluster of little words (for such it is) is recorded by Sir Thomas Browne as current in his time. It is now totally extinct. It stands thus in the eighth tract, 'On Languages.' Dr. Hickes has taken the liberty of changing it to *sammoditha*, and interprets it, 'Say me how dost thou,'—in pure Saxon, '*sæg me hu dest thu.*' But, as Spurdens amusingly points out, it is a mare's nest, and only a jumble up of the reply, ' Same unto thee.'

*Sammucking. Strolling aimlessly [*B. N.* 24]. See Sannikin.

Samp. To lull, either the wind or the sea [E. F. G.].

Sand Galls. *Vide* Galls.

*Sannick. Fancy [M. C. H. B.].

*Sannikin. Loitering, idling [Johnson]. See Sammucking.

Sannock. A freq. or intens. of Sanny.

Sanny. (1) To utter a whining and wailing cry without apparent cause. Sanna [Johnson]. (2) To fall or stagger from excessive weakness, &c. 'He *sannied* a little on one side, fell down, and died immediately' [Johnson].

Sap. Another of Sir Thomas Browne's words; of which neither Hickes nor Ray gives any explanation. [Probably the gipsy word *sap*, a snake. See Borrow.] E. S. T.

says *sap*, a silly fellow.   It is curious that now always, in scholastic slang, *sap* means a man who grinds hard on the sl*y* [W. R.].

Sapy.   Pallid, sickly; also meat that will not get firm [E. S. T.].   Johnson suggests sappy-headed, watery brain.   Spurdens says meat in the first state of putridity.

*****Sarn or Cern.**   '*Sarn* your bones, I'll ge yow a flogging' [Johnson].

*****Sarshen.**   See **Soshen.**

Sauce.   (1) Any sort of vegetable eaten with fresh meat. The ancient simplicity of rustic cookery, unacquainted with high and stimulating condiments, still seeks wholesome substitutes for them in the garden.   (2) Cheek, banter.   'Don't have none of your *sauce*' [M. C. H. B.].

*****Saucie.**   Full of spirits, of inarticulate animals even.   Ex. 'That bull is regular *saucie* this morning' [M. C. H. B].

*****Sawbill** = Merganzers and Goosanders [M. C. H. B.].

*****Sawnie.**   Silly [M. C. H. B.].

Say.   (1) A taste or trial, sufficient to give a hankering for more.   Ex. 'Now the sheep have got a *say* of this grass they cannot keep out of it.'   [**Assay** ?]

*****Sayces.**   Rows or layers of bricks.

Say-nay.   (1) To refuse.   (2) To forbid.

*****Scaithful.**   Given to breaking pasture; also liable to be overrun by stock, as open fields, &c. [Marshall].

Scald.   (1) To scorch; to affect with dry heat.   (2) A multitude; a collection of something paltry and insignificant. Ex. 'I found the whole *scald* on 'em '; perhaps of boys robbing an orchard.   (3) A patch in a field of barley, scorched and withered by the sun, in a hot dry season, and on a light soil.   A correspondent of *Broad Norfolk*, p. 28, gives scald as ' the highest part of a hilly field,' but there is little doubt he was only accidentally describing a scalded patch.

*Scald or Scalt. A 'scaled' head affected by ringworm [Spur.].

*Scale in. To plough with a shallow furrow [Marshall].

Scallion. An onion in an advanced period of its growth, in which its flavour becomes coarse and rank, and its substance tough. An onion sprouting in the second year to bear seed; or the new bulbs which are sometimes produced from the old one in that renewed growth.

*Scalps. Stones on a beach—especially at Hunstanton.

*Scamel. A godwit [B. N. 75].

*Scamp. The head or scalp. 'If you say so again I'll hit you a lick o' the scamp' [Johnson].

*Scandalized. A wherry is said to have her sail scandalized when it is half lowered, so as not to catch the wind; a slovenly way of getting out of reefing [W. R.].

Scant. (1) Insufficient, not competent. We talk of a 'scant pattern,' meaning a scanty pittance. (2) Narrow, a scant reach on the river [M. C. H. B.]. A scant wind.

Scantity. Scarcity, insufficiency. Ex. 'She has but a poor scantity to live on.'

Scare. (1) A cur to drive away the pigs and poultry. (2) Lean and scraggy, as applied to persons; scanty and flimsy, to apparel.

*Scarfing. Preparing two pieces of iron for welding, by beating them thin at the ends.

*Scarify. To rough harrow land [M. C. H. B.].

*Scatling Poles. Used in building scaffolding [M.C. H. B.].

Schisms. Frivolous excuses; roundabout reasonings; strained apologies; nice distinctions; whimsies; fancies and fooleries in general.

Scoeker. A rift in an oak-tree, particularly when blasted by lightning; but more frequently a scocker is occasioned by water soaking down into the body of a pollard oak from an unsound part in the head of the tree ; and when a severe frost follows, the expansion of the water, in freezing, splits the wood mechanically.

*Scoed. A disease among lambs; a sort of gout in the knee [Johnson].

*Scoles. Scales.

*Sconsed. Refused, neglected, shirked [Johnson].

Scoot. An irregular angular projection, marring the form of a field, garden, &c. ; also gore, probably askew [E. S. T.]. See also *B. N.* 12.

Scooter. 'To run like *scooter,*' i. e. very nimbly. Probably from Scout. Here is the origin of another American word [W. R.]. From the flight of the *scoter* duck, *Anas nigra,* Lin. This bird appears particularly active in pursuit of its prey.

*Score. A gangway down the cliff [Spur.].

*Scorf. To swallow or eat. 'I *scorfed* the lot' [W. B.].

Scotch. To spare, to refrain. Figuratively; the primary sense of the word being to cut or mince. So when we say 'I did not *scotch* to tell him my mind,' we mean 'I did not at all mince the matter.'

*Scotches. Scores or notches [Marshall].

*Scoulton-pie. The black-headed gull which nests on Scoulton mere [J. H. G.].

*Scour. Relaxed as to the bowels [M. C. H. B.].

*Scoused. Secluded or hidden. [M. C. H. B.].

Scove. To run swiftly, to scour along.

Scrab. (1) To scratch or claw. (2) The incipient nest of any ground-building bird is so called, especially that of game birds and plovers [M. C. H. B.].

Scrabbed-eggs. A lenten dish, composed of eggs boiled hard, chopped and mixed, with a seasoning of butter, salt, and pepper.

Scradge. To dress and trim a fen-bank, in order to prepare it the better to resist an apprehended overflow. All loose materials within reach are raked together, and such additions as are to be had are procured, and so applied as to heighten and strengthen the upper part on the side next to the flood.

Scranch, Scrange. (1) A deep scratch. (2) To inflict such a scratch.

Scrap. To scratch in the earth; as a dog or other animal having that propensity.

Scraps. The dry, husky, and skinny residuum of melted fat.

*Scrat. An hermaphrodite [Johnson].

*Screen. A sieve; also verb, to sift [M. C. H. B.].

Screet. Half a quarter of a sheet of paper.

*Scriggle. A quick motion caused by tickling, a wriggle [Johnson].

*Scrimmage. Skirmish, skrimmage [M. C. H. B.].

Scrimption, Scrimshuns. A very small portion, a miserable pittance.

Scringe. (1) To shrink or shrivel, as with sharp cold or dry heat. (2) To cringe, to shrink as it were from fear of chastisement.

*Scrinkled. Shrivelled or crumpled [M. C. H. B.].

*Scrog. To cut beans with a sickle or hook [B. N. 84].

Scroggy. Twisted, stunted.

Scrog Legs. Bandy legs, crooked shanks.

*Scrome. Screamed [M. C. H. B.].

*Scrovy (Scrubby). A shabby, ragged, and dirty appearance [Johnson].

*Scrunk. A shoal, generally of fish, but also used as of wild fowl, ships, and donkeys [E. F. G.].

Scruse. Truce, or perhaps excuse, probably a corruption of one of these words. A boy at play wanting to tie his shoe, or to leave off for any other momentary occasion, calls out *scruse*, and does not lose his place in the game.

*Scudding Pole. Part of a herring boat [M. C. H. B.].

*Scug. The squirrel [Johnson]. Nares has Scummer.

*Scule. For school.

*Scummering. The playful galloping of colts when let loose [Johnson].

Scuppit. A dimin. of Scoop. A sort of hollow shovel to throw out water ; also a common shovel.

*Scurrick. A small portion [Johnson].

*Scurrying Pole. A stick used to stir an oven fire [Johnson].

*Scutcheons. Wooden baskets with handles on top, to carry fresh herrings [E. F. G.].

*Scute. See Scoot.

Seal. Time, season. Hay *seal*, wheat *seal*, barley *seal*, are the respective seasons of mowing or sowing those products of the earth. But it goes as low as hours. Of an idle and dissipated fellow we say that he 'keeps bad *seals*'; of poachers, that they are ' out at all *seals* of the night'; of a sober, regular, and industrious man, that he attends to his business ' at all *seals*,' or that he ' keeps good *seals* and meals.' Sir Thomas Browne spells it Sele, but we seem to come nearer to the Saxon. 'To give one the *sele* of the day.' See Sele. [See Flight-seel and Shot-sele, W. R.]

*Sealable. Seasonable, opportune, but applied only to time. An inn is open at ' all *sealable* hours' [E. S. T.].

*Sea-pheasant. The pintail duck [J. H. G.].

*Sea-pie. The oyster catcher [J. H. G.].

*Sear. Dry, dead [Cull. Haw.].

*Search. Of physic. 'I feel it a *searching* on me' [M. C. H. B.].

*Searled up with cold. Pinched or nipped up [W. R., Tungate].

*Seat or Sitting. Enough eggs for a hen to sit on and cover nicely [M. C. H. B.].

*Seconding. The second time of hoeing turnips [M. C. H. B.].

*Sedge-marine. The sedge-warbler [J. H. G.].

Seed-lep. The basket carried by the seedsman. Sometimes it is applied with less propriety to the deep basket which holds chaff to feed the horses.

*See Sim. A child's game. If one of the party is blinded it is Blind Sim [Spur.].

*Seft. Saved, sparing [G. E.].

Seg. (1) Any animal emasculated when grown to maturity, as a bull *seg*. (2) Sedge [Spur.].

*Seggen. Made of sedges, as a *seggen* mattress, a *seggen* horse collar [Spur.].

*Sein Wheat. Mildewed wheat [Johnson].

*Sele. E.g. wheat *sele*, barley *sele*, hay *sele*, season for wheat sowing, &c. These words are pronounced short, thus— haysle, &c. [E. S. T.]. See Seal.

*Seles. Horsys harneys [*Prompt. Parv.*].

Sencion. The common groundsel.

*Sensible. Conscious, in cases of severe illness; the opposite to unsensed (N. Ess.) [C. D.].

*Sensible - crazy. A term applied to a lunatic who is sensible in some respects [H. B.].

*Sensible-make. To make understand. Local at Waldingfield [F. J. B.].

Serve. To impregnate.

Set. (1) To astound, to overcome with surprise. Ex. 'When she heard the news she was quite *set*,' q.d. motionless, *set* fast. (2) 'To *set* by,' to treat with attention and consideration. Ex. 'He was very much *set* by.' It is

O. E. : B. Tr., 'He that *setteth* not by himself.' (3) A situation, as an 'eel-*set*' [M. C. H. B.]. (4) To quant, a quant, a setting-pole. (5) To arrange, to set in order. (6) Sown, of seeds. (7) Set on, to put a man on to piece or job work. (8) Set out; of turnips, the final hoeing [M. C. H. B.].

*Sets. Of plants, the cuttings or offshoots. Also small potatoes used for 'setting' [M. C. H. B.].

Seven Year. A period of seven years collectively. A
. septennium. Ex. 'I have not seen him these two *seven years.*'

*Several. A portion of common land allotted to a certain person [M. C. H. B.].

*Sew. For sowed. 'He *sew* his wheat yesterday' [Spur.].

*Shabbley. Dull, showery [M. C. H. B.].

Shack. (1) To rove about, as a stroller and mendicant. (2) To turn pigs or poultry into the stubble fields, to feed on the scattered grain, in exercise of a right over common fields. [The custom of *shackage* was, that where lands were uninclosed but held in severalty in slips (see Seebohm), marked out by 'dole' stones, all the owners might turn out their pigs (and I think *all* cattle) to common over all the uninclosed land. Any one owner might inclose his slip, but then, of course, he lost his right of *shackage*. 'Injuste shakeraverunt' is a classical expression often found in Norfolk Court Rolls, W. R.] (3) A shabby fellow, lurking and prowling about, and living by his shifts. (4) The shaken grain remaining on the ground when harvest and gleaning are over; or, in woodland countries, the acorns or mast under the trees.

Shack Bag. Properly, one who carries a bag, *shaking* it to induce others to put something in, and holding it ready to receive whatever he can pilfer. But it is commonly used in the first sense of *shack*, substantive.

Shack Time. The time when pigs are at *shack*.

Shacky. Shabby, ragged, and shiftless, or shirtless.

*Shag. (1) 'To raise a man's *shag*' is to make him angry ('Get his wool up,' W. R.) [Johnson]. (2) Fat or bacon on which some of the coat, hair, or bristles remain [Johnson].

*Shag-trot. A slow pace.

Shail. (1) 'To *shail* about.' 'To run *shailing*' is to move as if the bones were loose in their sockets, like a ripe nut in its *shale* or shell [Forby]. (2) To throw a flat missile [Spur.]. A long string of barges being towed is said to go *shailing* about if it swings loosely across the river [W. R.]. (3) To drop out [F. J. B.]. (4) Sloping off [M. C. H. B.].

*Shake. A crack in timber [Spur.].

*Shaken. Timber is said to be shaken when from the violence of the wind its grain is separated; also **wany** [Johnson].

*Shaling. Gliding or slipping, slanting [M. C. H. B.].

*Shaling-off. Tapering or slanting [M. C. H. B.].

Shalm, Sharm, Shawm. To scream shrilly and vociferously.

Shamble. To drive away and disperse. Also to shout [*B. N.* 23].

*Shammock. A sloven [*B. N.* 92].

Shanny. Shatter-brained. Ray has **Shandy**, certainly the same word in somewhat different form. Sometimes *shanny*-pated [E. S. T.]. Johnson says, 'shy, wild in countenance, caused by affliction or an imaginary evil.'

*Sharm. See **Shalm**.

*Sharp. Hungry [M. C. H. B.].

Shaunty. Showy, flashy, affecting to be tasteful in apparel or ornament.

*Shay-brained. Foolish, silly [Blomefield].

Sheer. (1) Brittle. It is given in T. J. as an adv. and as a low word, in the sense of 'quick, at once.' Low let it be. It is nearly connected with our sense. (2) Bright red, shining with inflammation. (3) To reap [Marshall].

Shelled. Pie-bald, or partly coloured, as in **Sheldrake.**

***Sherb Corn.** [*Nolan's Poor Laws*, second edition, i. p. 501.]

Shere-man. Any man who had not the good fortune to be born in one of the sister counties, or in Essex. He is a sort of foreigner to us; and to our ears, which are acutely sensible of any violation of the beauty of our phraseology, and the music of our pronunciation, his speech soon bewrays him. 'Aye, I knew he must be a *shere-man* by his tongue.'

Sheres. A general name for all the counties in England, but Norfolk, Suffolk, and Essex, which are commonly called by us 'the three counties.'

Shet. To shut, e. g. a *shet knife* for a clasp knife [W. R.].

***Shew, Shue.** Interjec. to scare away [M. C. H. B.].

***Shife.** A slice or portion [Johnson]. But I doubt this, the example which he gives seeming to make it mean Sheaf [W. R.].

Shiften. (1) To change linen. (2) To shift stitches from one pin to another in knitting. Also **Shiffen,** to change linen [*B. N.* 89].

Shiftening. A change of linen. A poor woman begs of the overseer to give her boy, who is going out to service, 'only a *shiftening*, two of each sort, one on and one off.'

Shim. A narrow stripe of white on a horse's face.

Shimmer. To glimmer, to shine faintly.

Shimper. To simmer.

***Shinker.** A little curly-tailed long-coated dog [Johnson].

***Shinlog.** Refuse bricks used to stop the kiln mouth while burning [Johnson].

Shitten [Shut-in] Saturday. The Saturday in Passion Week, and should now be pronounced **Shutten,** or **Shut-in-Saturday**; the day on which the blessed Redeemer's body lay inclosed or shut in the tomb.

Shive. (1) A small and thin slice [Forby]. (2) A thick and broad piece [Johnson]. Also **Shiver** or **Sliver,** used for a slice of any size [W. R.]. (3) The small iron wedge with which the bolt of a window-shutter is fastened. In Suffolk this is called ' a **Sheer.**'

Shoaf. A sheaf [O. E., W. C.].

*****Shoal Furrow,** or **Fleet Furrow.** A shallow furrow, being the last ploughed before taking the balk up [Johnson].

*****Shoat.** See **Shot.**

Shod, Shud. A shed. Either may be the participle of the A. S. verb, It certainly means a shaded place.

Shoes and Stockings. The variety of primrose and polyanthus which has one flower sheathed within another.

*****Shog.** The pace of a horse, not an amble; a little out of a walk, but not a trot; also used to hurry up [Johnson].

Sholt. A cur, **Shoult** [Johnson].

*****Sholve.** A shovel [Spur.].

Shoo. To scare birds.

Shool, Shulve. To saunter, with such extreme laziness as if the saunterer did not mean to walk, but to shovel up the dust with his feet.

Shoring. Awry, aslant. From the oblique or slanting position of a shore or buttress.

*****Shortening.** Lard or butter for pastry-making [*B. N.* 22].

Shorts. Bran mixed with a small proportion of the flour.

*****Short-stuff.** Spirits. *Vide* **Spoon-stuff** [W. R.].

Shoshings. *Vide* **Ashoosh** and **Soskins.**

Shot, Shoat. A half-grown pig. It may, perhaps, be so called from its being of proper age and size to be fatted.

O

*Shotsele or Shutsele. The evening time, when birds give gunners the chance of a shot by a flight [W. R.].

Shove. (1) To cast the first teeth (pronounced like GROVE). (2) To germinate, to shoot. Neither of these senses is recognized in the Dictt.

*Show. For Shaw [E. M.].

Show. (Pronounced like COW.) To push or thrust. Certainly the same with Shove, but we seem to distinguish them by use. In *showing*, some force must be used. *Shoving* may be quietly and silently performed, as in the instances given under that word.

*Shrap or Scrap. A bait of chaff laid in the winter season to attract sparrows, &c., which are then netted with a contrivance called a '*shrap* net,' which it was once compulsory on parishes to provide [E. S. T.].

*Shrarm. *Vide* Shalm.

*Shreep. To clear away partially, as mist [E. F. G.].

Shreeve. The sheriff.

*Shrigger. A petty poacher and thief [Johnson].

*Shrook. For shrieked [Johnson].

Shrough. (Pronounced SHRUFF.) Fragments of sticks, bits of coal, cinders, &c., picked up by the poor for fuel. Occasionally applied, indeed, to any sort of refuse or sweepings.

Shrovy. Shabby, ragged, squalid. From Shrough.

*Shruck. For shrieked [W. R.]. 'She *shruck* a rum 'un' [E. M.].

*Shuck Dog. See Old Shuck.

Shuck Trot, Shug Trot. A low, lazy, and yet shaking trot. The butterwoman's rate to market. See Shog.

Shucky. (1) Long coated or long tailed, as a '*shucky* dog' [Johnson]. (2) Untidy in one's dress or person.

*Shud. For Shed [E. M.].

*Shuft. To push or crowd. 'I saw John *shuft* Tom into the ditch' [Johnson].

Shug, Shugging. To shake, shaking, concussion. Ex. 'Give the tree a good *shug*, and the fruit will fall.'

Shulve. A shovel. T., Sholve. Jen., Showl. W. C., Shool. Br., Shuil. Shulve [*B. N.* 22].

*Shy. Wild in conduct, amorous, *not* bashful [Spur.]. Also see *B. N.* 21 to same effect.

*Shywannicking [*B. N.* 74]. I think a coined word [W. R.]. See Skywannicking.

*Siberet. 'The *siberet* was asked at church,' the banns were published [Arderon]. Sybb-rit=*syb rede banna* [*Prompt. Parv.*]. Now usually Sibbits.

Sich. Such.

Side. Long, as applied to apparel. In the *P. L.* we find directions for making a short gown out of a *side* one. In modern usage, however, we seem to depart strangely from the ancient, and to use the word in the sense of strait. Ex. 'This sleeve is too *side*, it must be let out.' Or, 'It is too loose, it must be made *sider*.'

Sidlings. Aside, sideways. Women sit on horseback *sidlings*, and men straddlings. The words are respectively formed from *sidle* and straddle.

*Sight. A large quantity or considerable number; e. g. 'He has given me a *sight* of trouble' [J. H. G.].

*Sights. Spectacles; e. g. 'He was pakin about in *sights*' [H. B.].

Sile. (1) To strain, as milk, &c., to take out any dregs or impurity. (2) To allow a turbid fluid to remain unmoved, that it may deposit its sediment [Forby]. (3) The small fry of fish [E. F. G.].

*Sill Iron. The iron which connects the plough with the

standards, jigs, or carriage, of a Norfolk plough [Johnson].

Silly bold. Impertinently and unbecomingly free, assuming unseemly airs, applied to petulant and forward youth. '*Silly bold*, like Tom Johnson's owl' [E. S. T.].

*****Sim.** See **See-sim.**

Simper. To simmer. Skinner deduces these two words from the same etymon, and spells the latter of them **Simber**; most probably because it was so pronounced at that time in Lincolnshire, the county in which he was resident. This Mr. Todd ventures to call foolish. If the still existing use of *simper*, in the very next county, may be allowed to throw any light on that of *simber* one hundred and fifty years ago, we so far vindicate the most judicious, and generally most cautious, of our etymologists from such a censure.

*****Simpson.** Groundsel [W. B.].

Sin, Sen. Since.

*****Sine.** Then. 'First one, *sine* another' [Arderon].

*****Singular.** Long or single [Marshall].

*****Sink-hole Thief.** A despicable small thief, capable of creeping through a sink-hole [Arderon].

Sir Harry. A close stool. [Clearly a (k)night stool, W. R.]

Sirs. In O. E. sometimes written **Sers**, and thence, as we pronounce it, **Sars**. The common use of it, as a term of address, seems strangely inconsistent with the usual application of **Sir**. No respect is implied by it. It would be offensive to address it to superiors, or even to equals. It is a form of accosting inferiors only, as servants, and of both sexes. A farmer says to his domestics collectively, 'You may all go to the fair, *Sars*, for I shall stay at home.'

*****Sisserara.** A blow [*B. N.* 5, 59, 87].

Sithe. To sigh. O. E. *sihe*, of which our word seems a corruption.

*Sit ye merry. A phrase used at the end of a song. The suggested meaning is, *sich gemære*=behold the end.

Sizzle. To dry and shrivel up, with hissing, by the action of fire on some greasy or juicy substance, or green wood.

*Skein. A long line of flying duck [W. R.].

Skelp. (1) To kick with violence. It never means striking with the hand, or moving briskly, as in L. Sc. [S. W. Rix in *N. and Q.*, 2nd Ser., vol. vi. p. 372.] (2) A strong kick.

Skep. (1) A basket wider at top than at bottom [Forby]. Not to carry in the hand [Ray]. (2) A bee-hive is always a bee-*skep*.

Skew. To start aside, as a horse, at some object which scares him.

*Skewt. An irregular corner of a field [H. B.].

*Skife Nail. A long nail, having its head formed so as to suit or agree with the holes in the plat of a plough, and by which it is fastened firmly to the breast [Johnson].

*Skillagalee. Thin gruel [G. E.].

Skillet. A small pot of iron or copper with a long handle.

Skimmer. To flutter or frisk about lightly. It is a frequent. of *skim*. Pegge speaks of '*skimmering* light.' We should call it a *shimmering* light. The words may perhaps be connected.

Skinch. To stint; to pinch; to give short commons.

Skink. (1) To serve at table; particularly to serve the guests with drink [Forby]. (2) To avoid drinking in turn [Spur.].

Skinker. One who serves drink. In alehouse parties, in which the word is principally used, it is applied to one of the company who takes upon himself to fill the glasses or horns, and to call for more liquor, when it is wanted. The waiter, who brings it in, is not called the *skinker*, but the Tender, q. v.

*Skinks. Bricks immediately next the skovens or outside ones in a kiln or clamp [Johnson].

Skip-jack. The merry-thought of a fowl, converted into a little toy by means of a twisted thread and a small piece of stick [Br.].

*Skipping Block. A mounting block for horse [Johnson].

Skirl. To shrivel up something dry, by too much heat; as parchment, card, or paper *skirl* up before the fire. It may, however, be merely prefixing *s* to *curl*; and therefore to be spelled *scurl*.

*Skit. (1) A complaint incident to foals [Johnson]. (2) A hint; not direct information [Johnson].

Skive. To pare off the thickset parts of hides, to make them to uniform substance, in order to their being tanned. Sui.-G. *skifna*.

Skiwanikin, Skiwinckin. Awry, crooked, warped.

Skizzle. A large marble, rolled along the ground at others placed in ring, to displace as many of them as possible, as at the game of skittles.

*Skot Pig. See Shot.

*Skouch. To scrape the shoe awkwardly [G. E.].

*Skovens. The outside bricks in a kiln or clamp [Johnson].

*Skran. Dinner [*B. N.* 55].

*Skriggle. To wriggle or struggle away [E. S. T.].

*Skrimskin. A small piece [Johnson].

*Skrome. A scraping together of things as by a crome [Johnson].

*Skruse. A truce or temporary cessation. See Scruse.

*Skruzzle. Crackling or baked skin of pork [*B. N.* 35].

*Sky Wannikin. Shy, giddy, thoughtless [Johnson].

Slab. (1) The outer cut of a timber or other tree when sawn into planks. [Another American word—W. R.] (2) A slave; a drudge. The boy who serves the mason is called his *slab*. But perhaps, in this case, he may be called from the *slabby* stuff he carries to his master, or from his carrying it on a piece of a *slab*, and not corruptly from slave. (3) A puddle or collection of surface drainage [E. S. T.].

Slade. (1) A green road. (2) A sled or sledge. (3) A narrow slip of boggy ground [Spur.]. To carry on a sledge. Heavy weights are easily *sladed* on level ground [T.]. (4) To dislocate [M. C. H. B.].

*Slake. To be at slake, to be at leisure [Marshall]. Slack?

*Slaper. The bottom of a tree remaining in the ground after it is felled [Johnson]. [Is there any connexion between this word and the dry wood 'sleeper' of the railway?—W. R.]

*Slappy Bread. Not baked enough [Cull. Haw.].

Slar, Slare. To bedaub.

Slary. Bedaubed.

Slatter. To wash in a careless and *slatternly* manner, throwing the water about, &c.

Slattering-weather, Slavering-weather. A frequency or continuance of slight rain.

*Slaver. Nonsense [*B. N.* 55]. Of a soapy sort [*id.* 97].

*Slavering Bib. A child's chin-cloth [E. S. T.].

Slazy. Of loose and open texture, easily torn, and soon worn out; for which faults, it seems, the manufactures of Silesia were formerly remarkable.

Sled. *Vide* Slade.

Sleeper. (1) The stump of a tree left in the ground. (2) A rushlight [T.].

*Sleeping-room. A bedroom [H. B.].

Sleight. (1) The knack of doing anything. This sense is, perhaps, common enough, but not distinctly given in the Dictt. (2) Ready calculation, shrewd judgement. (3) To wear away clothes, shoes, &c. In Essex I heard the expression that a man was a 'slipe for boots,' i. e. that he wore his boots out very fast [W. R.]. 'A great *sleight* for butes' [E. M.]. Also *B. N.* 90.

Slent. A gentle slope in the surface of the ground.

*****Slicker.** A thick slice [Johnson].

Slift. The fleshy part of the leg of beef. The grand round of beef is the upper and under *slift* together. From **Sliver**; also **Slive.**

*****Slight.** Dexterous at any art [Arderon]. See **Sleight.**

Slimslacket. Of very thin texture, loose and flaccid.

*****Sling Horse.** The horse that follows the fore horse in a team [Johnson].

*****Slings.** A yoke to carry water [G. E.].

Slink. (1) To suffer abortion, as applied to a cow only. The cow *slinks* her calf, the mare **slips** her foal, the ewe **warps** her lamb. (2) A shifty fellow [C. H. E. W.].

Slink-calf. The abortion of a cow [W. C.].

Slink-veal. Miserable lean veal, which looks like the flesh of an abortion, L. Sc. W. C. Teut. *Schlenken,* abjicere.

*****Slipe.** For 'a wonder at;' generally, greedy. See **Sleight.**

*****Slite.** Wear and tear [E. F. G.].

*****Slithers.** Small pieces of leather put in between the sole of a shoe and the welt [Johnson, quoting *Norwich Mercury,* July 3, 1830].

Sliver, Sliving. A slice of flesh. Ch. seems to mean a small slice. We always mean a large one, and pronounce the *i* long, as directly from the verb **Slive.** A.S. *slifan,* findere. W. C., a thin slice.

Slod. (1) To wade through mire, half-dissolved snow, &c. (2) The accretion of soil, clay, or mould on one's soles [E. S. T.].

*****Slod, Slud.** A piece of dough with a pat of butter in the middle, put in to bake while the oven is heating [W. B.].

Slop. (1) An outside garment, reaching to mid-leg, worn by children, and by some workmen. (2) Underwood.

Sloven-wood. Southernwood.

Slub. (1) Thick mire, in which there is some danger of sticking fast. (2) To slub, to throw mud out of a ditch [M. C. H. B.].

Slug-horn. A short and ill-formed horn of an animal of the ox kind, turned downwards, and appearing to have been stunted in its growth.

Slump. (1) To sink suddenly and deep into mud or rotten ground. (2) Defeated, upset. An unsuccessful candidate is said to be *slumped*. 'Slumped again' [A. E. R.].

Slur, Slurry. Loose, thin, almost fluid mud. The reverse of slub.

Slurrup. To swallow any liquid greedily, and with a noise of the lips or in the throat.

Slush. (1) Loose mud. (2) Filthy talk. Figuratively. **Sluss** [*B. N.* 40].

*****Smeaa.** Marshland. 'Down by the carnser and over the *smeaa*' [*B. N.* 70]. Cf. **Marshland Smeeth** [W. R.], a smooth place.

Smeagre. Thin, lean.

Smeath. An open level of considerable extent, commonly pronounced and printed **Smee**.

*****Smee.** Widgeon (*Anas penelope*) [C. H. B.].

Smick, Smicket. Delicate diminutives of **Smock**.

*****Smite.** A small piece. 'They ate up every *smite*' [Johnson].

*Smittock. Ditto.

Smock-mill. A corn-mill, of a shape supposed to resemble that garment. If a mill of this form be mounted on a basement of stone or brick some few feet high, forming a storehouse under it, it assumes the more dignified appellation of a tower mill.

*Smoke-jacks. Cockades. [M. C. H. B.].

*Smolt. A calm [E. F. G.].

Smore. (1) To abound, to swarm. We say that a very numerous swarm of bees ‘come *smoring* out of the hive.’ (2) Contraction of *some more* [M. C. H. B.].

Smotch. (1) A blot or stain. (2) To defile. Ex. ‘I have *smotched* my fingers with the crock.’

Smouch. (1) To kiss him with a loud smack [Forby]. (2) To smuggle [Johnson].

*Smoulder. To smother, suffocate, quench, put out [Johnson].

*Smoultin. To get smooth. ‘The tide is a *smoultin* now —it gets kinder smoother when the tide is going out’ [*B. N.* 80].

*Smuddered. Smothered. Ex. ‘*Smuddered* to dead,’ choked to death, or stifled [M. C. H. B.].

Smur. Small misty rain, which seems to fill the air like smoke. It falls so lightly on the skin, as to seem rather to smear or anoint than to wet it.

*Smurry Day. A wet off-and-on sort of day [Tungate].

Snack, Sneck, Snick. A sort of fastening for a door. A snack must be of iron ; and is either a thumb-*snack*, in which the latch is lifted by pressing the thumb on the broad end of a short lever, which moves it; or it is a hand-*snack*, which acts upon the latch by a spring. In short, it is any sort of iron fastening which does not include a lock-*snack*.

*Snaffle. To talk nonsensically [Johnson].

Snag. (1) A rough knob or gnarl on a tree. (2) A tag of bootlace, or snack, or latch [M. C. H. B.].

Snaggy. Morose, coarse, and rough in temper. Not, properly, testy and peevish.

Snarl. To twist, entangle, and knot together; as a skein in winding off.

Snaste. The burning wick or snuff of a candle. [**Snaast,** *B. N. 6*].

Snasty. Captious, passionate. [**Snarlish,** *B. N. 12*.] 'To take a thing in snuff,' however low an expression it may now sound, was formerly used by very good authors in the most serious composition ; by Bishop Andrewes, for instance, in his sermons. It manifestly conveys the same idea as this word. To be angry is to take something in snuff. Easily annoyed.

Sneck. A door-latch [*B. N. 52, 90*]. See **Snack.**

Sneer. To make wry faces without intention of expressing contempt or insult, which the word in its general sense implies.

*Snettle. A noose [Johnson].

*Sniccups. The gapes. A disease which causes young birds to make a noise like ' sniccups ' [C. H. B.].

Snicker-snee. A large clasp-knife. This word was probably brought to us by the Dutch, in whose language it is said to have the same meaning.

Snickle, Snittle. A slip-knot. Ex. ' Tie it in a *snickle,* not in a tight knot.'

*Snick-snacks. Equal shares [Johnson].

Snickup. Begone! away with you!

Snickups. An undefined and undefinable malady, but not always easily cured. To say of a man that he has ' got the *snickups,*' means rather that he fancies himself ill, than that he really is so. It is by no means so alarming an ailment as a 'flap of cold,' q. v. It may have its name partly because it rhymes to hiccup ; and partly because it is not unlikely to be acted upon by the same, or by some similar medical treatment. It may be added that ' a poor *snickuppy* creature !' is sometimes applied to a pale-faced, petted, and pampered child, always pining and puling.

*Sniffle Snaffle. Trifling discourse, &c. [Johnson].

Snippock. A very small morsel. From *snip*.

*Snitch. The nose. Ex. 'Pull her *snitch* for her' [M. C. H. B.].

*Snob. A shoemaker, pronounced as shummaker [M. C. H. B.].

Snobbing. Horses biting one another gently [H. B.].

*Snooze. For noose. Ex. ' Defendant pleaded guilty to having *snoozed* the pike' [*Police Report*, 1886, Wroxham].

*Snotch. For notch [Johnson].

Snots. White bream (*Alramis blicca*) [M. C. H. B.].

Snoul. A short thick cut from the crusty part of a loaf or a cheese.

*Snuck. Dogs going after bitches are said to go *snucking* after them [Johnson].

Snudge. Such brisk motion as an aged person may use. Ex. ' The old woman went *snudging* along,' i. e. snugly wrapped up, with arms folded and head inclined, making the best of her way.

Snuskin. A nicety, a tit-bit.

Soak. To bake thoroughly. It is particularly applied to bread, which, to be good, must be macerated, as it were, in the caloric of the oven. If it be dough-baked, the complaint is that it has not been sufficiently *soaked*.

Sock. (1) The superficial moisture of land not properly

drained off [Forby].   (2) The lowest part of a wet field
from which there is no outlet for the water, therefore all
the *sock* (soak) is deposited there [Johnson].   (3) The
mouth or outlet from a ditch into the river.   (4) More
generally and correctly the ditch running parallel with the
river outside the wale [M. C. H. B.].   (5) Also Soggy,
wet, heavy, adhesive.

Soe.   A large tub carried by two men on a stout staff, or
stang, passing through two iron rings at its top, for
the conveyance of water, grains, hogwash, &c.

Soft-path.   One that may be ploughed.   A hard-path is
permanent [F. J. B.].

Soil.   To fatten completely.

Soiling.   The last fattening food given to fowls when they
are taken up from the stack or barn door, and cooped
for a few days.

So-ins.   In this or that manner, *taliter*.   We also say
So-fashions in the same sense.   *Vide* Siddlins.

Soldier.   To be disposed to give or take affront, to swagger,
to bully.

*Sole.   To beat violently [W. G. W.].

Soll.   To pull by the ears.   It is thus written because we
pronounce the *o* short.   In Suffolk it is pronounced
SOWL.

Soller.   A loft.   It anciently meant any loft or upper
room.   It seems now to be confined to a belfry, which is
sometimes called the bell *soller*, sometimes simply the
soller.   Sometimes Sollery [Spur.]

Sollop.   To lounge, to waste time in utter laziness and
inaction.

So-long.   Au revoir.   'Good-bye for so long as we are
apart' [M. C. H. B.].   [I doubt this being a genuine
Norfolk phrase, W. R.]

*Sona. For 'so.' Ex. 'I did not do that; I only did *sona*' [Johnson].

Sords. Filth, washings, offscourings.

Sore. Sorry, vile, worthless. Ex. 'He made a *sore* hand of it!'

Sore, Sorely. Very, exceedingly.

Sort. A great number. Ex. 'I have been there a *sort* of times' [Sh.]. 'I see a *sort* of traitors here' [B. Tr., Br.].

Sorzle, Sozzle. (1) To intermingle in a confused heap. Perhaps it may be connected figuratively with Soss, q. v. (2) An odd mixture of different things, generally applied to a compound of various ingredients boiled together for a medicine. Ex. 'How can she be well? she is always taking one *sorzle* or other.' (3) Slops [*B. N. 6*].

*Soshen. To cut at an angle [G. E.].

*Soshins. (In Suff., Shoshins), aslant, sloping.

*Soshways. Obliquely [Johnson].

Soss, Suss. A jumble, or mixed mess of food. Always used in contempt. See Suss.

*Sossen. Zigzag, right on the skew [W. R.]. Also see Soshins. Sarshen, *B. N. 65*.

Sotter. To boil gently. *Sottering*, in the case of a thick mixture of ingredients, seems to mean the same as the simmering of more fluid matter.

Soupings. Any sort of spoon meat.

Sow. (1) The insect called millipedes. (2) Sow-bug [M. C. H. B.].

Sow-pig. A gelded female [W. B.].

Sowse. (1) The paunch of an animal, usually sold for dog's meat. (2) Pigs' feet or ears pickled are called *sowse* in Suffolk [Forby]. (3) A smart slap rather than a blow, generally a box on the ear [Johnson].

*Spalt. Brittle [Cull. Haw.]. Used in Cambridgeshire.

*Span. 'I shall *span* you'=I shall spare you [Arderon].

*Spangles.   Oak spangles [M. C. H. B.].

Spank.   To move swiftly and stoutly.   Ex. 'How he did *spank* along !'

Spanker.   (1) A person who takes long steps with agility, a stout or tall person.   (2) Fine and large, conspicuous [M. C. H. B.].

Spanking.   (1) Moving nimbly, striding along stoutly. (2) Showy, conspicuous, especially if large.

*Spantree.   The threshold of a barn or outhouse [W. G. W.].

Sparch.   Brittle.

Spar Dust.   Powder off posts, dust produced in wood by the depredations of boring insects.   It is to be distinguished from Saw Dust.

*Spare.   To make, to be saving or careful [F. J. B.].

Spate Bone, Spaut Bone.   The shoulder bone of an animal slain for food.   Spade Bone, from its shape, is pretty common.

*Spear.   Of seeds, to germinate [M. C. H. B.].

*Spear-grass.   The usual term for twitch (*Triticum repens*) [H. B.].

Speck.   (1) The sole of a shoe.   The heel of the shoe is, by way of distinction, called the *heel speck*.   ' These old shoes must be *heel specked*.'   (2) The fish commonly called a sole, from its resemblance in shape.

*Specked.   Used of decay in its earlier stage.   ' More blades are *specked*, they'll soon be bad' [W. B.].

*Speets.   Long sticks or laths on which herrings are strung to dry [White's *Eastern England*, vol. i. p. 146].

Spend.   (1) To span with the fingers.   Apparently a mere corruption, but O. E. in P. B.   (2) To consume or expend.   Ex. 'We *spend* so much meat, flour, cheese, &c., in our family weekly.'

Spender. A consumer. A 'small *spender*' is a person who has very little appetite.

Spending-cheese. Cheese of a middling quality, used for family consumption in the dairy districts of Suffolk, considerably superior to the Bang, or Thump, for which they are so celebrated, but by no means equal to Gloucester.

*Spendlow. Dead wood made into fagots, and sold for kindling [Johnson].

Spere. A spire. Just as we use shere for shire.

Sperken, Sperket. A wooden peg to hang hats, &c., upon. See **Spiken** and **Spickot**.

Spikin, Spekin. A large nail with a round flat head. See **Spirket**.

Spile. A wedge of wood stoutly pointed with iron, used in clay or gravel pits, &c., to let down large quantities at once.

Spile-hole. The air-hole in a cask [Br.].

Spile-peg. The·wooden peg closing the hole for the admission of air into a cask when it is tapped.

*Spindling. Wasting away a good deal [Mrs. A. Leakey, of Acton].

Spink. (1) A chaffinch. (2) **Herring Spink**, the gold-crest [M. C. H. B.].

*Spinney. A small wood [H. C.].

Spire, or Spere. Anything that rises above the level of surrounding objects. Spere-grass, or couch-grass. The spires or young trees left in clearing underwood [F. J. B.].

Spirit. Electric fire; a blast of lightning. Ex. 'In the great tempest, a *spirit* lit upon the church steeple.'

*Spirket. An iron hook [M$_{oor}$, Blomefield]. Johnson gives it as a special word for a 'semicircular iron on which the hog is hung before it is bowelled.' But it is clear the word is for anything on which anything else is hung [W. R.].

Spit. The depth of a spade in digging. We talk of going two or three *spit* deep.

Spittle. A term of supreme contempt, or rather loathing. [O. E.] 'Oh, you nasty *spittle*!' q. d. filthy fellow! dirty creature! Arderon quotes the expression, 'You forlorn *spittle*!'

***Splarr.** To spread or sprawl [*B. N.* 27].

***Spoat.** Short-grained wood [*B. N.* 39].

Spoffle. To be over-busy about little or nothing. (**Spuffle.**)

Spolt. Brittle; chiefly applied to wood easily separable into fragments [Forby]. 'As *spolt* as steel' [Johnson].

Spong. (1) A long narrow slip of inclosed land, such as a strong active fellow might clear in **Spang** or leap. *Spong-water* is a narrow streamlet [Forby]. A low bog or morass [Johnson]. (2) '*Hot spong*,' a sudden power of heat from the sun comes from under a cloud [Johnson]. (3) A calm at sea [Spur.].

***Spoon-stuff,** or **Short-stuff.** Spirits [W. R.].

Spore. (1) A spur for a gate-post. The proper word. ? Shore [W. R.]. (2) To preserve fruit [W. G. W.].

***Spot Spoons.** Tadpoles [M. C. H. B.].

***Spotty.** Partial [E. F. G.].

***Spoutt.** Brittle [*B. N.* 40, 53].

***Sprags.** Sprays or spurs.

Spraid. To sprinkle, to spatter, to moisten with spray.

***Sprat-loon.** The red-throated diver [J. H. G.].

Sprawls. Small twigs, or branches of trees or bushes.

Spreckled. Speckled.

Spring. (1) Young plants of whitethorn, to make hedges [Forby]. (2) A lea, grass-land [Spur.]. (3) Run in eggs. *Vide* Run [M. C. H. B.]. (4) Excited by drink [*B. N.* 62].

Springe. (1) To spread lightly, to sprinkle. (2) A horse-hair or wire snare for birdcatching, &c. [M. C. H. B.].

Springer. A youth. In L. Sc. *springald.*

Sprink. A crack, a flaw. Sprunkt [Johnson].

Sprit. A pole to push a boat forward. A. S. *spreot,* contus.

Sprunny. Neat, spruce.

Spud. (1) Any person, or thing, remarkably short of its kind. (2) A chisel for weeds [G. E.].

Spuddy. Very short and stumpy.

*Spuds. Potatoes [W. B.].

Spuffle. To move hastily, with an ostentatious air of busi-ness and bustle. See **Spoffle.** [This is a much-used word.]

Spuffling. Moving as above. Ex. ' I saw Mr. A. *spuffling* along.'

*Spunking. A beating or thrashing with the hands [C. H. E. W.]

Spunky. Brisk, mettlesome. No uncommon vulgarism. In O. E. *spunk* is touchwood. A. S. *spoon,* fomes.

*Spurket. An iron hook on a wall [G. E.].

*Spurrer. A sparrow [M. C. H. B.].

*Spurway. A bridle-way [W. R.].

Squash. (1) To splash, to moisten by plentiful effusion. (2) To squeeze, so as to make soft, like a pumpkin squash. (3) Also pea-pods which look full but are really empty [W. B.].

Squat. To quiet, to put to silence. Ex. ' Pray, nurse, *squat* the child.'

Squatting Pills. An opiate in the form of pills. Ex. ' He got no rest till the doctor gave him some *squatting pills.*' In this, and the two preceding words, the *a* is pronounced as in *hat.*

*Squezzened. Suffocated [Johnson].

Squiggle. To shake and wash a fluid about the mouth, with the lips closed.

Squinder. To burn very faintly, or even insensibly, as damp fuel, which does not kindle into a flame, and gives out no heat, but yet it is consumed. It is said to *squinder*, or be *squindered* away. So is the candle which has a bad wick. Perhaps it is to be considered as a dimin. of Squander. The fuel or the candle is unprofitably wasted.

*Squink. To wink [Johnson].

Squinny. (1) To look asquint. Ex. ' Child, do not *squinny* your eyes so.' (2) Very lean, meagre, slender, shadowy, &c. Sometimes it is *squinny* gutted.

Squish. A dim. of Squash. The water *squishes* under our feet in the grass, if it be walked on too soon after rain. It is used by Swift.

Squit. (1) A word of supreme contempt for a very diminutive person. ' A paltry *squit* !' In O. E. it was Squib, but that word seems to be lost, and the more is the pity, for at any rate it was less offensively contemptuons. (2) Silly talk, for which onė feels contempt. Ex. ' Hold your *squit*.' (3) A syringe, a squirt [C. H. B.].

*Squoddy. Short of stature, sturdy [Spur.].

*Stacia. A comparative. ' That will do like *stacia*,' ' As drunk as *stacia* ' [Johnson]. Unknown to me [W. R.].

Stag. (1) A wren. (2) A cock turkey, killed for the table in his second year ; by which time he has often reached the weight of twenty pounds or more [Forby]. (3) A young bull [W. G. W.].

*Staith, or Staithe. A landing-place from a river, not necessarily for goods, as E. S. T. thinks [W. R.].

*Stale. The staff or handle of a rake or fork; also the stalk or reed of hemp [Spur.].

*Stalk. See Back Stalk.

Stam. (1) To astonish, to overcome with amazement.
Ex. 'It is a *stamming* story, indeed!' (2) A matter of
amazement.

*Stanch. (1) A lock with one pair of doors only [E. S. T.].
(2) Staunch. A hen when very broody and well settled on
her nest is said to be 'down' and 'stanch.' If she does
not go down well on to her eggs she is said to 'lift'
[M. C. H. B.].

Stanchions. (1) Iron bars, dividing and guarding a window, not used for a prop or support. (2) The timbers
or ribs of a row-boat.

Stand. (1) 'To *stand* in hand,' to concern, behove, or
interest. Ex. 'It *stands* you in hand to look to that.'
W. C. 'It *stands* you on.' (2) 'To *stand* holes,' to rest
content as one happens to be at present. It seems to be
an allusion to some game played by moving pegs from
one hole to another, as on a cribbage board.

*Stands. Young timber, trees under 6 in. timber girth, or
24 in. in circumference [Marshall].

Stank. A dam. In its nature a *stank* converts, in some
sort, into a pond that part of the water which it inter-
cepts ; so there is a connexion between the two senses.

Stannide. Stickleback [*B. N.* 35].

Stanstickles. Small fish, with many names.

*Star. (1) Starling (*Sturnus vulgaris*). (2) A showy
young woman, one to stare at [M. C. H. B.].

*Star. *Vide* Lead [M. C. H. B.].

*Starr Grass. Bents. A marsh between Martham and
Horsey is called *Starr Grass* Marsh [E. S. T.]. 'Starr
Gräs' is Norwegian for sedge [M. C. H. B.].

Statesman. The proprietor of an estate.

*Statue. A figure set up in a field as a scarecrow [F. J. B.].

*Stay. A lean-to post [C. H. B.].

*Stead. (1) To supply a space left vacant. Ex. 'I am at last *steaded*' with a servant, a house, a horse, or whatever else I have been in want of. (2) A place to stand on ; as a fair*stead* is the ground on which a fair is held.

*Steelfall. A spring trap [G. E.].

*Steelyard. A balance [G. E.].

*Steen. Spite or envy [Johnson].

*Stent. A task [G. E.].

Stepples. A short and neat flight of steps, as from the parlour window to the garden ; to reach the upper shelves of a book-case, or something else, in which appearance ·is to be considered.

Stetch. (1) As much land as lies between one furrow and another [Forby]. (2) A ploughed ridge [Johnson].

Stew. A cloud of dust or vapour; as from a much frequented road, a lime-kiln, a brew-house, &c.

Stifler. A stickler; one who is very busy and active in any matter; as it were raising a dust. Ex. ' She was a high *stifler* upon that occasion ' [Forby]. A stapler [Johnson].

*Still. Rest. Ex. ' There is no *still* in him ' [M. C. H. B.].

Stilts. Crutches. A lame man is said to walk with *stilts*.

Stingy. (1) Cross; ill-humoured. (2) Churlish; biting; as applied to the state of the air [Pe.].

*Stint or Stent. To allot work. Stinted=impregnated, of cattle [M. C. H. B.].

Stiony. A small itching and inflamed pimple among the eyelashes. It is sometimes Sty. [? Sty in eye, W. R.]

Stir-up Sunday. The last Sunday after Trinity ; of which the collect, in our Book of Common Prayer, begins with the words ' *Stir up*.'

*Stitch.   A space between two double furrows; a rig [*B. N.* 3].

Stith.   An anvil.

Stive.   (1) Dust.   (2) A smoke, a 'dutt' (dirt) [Arderon, also E. S. T. and Johnson].   (3) To raise dust.   Ex. 'Go gently, Tom, you *stive* the ladies'; said to an awkward fellow who kicks up clouds of dust in riding or walking.   (4) 'All of a stive,' all in a bustle [E. M.].

*Stiver or Stover.   Marsh litter or marsh stuff [M. C. H. B.].

*Stivven up.   A road is so when blown full of snow [Johnson].

Stock.   The back or sides of a fireplace; whence the simile, 'as black as the *stock*.'

*Stocken or Stocking.   'The barley will not get out of the *stocken*' [F. J. B.].

*Stock Frost.   (1) One which freezes the river, beginning at the bottom [Arderon].   (2) Ground or mare's ice [M. C. H. B.].

Stodge.   To stir up various ingredients into a thick mass.

*Stoeing.   The lopping or topping of pollards [Johnson].   Trees generally [W. B.].

*Stoggy.   Thick, broad, and strongly made [Johnson, Tungate].

*Stoly.   Dirty [Ray].

Stomach.   (1) Anger.   (2) To resent.   (3) To endure.   'I cannot stomach it' [F. J. B.].   (4) To lose one's stomach and find a greyhound = to recover one's appetite after an illness [M. C. H. B.].

Stomachful.   Resentful.

*Stondle.   A bearing tub [Marshall].

Stone Blind.   Totally blind, blind as a stone.   *Vide* Sand Blind.

*Stone Runner.   The ringed plover [J. H. G.].

Stoneware. Old-fashioned earthenware of a dusty white or greyish colour.

Stoop. An ancient sort of drinking-vessel. There are, or were a few years ago, in some colleges at Cambridge some very old ones, retaining their proper name.

Stoor. (1) To stir. (2) A stir, commotion, bustle [Br.]. (3) 'A *stoor* of yeast is a sufficient quantity for a brewing, be it large or small. It is not so called because kept in *store* (the common pronunciation), but that it is to be *stoored* (stirred) into the wort to excite fermentation.

*Stop. The bucket of a well; formerly any bucket. See *Prompt. Parv.* 'Mylke *stop*' [E. S. T.].

*Stoppages. Convulsions or fainting fits [H. B.].

*Store. For 'stir.' 'Boy, how you do *store*!' [Johnson].

*Stormified. Stormy-looking [M. C. H. B.].

Stound. (1) A while, a portion of time. Ex. 'He stayed a long *stound*.' (2) To stun. A man may be *stounded* by a blow on the head. (3) To overcome with astonishment.

Stour. Stiff, stout.

*Stove. To fumigate [*B. N.* 63].

Stover. Winter food for cattle.

*Stow. (1) To drive sheep, swine, horses, &c., into a corner, in order to catch them [Spur.]. (2) To put away, to store up [G. E.].

Stra or Strow. Straw.

Straddlins. Astride. In some counties it is **Astraddle.**

Straft. A scolding bout, an angry strife of tongues [Sir Thomas Browne].

*Straight Shop. A public-house in which liquor is sold at the same price indoors as outdoors [W. R.].

*Strakes. (1) The iron tire or rim of a wheel, Suffolk [Spur.]. (2) The boards forming the sides of a boat. Perhaps from *streaks.*

*Strake-tire. The tire of a wheel when made in sections; hoop-tire when the whole tire is in one piece [W. B.].

*Stramalkin. The gadding or loitering of a tall, awkward, dirty, and slovenly-dressed person, particularly a female [Johnson]. [A marvellously comprehensive word! W. R.]

*Strapping. Outstrapping others, a strapping great gal, very fine and large [M. C. H. B.].

*Streeking Board. The ironing-board [Spur.].

*Strif. Strife [M. C. H. B.].

*Strike. The flat bar by which all the grain above the measure is struck off.

Strings. The shafts of a wagon [Bevan].

Strinkle. To sprinkle.

Strip. To strip a cow is to milk her very clean, so as to leave no milk in the dug.

Strippings. The last milk drawn from a cow in milking. It is considered richer than the first milk. In Norfolk *strockings.*

Strit. A street.

Strockings. The last draining of the cow's milk, which can be got by *strocking* (stroking) the paps, after the full stream has ceased.

Strome. To walk with long strides. It may be figuratively connected with Stream, from the rapidity of motion [Forby]. E. S. Taylor, on the contrary, writes, ' It is a peculiarity in E. A. dialect to convey a variety in the meaning of a word by altering a vowel in it. A long vowel denotes slowness. Trip is to move quickly. Trape is to drag along heavily.' This is borne out by Spurden, who says to ' *stroam* ' is to wander idly about.

Strong - docked. Thickset and stoutly made about the loins and rump. It is a valuable qualification of labourers, male or female, employed in work requiring the exertion of the muscles of those parts of the body. 'Betty is a good shearer (reaper),' said an old labourer in commendation of his daughter; 'she is a fine *strong-docked* wench.'

Stroop. The gullet, or the windpipe. It seems indifferently applied to both.

Strout. A struggle, bustle, quarrel.

*Strul. Well. 'That will do *strul*' [Johnson].

Strum. (1) A battered prostitute. An abbreviation of Strumpet, as brim, in a like application, is from brimstone. (2) To make a noise on a musical instrument [M. C. H. B.].

*Strumel. A loose long head of hair [Johnson].

*Strunt. An animal's tail [Johnson].

Stry. To destroy, to waste.

Stry, Strygood. A wasteful person, a bad manager or economist.

Stryance. Wastefulness.

Stry-goodly. Wasteful, extravagant. Ex. 'A *stry-goodly* fellow.'

*Stub, Stump. Stub rabbits=rabbits that do not go to ground [M. C. H. B.].

*Stubley. Full of roots [M. C. H. B.].

*Stub Shot. A shoot growing from the *stub* [Johnson].

*Stud. (1) A steady careful person, who has the care and management of a business or family left to his trust, is said to be its *stud* and support [Johnson]. (2) A nickname given to a man from his love of venery (Wilton, 1877) [M. C. H. B.].

*Stuggy. Short, thickset, pluggy [W. G. W.].

Stulk Hole. *Vide* **Pulk Hole.**

*Stull. Any unusually large mackerel [E. F. G.]. Sir Thos. Browne talks of one caught at Lowestoft an ell long, in 1668. See **Sull.**

Stulp. A low post put down to mark a boundary, or to give support to something. A post standing up a little above ground [Arderon].

*Stunner. To signify something of uncommon merit, e.g. 'That's a *stunner*!' [C. H. E. W.].

Stunt. (1) A check in growth. Ex. 'That tree has got a *stunt*.' (2) To sprain [M. C. H. B.].

Stunt, Stunty. Short, blunt, crusty, unmannerly.

Stupe. A foolish and dull person.

Stuttle. *Vide* **Stanstickle.**

*Such-time. Time when [M. C. H. B.].

Suckling. (1) A honeysuckle. 'What she did admire, that was the *suckling*-room,' i.e. the honeysuckle-papered room [H. B.]. (2) The common purple clover. In Suffolk, however, the red clover is never called *suckling*, but that term is generally used for the white or Dutch clover.

*Sudges. Suds [Spur.].

Sue. To issue in small quantities, to exude as a fluid from a vessel not sufficiently tight to confine it [Forby]. A cow is *sue* or *sew* when she ceases to give milk [Johnson].

*Suecutret. Disappointment [M. C. H. B.].

*Sukey. A settle (Miss Ray, per C. S. P.); also in Herts [C. D.].

*Sull. A very large mackerel [*N. and Q.*, 2nd Ser. vi. p. 382]. See **Stull.**

*Summering. The summer growth, or summer feed or pasturing [M. C. H. B.].

*Summer-lamb. The common snipe in summer, when it 'drums' or 'lambs,' a noise somewhat resembling a 'ba, ba' [C. H. B.].

*Summer land, to. To lay it fallow a year [Ray].

*Summerly. A turnip fallow [Marshall].

Sump. (1) A dead weight. (2) A blockhead. (3) A fish-box to keep fish alive in water [M. C. H. B.].

Sumpy. (1) Heavy, lumpish, sullen. It is often applied to bread not sufficiently baked. (2) Saturated with water, as wreck timber [E. S. T.].

*Sun Dog. Halo round the sun [M. C. H. B.].

Sunket. (1) To pamper, cocker, cram with delicacies. (2) A contemptuous appellation of a silly fellow. (3) A tit-bit or dainty bit. (4) Spelt 'suncate' in Halliwell.

Sunkets. (1) Dainty bits, nice feeding [Forby]. (2) A small quantity of food or drink, especially if given grudgingly [Johnson].

Suss! Suss! An invitation to swine to come and eat their wash.

Suss. (1) To swill like a hog. 'I'll *suss* your pluck,' is a serious threat of an enraged vixen. (2) An uncleanly mess, looking like hog-wash. Possibly there may be some reference to the Latin word *sus ;* but *vide* Soss. (3) A pig that is thirsty, out of condition, e. g. 'She only *sussed*,' i. e. drained the liquid and left the meal. (4) 'He went *suss* into the water,' to tumble in headlong and make a splash in so doing. (5) Suss, v. to oppress [M. C. H. B.].

*Suttling or Swattling. Tippling, drinking a long time and to great excess [Johnson].

Swack. (1) To throw with violence. Teut. *swacken*, vibrare. L. Sc. *swak*. (2) A hard blow or violent fall. (3) Violently. Ex. 'I fell down *swack*.'

Swacker. Something huge, a bulky and robust person.

Figuratively, a great lie. Ex. ' That's a *swacker*.'
Whacker ? [W. R.].

Swacking. Huge, robust.

***Swad.** Pork *swad*=brawn [A. Grimmer]. See **Sward** and
Swerd.

***Swaggle.** To agitate in a jug [G. E.].

***Swaies,** or wands, occurs in the Churchwardens' Accounts
of St. Peter Mancroft, Norwich, 1630. See *Norf. Antiq.
Misc.*, vol. ii. p. 21. See **Sway.**

Swailing. Lounging from side to side in walking. [? **Shaling,**
W. R.]

Swake, Swike. The handle of a pump.

Swale. (1) A low place. (2) Shade, in opposition to sunshine. Ex. ' Let us walk, or sit, in the *swale*.' (3) To
melt away. Ex. 'The candle *swales*' by being placed in
a current of air [E. M.].

***Swallop.** A rolling, heavy, lounging walk [Johnson].

***Swan.** Swans' eggs are not supposed to hatch before there
has been a thunderstorm (to crack the hard shell ?)
[M. C. H. B.].

Swang. To swing with great force. 'To *swang* the door'
is a better phrase than to *slam* it. Also '*Swang* on to
him, give him a good smack ' [*B. N.* 91].

Swang-ways. Obliquely, aside.

Swank. To sink in the middle.

Swaper, Sway. A switch.

Sward Pork. Bacon cured in large flitches. But see **Swerd**
and **Swad.**

***Swarth.** For ' swaithe,' the row of cut grass.

Swash. To affect valour, to vapour or swagger.

***Swatch.** A narrow channel through a shoal [E. F. G.].

***Swattle.** To guzzle or drink.

*Swattock. A variety of 'swack.' An old woman at Beccles said, 'I fell down *swattock*, and there I lay gulsh' [E. S. T.].

*Sway. A small pliable twig or branch [Johnson]. A rod or switch [Marshall]. See Swaies.

*Sweepage. The right of cutting faggots, grass, &c., on a several or common allotment [M. C. H. B.].

Sweetful. Delightful, charming, full of sweets.

*Sweet William. Some salt-water fish. (Species I could not determine.) Lemon sole ? [M. C. H. B.].

Sweldersome, Sweltersome. Overpoweringly hot.

Swelking. Sultry. Ex. 'It is a *swelking* hot day.'

*Swerd. A Norfolk dish composed of the rind of pork seasoned, rolled up tight, boiled, and eaten in slices ; also called Mockbrawn [Johnson]. Now called Pork Cheese [Tungate]. See Swad. [It cannot be of the rind only, W.R.]

Swidge. A puddle or plash of water.

Swift. An eft or newt, a common species of lizard.

Swiggle. To shake liquor in an inclosed vessel.

*Swill. (1) A ped or hamper in which herrings are carried [Johnson]. (2) Pigs' food [C. H. E. W.].

*Swimmer. Light dumplings [*B. N.* 12].

*Swinge. A leash or couple by which hounds are led [Johnson].

Swingel. That part of a flail which swings. In Suffolk, the Tail-top. Also a Crank [Marshall].

Swingle. To cut off the heads of weeds, without rooting up the plants.

*Swingling. A process in dressing or preparing flax and hemp [Johnson].

*Swinny. A little crab, common on the Norfolk coast [W. G. W.].

Swipe. The lever or handle of a pump.

*****Swipes.** Small or very indifferent beer [C. H. E. W.].

*****Swish.** A pool of water [*B. N.* 25].

*****Swish Tail**, or **Switch Tail.** The tail of a horse uncut [Johnson].

*****Swiving.** Mowing with a reap-hook [*B. N.* 37].

Swob. (1) A very awkward fellow, who seems fit only for coarse drudgery. It is our form of the sea-term **Swabber**, one who sweeps and cleans the deck with a *swab* or mop. (2) Best explained in an Ex. 'If you stir it, it will *swob* over,' i. e. the liquor in a vessel so full that the slightest motion will throw it over the brim, leaving something to be *swabbed* or swept up.

*****Swobber.** To oscillate water, &c. [G. E.].

Swobble. To talk in a noisy, bullying, saucy manner, like a blackguard.

*****Swobble-cart.** One that goes more on other people's business than its owner's [W. B.].

Swobfull. Brimfull, so that an attempt to move the vessel would make its contents overflow.

*****Swop.** To exchange, to chop [C. H. B.].

Swottling. Corpulent, greasy, and sweaty.

*****Swuggle.** (1) To put liquor in motion in a tub, &c., when rinsing it [Johnson]. (2) To drink eagerly [Spur.].

*****Swulk.** The quantity of drink taken at one suction [Spur.].

Swullocking. A gross intens. of **Swelking**, q. v.

*****Swum.** Swam. In general use [H. B.].

Swurd. A sword.

Sybbrit. The banns of marriage. It is one of Sir Thomas Browne's words, and in full use at this day. See **Siberet.**

Ta, Te, To. The, this, that, it. If we write '*te* freeze,' or '*te* hail' (for 'it freezes,' or 'it hails') we must caution our readers to give to the vowel the same sound which it has on the French monosyllables, le, te, se, &c. *Tā* may, perhaps, be preferable. Ex. '*Ta* freeze?' 'Yes, and *ta* hail to.' 'Do it freeze?' 'No, *ta* don't freeze now, but *ta* wull at night' [Forby]. A child will say of the railway train, 'Here *ta* cum' [W. R.]. For the third form, *to*, we have common and general authority in *to*-day, *to*-night, and *to*-morrow, for *this* day or night, and the morrow.

Tab. (1) The latchet of a shoe, fastened with a string or thong. (2) The end of a lace; commonly, and perhaps more properly called a **Tag**.

Tack. (1) A trick at cards. (2) The handle of a scythe. Also **Sneed** [Johnson].

Tag. (1) The rabble. **Rag** and **Bobtail** are generally of the party. (2) To follow closely, as it were an appendage. Ex. 'He is always *tagging* after her.'

Tagney. Finery. 'Tagney clothes,' the Sunday best [M. C. H. B.].

*****Tail 'em.** To make an even exchange of animals [Johnson]. **Tale?** [W. R.].

*****Tailshotten.** A disease in the tail of cattle, in which the spinal marrow becomes so affected that the beast is unable to stand [Johnson].

*****Tail-top.** The swingle or short stick of a flail [*Norwich Mercury*, Nov. 15, 1828].

Taint. (1) A very dirty slut. A most expressive word, as if her dirt were contagious, and it were unsafe to come near her. (2) A large protuberance at the top of a pollard tree.

Take. (1) 'To *take* on,' to enlist, to *take* on himself the duties of a soldier, to grieve. Ex. 'She *took* on sorely for her husband's death.' To ache, as a wound, a strain, or a bruise, *takes on.* (2) To *take* to do, to *take* to task; to rate or reprove. (3) To *take* a talking to. Pretty much like the second phrase, but implying more of gravity and severity. Ex. 'I wish, sir,' said a good woman who had a graceless whelp of a son, 'you would be so good as to send for my Tom into your study, and *take* a talking to him. I hope ta would daunt him.' (4) To take a thing next the heart, to take it on an empty stomach [M. C. H. B.].

Tam. The familiar abbreviation of the female name Thomasine, probably used to distinguish it with proper delicacy from the coarse masculine Tom.

Tan. Then. We very commonly pronounce it *than.*

Tang. A strong flavour; generally, but not always, an unpleasant one.

*****Tangle.** Sea-weed wrack [M. C. H. B.].

*****Tangle-leg.** Strong beer [M. C. H. B.].

Tantablet. A sort of tart, in which the fruit is covered by a crust, but fancifully tricked and flourished with slender shreds of pastry.

*****T'antony's Fire.** The erysipelas.

*****Tap-lap.** Ordinary beer, the droppings of the tap [Johnson]. *Sed quere* Cat-lap [W. R.].

Tappis. To lie close to the ground. A sportsman's phrase. Ex. 'It is so wet the birds cannot *tappis.*'

Tardry. (1) Immodest, loose, whorish. (2) Shabby genteel, cheap finery [M. C. H. B.].

*****Tarmarl.** Tarred string.

*****Tarmit.** For 'turnip' [Johnson].

*****Tarra-diddle.** A falsehood of the lesser kind.

Tass. A dish or a dram; as a *tass* of tea, or a *tass* of brandy.

Tatho. (1) Manure dropped upon the land by the cattle depastured upon it, principally of sheep. **Teath** [Johnson]. (2) To manure land with fresh dung by turning cattle upon it.

Tatter. To stir actively and laboriously. It is commonly used in conjunction with **Tow** (pronounced like cow), which, if not equivalent, is closely connected in meaning, q. v. Ex. ' He is a very painstaking man, always *towing* and *tattering* after his business ' [Forby]. Scolding, continually lecturing [Johnson].

Taunt. To tease ; to pester with silly questions, importunate entreaties, or any mode of minute vexation. Ex. ' How this child does *taunt* me ! ' (pronounced like aunt).

*****Taut.** (1) Tight, close, fast. (2) Watertight, of a boat [M. C. H. B.].

*****Tavaels.** Cat's claws or talons of a hawk.

*****Taw Maker.** Work in weaving which makes flowers [Arderon].

*****Teagle.** Tackle [Spur.].

*****Team.** A team of links = a string or chain of sausages [Spur.].

*****Team, Teamer.** To pour out copiously. We use it also metaphorically of a multitude pouring along like a stream : of a thronged congregation issuing from a church, or a crowded audience from a theatre, it is said ' how they came *teamering* out.'

*****Teamer.** A team of five horses [Marshall].

*****Teath, Taythe.** The manure of sheep, particularly when the field is regularly folded [Johnson].

Teen. Trouble, vexation.

*****Teeniest.** Tiniest, very smallest [M. C. H. B.].

*****Teeter-cum-tauter.** A see-saw [Johnson]. Still in common use [W. R.].

*Tell. To count or recount. 'I never heard *tell* on it afore.'

*Tempanus or Tempus Fire. Erysipelas (? St. Antony's fire).

*Temper. In Norf. = to ease ; in Essex, first to clean plough the land shallow, then to rove across, then stetch up and plough once more. See Young's *Agric. of Ess.*, i. 261, or full quotation in Murray's case [C. D.].

*Tempest. Thunder-showers.

Tench Weed. A sort of pond weed, having a slime or mucilage about it; supposed to be very agreeable to that fat and sleek fish. It is *Potamogeton natans*, Lin.

Tend. (1) To wait on company at table. (2) To take care of children, cattle, poultry.

Tender. A waiter at a public table or place of entertainment.

Terrify. To seize; to irritate annoy. A blister or a caustic is said to terrify a patient. To shake [*N. and Q.*, 3rd Ser. iv. p. 126]. To tear out, p. 178 [F. C. H.].

*Tetchy. Irritable [C. S. P.].

Tew, Tow. (1) To pull, tear, and tumble about, as hay with the fork and rake, a weedy soil with plough and harrow. (2) Tew, two [M. C. H. B.].

*Tewel. The vent or fundament of a horse.

*Tewey. To be squeamish in eating [C. S. P.].

Thack. To thatch ; or the material for thatching ; as straw, sedge, reeds, &c. ; also to thwack [Johnson, and Em.].

Thackster. A thatcher.

Thapes. Gooseberries. E S. T. says, 'I have never heard Fapes used. My grandmother invariably called gooseberry-tart, "thape pie."' Tungate agrees with this, so does Marshall [Sir Thomas Browne]. *Vide* Fapes.

*Thatney. That fashion [Arderon].

That'ns. In that manner.

The. Used as an inflexion on It   Ex. 'The child will cut *theself*, if you do not take away the knife' [O. E.].   '*The* own accord' [Arderon].

Thead. The tall wicker strainer placed in the mash-tub over the hole in the bottom, that the wort may run off clear.   It is perhaps more commonly called a **Fead**.

There and there-aways. Thereabouts.   Ex. 'Is the horse worth twenty pounds?'   '*There and there-aways.*'

Thight. Close, thickset, &c., as in crops [Marshall].

Thiller. The shaft horse [W. R.].

Thinder. *Vide* **Yinder.** *Th* and *y* have in many instances been confounded, not from any cognatio literarum, but from some similarity of A. S. characters.   This is the origin of the common abbreviations, y^e, y^t, &c.

Thiseney. This fashion [Arderon].

Thisness. In this manner or way [Johnson].

This'ns, Thus'ns, That'ns. In this or that manner.

Thite. (1) Tight; as applied to the fitting of apparel.   (2) Compact, not leaky, water-tight.

Thokish. Slothful, sluggish [Sir Thomas Browne and Johnson].

Thongy. The heat between two showers [*B. N.* 2].

Thorough. Short or pin.   A spavin which shows itself on both sides of a horse's hough or hock [Johnson].

Thoughts. Opinion.   Ex. 'It is my *thoughts* that,' &c.

Thow. For **Thaw** [Johnson].

Thrattles. Sheep's dung in pellets [Johnson].

Three-releet. *Vide* **Releet.**

Throat-latch. (1) The narrow thong of the bridle which passes under a horse's throat.   Throat-band [Johnson].   (2) The strings of a hat, cap, &c., fastened under the chin.

Thrum. To purr, as a cat.

Thumb-snack. (1) A simple mode of fastening a door. *Vide* Snack. (2) Or thumb-bonds, in thatching [M. C. H. B.].

Thump. A sort of hard cheese. *Vide* Bang.

Thunder. 'March *thunder* makes all the world wonder' [M. C. H. B.].

Thurck. Dark. So say Hickes and Ray, and so it may have been for aught we can say to the contrary [Sir T. Browne].

*Tibs. The extreme ends of a cart. I never heard it used to those of a wagon [Johnson].

Tick. (1) A very gentle touch, by way of hint, or as a token of endearment. Br. *tig*, Fr. *tic*. (2) To toy. Indeed, the two are often used together, and seem to defy discrimination; two fond sweethearts are sometimes seen '*ticking* and toying.'

Tiddling, Tittling. Topmost. 'The *tiddling* top' means the very highest point, the same as **Tip-top**. The meaning may perhaps be, that a thing so placed must stand *ticklish* or *tittlish*.

*Tidiff. The titmouse or oxeye. In Norfolk, the **Pickcheese** [Johnson].

Tidy. A light outer covering worn by children to keep their clothes from dirt and grease.

*Tidy, Tidily. (1) 'I fare pretty *tidy*, kind o' middling,' a little more than moderate. 'I'm a-doing pretty *tidily* now, I'm a-mendin'.' (2) A good *tidy* stroke=quickly [M. C. H. B.].

*Tied up. (1) Confused, constipated [Johnson]. (2) Married. (3) Tied house, a retail house bound to deal with a certain wholesale house [M. C. H. B.].

Tiff. A pet, slight anger. Ex. 'She was in a *tiff*.'

Tiffle. To be mightily busy about little or nothing.

Tight. (1) Prompt, active, alert. 'A *tight* fellow!' (2) Drunk. 'He is *tight*.' (3) Tidy. '*Tight* yourself up' [W. B.].

Tightly. Promptly, actively, alertly.

Tight Lock. Any species of coarse sedge growing in marsh ditches. So called from its being used to bind the sheaves of beans or oats, growing very luxuriantly on such land.

Tild. To incline. It is particularly applied to a cask, so raised at one end as that the liquor, when it is become low, may flow out at the other. We also say of anything which stands inclined, and in apparent danger of falling, that it 'stands *tilding*,' or 'upon the *tilt*.' In T. J. both verb and substantive are *tilt*. So, indeed, they very commonly are with us. But there is fair analogy for the difference in spelling.

*Tile-loose. A harmless lunatic, shanny [M. C. H. B.].

Tilesherd. A fragment of a tile, as potsherd of a pot, q. d. Shred.

Tiller. (1) The handle of a spade. (2) To throw out many stems from the same root. (3) Of land, in good tiller or tilth. (4) In good heart, or in good working order [M. C. H. B.].

*Timberwhim. A gill [M. C. H. B.].

*Time I do this＝while I do this [Em.].

*Tine. The prong of a fork [Johnson]. Compare a stag of ten tynes [W. R.].

Ting. To ring a small bell. 'To *ting* bees,' is to collect them together, when they swarm, by the ancient music of the warming-pan and the key of the kitchen door; the melody of which is still believed to be very efficacious.

Ting-tang. . A small and shrill bell, to summon the family to dinner, the congregation to prayers, &c.   The sanctus or saunce bell.

Tip.   A smart but light blow.

Tipe.   To kick up, or fall headlong, from being top-heavy. The word seems connected with *top* through *tip* [Forby]. To *tip* up a cart [Johnson].

*Tippling.   Haymaking [Halliwell].   Neither Johnson nor I know this [W. R.].

Tissick.   A tickling faint cough; called also a '*tissicky* cough.'

*Titchy.   Touchy, irritable [M. C. H. B.].

Titter.   To ride on each end of a balanced plank.   Otherwise **Titter-cum-totter.**   A common sport among children, sometimes ending in broken heads or limbs.   See **Teeter-cum-tauter**, a see-saw.   Commonly **Tittem-a-tauter.**

Titter.   (1) A pimple.   (2) The teat [M. C. H. B.].

*Titteravating.   Perplexing, teasing [Johnson].

*Titterish, otherwise **Totterish.**   Tittery, tottery, unstable, easily overset [Spur.].

Titter-worm.   A cutaneous efflorescence, a series or confluence of minute pimples.

Tittle.   To tickle.

Tittle-my-fancy.   Pansies.   *Viola tricolor*, Lin.

Titty, Titty-totty.   Very small, tiny, sometimes pleonastically, little *titty*.

Tiver.   (1) A composition of which tar is the principal ingredient, to colour and preserve boards exposed to the air [Johnson].   (2) Marked with ochre.   'The sheep are *tivered* across the loins' [Johnson].

*Toad-in-the-hole.   Meat and batter baked pudding [M. C. H. B.].

Toad's Cap.   A fungus.

*Toad Skep.   A fungus produced from ash-trees [Johnson].

Tod. (1) The head of a pollard tree [Forby]. (2) The upright stake of a 'wan' hurdle, the bottom of a tree left in the ground. See Slaper [Johnson]. (3) To amount to a *tod*, or twenty-eight pounds of wool.

To-do. A stir, a bustle. Ex. 'He made a great *to-do* about it.'

***Tog.** A crab [W. R.].

Together. Seemingly, but not really, an adverb converted to a noun, and used in familiarly addressing a number of persons collectively. Ex. 'Well, *together*, how are ye all?' 'Where are you going *together*?' i. e. both of you [W. R.].

Tolc. To tempt, coax, &c. Ex. 'Good sauce *tolcs* down the meat.' In Suffolk it is Tole.

***Tole away.** (1) To draw away or persevere in drawing [Spur.]. (2) To tole, to talk into or over [M. C. H. B.].

Tolerate. To domineer, to tyrannize.

***Tom Breezer.** The dragon-fly [M. C. H. B.].

***Tomma.** A brown loaf [Johnson]. But surely *tommy* is recent slang for any bread [W. R.].

Tommy. A small spade to excavate the narrow bottoms of under-drains. Also a small wrench used by engineers.

Tom Poker. The great bugbear and terror of naughty children, who inhabits dark closets, holes under the stairs, unoccupied cock-lofts, false roofs, &c. Such places are often called from him Poker-holes.

Tom-tommy. A plough with a double breast, to clear out furrows.

Tongue. A small sole, from its shape. A distinction used by our fishermen.

Toon. Too [? W. R.].

Top Latch. The thong by which the sales of the horse-collar are tied together.

*Top and Tail. To top and tail turnips, to cut their leaves and roots off, generally called 'tailing tunnips' [M. C. H. B.].

Toppings. The second skimming of milk, the first being properly called cream.

Topple. To tumble, to bring the head to the ground and throw the heels over.

Toppler. A tumbler, who, among various antic postures, throws his heels over his head.

Tosh. A tusk, a long and somewhat curved tooth. It is but another form of the commoner word.

Toshnail. A nail driven in aslant or diagonally, so as to have the stronger hold, like the teeth of some animals. It is also used as a verb.

*Toshy. Muddy or sticky [G. J. C.].

*Totald. Killed or injured [Johnson].

*Tote. The whole or all. 'The whole *tote* of them' [Johnson].

Totty, Totty-headed. (1) Dizzy. Particularly from the effect of too much drink [Ch.]. (2) Totty, tiny [M. C. H. B.].

*Tou. Snares for taking game. Sometimes applied to greyhounds [Johnson]. No doubt the same as Tow.

*Touchwood. Dry rotten wood [G. E.].

Tow. Necessary tools, tackle, or apparatus for any purpose (pronounced like cow) [Forby]. An angling rod and line is called in Norfolk, a fishing *tow*. A farmer's stock of implements is called his *tow* [E. S. T.].

*Toward. Quiet, easily managed. As of a colt [W. B.]. Of a child [C. S. P.].

To-ward. (1) The substantive is to be inserted between the two syllables of the preposition. Ex. '*To* London *ward*,' i. e. toward London [O. E., P. L.]. (2) To be tame or fond [G. E.].

*Tow Bowen. A blown herring [W. R.].

*Town. Any village. 'I have the best turnip in the *town*' [M. C. H. B.].

*Towty. Cord become untwisted and in nearly the same state as before twisting, that is, hemp or tow [Johnson].

Trade. Line·of conduct, course of action, practice, habit, custom. Ex. 'If this is to be the *trade*,' &c. Here is the source of another 'American' word.

Traffing Dish. A bowl through which milk is strained into the tray in which it is set to raise cream.

Trape. To trail, to be drawn along. Ex. 'Her gown *trapes* after her on the floor' [Forby]. It is strange that throughout Forby's examples he inserts the final *s*. This should have read, 'Her gown *trape* after her' [W. R.].

Traptles. The small pellets of the dung of sheep, hares, rabbits, &c.

Traverse. A smith's shoeing shed.

Treaden. Made of thread. Within our memory '*threaden* stockings' were an article of Sunday apparel for village servants and apprentices.

*Treen Plates. Trenchers [Spur.].

*Trickle, Trittle. To bowl. Ex. '*Trickle* me an orange across the table.' 'The crowd was so thick, one might have *trickled* balls on their heads.'

*Tricky. (1) Mischievous. (2) Spitefully ill-humoured. (3) Artful.

Triculate. To adorn. It seems to be fancifully formed from the phrase 'to *trick out*.' It is used by masons for putting the last hand to what they mean to be smart and showy.

*Trids, Tirds. Foeces [M. C. H. B.].

Trig. (1) To trot gently, or trip as a child does after its nurse. 'They *trigged* off together.' (2) The mark from which a ball is delivered [Johnson].

Trip. (1) A small cheese, made in summer, to be eaten in its soft and curdy state, or it soon becomes dry, tough, and uneatable [Forby]. (2) A few sheep [Ray].

Trip-skin. (1) A piece of leather, worn on the right-hand side of the petticoat, by spinners with the rock, on which the spindle plays, and the yarn is pressed by the band of the spinner. (2) The skinny part of roasted meat which, before the whole can be dressed, becomes tough and dry, like a *trip* overkept, or the leather used by old women for cleaning.

*Trivet. A rest for the kettle on the hob [M. C. H. B.].

*Troat. The throat [M. C. H. B.].

*Troison. A taste or savour [Arderon].

Trollibags. The intestines.

*Trollies. The long narrow Yarmouth cart adapted to go up the 'rows' [W. R.]. See **Currie.**

*Troned. For 'trained.' 'He have ollost been *troned* up t'ut' [Johnson].

*Trope. To saunter or loiter. See **Trape** [Johnson].

*Trosh. To beat out grain with a flail [G. E.].

*Troshel. Threshold, a step [G. E.].

*Trotter. A woman of the town [W. B.].

Trouble. A woman's travail. Ex. 'She is now in her *trouble.*' Perhaps a corruption.

Trounce-hole. A game at ball, very like trapball, but more simple; a hole in the ground serving for the trap, a flat piece of bone for the trigger, and a cudgel for the bat.

Trow. A trough [E. S. T.].

*Truck. Rubbish of any sort which requires removing [F. J. B.].

Trunch, Trunch-made. Short and thick; compact and squab in figure.

*Trundle. To saunter [Em.].

Trunk. A wooden box with air-holes, submerged in the broads and rivers, in which fish when caught is kept if not wanted immediately for market.

*Trunket. A game at ball, played with short sticks, and having a hole in the ground instead of a wicket [Johnson]. **Two Stone Trunket,** the same game, but the boy who wields the stick is put out by one of the other players throwing the ball between the stones.

Trunk-way. A watercourse through an arch of masonry, turned over a ditch before a gate. The name arose, no doubt, from the trunks of trees used for the same purpose in ancient and simpler times, and even now, in the few wooded parts of both counties.

Try. To melt down by fire, for the purpose of purifying; usually applied to melting the suet of hogs, or other animals, to get rid of the skinny and impure parts. The purified lard is then kept for domestic use.

*Tucks. Iron pins usually put in the upper part of the blocks of a four-wheeled carriage for timber, to prevent the timber slipping off [Johnson]. Sometimes pronounced **Stucks** [W. B.].

*Tumble. To agree, to understand; e. g. 'He would not *tumble* to it' [M. C. H. B.].

Tumbler. A tumbril. Our name is exactly descriptive. A *tumbler* is made open behind, and occasionally closed by a tail-board. On the removal of this, and a strong wooden bar before, which, passing through two iron hold-fasts, secures the body to the shafts, the carriage *tumbles* backwards and discharges the load.

Tunder. Tinder.

*Tundey. Rotten; of wood shining with a phosphoric appearance. 'It's nothing but an old *tundey*-log' [W. B.].

*Tune. Order or temper. 'That farm is in good *tune*' [Johnson].

Tunmere. The line of procession in parochial perambulations.

Tunnel. A funnel.

*Tupe. To drink a quantity at a draught [*B. N.* 27]. From **Tope** ?

Turf. Peat, fuel dug from boggy ground. The Dictt. interpret the word as meaning only the surface of the ground pared off. These we call flags, and they are cut from dry heaths, as well as from bogs. The substance of the soil below these is *turf.* Every separate portion of it is a *turf.*

*Turfer. A woman of the town [W. R.].

*Turnover. An article in pastry [G. E.].

Tussle. A struggle.

Tussock. A hassock, q. v. ; a thick tuft of coarse grass in pastures, or of rank growth in corn.

*Tussick. To cough.

*Tutnose. A short snub nose [Johnson].

Tutter. Trouble. 'What a *tutter* he make of it!'

*Tuttle Box. An article used by ploughmen to keep the horses apart from each other, that they may see forward and between them to make a straight furrow [Johnson].

*Tuzzle for Tussle. A struggle.

*Tuzzy. Muzzy, ruffled, ragged, dishevelled [Johnson]. But very intoxicated [W. R.].

*Twack. To turn quickly; to change or alter one's opinion [Johnson].

*Twadeling. Slow, inactive, spiritless [Johnson].

*Twadle. A long whistling [G. E.].

Twank. (1) To let fall the carpenter's chalk-line, which makes a smart slap upon the board. (2) To give a smart slap with the flat of the hand, on the breech, or other fleshy part.

Twiddle. A small pimple. Sometimes a **Widdle** [Johnson]. To be busy and bestow seeming pains about the merest trifles. Ex. ' What are you *twiddling* about there ?'

Twig. (1) To give such a slight, but smart, correction as may be inflicted with a twig. (2) Figuratively, to give somewhat sharp, but not angry and severe reproof [Forby]. (3) To sway sideways [Spur.].

*Twiggers. Tusser has this, but the meaning is obscure.

Twil. Until. It is a word compounded of the prep. *to* and the subst. *while*; and means ' to the time.'

Twill. A sort of coarse linen cloth, of which loose frocks, trowsers, &c., are made for working-men.

Twilt. (1) A quilt, here as well as in the North [T. J.]. (2) To quilt [Br.]. (3) To beat. An expressive word, inasmuch as it is implied that weals are left, like the stripes or ridges in quilted work. Boys used to show with pride balls they had *twilted*, that is, quilted with twine.

Twinny. To rob a cask before it is broached. A thievish wench *twinnies* her dame's cask of mead or made wine.

*Twinters. Two winters. Beasts two winters old [*B. N.* 87].

*Twister. To twist or turn [G. E.].

Twit. (1) A fit of hasty ill-humour, snappishness. (2) To taunt [C. H. E. W.].

*Twitchy. Said of the wind blowing in gales, unsteady. Also irritable.

Twitty. Cross, snappish.

Twizzle. To turn a thing round and round between the fingers, quickly and repeatedly. It is sometimes used in a neuter sense. Ex. ' He came *twizzling* down.'

Tye. An extensive common pasture. There are several *tyes* a few miles south of the central part of Suffolk; but in no other part of East Anglia. There are also some on the northern border of Essex.

*T'year. This year [M. C. H. B.].

Undeniable. Unexceptionable, with which no fault can be found.

Under Butter. The butter made of the second skimmings of milk in the dairy districts of Suffolk. It is kept for domestic purposes, or sold to near neighbours for prompt use ; never put up in firkins and sent to market. Though good for present consumption it will keep but a short time.

Under Deck. The low broad tub into which the wort runs from the mash-tub. [Under Beck ?] Underback rather than Underbeck [W. B.].

Under Grub. To undermine.

Under Grup. An under-drain, a concealed watercourse in wet soils.

*Underly. Backward, behind time [M. C. H. B.].

*Underming. To undermine [M. C. H. B.].

Under Nean [Under Nane, W. R.]. Underneath.

Uneathily. Unwieldy, hard to be put into motion.

Unfaceable. Unreasonable, indefensible. A proposal, or an assertion, which a man could not have the face boldly to make or to maintain, is said to be an *unfaceable* one.

Ungain. Inconvenient, intractable. Ex. 'The land lies *ungain* for me.' 'My horse is very *ungain*.'

Unsensed. (1) Stunned, as by a blow or fall. (2) Stupefied, as by excess of drink. (3) Insane.

*Up. Said of birds in full breeding plumage [M. C. H. B.].

Upland. Higher and drier ground, as contradistinguished from fen-land.

*Upright, to live=live on income from money or land.
'She lived *upright*' would be intended as a high com-
pliment to one deceased [F. J. B.].

Upstart. The deep impression of a horse's foot in a clayey
soil, soon filled up with water, which, when another
horse happens to tread in the very same place, starts
upwards and plentifully bespatters the rider.

Urgeful. Urgent, importunate, teasing.

*Valuation. Time, quantity. 'I lost the *valuation* of eight
sacks of potatoes.' 'Let it stay there the *valuation* of two
days' [Marshall].

*Vance Roof. The garret [Marshall].

*Vardle. Bottom hinge of a gate [*B. N.* 86].

Vast. A very great quantity. 'We had a *vast* of rain in the
last quarter of the year 1824.'

Vessel. (1) Half-a-quarter of a sheet of writing paper (?).
(2) A wooden cask to hold fermented liquors.

Vine. Any trailing fruit-bearing plant, which must spread
itself on the ground if it be not supported, as cucumbers,
melons, strawberries, &c. This is another 'American'
word [W. R.].

Voke. To make an effort to vomit. *Vide* Boke and Puke.

*Wab. An artificial teat, used in rearing young children
or animals [Spur.].

*Wack [Whack, W. R.], a quantity, enough.

*Wacken. Large. 'A *wacken* boy' [Johnson]. But
surely this is only the common expression 'whacking'
[W. R.].

Wad. Woad. A plant of great use in dyeing. By mixture
it contributes to produce many colours. What it yields
of itself is blue. 'As blue as *wad*.'

*****Wad.** The edge of grass, hay, or stubble left higher than other parts between each mower's work in mowing a field [Johnson].

*****Wade.** To have liberty; as the tension in a mortice or other joint, from the wood having shrunk, is said to *wade* [Johnson].

Wadmal. A very coarse and thick kind of woollen manufacture. What is thus called by us is only the winter clothing of rustics.

*****Wake.** A piece of open water, in the midst of a frozen river or broad. In Norway called WAK [M. C. H. B.].

*****Wale.** The forefront of a horse-collar [Johnson].

Walk. (1) An uninclosed cornfield [Forby]. (2) A fair or wake [Spur.].

Walks. A large extent of country so circumstanced is called 'The Walks.' The name is, no doubt, from the ancient manorial right of sheep-*walk* over such lands during a considerable part of the year.

*****Wall.** (1) To lie by the. Ex. 'He lies by the *wall*,' is, he is dead. Spoken between death and burial [Cull. Haw.]. (2) Marsh or river wall, an artificial earth embankment against water [M. C. H. B.].

*****Wall - bird.** The spotted flycatcher. From the usual situation of its nest [J. H. G.].

*****Walland band.** The leather used in spinning [E. S. T.].

*****Wall-eyed.** When the two eyes are of a different colour [M. C. H. B.].

Wallis. The withers of a horse.

Wallop. To move as fast as possible, but not without much effort and agitation. The gallop of a cow or a cart-horse is a good specimen of *wallopping* [Forby].

Walter, Wolter. (1) To roll and twist about on the ground; as corn laid by the wind and rain; or as one who is rolled in the mire. (2) To cause extreme fatigue, whether by the above-mentioned discipline, or any other exhausting exertion. Ex. 'I am right on *woltered* out by my day's work,' long walk, or whatever else. See **Wankered**.

Wan. A long rod to wave into a wattled hedge.

Wancle, Wanky. Weak, pliant, sometimes *winky-wanky*.

*Waney. A long talk [G. E.].

*Wankered (see **Woltered**). Fatigued or exhausted; a corruption from 'vanquished' [E. S. T.].

*Wanklin. A weakling [*B. N.* 92].

*Wanting. Wanted, e. g. rain was wanting (N. Ess.) [C. D.].

*Wanty. The belly-band of harness [M. C. H. B.].

*Wany. Partly unsound timber.

Wanze. To waste, pine, wither.

Wap. (1) To wrap. (2) To beat; with some figurative allusion to the former sense.

Wapper-jaws. A wry mouth, a warped jaw.

Wappet. A yelping cur. *Vide* **Yap**.

Waps, Wapsy. A wasp. The original word.

Warble, Warblet. A hard swelling in the hides of cows and other cattle, caused by the growth of a larva or large maggot, from the egg of a fly deposited there. Warbeetles [Johnson].

Ward. Callosity of the skin, on the hands from hard labour, and on the feet from much walking.

*Warded off. Started off work [M. C. H. B.].

*Warp. (1) A lamb cast some time before its maturity [Johnson]. (2) Of herrings, is four [E. F. G.].

*Warted. The situation of a dog and bitch when together [Johnson].

R

*Was. Short for 'vast,' in sound like 'worse'; e. g. 'T'aint a *worse* sight better than 'twas afore.'

*Wase. To breathe with difficulty, as in asthma [Johnson].

*Wash. Sweat; as 'The horse is all of a *wash*' [W. B.].

*Wasket. A heavy block of wood for levelling turf [M. C. H. B.].

*Wasking. A beating [Johnson]. 'I'll *warsk* yar weskit' [Em.].

*Waste. To bang or cudgel.

*Waster. (1) A defective wick to a candle, causing guttering and waste [Johnson]. (2) A rabbit or other animal that looks like a dier, wasting away [M. C. H. B.].

Water Dogs. Small clouds of irregular but roundish form, and of a darker colour, floating below the dense mass of cloudiness in rainy seasons, supposed to indicate the near approach of more rain.

*Water-frolic. A regatta on the broads [H. B.].

*Water-ranny. The short-tailed field-mouse.

*Water-ret. The steeping hemp in water [Johnson].

Water-slain. Overcome with superabundance of water.

Water Springe. A copious flow or springing of saliva, which often precedes and attends nausea.

Water Sprizzle. A disease in goslings and ducklings, of which no intelligible account can be obtained from those who are most conversant with the diseases of those animals.

Water Taking. A pond from which water is taken, in default of a pump for the use of the house.

Water Whelp. A dumpling kneaded without either yeast or eggs, and of course very hard and heavy.

*Waxspunsends. Waxed thread [G. E.].

*Weam. A rent or tear in a garment or cloak [Johnson].

Weariful. Tiresome, giving exercise to patience. Ex. ' I have had a *weariful* bout of it.'

Weary. (1) Feeble, sickly, puny. Ex. ' It is a poor *weary* child.' (2) Troublesome, vexatious [Br.].

*****Weather.** Stormy weather. ' What a day of *weather* ' [M. C. H. B.].

*****Weather-breeder.** An unseasonably ' still ' or fine day [M. C. H. B.].

Weather-head. The secondary rainbow.

Weather-laid. Stopped on an intended journey by stress of weather.

Web. (1) ' The *web* of the body,' the omentum. (2) The film of the eye.

*****Weeping.** The plaintive note of the golden-crested wren (*Regulus cristatus*) [E. T. Booth].

Weeping Tears. A very old pleonasm, but in very common use for excessive sorrow. Ex. ' I found poor Betty all in *weeping tears*,' i. e. shedding them profusely.

Weer. Pale and ghastly in aspect.

*****Weesh, or Weesh away.** Horse language for ' to the right ' [Em.]. See **Come** or **Cope hardy** or **harby,** for the left.

*****Wee-wo.** See **Wew-wow.**

Welk, Welt. (1) To soak, roll, and macerate in a fluid. (2) To expose to sun and air, and turn over in order to be dried, as grass to be converted to hay; garden plants to save their seeds, as peas and beans, or to be preserved for winter use when their moisture is exhaled, as onions. (3) To give a sound beating, which is likely to raise *weals, welks,* or *welts* (ridges).

*****Well.** Healthy. ' The doctor saw he was never a *well* child ' [C. S. P.].

Well to live. Having a competence. Ex. ' Is Mr. A. a rich man ? ' ' Pretty *well to live*,' or ' *to do*.'

*****Welter.** To fade, applied to flowers [C. S. P.].

Wellum. The filling up of a ditch at a gateway to afford access to a field [M. C. H. B.].

Wem. A small fretted place in a garment. A. S. *wem*, macula [W.].

*****Wench.** A woman of the town, or other immoral female [W. R.].

*****Went.** The mesh of a net [E. F. G.].

Wennel. A weaned calf [T.].

Wet Shod, or **Shed.** Wet in the feet.

*****Wewling** (? Mewling). A plaintive note in crying, commonly with a view to excite charity [Johnson].

*****Wewting.** The whistling of a boy without any regard or idea of time or harmony [Johnson]. See **Whewt.**

Wew-wow. To wring and twist in an irregular and intricate manner. Wee - wo, ' All of a *wee - wo*.' Not straight [Em.].

*****Weybreds.** Warts, anburies [Johnson].

*****Whale.** Swarth, double-whale. When a marsh is not cut for two years, it is called a double swarth or double whale [M. C. H. B.].

Whart-whartle. To cross, tease, and exhaust patience. It is certainly another form of **Thwart;** as in the instance of over-whart.

Whaul. *Vide* **Yawl.**

Wheelspun. A very stout worsted yarn, spun on the common large wheel, of which the coarsest stockings, gloves, caps, &c., are made.

Wheel Spur. In the old state of our cross-roads, the horse-path was in the midway between the two wheel ruts.

Between that and each rut was the *wheel spur*, much higher than either. If, to avoid the deep rut, a carriage drawn by a single horse was ventured upon the quarter, the horse was obliged to make the *wheel spur* his path, often a very unsafe one, particularly in stiff soils.

Whelm. (1) Half a hollow tree, placed with its hollow side downwards, to form a small watercourse. (2) To turn a tub, or other vessel, upside down, whether to cover anything with it or not. Ex. ' *Whelm* it down.'

*Whereby. By or on account of which [M. C. H. B.].

Wherret or Worrit. To pester, annoy, harass. [worry?]

*Wherry. A sailing barge, with one sail, and mast stepped right forward, the successor of the ' keel.'

*Whet. A drinking among harvest men on the first day of harvest [Johnson].

Whewt. (1) To whistle. (2) To squeak faintly, as a young bird. Perhaps formed from the sound. See **Wewting.**

*Whid. A dispute or quarrel [Johnson].

Whiffler. One who goes at the head of a procession to clear the way for it. In that of the Corporation of Norwich from the Guildhall to the Cathedral Church, on the Guild-day, the *whifflers* (for they are so called) are two active men very lightly equipped (*milites expediti*), bearing swords of lath or latten, which they keep in perpetual motion, *whiffling* the air on either side, and now and then giving an unlucky boy a slap on the shoulders or posterior with the flat side of their weapons.

While, Whilst. Until. Mr. Pegge says the word is invariably so used in the Northern counties. It is nearly so in the Eastern. Thus, ' Stay *while* I go in,' i. e. ' Stay in the time (while) of my going in,' ' Stay *while* I return,' i. e. stay *to* the time (while) of my return.

Whinnock. Intens. of *whinny* in the second sense, q.v.

Whinny. (1) To neigh like a foal. (2) Fig. to snivel and whimper like a child. Lat. *hinnio*.

*****Whins.** Furze bushes [Tungate].

Whippet. A short light petticoat.

Whipple Tree. A short bar by which horses draw. *Tree* used again in the simple sense of *wood*. **Wimple Trees** [*B. N.* 60].

*****Whisk.** A contrivance for winnowing or blowing dirt, &c., from corn [Johnson].

Whisket. A small parcel.

White Back. The white poplar, *Populus alba*, Lin. So called from the whiteness of the under side of the leaves.

White Herring. A fresh herring.

*****Whitester.** A bleacher. Down in Surrey a whitester is a 'cock laundress.'

*****Whittawer.** A tanner who makes white leather by using alum instead of bark [Johnson].

Whittery. Pale and sickly. Chiefly, if not solely, applied to puny children. Ex. ' It is a poor *whittery* brat.'

Whole-footed. (1) Treading flat and heavy, as if there were no joints in the feet [Forby]. (2) Stiff, congested [W. G. W.]. (3) Very intimate, closely confederate. A figurative expression doubtless. But it is not easy to comprehend what the figure is meant to be. **Whole-handed**, which is used in the same sense, is far more intelligible. Hand joined in hand is a good image of intimacy and confederacy.

Whop, Whap. (1) A heavy blow [Jen.]. (2) To beat severely.

Whybibble. A whimsy, idle fancy, silly scruple, &c.

*****Wicker.** (1) To neigh. (2) A corner, e. g. *wickers* of the mouth.

Widdles. (1) Very young ducks [Forby]. (2) Small pustules causing considerable itching [Johnson].

*Wiff. (1) A sudden glance [Johnson]. (2) The sudden turning of a hare when coursed [Id.].

*Wiffle. To be unsteady, uncertain [Johnson].

Wilch. The wicker strainer set upright in the mash-tub, to prevent the grains running off with the wort. *Vide* **Thead.**

*Wile-time, Pastime. 'Now that is a nice *wile-time* for you ladies, to come and see we poor people' [C. S. P.].

*Will. To wait your grandmother's will = to wait till some one asks you to marry [M. C. H. B.].

Will-a-wix. An owl. **Billy-wix** usually [W. R.].

*Will-led. See **Led-will** [M. C. H. B.].

*Willock. A guillemot [E. F. G.].

Wind Egg. An addle egg, or an egg without a yolk.

Winders. The women who perform the office of giving the last attire to the dead, and watch the body till the time of burial.

Winding. The wool in which the bodies of the poor are wrapped, or rather covered, when deposited in their coffins. A single pound is so drawn out and artfully disposed as to suffice for a large body. In Suffolk the flannel which is wound round a corpse is called a *winding.*

*Windle. A skep or basket [Johnson]. For winnowing corn [W. G. W.].

Windrow. (1) A row of mown grass, put together in the process of haymaking to be ventilated, when far advanced towards completion. (2) To put the nearly-made hay into such a form.

Winge. To shrivel, as fruit over-kept.

*Winne. The pensive crying of a child; also the neighing of a horse. [**whinny,** Johnson.]

***Winnick.** A weak crying [G. E.].

Winnol Weather. The stormy weather which is common in the beginning of March. The third day of that month is the anniversary of St. Winwaloe, a British saint.

***Winter-proud.** Said of wheat when strong above ground before the spring [M. C. H. B.].

***Wippet.** A child small of its age, perhaps from puppet [Johnson] Whippet is North Country for a small racing dog [W. R.].

***Wips and Strays.** Heads and straws, of corns (Danish) [Miss Gurney].

***Wirriwibble** or **Wivivvel.** The sea-buckthorn.

Wishly. Earnestly, wishfully, with longing. Ex. ' The lad looked so *wishly* at her.' ' The children eyed the plum-pudding *wishly.*'

***Wisp.** A rowel or seton [Marshall].

***Wisp** or **Whisp.** A small flock [M. C. H. B.].

Wit. Common sense [Ch., &c.]. Ex. ' He did it without fear or *wit*,' q. d. with a foolish want of thought.

Without. Unless. Ex. ' I will not go *without* you will go with me ' [Pe.].

***Witles.** Vitals, heart and lungs.

***Wittery.** Weak or frail [*B. N.* 94].

***Wittles.** Victuals [M. C. H. B.].

Wizzen. To wither, shrivel, dry up.

Wo. Stop, check. Ex. ' There is no *wo* in him.' ' He knows no *wo.*'

***Wob.** A piece of linen containing sugar or some sweet-meat, which is given to an infant as a substitute for the breast [Johnson].

Wobble. To reel, totter, or move uneasily and laboriously.

*Woe. Mourning. 'Blinds down for the week are said to be *in woe*' [W. R.].

Wolder. A rolled bandage (or Woulder).

*Wolt. To harass, worry, fatigue to death [E. S. T.].

Wong. (1) An agricultural division or district of some uninclosed parishes. Spelman says it is rather of arable than of pasture land. (2) Meadow, *green* field? always wet [*N. and Q.* 2nd Ser. i. p. 522].

*Wonmell. *Wonmell* cheese, i. e. one meal [Spur.].

Wooch, Woosh! '*Wooch wo!*' means 'Go to the right!'

Woodlands. The district usually called High Suffolk is still distinguished by the inhabitants of the eastern coast of that county by the name of *The Woodlands*, though now the name is far from applicable. Formerly, indeed, and within living memory, it was very thickly wooded.

Wood-sprite. The woodpecker.

*Wooflt. An oaf, an ignorant person. Sometimes used as a term of endearment to infants [Johnson].

*Wooser. A hard blow [G. E.].

Wop. To produce an abortive lamb. The word is as peculiarly applied to ewes, as *slip* is to cows. The ewe *wops* her lamb, the cow *slips* her calf.

*Worbitten. Used of growing timber pierced by the larvae of beetles [Johnson].

*Wor-bush. A piece of reed-ground or margin of Hickling Broad [M. C. H. B.]. Said to be where the Hickling men hid to avoid being pressed in time of war.

Word. To dispute, to wrangle. Ex. 'They *worded* it a long while.'

Wore for Worn. My hat is wore out [M. C. H. B.].

Work. To ache, to throb. In violent headache the head '*works* like a clock.'

Work-wise. In a workmanlike manner, as such work (whatsoever it be) ought to be done. Ex. 'I thought he did not handle his tools *work-wise*.'

*Worl or Whirl. (Commonly pronounced WALL.) The ring put on a spindle to give it steadiness [Johnson]

*Worrok. To tease, perplex, or vex [Johnson].

Worthy. Lucky enough. Ex. 'If I had but been *worthy* to know that.' Sometimes *worthy* is added at the end of another word, to convey the idea of being capable of, or fit for. Ex. 'I will level this pit to make the land plough-*worthy*,' i.e. capable of being ploughed, fit for the plough.

*W(h)ortle Berries. Bilberries [Johnson].

*Woultered. Fatigued, exhausted [Johnson]. Sometimes 'right on jowered out' [W. R.].

Wowl. To howl, to wail vociferously.

*Wrapped up in. Very fond of. Ex. 'I ain't much *wrapped up* with it' [M. C. H. B.].

Wrastle. To dry or parch.

Wrastling Pole. A pole to spread fire about the oven, or to beat walnuts from the trees. Both these processes seem to include the idea of drying or parching.

Wret. (1) A wart, [or writ, Em.]. To cure, cut as many 'scotches' in an ashen tree as you have wrets [M. C. H. B.].

Wret Weed. Any wild species of euphorbia.

Wrigglers. Small fish, of which commoner names are Sand-eels or Lance-fish.

*Wrinch. (1) A sprain [Johnson]. (2) A piece of cord put through a hole in a staff, by means of which it is twisted on the nose of a horse to keep him still during an operation [Johnson].

*Writ. See Wret.

Wrong. (1) Deformed, misshapen in person. (2) A crooked bough.

Wry. To cover close [Forby]. To rake up the fire [Johnson].

Wrying. Covering, of bedclothes, &c., not of apparel.

Wry-rumped. Having an obliquity of form in the lower part of the back.

*Wunt. To sit, as a hen [Miss Gurney].

*Wypes (or **Pywypes**). The lapwing or plover [Johnson].

*Yag. To irritate (**Nag** ?) [Spur.].

Yale. A small quantity.

Yangle. To tether a horse by fastening a fore-leg and hind-leg together.

Yap. (1) To yelp. (2) A yelping cur. We have the venerable authority of Dr. Caius for *wappe*, which comes very near our word. And we have its dimin. *wappet*.

Yard. The garden belonging to a cottage or ordinary messuage is very often called the *yard*; perhaps from humility, as unworthy to be called a garden. Ex. ' We have a sort of fape bushes in the *yard*.'

*Yarden. A yard measure [Spur.].

Yardman. The hind who has the particular care of the . farmyard, and of the cattle fed there.

Yarm, Yawm. To shriek or yell.

Yarroway. The common yarrow.

Yawl. (1) The large open sea boat used on the Norfolk coast. (2) To squall or scream harshly, like an enraged cat ; or the cry of a peacock is an excellent instance of yawling.

Yelk, Yulk. (1) To knead clay with straw or stubble, to prepare it for dauber's work. (2) The yolk of an egg [M. C. H. B.].

Yelm. (1) To lay straw in convenient quantities, and in regular order, to be used by a thatcher. (2) A portion of straw laid for that purpose.

*****Yelt.** A pig [M. C. H. B.].

*****Yeow.** You [*N. and Q.*].

Yerbes. Herbs.

Yerth. Earth.

*****Yet.** As yet [M. C. H. B.].

Yin. Yon.

Yinder. Yonder.

Yip. To chirp like a newly-hatched chicken, or other very young bird.

Yipper. Brisk.

*****Young-youth.** A young person of either sex [C. S. P.].

Yowe. An ewe.

*****Yowl.** See **Yawl** [Em.], and (2) to howl or complain [M. C. H. B.].

Yulk. A heavy fall.

PE
1884
H4P35

Palgrave, Francis Milnes
Temple
    A list of words and
phrases in every-day use by
the natives of Hetton-le-

CALL NO	AUTHOR.
PE 1884 H4	Palgrave, F.
P 35	TITLE: List of w... phrase... in every-day use by the natives of Hetton-le-Hole

Lightning Source UK Ltd.
Milton Keynes UK
UKHW021615261118
332986UK00012B/1012/P